THE

CUSTOMER SCIENCE HANDBOOK

Using Behavioral Insights to Create
Breakthrough Customer Experiences

ALEXANDER CHERNEV

Kellogg School of Management
Northwestern University

SECOND EDITION

The Customer Science Handbook

Using Behavioral Insights to Create Breakthrough Customer Experiences

Second Edition | January 2025

ISBN: 978-1-936572-84-7 (paperback)

ISBN: 978-1-936572-88-5 (hardcover)

Published by Cerebellum Press, USA

TABLE OF CONTENTS

About the Author

Alexander Chernev is a professor of marketing at the Kellogg School of Management, Northwestern University. He holds a PhD in psychology from Sofia University and a second PhD in business administration from Duke University.

Dr. Chernev's research has been published in the leading marketing journals and has been frequently quoted in the business and popular press, including *Scientific American, Associated Press, The New York Times, The Washington Post, The Wall Street Journal, Financial Times, Forbes,* and *Harvard Business Review.* He was ranked among the top ten most prolific scholars in the leading marketing journals by the *Journal of Marketing* and among the top five marketing faculty in the area of consumer behavior by a global survey of marketing faculty published by the *Journal of Marketing Education.*

Alexander Chernev has served as guest editor and area editor for the *Journal of Marketing, Journal of Retailing,* and *International Journal of Research in Marketing,* a guest area editor for the *Journal of Consumer Psychology* and *Marketing Science,* and on the editorial boards of leading research journals, including the *Journal of Marketing Research, Journal of Consumer Research, Journal of Consumer Psychology,* and *Journal of the Academy of Marketing Science.*

Dr. Chernev's books — *Strategic Marketing Management: Theory and Practice, Strategic Marketing Management: The Framework, Strategic Brand Management, The Marketing Plan Handbook,* and *The Business Model* — have been translated into multiple languages and are used in the top business schools around the world. He is also a co-author of the new editions of Philip Kotler's seminal *Marketing Management* textbook.

Alexander Chernev teaches marketing strategy, brand management, and behavioral science in MBA, Executive MBA, PhD, and executive education programs at the Kellogg School of Management. He has also taught in executive programs at INSEAD in France and Singapore, at IMD in Switzerland, and at Hong Kong University of Science and Technology. He has received numerous teaching awards, including the Core Course Teaching Award, Faculty Impact Award, and the Top Professor Award from the Kellogg Executive MBA Program, which he has received fifteen times.

In addition to research and teaching, Alexander Chernev has served as an Academic Trustee of the *Marketing Science Institute* and advises companies around the world on issues of marketing strategy, brand management, behavioral science, and consumer behavior. He has advised Fortune 500 companies on ways to reinvent their business models, develop new products, and gain competitive advantage. He also serves as an expert witness in behavioral science, consumer behavior, brand management, and marketing strategy matters.

ACKNOWLEDGMENTS

This book has benefited from the wisdom of many of my current and former colleagues at the Kellogg School of Management at Northwestern University: Chethana Achar, Nidhi Agrawal, Eric Anderson, Jim Anderson, Robert Blattberg, Ulf Böckenholt, Galen Bodenhausen, Miguel Brendl, Bobby Calder, Tim Calkins, Greg Carpenter, Moran Cerf, Yuxin Chen, Anne Coughlan, Patrick Duparcq, David Gal, Kelly Goldsmith, Kent Grayson, Karsten Hansen, Julie Hennessy, Dawn Iacobucci, Dipak Jain, Robert Kozinets, Lakshman Krishnamurthi, Aparna Labroo, Jim Lecinski, Eric Leininger, Sid Levy, Eyal Maoz, Blake McShane, Kevin McTigue, Vikas Mittal, Ilya Morozov, Vincent Nijs, Tom O'Toole, Sergio Rebelo, Neal Roese, Derek Rucker, Mohan Sawhney, John Sherry, Louis Stern, Brian Sternthal, Jake Teeny, Artem Timoshenko, Rima Touré-Tillery, Anna Tuchman, Alice Tybout, Caio Waisman, Philip Zerrillo, Florian Zettelmeyer, and Andris Zoltners.

I owe a considerable debt of gratitude to the "father" of modern marketing, mentor, colleague, and co-author Philip Kotler, who sparked my interest in marketing management and applying behavioral science to solving business problems. I am also indebted to Jim Bettman, Julie Edell, Joel Huber, John Lynch, John Payne, and Rick Staelin at Duke University for sparking my interest in behavioral science and for their advice and support at the outset of my academic career.

Thanks are also due to researchers in the field of behavioral science whose insights have helped shape this book: Dan Ariely (Duke University), Jonah Berger (University of Pennsylvania), Simona Botti (London Business School), Pierre Chandon (INSEAD), Robert Cialdini (Arizona State University), Ravi Dhar (Yale University), Ayelet Gneezy (University of California, San Diego), Chip Heath (Stanford University), Christopher Hsee (University of Chicago), Sheena Iyengar (Columbia University), Eric Johnson (Columbia University), Daniel Kahneman (Princeton University), Barbara Khan (University of Pennsylvania), Ran Kivetz (Columbia University), George Loewenstein (Carnegie Mellon University), Ann McGill (University of Chicago), Tom Meyvis (New York University), Steve Nowlis (Washington University), David Reibstein (University of Pennsylvania), Baba Shiv (Stanford University), Itamar Simonson (Stanford University), Richard Thaler (University of Chicago), and Klaus Wertenbroch (INSEAD).

I would also like to thank Ryan Hamilton (Emory University) for his valuable comments and suggestions on the early drafts of this book. I am also very grateful to Joanne Freeman for editing this book with a very keen and helpful eye.

Preface

Successful marketing of any product or service is based on understanding the customer.

We live in an era of rapid change, when traditional industries are frequently disrupted by innovative business models. Technology has reshaped the business landscape with advancements in online shopping, mobile connectivity, social media, and data-driven marketing.

Yet, when it comes to customer experience, not much has changed. It begins with customers recognizing a need to be fulfilled. As they seek ways to meet this need, they interact with the company and its offerings. At the end of this interaction, they want to feel satisfied and happy. None of this has changed: Identifying and fulfilling customer needs is the basic premise of any viable business.

The core principles of designing customer experiences and creating customer value are the focus of this book. We analyze the customer experience from three perspectives: (1) what customers do—how they identify a problem, seek a solution, interact with the offering, and what they think and feel during this process; (2) the specific actions a company should take to manage the customer experience; and (3) the key behavioral insights that can guide a company's actions when creating an optimal customer experience.

Taking a systematic approach to understanding customer needs and crafting experiences to meet these needs is crucial. As products and services increasingly become commoditized, creating meaningful customer experiences is the new competitive frontier. Drawing on insights from psychology, behavioral economics, and marketing, this book helps managers understand the forces that shape customer behavior and develop a systematic approach to delivering breakthrough experiences.

The organizing principle of this book is the Customer Experience Canvas, which outlines the key stages of the customer experience and identifies strategies for managing this experience at each stage. Across the different aspects of the customer experience—from triggering a dormant customer need and engaging customers with the company's offerings to designing impactful consumption experiences and building enduring customer loyalty—this book helps managers create superior customer value.

Creating breakthrough customer experiences is both challenging and rewarding. As Steve Jobs put it, "When we use price, product, placement and promotion techniques, people call it marketing. When we orchestrate a consumer experience that delights, people call it magic." Understanding how customers think, feel, and act, and what motivates their behavior, is the first step toward creating this magic. The key behavioral science insights and the ways they can be applied to diverse business scenarios to create meaningful customer experiences are at the heart of this book.

CHAPTER ONE

MANAGING THE CUSTOMER EXPERIENCE

The purpose of business is to create and keep a customer.

—Peter Drucker

Creating a meaningful customer experience starts with a deep understanding of customers' thoughts, feelings, and motivations as they engage with a company's offerings. Managers can gain valuable insights by analyzing the factors that drive customer behavior. This chapter outlines a systematic approach to understanding a company's customers and provides a framework to guide managers' decisions in creating a meaningful customer experience.

Managing the Customer Experience: From Intuition to Science

Managers often rely on their intuition to solve complex problems, even when alternative sources of information are available. Some argue that the higher up in the corporate structure managers are, the more they need to rely on their gut feeling. In the words of Ralph Larsen, the long-term chairman and CEO of Johnson & Johnson, "Often there is absolutely no way that you could have the time to thoroughly analyze every one of the options or alternatives available to you. So you have to rely on your business judgment."[1]

Clearly, intuition can benefit managerial decisions. In an environment that requires processing vast amounts of incomplete information in a relatively short amount of time, it is natural to turn to one's "gut feel." Our mind continuously processes much more information than we are consciously aware of, generating potential solutions to complex problems without us being cognizant of how we reached a specific decision. When we use our intuition, we often draw on principles and patterns that are difficult to articulate. As a result, we are aware of the outcome of our intuition but not the specific steps that led to it.[2]

Deciding by intuition helps avoid analysis paralysis, which occurs when we become overwhelmed with information and cannot make a decision. By relying on rapid, non-conscious, and holistic associations—the hallmarks of intuitive decision making—we can avoid the emotional consequences of analysis paralysis. This way, the fear of making an error does not outweigh the benefits of making a timely decision.

Despite its benefits, relying solely on intuition has important drawbacks. Since most managers work within a specific industry, their experience is limited to that industry, preventing them from identifying and adopting new trends and practices developed in other fields. Managers' experience is also often limited to the types of problems they have faced in the past. As a result, their intuition might be irrelevant—or even outright wrong—when presented with a problem they have not previously encountered.

Another potential issue with managers' reliance on intuition is that it is often based on their "personal truths"—beliefs they hold strongly but have not been rigorously tested and might not withstand scientific scrutiny. Consider a manager who runs an advertising campaign during major holidays each year, believing that without this promotion, sales will drop sharply. This belief stems from many years of experience; the manager has been advertising during holidays for over a decade, and sales always go up. But was advertising responsible for the sales increase? Although the manager strongly believes it was, the increase in sales might have been a mere consequence of the increased store traffic during that week.

Behavioral science can help managers reach better decisions by providing insights that augment their intuition. Consider the following scenario: You have just been promoted, and as part of your new responsibilities, you are tasked with improving sales revenues from the company's existing customers. You already have prior experience launching new products but have not directly worked on customer retention and revenue growth. Relying on intuition in this case might not prove very helpful since it is the first time you have encountered this specific problem.

Of course, you might gather additional data by conducting problem-specific marketing research. However, this is not a trivial undertaking. You will need to decide what specific questions to ask, design the research questionnaire or experimental study, and ensure that the research output is both valid and relevant to the question you aim to answer. Even if some combination of intuition and marketing research proves to be relevant, what would you do if the recommendations from these different sources contradict each other? Which ones do you follow, which ones do you ignore, and how do you justify your decision to your team or senior management?

An alternative approach is to step back and, rather than asking the specific question of how to improve sales from the company's existing customers, ask the more general question: how to design a customer experience that engenders loyalty. The answer to this question calls for understanding how customers make purchase decisions and what factors are likely to influence these decisions. By applying knowledge accumulated over decades of academic research to specific business problems, behavioral science elevates our understanding from personal truths to verified truths, thus helping to ensure that we make informed decisions.

Using behavioral science to facilitate our intuition involves three key steps (Figure 1). The first step is to abstract from the specific problem to a more general one. Once the general problem has been formulated, the next step is to use a behavioral science framework to address this problem. The Customer Experience Canvas, outlined later in this chapter, is one such framework. The final step is to apply the general solution to the problem at hand and develop a specific course of action.

Figure 1. Behavioral Science as a Decision Framework

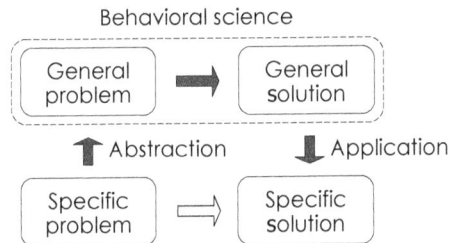

To illustrate, imagine you are tasked with creating a new breakfast cereal. This endeavor presents a series of critical decisions. How do you determine the right balance between taste and nutrition to ensure customer satisfaction? How can you create awareness among and engage your target customers? What strategies can you employ to communicate the cereal's benefits effectively? How can you persuade customers who purchased the cereal to consume it more frequently and ensure their continued satisfaction and loyalty?

Rather than relying solely on intuition and project-specific market research, you could adopt a broader perspective. Launching a new cereal brand is, at its core, about introducing a new product to the market—a challenge that many companies have faced in the past and that has been extensively studied by academic research. The general principles of creating a meaningful customer experience are applicable to launching a new cereal, just as they are in other contexts. The challenge lies in adapting these overarching strategies to the specific nuances of your cereal brand.

The ultimate purpose of a behavioral science framework in marketing is to distill the fundamental principles of how people think, feel, and behave and present them in a way that facilitates managerial decisions. By drawing on insights accumulated across various contexts over time, behavioral science enables managers to streamline their actions and sidestep potential pitfalls. Behavioral science is not a substitute for intuition but a tool that helps guide and enhance this intuition, strengthening the accuracy and efficiency of managers' decisions. The key insights from behavioral science and their application in creating meaningful customer experiences are at the core of this book.

The Customer Experience as a Process

A common mistake managers often make is focusing on certain aspects of the customer experience while ignoring others. It is not unusual for companies to zero in solely on the moment when the customer is using their offerings, neglecting the fuller experience, which includes what occurs before and after the purchase. For example, a hotel manager might define the customer experience only in terms of what happens from the moment customers enter the hotel to the moment they exit. Similarly, a product manager might focus only on how customers use the company's offering, without considering how they discover information about it, choose it from among many competitive options, and what they do after consuming it.

This approach reflects the erroneous belief that the customer experience is limited to the actual usage of the offering. It ignores the fact that the customer experience often begins long before they use the offering and includes various interactions before, during, and after the actual usage, each contributing to the overall experience. To be effective, managing the customer experience must start long before customers purchase the company's offering and requires a holistic understanding of all aspects of how customers interact with it.

Great customer experiences rarely happen by accident. Most often, they stem from a company's strategic vision of what constitutes a meaningful customer experience. To cultivate such a vision, managers must develop a deep understanding of their customers' needs, the benefits these customers expect to receive from the company's offering, and the way they encounter and interact with the offering—from the moment a particular need emerges to the moment when this need is fulfilled and eventually reoccurs. Specifically, the customer experience can be viewed as a series of seven interconnected stages: *need activation, search, evaluation, choice, purchase, consumption,* and *repurchase.* These building blocks of the customer experience and the relationships among them are depicted in Figure 2 and outlined in more detail below.

Figure 2. The Customer Experience Map

- *Need activation.* Customers do not strive to fulfill all needs at all times; rather, at any given moment, they focus on active needs. A need becomes active when customers are confronted with a gap between what they desire and what they currently have. The realization of such a gap activates the relevant need and motivates them to seek ways to close the gap and fulfill the active need. For example, the desire for a new car may be triggered by a pay raise at work, which can create a preference for a more prestigious car. Alternatively, this need might be activated by witnessing a car accident and realizing the importance of safety features that their current car lacks.

- *Information search.* Once a need has been activated, customers often seek information pertinent to deciding how to fulfill that need. This process involves searching—both from external sources and from memory—for relevant information, including specific products, services, and brands that are likely to fulfill the active need. The information search often leads to the creation of a consideration set containing options most relevant to the active need. For example, when seeking to buy a car, consumers might create a consideration set of five models, which, upon further consideration, might be reduced to two options.

- *Evaluating the alternatives.* As customers gather information about the available options, they also evaluate these options based on their ability to fulfill the active need. This determines which attributes are considered, how important these attributes are to customers, and how well the available options are expected to perform in these areas. For example, when purchasing a car, consumers might focus on the car's power, safety, fuel efficiency, and style. They may also decide that style is the most important attribute, followed by power, safety, and fuel efficiency, and evaluate the cars under consideration based on these attributes.

- *Making a choice.* The evaluation of available options typically culminates in choosing the one deemed most attractive. When none of the options dominate the others on all attributes, customers must trade off the benefits and costs of different options to select the one that best meets their needs. For example, when choosing between a car that is more fuel-efficient but less powerful and one that is more powerful but less fuel-efficient, consumers might sacrifice performance for better fuel efficiency.

- *Making a purchase.* Even though many purchases occur soon after a choice is made, choice and purchase can be temporally separated. This might be due to various factors such as unavailability of the offering, procrastination, or lack of financial resources. For example, after choosing a particular car, consumers might not immediately purchase it due to budgetary constraints or the limited availability of the car in nearby dealerships.

- *Using the offering.* Usage involves the actual consumption of the product or service, dealing with any problems that occur during consumption, and disposing of the offering. Using the car example, this includes driving the car, performing the required maintenance, and ultimately trading in the car for a new one.

- *Repurchasing the offering.* Because many needs tend to recur, the customer experience is often an iterative process. Based on prior experience, customers might simply repurchase the same offering without considering other options, or they might restart the process by forming a new consideration set, evaluating the options in this set, making a choice, and purchasing the chosen option. For example, consumers might trade in their car for a newer model or decide to make a fresh start by exploring all available market options.

It is important to note that the customer experience does not always involve a series of clearly delineated steps as shown in Figure 2. Searching for information, evaluating the available options, and making a choice can be intertwined and sometimes occur simultaneously. Furthermore, the sequence of the different stages of the customer experience might vary, with customers reassessing and modifying earlier steps.

For example, customers might deprioritize an active need, modify the consideration set, change the criteria used to evaluate the considered options, use different decision rules to make a choice, and then change their mind and ultimately purchase a different option. This is why the customer experience map is only a generalized outline of the key components of the customer experience and the relationships among them.

Designing the Customer Experience

Once the key aspects of the customer experience have been identified, the company must tailor its actions to address each aspect of the experience. This process involves identifying opportunities in how customers seek to fulfill their needs and interact with the company's offering, and then developing a course of action to capitalize on these opportunities. This holistic approach to managing the customer experience goes beyond merely focusing on customer touchpoints—the instances when customers encounter the company and its offerings through marketing communications, sales interactions, and product and service experiences.

Focusing on touchpoints is not an issue in itself, as they can help identify opportunities to interact with customers and promote the company's offerings. The problem arises when companies limit their efforts to managing customer touchpoints, ignoring the end-to-end customer experience. This is problematic because touchpoints reflect only one aspect of the customer experience, overlooking interactions that occur beyond the company's immediate control.

One reason managers tend to focus on touchpoints rather than the overall customer experience is that they view the customer experience only from the company's standpoint: seeking ways to attract and retain customers. This mindset makes touchpoints attractive because they are actionable, making it easier to build marketing programs around them. However, programs that focus only on touchpoints are tactical in nature.

What is missing is a strategy to guide these tactics. Such a strategy must clearly articulate the needs of the company's target customers and specify the value the company will create for them.

A strategic approach to managing the customer experience must define the company's goals at different stages of the customer journey. To this end, a manager must first establish whether the need that the company aims to fulfill is prominent in customers' minds and whether customers are aware of the company's offering. Next, the manager must ensure that the offering creates value for customers, clearly articulate this value, craft the optimal choice architecture, and nudge customers toward purchase. Once customers have acquired the offering, the company's goal is to create a meaningful consumption experience and build long-term customer loyalty. The key aspects of the customer experience and the specific goals the company aims to achieve at each stage are illustrated in Figure 3 and discussed in more detail next.

Figure 3. Company Goals in Managing the Customer Experience

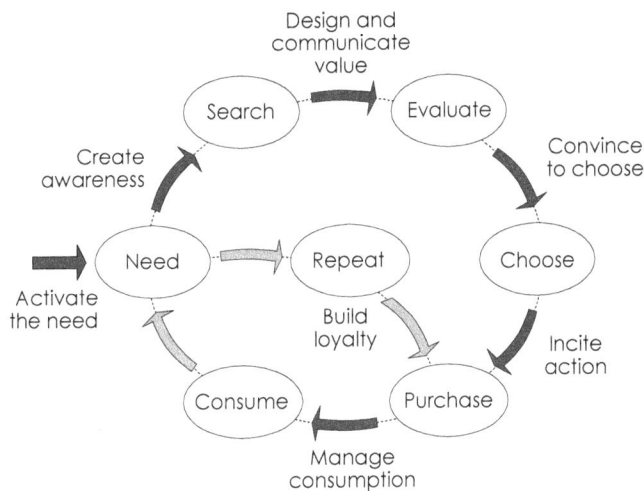

- *Activating a need.* At the very outset, a company must ensure that the customer need it aims to address with its offering is prominent in customers' minds. The specific questions a manager must ask to evaluate this need include: "What need does the company's offering address? Do customers see this need as a problem that must be solved? Are they actively trying to address this need?" For example, a car dealer can benefit from understanding what motivates different customers to consider buying a new car and how the ownership of a new car will help them achieve their goals.

- *Creating awareness.* Once the focal need is active, the company's goal is to make its target customers aware of the offering and ensure they are actively considering it. To assess customers' awareness of the company's offering, a manager should ask, "Do customers know about the company's offering? Are they aware of the specifics of the offering? Is this offering part of customers' consideration set?" For example, a car dealer's goal here is to engage customers so that they become aware of the company's offering and include it in their consideration set.

- *Designing and communicating the value of the offering.* As customers evaluate the available offerings, the company must ensure that its offering is designed and communicated in a way that creates value for these customers and allows customers to readily see its benefits. An offering's ability to create customer *value* is assessed by asking "Do customers understand and value the attributes of the offering? Do customers think that the benefits of the offering outweigh its costs? Do they think that the company's offering is superior to the alternative means of fulfilling their need?" For example, a car dealer must ensure that customers understand the benefits associated with the different attributes of the car and feel that these benefits outweigh the costs associated with the car.

- *Convincing customers to choose the offering.* Next, the company must give customers a compelling reason to choose its offering. At this stage, a manager should ask, "Are customers likely to choose the company's offering? Are there impediments to choosing our offering? Can the choice process be streamlined?" For example, a car dealer might present customers with a subset of available cars arranged to underscore the benefits of a given option, thus streamlining the customers' choice while steering them toward an option that also benefits the dealer.

- *Inciting action.* After customers have made a choice, the company must incite action and nudge them into making the purchase. The key questions a manager should ask are, "What will motivate customers to proceed with the purchase of the chosen offering? Is there an easy path from choice to purchase? Are there barriers to purchase?" For example, a car dealer might offer additional incentives to encourage customers to act on their choice while simultaneously streamlining the purchase process to make it easier and more convenient.

- *Managing consumption.* As customers use the offering, the company should focus on managing consumption to ensure that customers utilize the benefits of the offering and enjoy the experience. Here, a manager should ask, "Do all aspects of the consumption experience create customer value? Is this experience memorable?" For example, a car dealer might spend extra time explaining the different features of the car to ensure that customers know how to use them and can maximize the value they derive from owning and driving the car.

- *Building loyalty.* The company should ensure that when the focal need re-emerges, customers repurchase its offering without considering alternative options. The key questions a manager must ask at this juncture include, "Does the customer experience foster loyalty? Does it lead to habitual repurchase and consumption?" For example, a car dealer might offer a loyalty program that rewards returning customers and provides an attractive trade-in offer for their current vehicle.

The key aspects of managing the customer experience are summarized in the *Customer Experience Canvas*, or *CX Canvas*, a practical tool that helps managers develop meaningful action plans. It is structured around the seven main elements of the customer experience: need activation, search, evaluation, choice, purchase, consumption, and repurchase. For each of these elements, the CX Canvas helps analyze the underlying customer need, the extent to which the company's offering meets this need, and then outlines the proposed course of action. The CX Canvas is discussed in more detail at the end of this chapter.

Using Behavioral Science to Manage the Customer Experience

When designing customer acquisition and retention strategies, managers sometimes focus solely on customer behavior while neglecting the psychological factors such as beliefs, emotions, and motivations that guide this behavior. One reason for this oversight is that, unlike behavioral outcomes, customers' beliefs, emotions, and motivations are not readily observable. This tendency to overemphasize the observable and ignore the unobservable is problematic because without understanding the forces that drive and shape behavior, it is difficult to develop a meaningful customer experience.

As the popular saying goes, "what gets measured, gets managed." When managing customer loyalty, managers tend to focus exclusively on observable factors such as how often customers repurchase the company's offerings and whether they also purchase competitors' offerings. This behavior is easily detectable and directly translates into sales revenue and profits, so managers often do not see the need to dig deeper into the psychological drivers of this behavior. However, without understanding the factors that motivate customers, loyalty is rarely sustainable. Loyalty is a consequence of customers' beliefs, attitudes, and emotions toward the company's offering. Without a psychological commitment, customers are unlikely to remain loyal.

A company's ability to create impactful customer experiences hinges on managers' understanding of the factors that shape customers' beliefs, choices, and actions. To develop an effective action plan for managing the customer experience, managers must consider how customers think, what they feel, and why they behave the way they do. Gaining this understanding is significantly enhanced by applying insights from behavioral science.

The key customer insights that should guide managers' actions can be linked to different stages of the customer experience (Figure 4). To activate a particular customer need, managers need to design meaningful triggers. To reach their target customers, they must know how to create an engagement mindset. When designing and communicating their offering, they can benefit from understanding how to create customer value. To convince customers to choose their offering, managers must be able to craft effective choice architecture. To incite action, managers must know how to nudge customers to act. To ensure that customers use the offering in a way that enables them to receive maximum benefit while also creating value for the company, managers should know how to design meaningful experiences. Finally, to foster repurchase, managers should follow the key principles of building customer loyalty.

Figure 4. Using Behavioral Science to Manage the Customer Experience

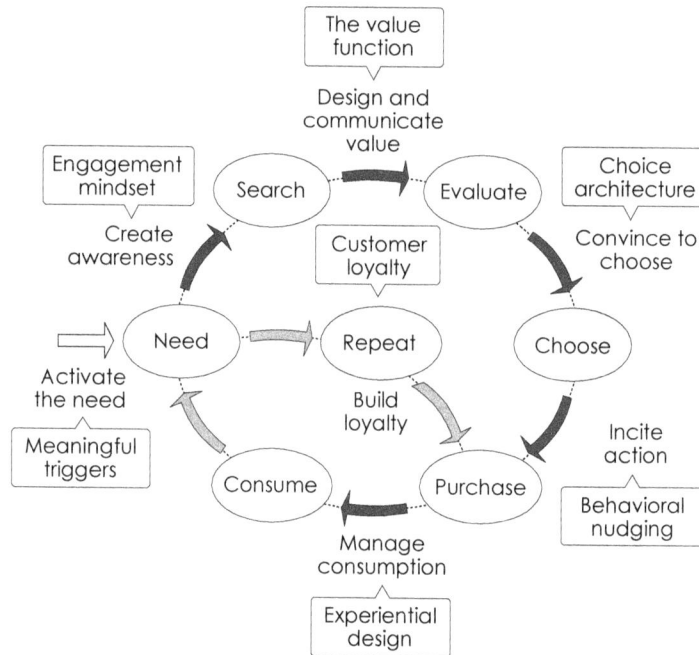

The key behavioral insights that managers must consider at each stage of the customer experience—designing meaningful triggers, creating an engagement mindset, designing and communicating customer value, crafting the choice architecture, nudging purchase, orchestrating the consumption experience, and building customer loyalty—are outlined below.

- *Designing meaningful triggers* starts with understanding how triggers activate customer needs. Managers can benefit from knowing the various types of customer needs, their hierarchy, how they evolve, and how to determine which needs to trigger. It is also crucial for managers to distinguish between triggers that aim to activate functional needs, those that target affective needs by evoking positive or negative emotions, and triggers that focus on identity needs such as the desire for attaining status and expressing one's personality.

- *Creating an engagement mindset* builds on the science of how to make an offering stand out and become part of customers' consideration set. Here, managers can benefit from understanding how people search for and process available information, what factors draw attention, and how the two systems of human thinking influence decision outcomes. Managing customer engagement also requires understanding the role of attention in evaluating information, why things that become a focus of attention are perceived as more important, the role associations play in creating and changing beliefs, and the danger of overestimating customers' level of involvement.

- *Designing and communicating customer* value relies on the principles of value creation: how customers form value judgments, how product features drive value, and how companies must design their offerings to create customer value. Here, managers must understand the relationship between the attributes of their offerings and the customer value these attributes create. They must also be cognizant of how the three key properties of the value function—reference dependence, loss aversion, and diminishing marginal value—define the benefits and costs customers receive from a company's offerings. Additionally, managers must recognize the three types of value a company can create for its customers—functional, psychological, and monetary—and avoid the pitfalls of focusing exclusively on a single type of value.

- *Crafting the choice architecture* builds on research insights about how people make choices and the forces that guide their decisions. Managers can benefit from understanding the decision heuristics people use when making choices and how these heuristics influence decision outcomes. Key insights include the importance of reasons in choice, the impact of categorization and qualitative thinking on decision outcomes, and the role of the choice context in guiding decisions. Choice architecture can also explain why offering too many options can be counterproductive, how decision fatigue depletes mental resources and influences choices, and the powerful role of default options as one of the most effective tools available to choice architects.

- *Nudging purchase* aims to address the gap between behavioral intentions and actual behavior by identifying ways to motivate customers to act and remove impediments to purchase. Here, managers can benefit from defining the factors that drive action as well as from understanding the key cognitive, emotional, and implementational barriers to action. Specifically, managers must understand the roles of uncertainty, anticipated regret, and effort in deterring customer action.

- *Orchestrating the consumption experience* builds on insights about how customers use a company's offerings and the value they derive from this process. Here, managers can benefit from understanding all aspects of the customer experience: from the anticipation of using the offering to its actual usage and end-of-usage disposal. Managers can also benefit from understanding why things often become less exciting over time and what a company can do to mitigate this effect. Additionally, managers must understand the importance of engaging customers on an emotional level and how to create such engagement. They should also be aware of the role of retrospective evaluations and how to create truly memorable experiences.

- *Managing customer loyalty* focuses on the factors that drive repeated purchases and how loyalty benefits both the company and its customers. Here, managers can benefit from understanding the role of the functional, emotional, identity, and behavioral aspects of loyalty. Specifically, they should understand the role of satisfaction in creating loyal customers and the key principles of designing loyalty programs. Managers should also be aware of the importance of connecting with customers' feelings, the power of customers' need for self-expression, the impact of brands on fostering loyalty, and the importance of creating and sustaining habits.

The seven stages of the customer experience and the behavioral insights that guide managerial decision making at each stage are the organizational principles of this book. Chapter 2 outlines the key principles for designing meaningful triggers. Chapter 3 addresses the process of creating an engagement mindset. Next, Chapter 4 outlines how a company can create and communicate customer value. Chapter 5 then discusses the key aspects of crafting the choice architecture, and Chapter 6 outlines the process of behavioral nudging. Chapter 7 focuses on the key aspects of designing impactful experiences, and Chapter 8 discusses how to build customer loyalty. Finally, Chapter 9 delves deeper into the different methods for gathering customer insights.

By linking each stage of the customer experience to the relevant behavioral insights, this book presents a systematic and managerially relevant approach to understanding the scientific principles behind designing impactful customer experiences. Encapsulated in the Customer Experience (CX) Canvas, this approach can help foster brand loyalty and maximize value for both customers and the company.

SUMMARY

Behavioral science can guide and enhance *managerial intuition*. Managers' intuition is often based on their "personal truths"—strongly held subjective beliefs that have not been rigorously tested. Intuition is also subject to various decision biases that can lead to erroneous conclusions. By relying on the cumulative knowledge of human behavior rather than solely on individual experience, behavioral science helps managers be more objective in designing breakthrough customer experiences.

Creating a meaningful customer experience starts with thoroughly understanding how customers interact with a company's offering to fulfill their needs. The customer experience comprises seven interconnected steps: need activation, search, evaluation, choice, purchase, consumption, and repurchase. These steps form the key building blocks of the *customer experience map*. By using this map as a guiding principle, managers can gather insights into how their customers think, feel, and behave, enabling them to design effective strategies to fulfill customer needs.

Defining the key aspects of the customer experience enables the company to tailor its actions to the different stages of this experience. Because the customer experience involves a series of interconnected steps, a manager must set specific goals for each stage. At the very outset, a company must activate the customer need it aims to address with its offering. Once the need is active, the company must make customers aware of the offering and ensure they are actively considering it. As customers evaluate the available offerings, the company must ensure its offering is designed and communicated in a way that creates value for these customers, making the benefits of the offering readily apparent.

Next, as customers make a choice, the company must convince them to choose its offering. After customers have made their choice, the company must incite action and nudge them toward making the purchase. As customers use the offering, the company should focus on managing consumption to ensure customers utilize the offering's benefits and enjoy the experience. When the focal need re-emerges, the company needs to foster repurchase, encouraging customers to return to its offering without considering alternative options.

The key aspects of managing the customer experience are outlined in the *CX Canvas* — a practical tool to help managers develop meaningful action plans. This canvas is organized around the seven main elements of the customer experience: need activation, search, evaluation, choice, purchase, consumption, and repurchase. For each of these elements, the CX Canvas provides an analysis of the performance of the company's offering and outlines the proposed course of action. By directly linking customer experience to company actions, this canvas serves as the blueprint for designing and managing the customer experience.

Behavioral science can offer valuable insights for managing the key stages of the customer experience. When managers aim to activate a particular customer need, behavioral science informs them on how to design meaningful triggers. As they strive to reach their target customers, it offers advice on creating an engagement mindset. When designing and communicating the company's offering, managers can benefit from insights on creating customer value. To convince customers to choose the company's offering, behavioral science provides insights on crafting the choice architecture. To incite action, behavioral science helps managers learn how to nudge customers effectively. When optimizing the consumption experience, managers can use insights to design meaningful and memorable experiences. Finally, behavioral science can help foster repurchase by delineating strategies to build customer loyalty.

Key Takeaways

Let analysis guide actions. Managers' actions should be based on a deep understanding of customers' needs and their interaction with the company's offering.

Define the customer experience. Identifying the key aspects of the customer experience, starting with the needs customers aim to fulfill, is the backbone of creating customer value. The customer experience map is a practical framework for defining the key components of this experience.

Delineate the company goals. A company's actions are guided by a set of specific goals at different stages of the customer experience. The CX Canvas is a practical tool for pinpointing problem areas and identifying opportunities to create superior customer value.

Use behavioral science to facilitate managerial decisions. Insights from behavioral science provide a framework for understanding how customers think, what they feel, and why they behave the way they do. Applying these insights to identify unmet customer needs and design offerings to fulfill these needs is the roadmap for creating superior customer experiences.

SPOTLIGHT: BEHAVIORAL SCIENCE IN BUSINESS MARKETS

Behavioral science insights are not limited to consumer markets; they are also relevant in business markets. A company's customers might include both individuals seeking to fulfill their own needs and managers aiming to achieve their organizations' goals. Managers are also consumers in their private lives, and the way they think about business offerings is influenced by how they think as consumers. Since both types of decisions—business and consumer—are ultimately made by the same individuals, these decisions are guided by similar behavioral principles.

Despite their similarities, business and consumer decisions differ in several important aspects. First, business decisions often involve *multiple entities*. A business decision-making unit typically consists of representatives from various departments within an organization, including finance, accounting, marketing, sales, information technology, operations, and purchasing. These entities can play distinct roles: Some might initiate the decision process, others might act as gatekeepers imposing restrictions, some might have the final say, and others might oversee the purchase of the selected offering. The end-users might not always be a part of the decision process. In fact, some businesses have a centralized decision-making process that does not seek direct input from end-users, which can result in outcomes that do not fully align with their needs.

Another important distinction is that managers often have *different goals* and, consequently, pay attention to different aspects of the offering. Project leaders, end users, and research and development teams often focus primarily on the functional benefits of the offering, such as performance, reliability, and durability. In contrast, senior management, along with the finance, accounting, and purchasing departments, tend to focus on the monetary aspects of the offering. Additionally, some managers might face conflicts of interest when choosing between outcomes that benefit the company and outcomes that are self-serving, such as enhancing their power and status within the organization, gaining recognition, and satisfying their ego.

Another relevant aspect of business markets is that the decision-making process is often driven primarily by *functional benefits* rather than emotions. While emotions might play a role in business decisions, these decisions typically involve multiple entities, so the emotional state of any individual decision maker is often not the key driver of the decision outcome. Business decisions tend to be driven by practical considerations and focus on the performance aspects of the available options—a process that is less likely to be emotional in nature.

Because business purchases typically involve offerings related to the company's operations, managers tend to have a higher level of understanding and knowledge of the available options. This greater expertise enables managers to determine the value of offerings by examining their attributes. In contrast, consumers, who often lack such expertise and have difficulty deciphering the meaning of specific attributes, are more interested in an offering's benefits and costs.

The differences between consumer and business markets have led some managers to believe that these markets are fundamentally different, and that relevant knowledge only comes from business-to-business companies operating in the same industry. This belief is rather myopic. Not only do the core principles driving the customer experience apply to both consumer and business markets, but consumer markets often present managers with more complex problems. Consumer companies usually deal with a larger number of customers with more diverse needs, who are less knowledgeable about the offerings they buy and their own preferences. The ever-increasing competition in consumer markets has forced many consumer goods companies, including Amazon, Netflix, and Airbnb, to attain high customer experience standards in a scalable way that many companies operating in business markets have yet to achieve.

Understanding how people, whether individual consumers or business managers, think and behave can benefit companies by providing powerful tools to create impactful customer experiences and deliver superior customer value. By leveraging the knowledge accumulated through decades of academic research, behavioral science can help companies design marketing strategies that resonate more deeply with their business customers, enhancing their engagement, satisfaction, and loyalty.

The CX Canvas: The Big Picture

The Customer Experience Canvas, or CX Canvas, is a practical tool for developing effective action plans for managing the customer experience. It is organized as a matrix with seven cells, each corresponding to a different stage of the customer experience: need activation, search, evaluation, choice, purchase, consumption, and repurchase. Since value creation is the ultimate goal of managing the customer experience, the Value cell is particularly important and is therefore double in size. The key elements of the CX Canvas and the corresponding questions you must ask at each step are outlined in Figure 5.

For each of the seven stages of the customer experience, the CX Canvas involves two key components: (1) analyzing the underlying customer need and the company's ability to fulfill this need across all aspects of the customer experience, and (2) developing a course of action to create long-term customer value. By linking the analysis of the different stages of the customer experience to the company's actions, the CX Canvas enables companies to take a focused, logic-based approach to building breakthrough customer experiences.

Figure 5. The CX Canvas

▸ **Need**	▸ **Awareness**
- *Analysis:* What need does the company's offering address? Do customers see this need as a problem that must be solved? Are they actively trying to address this need? - *Action:* Activate the customer need targeted by the company's offering	- *Analysis:* Are customers aware of the company's offering? Are they aware of the specifics of the offering? Is this offering a part of customers' consideration set? - *Action:* Make customers aware of the offering and its specifics, and ensure that they are actively considering it

▸ **Value**	
- *Analysis:* Do customers understand the benefits and costs of the offering? Do they see the offering's benefits as relevant to their needs? Do customers think that the benefits of the offering outweigh its costs? - *Action:* Design the offering to address a relevant customer need and communicate its value to customers	

▸ **Choice**	▸ **Purchase**
- *Analysis:* Is it easy for target customers to make a choice? Does the decision context facilitate the choice of the company's offering? - *Action:* Optimize the choice architecture to provide compelling reasons for customers to choose the company's offering	- *Analysis:* Are there opportunities to enhance customers' motivation to act? Are there any functional, emotional, or implementational barriers to purchase? - *Action:* Streamline the purchase process to nudge customers to buy the chosen option

▸ **Consumption**	▸ **Loyalty**
- *Analysis:* Do all aspects of the consumption experience create customer value? Does the experience engage customer emotions? Is the experience memorable? - *Action:* Design the customer experience to maximize the functional, psychological, and monetary benefits customers derive from it	- *Analysis:* Are customers satisfied with the performance of the offering? Do they feel an emotional connection with it? Do they see it as related to their identity? Have they formed habits to buy and use the offering? - *Action:* Optimize all aspects of the customer experience to build long-term loyalty

Throughout this book, we discuss the use of the CX Canvas at various stages of the customer experience. After exploring the behavioral insights that define the customer experience at each stage, we outline the main issues a manager should consider and the subsequent actions the company might take. This systematic approach makes the CX Canvas a comprehensive tool for designing and managing the customer experience.

CHAPTER TWO

DESIGNING MEANINGFUL TRIGGERS

Every battle is won before it is fought.
—Sun Tzu, Chinese military strategist

The customer experience usually starts with an active need that customers aim to fulfill. This need can be activated in two ways. First, customers might realize a deficiency on a particular dimension, such as hunger or thirst, and seek ways to reduce this deficiency. Alternatively, a customer's need might be triggered by a company's actions that highlight a deficiency and, typically, identify means to fulfill it. In either case, once customers realize that there is a gap between their current and desired state, they tend to seek ways to close this gap. To this end, they search for options that can fulfill the active need, evaluate these options, choose and purchase the most attractive one, consume that option, and if satisfied with the experience become loyal customers (Figure 1).

Figure 1. The Customer Experience Map: Triggering a Need

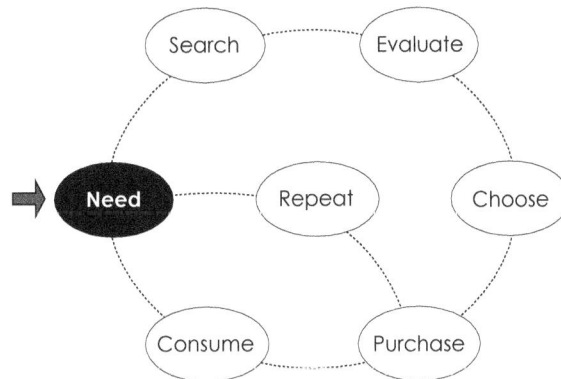

Triggers aim to activate dormant customer needs and serve as the driving force to jump-start the customer experience. In addition to providing the impetus for customers to act, triggers help shape their experience by bringing unmet needs into focus. Because triggers play a key role in defining the customer experience, choosing the right trigger is crucial for the success of a company's offering. Consider the following scenarios:

- You are the CEO of a paint manufacturing company and would like to grow sales. How can you motivate consumers to repaint their houses?

- You are launching a new product that offers superior functional benefits relative to the existing offerings in the market. Most of your target customers are generally satisfied with the performance of the offerings that are already available. You are considering using infomercials to promote your new product. Is this a good idea? Why?

- Your company is a market leader with an established brand and reputation in an industry that is becoming increasingly commoditized. Most of your customers are other businesses. The marketing team suggests two alternative positioning strategies: one focusing on the utilitarian benefits and one focusing on the emotional benefits. What would you do? Why?

- You are advising a company selling luxury goods on their pricing strategy. Research shows that if the company lowers prices, it can quickly grow its market share and increase its sales revenues. What factors do you need to consider when making the decision?

In this chapter, we address these questions as we discuss the importance of triggers and the role they play in activating customer needs. We start by examining the different types of customer needs, their hierarchy, and dynamics. We zero in on how triggers activate dormant needs, the different types of triggers, and the importance of deciding which needs to trigger. Next, we discuss functional and monetary triggers that aim to activate utilitarian needs. We then address triggers designed to activate emotional needs, focusing on those that activate positive and negative emotions. Finally, we consider status and personality triggers, which aim to activate identity needs.

The discussion of the conceptual issues involved in designing meaningful triggers is complemented with examples of companies that have used these triggers to achieve market success. Specifically, we will discuss how Pepsodent changed Americans' toothbrushing behavior; why TiVo, the first digital video recording device, failed to gain traction in the market; how Ginsu convinced customers that they needed to buy another set of knives; how Listerine prodded Americans to use mouthwash regularly; how potatoes went from being viewed as a product of witchcraft to becoming a staple of German cuisine; and how Betty Crocker managed to increase sales by making its products more difficult to use.

We explore factors that are likely to spark customer needs, the different types of triggers, and the ways managers can motivate customers to seek their offerings in the following sections.

Needs and Triggers

Most decisions are driven by unmet needs that people aim to fulfill. These needs motivate their behavior and are the primary forces guiding their actions. Without understanding the underlying needs that drive behavior, it is difficult to design offerings that meet these needs and create customer value. We address the role of needs as the impetus for customer behavior, the different need states, and the dynamics of customer needs in the following sections.

Needs as Drivers of Customer Behavior

Customer needs come in many forms, from those rooted in the biological requirements that sustain life and those that shape our social status to passing fancies and transitory desires. Understanding customer needs requires understanding customer need states, how various need states differ from one another, and how needs evolve over time.

Needs, Wants, and Preferences

A *need* is a physiological or psychological necessity for the well-being of an individual. When we become aware that a particular need is unmet, we are motivated to take specific actions to fulfill this need. Unmet needs can be defined by two main factors: their *strength*, which reflects the magnitude of tension created by the state of deficiency and the urgency a person feels to reduce it, and their *direction*, which reflects the desired end state and serves as a goal that guides our decisions and actions.

Needs are closely related to *wants* in that they reflect a psychological necessity. However, they differ in their level of generality. Needs are a general requirement for an individual's well-being, whereas wants are specific manifestations of these needs. Wants are often associated with a particular category or even a specific product or service that can satisfy a need. For example, hydration, transportation, and entertainment are needs; the desire to drink a particular brand of carbonated beverage, to drive the newest electric car, and to watch a particular movie are specific wants.

Preferences are also closely related to needs and refer to the specific benefits that individuals expect to receive from a given product, service, or brand. Preferences are often expressed in terms of comparisons with other relevant offerings. In this context, preferences can be thought of as the most attractive means for fulfilling a given want. For example, consumers might prefer Pepsi to Coke as a carbonated beverage, prefer Tesla Model S to a Chevrolet Volt as an electric car, and prefer Netflix to Amazon Prime Video as a means of watching movies on demand.

Because needs are an innate aspect of human beings, they cannot be created. Companies do not "create" needs; instead, they activate and shape existing needs to create specific wants and preferences. For example, Coca-Cola did not create a "need" for Coke; instead, it promoted the idea that Coke satisfies people's innate need for hydration, stimulation, and self-expression. Because the concepts of needs, wants, and preferences are intricately related, throughout this book the term "needs" is used in a more general sense to include specific wants and preferences.

The Hierarchy of Needs

All needs are not created equal. Some are more important than others. One of the most popular and widely referenced theories of the hierarchical organization of human needs was advanced by American psychologist Abraham Maslow nearly a century ago. This theory delineates five basic human needs, often depicted as levels within a pyramid, frequently referred to as Maslow's Pyramid of Needs. From the bottom of the hierarchy upward, the needs are physiological (food, water, sleep), safety (avoiding danger), love and belonging (affection and friendship), esteem (respect and appreciation), and self-actualization (self-fulfillment and self-expression). Maslow's theory is described in more detail at the end of this chapter.

From a marketing perspective, needs can be organized into three general categories: utilitarian, emotional, and identity needs. Broadly speaking, utilitarian needs correspond to physiological and safety needs, emotional needs correspond to the need for love and belonging, and identity needs correspond to the need for esteem and self-actualization in Maslow's pyramid.[1] These three types of needs are defined as follows:

- *Utilitarian needs* are those that can be met by the functional attributes of an offering. These needs include physiological needs like hunger, thirst, and physical intimacy. Another common utilitarian need is the need for safety. Offerings such as insurance, home security products, and safety gear are designed to appeal to the need for safety. Utilitarian needs also encompass resource preservation, such as minimizing effort, time management, and the accumulation of financial resources.

- *Emotional needs* reflect an individual's desire to experience pleasure and avoid pain. These needs are typically concerned with entering or maintaining a positive emotional state or leaving a negative one. Common positive emotional states involve sensory pleasure, enjoyment, love, happiness, and peace of mind. Offerings such as vacations, entertainment services, and experiential products are designed to appeal to the need for emotional stimulation.

- *Identity needs* are associated with how individuals define themselves, both to others and to themselves. These needs reflect people's desire to belong to certain ingroups, such as family, friends, work colleagues, and society at large, while also wanting to be unique and distinguish themselves from out-groups. Identity needs can be directed toward others, such as the need for self-expression, and toward the self, such as the need for self-identification. These needs broadly correspond to the needs for esteem and self-actualization in Maslow's hierarchy.

Needs vary in their importance: Some needs are more important than others. Identity needs are typically the most personally relevant, while utilitarian needs are the least personally relevant (Figure 2). This hierarchy stems from Maslow's theory, which views physiological needs as lower level needs compared to the need for sustaining a positive emotional state and, ultimately, the need for self-actualization and reaching one's full potential.

Figure 2. The Hierarchy of Customer Needs

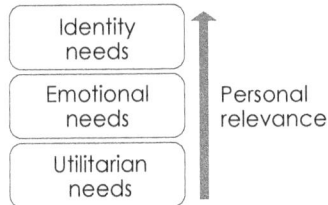

These three types of needs operate in concert to drive people's behavior. To illustrate, consider how the need for food interacts with higher order emotional and identity needs. All humans need to eat to obtain the nourishment necessary to survive, but which foods are chosen and which are rejected is often determined by people's emotional and identity needs. Even when the physiological need for food is active, a person might avoid indulgent foods that would put them in a negative emotional state such as regret or guilt. Similarly, food choices can be affected by identity needs. For example, a person who self-defines as a vegetarian will avoid meat products even when very hungry, since eating meat would run contrary to their self-identity.

The Dynamics of Customer Needs

Not all needs are active all the time. Many needs, especially utilitarian ones, remain dormant until individuals experience a deficiency, such as hunger, thirst, or safety. The realization of a gap between the current state and the desired state activates the relevant need. This creates a state of tension that drives the individual to reduce or eliminate it. The process of reducing this tension—referred to as need fulfillment—involves seeking means to close the gap between the actual and desired states.

When a particular need is active, individuals focus their attention on finding ways to gratify this need and often overestimate the importance of means that can fulfill it. For example, studies have shown that poor people tend to perceive coin sizes as larger than wealthier individuals do, and smokers deprived of nicotine perceive cigarettes to be longer. Similarly, it has been shown that hungry shoppers tend to purchase more groceries than originally planned and are also willing to pay more for them.[2]

Needs vary in the degree to which they are active in an individual's mind. The different levels of need activation are determined by the importance of the need and the magnitude of the gap between the current state and the desired state. People can have varying levels of awareness of a need, different degrees of urgency to fulfill it, and different thresholds for the obstacles they are willing to overcome to satisfy it. The more active a need is, the more likely it is to involve high levels of awareness, urgency, and willingness to overcome obstacles.

Active needs become goals that individuals aim to attain. The intensity with which individuals pursue a given goal is determined by their need state. Based on the degree to which a given need is prominent in people's minds, there are four main need states: *delight*, where the need has been fully met; *indifference*, where the need is reasonably met but there is room for improvement; *discomfort*, where individuals are aware of an unmet need but do not act to address it; and *problem*, where there is a prominent unmet need that individuals are actively seeking to address. These four types of need states are illustrated in Figure 3 and discussed next.

Figure 3. Customer Need States

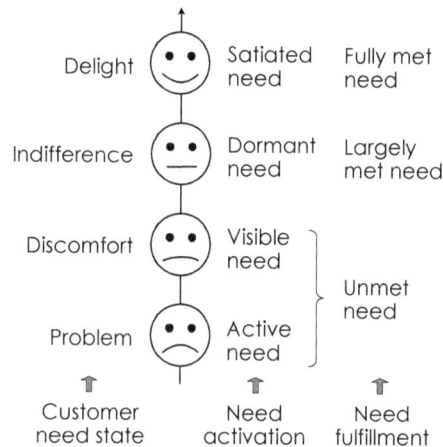

- *Delight*. Customers are delighted when they are extremely satisfied with the current means of fulfilling an active need, believe that this need has been fully addressed, and largely ignore alternative solutions. The state of delight typically occurs when expectations are completely met or exceeded, and there is no reason to expect that further improvement is necessary or even possible. This state of delight can persist until the relevant need re-emerges or until individuals encounter a way to improve their current situation.

- *Indifference*. Customers are indifferent when they are reasonably satisfied with the current options and prefer to avoid taking action. Even if their needs are not perfectly met and better alternatives exist, indifferent customers do not view this as a problem and are not actively seeking better options. Indifference occurs when an offering does a reasonably good job of fulfilling a need, and individuals do not have a compelling reason to change their behavior.

- *Discomfort*. Customers experience discomfort when they become aware of an unmet need and realize there is a gap between their current state and the ideal state. This discomfort typically manifests as a sense of uneasiness without necessarily being seen as a problem that needs to be solved. Although customers recognize that their situation could be improved, they do not prioritize addressing it and put it on the back burner.

- *Problem.* A need is perceived as a problem when customers not only recognize that they have an important unmet need and are dissatisfied with the status quo but also actively seek a solution. Clayton Christensen, the author of the theory of disruptive innovation, refers to these needs as "jobs to be done." Needs become "jobs to be done" when customers identify a goal they aim to achieve and face an impediment to reaching that goal. The "job" in this case is the progress that the individual is trying to achieve.[3]

Different need states vary in the degree to which they motivate customers to act. Those facing a well-defined problem are more likely to proactively seek to address the unmet need that they perceive as a pain point than those whose needs have been largely met and who are satisfied with the status quo. This is because customers expect to receive greater benefits from solving an important problem than from enhancing an already satisfactory experience. As a result, problem-solving offerings that aim to fulfill an active need tend to be adopted much faster than experience-enhancing offerings that merely improve a satisfactory experience.

For example, when Uber was launched, many people were dissatisfied with the status quo. Tasks such as hailing a taxi on the street often ranged from difficult to impossible, and arranging for a pick-up required significant time and effort. As a result, Uber gained popularity rapidly without a significant investment in advertising. Satisfied customers were happy to spread the word and promote the service. Likewise, companies like Airbnb, Dollar Shave Club, and Warby Parker, which found a way to solve an active unmet need, enjoyed rapid customer adoption, enabling them to reach billion-dollar valuations in record time.

Unlike offerings that address a problem people are actively trying to solve, offerings targeting those whose needs are largely met have much slower customer adoption. For example, even though Gillette's research showed that its five-bladed Fusion razor was preferred over the three-bladed Mach3, most men were satisfied with the shave quality of their current razor and were in no hurry to trade it in for the new version. Similarly, even though ultra-high-definition TVs could provide a better viewing experience, most consumers were reasonably satisfied with their existing high-definition TVs, resulting in slow adoption of the new technology.

Triggers as Action Drivers

Most needs remain dormant until they're awakened by an impulse—a trigger that signals a deficiency in some aspect of our lives. Any factor, whether internal or external, that highlights the potential for improvement becomes a catalyst, motivating us to act. Once activated, these needs drive behaviors that aim to achieve a more desirable state.

The Essence of Triggers

Triggers reveal unmet needs and motivate individuals to fulfill these needs with the company's offerings. Triggering a need is important because unless a need is active, individuals might not see the value of an offering that can fulfill that need. The essence of triggers as a mechanism for activating dormant needs and the different types of internal and external triggers are discussed in more detail below.

Activating Dormant Needs

The role triggers play in activating dormant needs can be related to the four types of need states—problem, indifference, discomfort, and delight—outlined earlier in this chapter. When customers are aware of a deficiency on a particular dimension and see it as a problem to be solved, triggers are largely irrelevant since the need has already been activated. At this stage, the main purpose of triggers is to frame the active need in a way that aligns with the benefits provided by the company's offering. For example, individuals actively planning a summer vacation but undecided on the specifics might be influenced by an advertisement for a Caribbean cruise. In this case, the advertisement's role is limited to channeling an already active need for an escape from the daily routine into a specific type of vacation experience—a Caribbean cruise.

When customers are aware that their situation can be improved but are reluctant to act, triggers can nudge them toward taking action by highlighting the benefits of addressing the need and showcasing a specific offering. For those whose needs have been largely met and who are generally happy with the status quo, triggers can reactivate these needs by making individuals aware that their current situation can be improved. To this end, triggers highlight the gap between the current and desired state and point individuals toward the benefits provided by the company's offering. For example, the need to replenish one's mental and physical resources might be made salient by viewing an advertisement for an exotic vacation, passing the window display of a travel agency, or listening to friends' accounts of their holiday break.

Triggering an action from a state of delight is much more difficult than simply activating a dormant need. It is a challenge to convince customers, whose needs are largely met and who see no reason to change their current circumstances, that their situation can be improved. In this case, triggers often set a new reference point that raises customers' expectations, creating a gap between their current and desired states. A common example of triggers that engage customers who are delighted with their current state is showcasing new offerings that provide superior benefits. For instance, after learning of a new mobile phone with superior functionality, individuals who have been delighted with their current phone might feel a strong urge to upgrade.

Based on their origin, triggers can be internal and external. Internal triggers are rooted in personal feelings, desires, or physiological states, whereas external triggers come from the surrounding environment, including significant life events and marketing activities.

Internal Triggers

Internal triggers, as their name implies, originate from the individual. They are idio-syncratic and occur at different points in time across different individuals. Based on the type of need they activate, internal triggers can be physiological or psychological.

Physiological triggers activate the most fundamental biological needs, such as hunger, thirst, rest, and sexual gratification. These needs are usually triggered automatically by our brain to sustain normal body function. Because these needs are essential for sur-vival, most of them are triggered regularly and follow a predictable pattern. For in-stance, hunger typically occurs several times a day, prompting us to seek food.

Psychological triggers involve the realization of a deficiency in a particular aspect of one's identity. A person might suddenly realize the presence of a gap between the cur-rent and the ideal fulfillment of a higher level need, such as the need for belonging, love, esteem, social status, and self-actualization. For example, the realization of one's advancing age, coupled with a sense of inevitable mortality and a feeling of lacking accomplishments in life—symptoms of a state we often refer to as a midlife crisis—can trigger the need for self-expression and make an individual buy the proverbial red con-vertible sports car.

Both physiological and psychological triggers stem from our own biological or men-tal activities rather than from external factors. On many occasions, however, our needs can be triggered by external events that occur in our environment. We discuss the dif-ferent types of external factors next.

External Triggers

External triggers are the various environmental factors that have the potential to activate a particular dormant need and motivate an individual's actions. For our purposes, we can distinguish two types of external triggers: *situational triggers*, which arise from the circumstances surrounding the individual, and *marketing triggers*, which are deliberately created by companies to activate a specific need. Both types of triggers—situational and marketing—aim to activate dormant needs that might otherwise go unnoticed.

Situational triggers are events or objects that make us realize we have an unmet need. Common types of situational triggers involve a change in a person's life circum-stances. Thus, major changes in an individual's lifestyle will frequently activate a set of needs associated with the change. Some of these lifestyle changes include going to college, graduating, moving to a new city, marrying, having kids, buying a house, and retiring. Consider the situational need triggers likely associated with retirement. Pri-mary among these will be a need to occupy the time previously spent at work. These newly activated needs will subsequently lead to new preferences. For example, a house that was satisfactory pre-retirement may now be deemed too large and too far from the golf course.

Another common type of situational trigger involves temporal events associated with a particular need. For example, events such as Valentine's Day, Mother's Day, Father's Day, Thanksgiving, and the New Year are likely to activate a particular set of needs that will, in turn, motivate specific activities aimed at fulfilling these needs. These occasions often prompt individuals to buy gifts, plan celebrations, and engage in traditions that align with the event.

One trigger that leads to the realization of an unmet need occurs at the start of each new year. People are often encouraged to engage in self-reflection and self-improvement by making New Year's resolutions, which for many Americans frequently involve the goal to lose weight. To achieve this goal, many individuals go online and start searching for a diet that will help them reduce calorie intake and ultimately shed unwanted pounds.

The impact of this trigger can be readily observed using Google Trends—a website that analyzes the historical patterns of top search queries on Google. One might predict that general interest in topics such as health and dieting remains relatively constant over time, as these topics reflect lifestyle choices and require long-term commitment. However, examining the popularity of searches for words like "diet" and "calorie" reveals a surprisingly consistent pattern that contradicts this prediction. Interest in health and dieting peaks around New Year's Day and declines throughout the rest of the year, only to peak again during the next resolution season (Figure 4). This trend suggests that people's interest in health- and dieting-related topics is highly influenced by the tradition of setting New Year's resolutions, which serves as an external trigger and motivates their behavior.

Figure 4. Information Search Pattern for the Word "Diet"

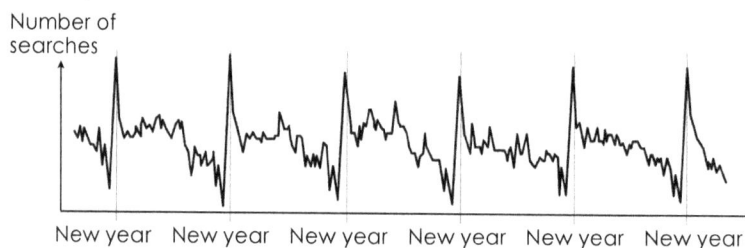

Because situational triggers reflect a change in an individual's circumstances rather than being internally evoked, they can be readily observed and, in many cases, anticipated. As a result, companies can coordinate their promotional activities in a way that is aligned with the needs triggered by the change in an individual's life circumstances.

Marketing triggers stem from a company's promotional activities aimed at motivating its target customers to take a particular action. These triggers often act in conjunction with situational triggers. For example, in anticipation of New Year's resolutions, a company might strategically advertise the benefits of a healthy diet and promote its weight-loss offerings. In addition to relying on circumstantial events, marketing triggers can also activate needs that might otherwise remain dormant.

One prominent example of a marketing trigger is Pepsodent's campaign designed to promote the habit of brushing teeth (with Pepsodent, of course). Surprisingly, in the early 1900s, tooth brushing was not common in the United States. Even when door-to-door salesmen convinced someone to buy toothpaste—the primary way dental products were sold at the turn of the last century—it would usually not be used very often. Pepsodent faced a seemingly insurmountable challenge: trying to sell toothpaste to people who gave little thought to brushing their teeth.

Pepsodent approached this challenge strategically. First, it identified a goal that would be meaningful to most consumers and likely to motivate them to act: showcasing a beautiful smile. This positioning was not just about oral hygiene but also about giving women a sense of confidence and self-esteem. The next challenge was to ensure that consumers associated this need with brushing their teeth.

To address this challenge, Pepsodent identified an impediment to having a beautiful smile—the film (plaque) that naturally builds up on teeth. This film is virtually invisible, and most consumers had not paid much attention to it. To create awareness of the film, Pepsodent bombarded consumers with messages such as "Note how many pretty teeth are seen everywhere. Why would any woman have dingy film on her teeth?"

Then, Pepsodent took on the challenge of making consumers realize that this film detracted from their appearance. To make the problem more prominent in consumers' minds, Pepsodent introduced the so-called tongue test. "Just run your tongue across your teeth," stated its ads. "You'll feel a film—that's what makes your teeth look 'off color' and invites decay." The solution to that problem was to brush with Pepsodent to achieve a bright, plaque-free "Pepsodent Smile." This campaign not only propelled Pepsodent to become one of the best-known U.S. consumer products but also helped make tooth brushing a daily routine. And all this stemmed from identifying a relevant trigger to appeal to a deep-seated psychological need.

Deciding Which Need to Trigger

Companies often focus on the tactical question of how to trigger a need, overlooking the strategically more important question of which particular need to trigger. Deciding which need to trigger is crucial because different needs can evoke different responses to the company's offering. For example, an important aspect of Pepsodent's success was activating the psychological need for social acceptance by stressing the advantages of a beautiful smile rather than the utilitarian need of maintaining dental health.

The specific need to trigger can vary across customers. For example, a toothpaste manufacturer might identify different age-related customer segments—teenagers, adults, and seniors—based on the benefits they are likely to seek in a toothpaste. For teenagers, who tend to be concerned with the social benefits of toothpaste, a company might emphasize that its toothpaste makes them more "kissable" and attractive to their peers. Adults, on the other hand, might be more interested in the health benefits of the toothpaste, so the company might promote its product by focusing on preventing cavities. Finally, because seniors are likely to be concerned with preserving and restoring their teeth, the company might position its toothpaste by highlighting its corrective benefits, such as repairing tooth enamel.

Imagine that you are designing an advertising campaign for a paint company like Benjamin Moore or Sherwin-Williams. How would you encourage consumers to repaint their home? The key to answering this question is identifying the higher level needs that might make consumers want to paint their house. For some, this need might have already been triggered internally because new furniture has prompted more redecorating, there's been some water damage, or the walls have just gotten too scuffed and worn. These consumers have already identified a problem to be solved and will seek out the paint that best meets their needs.

But many consumers do not have a pressing reason to repaint their homes. What can the company do to motivate them? One approach is to focus on the utilitarian benefits of repainting. For example, a company can highlight the fact that new paints are more technologically advanced, making them easier to keep clean and remove scuff marks and pencil scribbles. Alternatively, the company can promote the emotional benefits, such as making the home feel cozy, inviting, or invigorating. Here, paint can be advertised as a means for making consumers feel happy when they walk into a bright and cheery kitchen in the morning. Another approach is to promote the self-expressive benefits of having a home that reflects one's individuality or fashion sense.

The three types of benefits outlined above aim to trigger different types of needs. Based on the type of need they seek to activate, there are three main types of triggers: *utilitarian triggers*, which focus on activating more basic human needs; *emotional triggers*, which focus on activating the need for emotional gratification and well-being; and *identity triggers*, which focus on activating the need for self-actualization and self-expression.

These triggers are not mutually exclusive and can be activated simultaneously. For example, Starbucks is positioned as a purveyor of high-quality coffee (functional benefit), as well as a place where customers can feel at home (emotional benefit) and have a customized drink that becomes part of their self-image (identity benefit). Similarly, Harley-Davidson can trigger the need for emotional gratification associated with the joy of riding a bike, as well as the need for self-expression tied to the perception of being a free individual in control of their own destiny. We will discuss these three types of triggers—utilitarian, emotional, and identity—in more detail in the following sections.

Utilitarian Triggers

Utilitarian triggers aim to activate needs related to individuals' physical existence and their ability to accomplish specific tasks. Utilitarian triggers can activate physiological needs such as hunger, thirst, and safety, as well as needs related to preserving resources like effort, time, and money. Based on the way they create value, utilitarian triggers fall into two broad categories: *functional* triggers, which focus on maximizing benefits, and *monetary* triggers, which focus on minimizing financial expenses. These two types of triggers are discussed in more detail below.

Functional Triggers

Functional triggers are aimed at meeting or enhancing an individual's functional needs, emphasizing the acquisition or maintenance of positive outcomes. These triggers help individuals recognize a discrepancy between their current state and an ideal state, activating an otherwise dormant need and motivating them to act. Without activating a relevant need, a company's offerings might be overlooked by target customers despite their potential value.

Consider the case of TiVo. Introduced at the turn of the century, it was the first commercially available digital video recorder. TiVo offered a long list of novel features, including the ability to pause, play in slow motion, and instantly replay live shows; automatically record favorite programs regardless of time slot; provide direct access to all pre-recorded programs without fast-forwarding through previous recordings; skip commercials; and recommend programs the viewer was likely to enjoy. One might think that with such an abundance of features, TiVo would have become an immediate hit and a must-have household device. Yet, the reality was quite different: Apart from a relatively small number of early adopters, most consumers shrugged off TiVo's commercials and continued watching television the way they always had.

Why did TiVo fail to win the hearts and minds of consumers the same way the iPhone, Uber, and Airbnb did? After all, TiVo offered many unique benefits that had the potential to create value for its customers. The problem was that even though we now take most of these features for granted and consider them an essential part of the viewing experience, at the time TiVo was introduced most consumers were generally satisfied with their television-viewing experience. If anything, the concern was the size and the quality of the television sets. Rather than educating consumers about the specific benefits of TiVo, thus triggering a need to upgrade their viewing experience, the company assumed that the benefits were self-evident and would immediately resonate with consumers. They did not. Consumers did not understand the benefits TiVo could bring them and did not see an urgent problem that needed solving. And in the absence of a prominent need to be solved, most consumers did not rush to buy TiVo.

An informative example of successfully triggering a dormant need is Ginsu knives. Most consumers who ended up buying Ginsu knives were satisfied with the knives they already had in their kitchen. Even if some consumers were aware that their knives were not the sharpest, they did not give it much thought because their knives did the job reasonably well—until they saw the Ginsu infomercials.

Ginsu's challenge was to build demand for a product people did not realize they needed. "We were mindful," shared one of the company co-founders, "that the last thing anyone wanted was another set of knives. The challenge was to position the product so that it made every other knife you owned obsolete." This type of challenge is often addressed with infomercials. When it comes to triggering a need, infomercials can be very effective because their length allows a company to engage viewers, make them realize the benefits of the advertised product, and even envision themselves using the product and experiencing its benefits. Ginsu infomercials were ubiquitous in the 1980s, as the company bought more commercials per year than Coca-Cola.

Ginsu infomercials not only triggered a need but also provided viewers with an option to act on this need. The company was among the first TV advertisers to use direct-response marketing featuring 800 numbers. Another important factor in Ginsu's success is its name. Contrary to popular belief, Ginsu knives are not designed in Japan using an ancient sword-making secret but are made by the Ohio-based company Qui-kut. The Ginsu brand is a made-up name designed to be associated with the exceptional sharpness and durability of Japanese samurai swords.

Triggering a particular need before touting a company's features can greatly facilitate customers' ability to translate these features into meaningful benefits. For instance, Volvo's performance is more meaningful to those apprehensive about safety, Porsche's performance is more relevant to those concerned with speed and agility, and Toyota's performance is more relevant to those who care about reliability. Triggering a need makes the product's benefits more prominent in people's minds, prompting them to pay greater attention to seeking a means for fulfilling this need.

Functional triggers are particularly effective when the available options do not adequately fulfill a specific practical need, leaving this need either unmet or only partially fulfilled. This often occurs at the early stages of the product cycle when the performance of available offerings is deficient, leaving ample room for improvement. As the ability of the market offerings to deliver meaningful benefits that satisfy customers' needs improves and these benefits become more uniform across different offerings, functional triggers tend to become less effective, prompting companies to consider triggering different types of needs.

Monetary Triggers

Rather than focusing on functional benefits, a company might focus on the financial resources associated with fulfilling a particular need. Unlike functional triggers that aim to maximize benefits, monetary triggers focus customers' attention on minimizing monetary costs and saving money.

Consider the case of Dollar Shave Club. Launched in 2012, it quickly gained popularity through its humorous YouTube video that went viral, accumulating millions of views and generating widespread media coverage. In contrast to Gillette's focus solely on performance, Dollar Shave Club, as its name suggests, emphasized price. The message was simple: These days, all razors are good, and what really matters is the price.

By triggering the need to save money, Dollar Shave Club was able to shift consumers' attention from maximizing the benefits of shaving to minimizing its costs. The message resonated with consumers who were frustrated with Gillette's high prices and felt that the company was taking advantage of them. As a result, Dollar Shave Club quickly gained on Gillette—no small feat in a mature industry—and established a market footprint large enough to ultimately be acquired by Unilever for $1 billion only four years after its launch.

Dollar Shave Club is not alone in creating customer value by triggering the need to preserve financial resources. Retailers ranging from Walmart, Aldi, and Lidl to Dollar General, Family Dollar, and Dollar Tree owe their success to their razor-sharp focus on low prices and their promise to help customers save money. Triggering the need to preserve financial resources is relatively easy because money already has top-of-mind awareness for most consumers. The key to triggering this need is clearly communicating the importance of savings and, of course, ultimately being able to deliver on fulfilling this need.

Emotional Triggers

Emotional triggers aim to tap into a person's feelings and focus on affective benefits. Evoking an emotional reaction is not limited to emotional triggers; utilitarian needs can also provoke a distinct emotional response that signals the severity of the need. However, in the case of utilitarian needs, the emotional response is secondary and typically disappears once the underlying need is fulfilled. In contrast, emotional triggers directly target people's emotional needs, driven by their desire to experience pleasure and avoid pain. Depending on the valence of the activated need, emotional triggers can be broadly classified as positive or negative.

Positive-Emotion Triggers

Triggers designed to elicit positive emotions typically focus on creating or sustaining a positive emotional state. Because our behavior is often guided by the desire to feel good and experience positive emotions, companies frequently position their offerings as sources of positive affect. Emotions commonly triggered by marketers include sensory pleasure, enjoyment, love, nostalgia, and peace of mind.

Sensory pleasure is the emotional reaction to the design and aesthetics of the objects we encounter. The contoured, fluted lines of the iconic Coca-Cola bottle — one of the most famous shapes in the world — gratify our senses, triggering an emotional response when we see and touch the bottle. The first iMac sent shockwaves through the industry with its egg-shaped, translucent design that came in a variety of bright colors, creating an instant emotional connection with consumers. Method's line of household cleaning and hygiene products not only grabbed consumers' attention but also evoked a strong emotional reaction. All these products have one thing in common: They use design to evoke emotions that result in positive customer experiences.

The impact of design and the overall look and feel of an offering become increasingly important as utilitarian benefits are commoditized and consumers' attention shifts from performance aspects to an internal assessment of how they feel about the offering. Car manufacturers realized long ago that our car choices are often determined not by the car's actual performance but by its ability to trigger emotions. This emotional reaction stems from the fact that we often think of cars as having human-like features, associating headlights with eyes, the center part of the grille with the nose, and the air intake with the mouth. Anthropomorphizing cars triggers our feelings and helps create an emotional relationship with the car rather than a purely utilitarian one.

Enjoyment is another commonly triggered emotional reaction. A great example of designing an offering that triggers the need for excitement and enjoyment is Las Vegas. Promoted as The Entertainment Capital of the World, it is one of the planet's most visited tourist destinations. Not only does it offer various emotionally charged experiences, including gambling, shopping, fine dining, entertainment, and nightlife, but its slogan, "What happens in Vegas, stays in Vegas," connotes adventure, fun, and having a good time. In fact, for some, merely thinking of Las Vegas can trigger an emotional reaction.

Another example of the role of triggering emotions to activate dormant needs is the timeshare industry. The concept of timeshare ownership is based on creating excitement among potential customers during the sales presentation by showcasing appealing destinations, perks, options, and possibilities. More important, because presentations are usually done at the actual vacation destination, they create a pleasurable and fun experience, encouraging prospects to imagine what it would *feel* like to own a timeshare. This association between the positive state that potential buyers experience during the presentation and the benefits of owning a timeshare often occurs on a subconscious level.

Different products trigger enjoyment in different ways. Consider a seemingly trivial question: Why do people buy ice cream in the summer? The obvious answer involves a purely functional benefit: to cool down during hot summer days. But if this is true, then countries with warmer climates, like Italy, should consume more ice cream than countries with cooler climates, like Sweden. Yet, this is not correct: Swedes consume nearly twice as much ice cream annually compared to Italians.[4] The real benefit of ice cream is not just to cool down but to generate positive emotions and feel good.

Another powerful emotional trigger is *love*. A company that achieved great success by using affection as a trigger is De Beers. During the first half of the 20th century, there was no Western tradition of buying expensive diamond engagement rings. In fact, before World War II, only about ten percent of engagement rings contained diamonds. De Beers, which controlled the diamond supply, changed that by associating diamonds with everlasting love in its unforgettable advertising slogan: "A diamond is forever." As a result of this highly romanticized positioning, which triggered the need to express (and later reaffirm) love and commitment, the sales of diamonds in the United States increased nearly a hundredfold.

Nostalgia is another popular emotional trigger, connecting a company's offering with positive events or ideas from the past. It taps into familiar concepts that customers already love and have fond memories of. When Volkswagen launched a redesigned version of the iconic Beetle half a century after the introduction of the first model, it counted on consumers' nostalgia for the irreverent, youthful spirit of the 1960s and 1970s. This strategy paid off, ultimately translating into strong sales and a revitalized brand image, highlighting Volkswagen's ability to innovate while respecting its heritage.

The role of nostalgia as an emotional trigger is particularly relevant as we age and during times of uncertainty. Nostalgia gives us a sense of continuity and meaning by triggering happy memories and providing comfort. Similarly, in times of anxiety or uncertainty, nostalgia evokes a sense of security and helps us recall the best memories from our past. By anchoring new experiences in familiar emotions, nostalgia helps us navigate change, providing a stable reference point in an ever-evolving world.

Creating *peace of mind* triggers positive emotions by helping reduce anxiety and perceived risk. For insurance companies, peace of mind is a key component of their value proposition. Advertising slogans like "You're in good hands with Allstate" trigger the need for safety and emphasize the importance of reducing uncertainty. Similarly, the belief that "Nobody ever got fired for choosing IBM" became a key driver of IBM's sales by focusing customers' attention on the psychological benefits associated with their purchase. When IBM was the default option for mainframe computers, choosing its products was an easy-to-justify decision even if something did not work out. This ease of justification is one reason why market leaders are often successful despite having higher prices and, sometimes, subpar functionality.

Negative-Emotion Triggers

One of the most used negative-emotion triggers is *fear*. Fear is our emotional response when facing various types of physical, financial, and social risks. Companies use negative-emotion triggers by focusing our attention on the negative consequences of a particular type of risk that we either did not know existed or had not paid much attention to. This newly created awareness of potential risk naturally evokes an emotional reaction that can range from uneasiness to outright fear. Once a sense of uneasiness has been created, a company showcases its offering as the best way to alleviate the risk and neutralize the potential threat.

Although triggering fear can backfire by associating negative feelings with the offering, some companies adopt this approach, believing that highlighting a problem customers were not aware of and evoking a strong emotional reaction will trigger interest in their products. An example of the effectiveness of triggering fear to promote consumption is Listerine's advertising campaign designed to convince American consumers to start using mouthwash.

Listerine's history dates back to 1879 when Dr. Joseph Lawrence, inspired by the research of British surgeon Joseph Lister on sterilization techniques, created a unique antiseptic called Listerine. Initially, Listerine was sold in drop-like glass bottles and promoted for use in surgeries. Studies conducted over the next few decades showed that it was also effective in killing germs in the mouth. Building on this research, Listerine mouthwash in 1914 became the first product in the United States to be sold over the counter and advertised as an oral germ killer. However, it was slow to take off because most consumers did not perceive a problem that it could solve. To address this challenge, the company decided to identify a need that could be met with Listerine.

The solution was to present bad breath as a medical condition with adverse consequences if left untreated. And to make it more convincing, the company dug up a Latin word—halitosis, meaning "unpleasant breath"—and launched it into general usage. This scientific-sounding name made many consumers pay attention and take the bad breath problem seriously. The medical-sounding name was just the beginning. Listerine's ad campaigns framed halitosis as a health condition that was keeping people from achieving their true potential in life.

Many of Listerine's ads presented readers with dramatic stories featuring young women struggling to find romantic partners and ultimately get married. One ad told the following story: "Enter Edna, a beautiful young woman with all of the charm and social graces that made her desirable, except for one fatal flaw—Edna suffered from halitosis. What made it worse was that she didn't even know it! Not even her closest friends would tell her and so poor Edna, despite all of her charms, was 'always the bridesmaid and never the bride.'" The campaign became so popular that the last phrase became a common expression.

Although considered rather offensive nowadays, the fear appeal worked a century ago: Listerine's "halitosis" campaign resulted in a tenfold increase in revenues in just a few years. Notably, although Listerine was a hygiene product with distinct functional benefits, what made it a household name was not its medical benefits but the fear of social and romantic rejection. Listerine's story is one of many examples showing that triggering fear can be a powerful driver of human behavior.

A more recent type of fear appeal is the *fear of missing out* (FOMO), which refers to the anxiety stemming from the belief that one might miss a unique, attractive opportunity. This fear is often related to unmet social needs, such as the need to belong, form meaningful interpersonal relationships, and stay connected with others. This social aspect of the fear of missing out reflects the belief that others are having better experiences and living better lives while one is stuck in a rut.

The fear of missing out is not limited to social experiences; it can also stem from a broader set of missed opportunities, such as financial gains or acquiring unique objects. In this context, triggering the fear of missing out aims to motivate individuals to act by evoking anxiety and a feeling of regret at missing opportunities that could improve their lives.

Identity Triggers

Identity triggers go beyond utilitarian and emotional needs to focus on an individual's need for self-realization, belonging, esteem, and respect. These identity needs have the highest personal relevance and occupy the top of Maslow's hierarchy of needs. Because of their fundamental role in regulating an individual's behavior, the needs to self-actualize and express one's identity play a crucial role in motivating behavior.

Based on the type of identity need they aim to activate, identity triggers can be broadly divided into two types: status triggers and personality triggers. Status triggers target individuals' need to express their socioeconomic class and are typically related to factors such as social status, wealth, and power. Personality triggers, on the other hand, involve factors that showcase the unique aspects of an individual's personality, such as their value system, beliefs, and taste. Let's examine these two types of triggers in more detail.

Status Triggers

Status triggers activate individuals' desire to demonstrate their membership in a particular socioeconomic class. These triggers might target members of a higher class to encourage consumption that distinguishes them from members of a lower class. Alternatively, status triggers might target members of a lower class to spur consumption of offerings that will present them as members of a higher class.

A revealing example of the impact of status triggers dates to the 18th century and involves King Frederick II of Prussia, who became known as Frederick the Great. Facing the risk of famine in his country, the King decided to promote the growth and consumption of potatoes. Although the potato had been brought from Peru by Spanish explorers several centuries earlier, it was slow to take off in Europe. Even though it was a vital source of nutrients and was easy to grow, it was widely considered unsuitable for human consumption, and, sometimes even viewed as a product of the devil or witchcraft.

Frederick's initial efforts to encourage his subjects to grow potatoes fell on deaf ears. Peasants' resistance to the unsightly vegetable was captured in the saying that was popular in Prussia at the time, "What the peasant doesn't know, he will not eat." Even when Frederick decreed the growth of potatoes, it proved ineffective. One town responded to the order with a rhetorical question: "These things have neither smell nor taste, not even the dogs will eat them, so what use are they to us?"

Ultimately, Frederick decided to take a different approach. Rather than trying to encourage peasants to eat potatoes, he declared them a royal vegetable, suited only for the king and the royal family. He had fields of potatoes planted around the capital and ordered the army to guard these fields to protect the potatoes from being stolen by peasants. This protection, however, was for show only; guards were instructed to look the other way and let peasants steal some potatoes. The real purpose of having guards was not to protect the fields but to create the impression that, like truffles, potatoes were a treasure worthy of being consumed only by royals. By triggering the need for social status among peasants seeking to associate themselves with the higher class, Frederick helped make potatoes not only widely cultivated but also a staple of German cuisine.

The effectiveness of status triggers is rooted in the Veblen effect, named after American economist Thorstein Veblen. This concept describes the tendency to acquire goods primarily to display social status, income, and wealth. Veblen introduced the idea of conspicuous consumption to explain why affluent individuals often put on a highly visible show of consuming goods that showcase their wealth and social standing. He wrote, "To gain and to hold the esteem it is not sufficient merely to possess wealth or power. The wealth or power must be put in evidence, for esteem is awarded only on evidence." This evidence is provided through conspicuous consumption, where high-priced goods are acquired not for their functional value but for their ability to signal status.[5]

The desire to signal socioeconomic status is particularly prominent in environments characterized by the creation of new wealth and the upward mobility of certain social groups, such as the emergence of an upper and middle class in developing countries. In this context, status triggers can be very effective for luxury brands purchased by consumers seeking to showcase their wealth. In fact, the entire luxury industry is largely based on the notion of social hierarchy. One of the primary goals of luxury products is to signal social status and create a sense of exclusivity by separating those with means from those without. The exclusive nature of luxury is reflected in the tagline from a 1980s advertisement for Krug Champagne: "For most, Krug will remain out of reach." Without invoking social status and exclusivity, the appeal of luxury is lost.

Personality Triggers

Instead of appealing to the desire to express socioeconomic status, personality triggers aim to tap into the need to express one's unique values, beliefs, and preferences. While status triggers are usually linked to belonging to a high socioeconomic class rather than highlighting individual traits, personality triggers focus on the need to showcase personal identity, reflecting a person's aspirations, abilities, and tastes.

By activating the need to express oneself, personality triggers can significantly impact people's decisions and actions. For example, one study showed that merely asking participants a question related to certain aspects of their personality—such as "Do you consider yourself to be somebody who is adventurous and likes to try new things?"—led to significantly higher levels of willingness to try a new product.[6]

The need to define one's identity is closely associated with the need for self-expression. Self-expression allows people to distinguish themselves from others, define their own values, beliefs, and needs, and validate their self-identity. The backbone of a person's identity is the value system that reflects the principles, standards, or qualities that this person holds in high regard. Consider the case of Betty Crocker.

In the mid-'50s, Betty Crocker—a popular brand known for providing homemakers with recipes and cake mixes—introduced its latest creation: an easy-to-make cake mix. The company's goal was to simplify the food preparation process, reducing the time and effort required. The concept seemed logical: homemakers, who are often very busy and have many responsibilities, would appreciate an instant cake mix that required just adding water before baking. Yet, despite the company's high hopes for the new product, consumers' reaction was lukewarm, and the sales were disappointing.

Research commissioned to address the problem identified one potential source of consumers' tepid response: It had less to do with how the cake tasted and more to do with how consumers viewed the benefit of the easy-to-make cake. Contrary to conventional wisdom that products requiring less effort are always better, studies showed that in this case, the opposite was true. An important aspect of the self-identity of many of Betty Crocker's customers in the 1950s was taking care of the family, and as a result, they felt guilty about making a cake so easily.

Based on this insight, the company altered the recipe to require consumers to add fresh eggs to the mix. The intention was not so much to enhance the cake's flavor but to change how consumers perceived the process of making the cake, particularly in relation to their identity as caregivers for their families. Along with the recipe change, the company highlighted this added effort in its advertising, with the tagline, "Because you add the eggs yourself." By emphasizing the homemaker's involvement, this repositioning tapped into the identity-driven need to care for one's family, ultimately turning the cake mix into one of the company's bestsellers.

Betty Crocker's experience is not unique. Around the same time, Nestlé discovered a problem with the positioning of its instant coffee, Nescafé. It started with an experiment conducted by Berkeley professor Mason Haire, who examined how the type of coffee purchased—instant or drip ground—influenced people's perceptions of the buyer. He devised two shopping lists that contained commonly purchased food items like bread, hamburger patties, carrots, baking powder, canned peaches, potatoes, and coffee. The two lists were identical in all aspects except that one contained Nescafé, an instant coffee, and the other Maxwell House, a drip ground coffee. He then gave each of these lists to different groups of respondents and asked them to describe the type of woman who would purchase the listed groceries and write brief descriptions of her personality and character.[7]

Simply switching the type of coffee on the shopping list had a dramatic impact on people's perceptions of the shopper. Nearly half the respondents described the woman who bought Nescafé as a poor planner of household purchases and outright lazy, compared to only 4% who deemed the Maxwell House buyer lazy and 12% who felt she was a poor planner. The Nescafé buyer was characterized as a spendthrift by 12% of the respondents, a trait not attributed to the Maxwell House buyer. Additionally, 16% of the participants described the beleaguered Nescafé buyer as "a bad wife," while nobody thought that of the Maxwell House buyer. As in Betty Crocker's case, making things easier backfired because it clashed with the self-image of many of Nestlé's customers, who viewed their main responsibility as taking care of the family. Ultimately, Nestlé repositioned its instant coffee away from ease and convenience to better reflect the personality of its target customers.

Note that, like most other needs, the need to express one's identity is context dependent. Betty Crocker's approach was successful given the beliefs and value system of women in the 1950s. At that time, a product that required greater effort but helped consumers reaffirm their identity as homemakers was valued more than a product that required less effort but was inconsistent with that identity. As society has moved away from gender stereotypes and consumers have been given multiple ways to express their self-identity, products offering convenience and ease of use tend to be preferred today. This shift highlights the importance of understanding the evolving cultural and social contexts when triggering self-expressive needs.

SUMMARY

Most actions are motivated by active needs that people aim to fulfill. Needs can be divided into three general categories: *utilitarian*, *emotional*, and *identity*. Not all needs are active at any given point in time; many needs are dormant until individuals experience a deficiency on a particular dimension, such as hunger, thirst, or safety. Active needs become goals that individuals aim to fulfill. Based on the degree to which a given need is prominent in people's minds, there are four main need states: delight, indifference, discomfort, and problem. Offerings addressing a problem are adopted much faster than offerings targeting customers who are satisfied with the current situation and do not have an urgent need.

Most needs are not active until they are awakened by a trigger — an impulse that signals a deficiency. Based on their origin, triggers can be internal or external. Internal triggers originate from the individual and can be physiological or psychological in nature. External triggers are the various environmental factors that have the potential to activate an otherwise dormant need. External triggers can be situational, arising from individuals' circumstances, or marketing, which are deliberately created by companies to stimulate demand for their products.

Based on the type of need they aim to activate, there are three types of triggers: utilitarian, emotional, and identity triggers. *Utilitarian triggers* aim to activate needs related to individuals' physical existence—their ability to accomplish specific tasks and obtain satisfactory outcomes. Utilitarian triggers fall into two broad categories: functional triggers, which aim to maximize gains by activating physiological needs such as hunger, thirst, and safety; and monetary triggers, which are focused on attaining and preserving financial resources.

Emotional triggers tap into emotional needs by targeting individuals' desire to experience pleasure and avoid pain. Based on the valence of the activated need, emotional triggers can be positive or negative. Positive-emotion triggers focus on creating or maintaining a positive emotional state. Positive emotions commonly triggered by marketers include sensory pleasure, enjoyment, love, nostalgia, and peace of mind. One of the most common negative-emotion triggers used by marketers is fear—the affective response to various types of physical, financial, and social risks. A more recent type of fear appeal is the fear of missing out—the anxiety stemming from the belief that one might miss a unique and attractive opportunity.

Identity triggers focus on an individual's need for self-realization, belonging, esteem, and respect. These triggers typically concentrate on either status or personality. Status triggers target individuals' desire to express their socioeconomic status, including social standing, wealth, and power. In contrast, personality triggers focus on people's need to express their own identity, as reflected in their beliefs, aspirations, abilities, and tastes.

KEY TAKEAWAYS

Trigger a need. An offering can create value only if it addresses an active customer need.

Identify the focal need. Before deciding *how* to trigger a need, decide *which* need to trigger.

Functionality has limits. In the age of commoditization, creating value solely by fulfilling utilitarian needs can be difficult to sustain.

Spark emotions. Emotional triggers can have a strong effect on customers' behavior.

Engage the self. Identity triggers activate needs that have the highest personal relevance and can be a long-term driver of customer behavior.

SPOTLIGHT: MASLOW'S THEORY OF HUMAN NEEDS

The theory introduced by American psychologist Abraham Maslow is one of the most widely recognized classifications of human needs. The basic premise of this theory is that motivations arise from unfulfilled needs, which might be physiological, like the need for food, or psychological, like the need for love, friendship, or respect. Maslow identifies five basic types of needs: physiological, safety, belongingness and love, esteem, and a need to reach one's potential, referred to as self-actualization. These five needs are arranged in a hierarchy and often depicted as levels within a pyramid, such that lower level needs tend to subside as they are increasingly satisfied and are replaced by newly emerging higher level needs (Figure 5).[8]

Figure 5. Maslow's Hierarchy of Needs

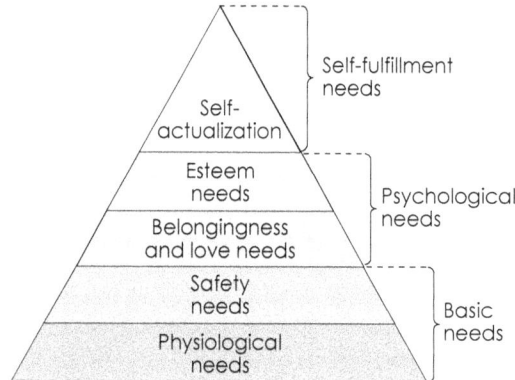

- *Physiological needs.* The lowest and most basic needs in the hierarchy are physiological, which must be satisfied for human survival. Common examples of physiological needs include essential resources such as food, water, sleep, and rest. When these needs are not met, and individuals experience extreme deficiency in any of these areas, fulfilling them tends to become a dominant and overwhelming driver of behavior, often overshadowing all other needs.

- *Safety needs.* The need for safety involves the desire for personal security by avoiding uncertainty, risk, and danger. Unlike physiological needs, which focus on achieving positive outcomes like alleviating thirst, safety needs are centered on preventing negative outcomes, such as avoiding physical harm, injury, or pain. As with physiological needs, individuals whose need for safety is not adequately met will be primarily motivated by this need, organizing their behaviors and decisions around ensuring their protection and stability.

- *Belongingness and love needs.* Belongingness refers to the fundamental human need for connectedness, meaningful interpersonal relationships, and a sense of being part of a group or community. Beyond the basic need to belong, humans also have a deep-seated need to love and be loved, both sexually and non-sexually. The need for love can be seen as a more intense and profound expression of the need for belongingness, characterized by deeper emotional bonds, closer connections, and a heightened level of emotional intensity.

- *Esteem needs.* The need for esteem is centered around people's desire for respect and appreciation. It involves two components: the need for respect from others, which reflects the desire for status, recognition, fame, and attention, and the need for self-esteem, which reflects a sense of dignity, achievement, and independence. According to Maslow, these two types of esteem vary in their relative importance. The need for respect and recognition is considered a lower level need compared to the higher-level need for self-respect and self-esteem.

- *Self-actualization.* The need for self-actualization is the pinnacle of the hierarchy of needs. This need can be broadly described as a need for self-fulfillment, which stems from the realization of one's full potential; it is the drive to accomplish everything that one can be. The need for self-actualization manifests differently across individuals: For some, it might manifest as a desire for self-expression through art; for others, it might lead to advancing their social status; and for yet others, it can take the form of athletic or academic excellence.

Introduced nearly a century ago, Maslow's theory is still very influential today. However, it also has limitations. While people generally progress up the hierarchy from physiological needs to self-actualization, higher needs can sometimes take precedence even when lower needs are unmet. For instance, a person might sacrifice basic needs like affection and safety for the sake of a cause. Accordingly, Maslow's theory should be viewed as a framework for understanding human needs rather than a rigid sequence in which these needs are fulfilled.

THE CX CANVAS: TRIGGERING A NEED

Designing the customer experience starts with identifying a customer need that the company's offering aims to fulfill. This involves two key components: (1) analyzing the company's target customers to determine their underlying needs and, if necessary, (2) developing a course of action to activate the identified need (Figure 6).

Figure 6. Triggering a Customer's Need: The Big Picture

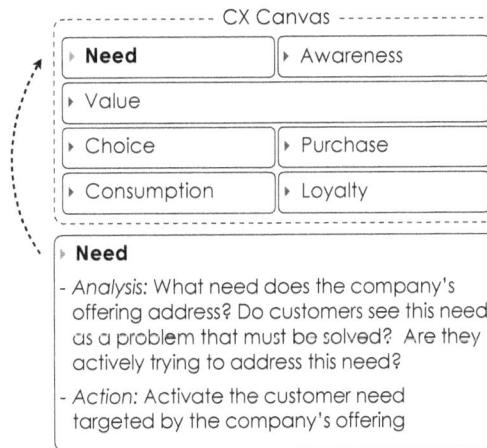

The analysis of a customer's need state identifies the need that the company aims to fulfill with its offering, the extent to which customers are aware that this need has not been met, and their intention to act to fulfill it. Here, a manager must ask the following questions:

- *What need does the company's offering address?* This question aims to identify the customer problem—the pain point—that the offering is designed to solve. Customers' needs can be defined along three dimensions: utilitarian (what practical problem does the offering solve?), emotional (how does the offering make customers feel?), and identity (how does the offering help customers express their values and beliefs?).

- *Do target customers see this need as a problem that must be solved?* This question aims to determine whether the focal need is active, meaning that target customers think their current situation is deficient and can be improved. The answer to this question shows the level of interest target customers are likely to show in the company's offering.

- *Are target customers actively trying to address this need?* This question aims to determine the importance of the given need and the extent to which customers are actively seeking means to fulfill this need. The answer to this question indicates customers' readiness to engage with the company's offering.

The ultimate purpose of this analysis is to identify the need that must be active for customers to appreciate the benefits of the company's offering and to assess the extent to which customers are aware of this need and recognize its importance. The course of action a company should take depends on whether customers perceive the need as a problem that must be solved and whether they are actively seeking solutions. Based on customers' need states, there are two core challenges, each requiring a distinct approach:

- *Dormant need.* These customers are unaware that their current situation can be improved and are content with the status quo. A company's goal here is to trigger the dormant need by raising customers' awareness of the gap between the desired and actual state of affairs. This can be achieved by showing customers how certain aspects of their lives can be improved, thus creating a sense of deficiency that impels action.

- *Passive recognition.* These customers are aware that the focal need has not been fully met but are not actively seeking a solution. A company's goal here is to move customers from a passive mindset that merely recognizes a deficiency to an implementational mindset focused on action. This can be achieved by raising the perceived importance of the need so that fulfilling it becomes a priority in customers' minds.

The challenges of activating a customer's need and the corresponding company actions are outlined in Figure 7. Dormant needs tend to require more effort from the company, as it must both raise customers' awareness of the unmet need and emphasize its importance. In contrast, needs that are already active require relatively less effort, allowing the company to focus on prioritizing the focal need to incite action.

Figure 7. Triggering a Customer's Need: The Action Plan

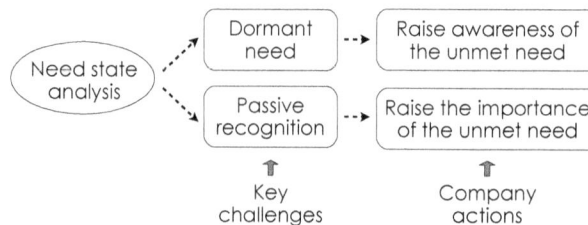

Consider a company that has developed a novel sensor that continuously monitors body hydration levels and sends notifications to a mobile device, informing users exactly when, what, and how much to drink. When designing the customer acquisition strategy, the first question to ask is whether target customers are concerned with monitoring their hydration levels. Note that the issue is not whether customers believe hydration is important, but whether they think it is crucial to know their current hydration status. Indeed, if customers are only concerned about staying hydrated, they can address this by drinking plenty of liquids and keeping a water bottle or other hydration source handy.

Further analysis might reveal that while knowing their hydration level is important for those actively involved in sports—such as marathon runners, triathletes, and competitive cyclists, it is not a top priority for most consumers. This suggests that for the company to succeed among the general public, it must raise awareness about both the benefits of staying hydrated and the importance of monitoring optimal hydration levels.

Merely promoting the benefits of staying hydrated is insufficient, as this need can be met by simply consuming more liquids. The goal is to create awareness and emphasize the importance of monitoring hydration levels and maintaining optimal hydration, not merely staying hydrated. Without ensuring that target customers understand the importance of monitoring their hydration levels, they are unlikely to pay attention to, evaluate, decide on, and purchase the device.

Finally, for those actively involved in sports and likely aware of the importance of hydration, the company does not need to spend resources to trigger this need. Instead, it should focus on creating awareness of its offering and engaging customers to ensure that its hydration sensor is a part of their consideration set.

CHAPTER THREE

CREATING AN ENGAGEMENT MINDSET

The conscious brain thinks it's the Oval Office when actually it is the press office issuing explanations for actions we've already taken.
—Jonathan Haidt, American social psychologist, author of *The Righteous Mind*

The customer experience typically begins with an active need that customers are looking to satisfy. When customers recognize a gap between where they are and where they want to be, they embark on a journey to bridge this gap. This journey involves searching for a product or service capable of meeting their need (Figure 1). To achieve this, customers form a consideration set, a shortlist of potential options from which they choose the one that best addresses their need. In this chapter, we will explore how customers gather information, what motivates their engagement, and strategies companies can use to ensure that their offerings are included in the customers' consideration sets.

Figure 1. The Customer Experience Map: Creating an Engagement Mindset

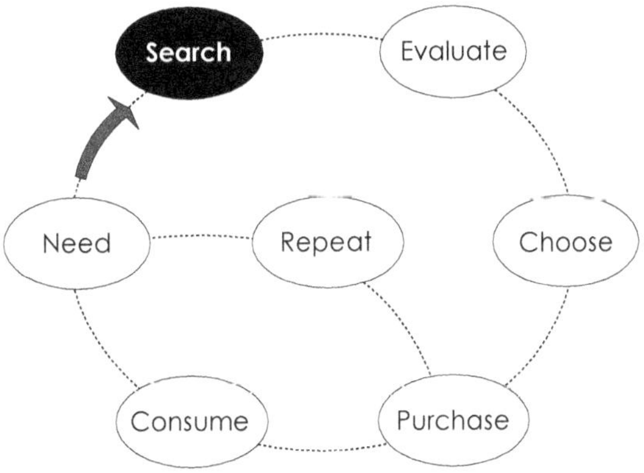

To be chosen, an offering must first be considered. In the words of James Patterson, a former advertising executive and a bestselling author whose books have sold over 300 million copies worldwide, "No book has ever been bought without first being picked up." Engaging customers with the company's offering is key for this offering to be considered. The importance of engagement in managing the customer experience raises the question: What are the key factors that determine whether a company's offering will be actively considered? Or more generally, what drives customer engagement? Consider the following scenarios:

- Your client, a large wine retailer, is trying to encourage customers to consider buying French wine. What in-store activities would you propose?

- You are advising a grocery store on the shelf placement of different cereal brands. What factors should the store consider when making this decision?

- You are a service manager at a high-end hotel chain known for offering exceptional customer service. You are contemplating asking customers to evaluate their experience following their stay. What factors do you need to consider when making this decision?

- You are the manager of a popular brand of snacks and are challenged with the task of increasing its top-of-mind awareness. What are the different strategies for achieving this goal?

- You are advising an advertising agency on a campaign that highlights the benefits of the company's offering by depicting undesirable outcomes for customers who choose a competitor's offering. What are the pros and cons of this approach?

In this chapter, we discuss the science behind making an offering stand out and become part of a customer's consideration set. We start by examining how people process available information, outlining the two systems of thinking and describing how they influence decision outcomes. We then discuss how people search for information and delineate factors that tend to draw their attention. Next, we address the role of attention in evaluating available information and why things that become the focus of attention are perceived to be more important. We then consider the role of associations in creating and changing beliefs and identify strategies for creating impactful associations. Finally, we address the issue of involvement gaps and the danger of overestimating the level of customer involvement.

The discussion of the conceptual issues entailed in creating an engagement mindset is enriched by examples of managerial decisions illustrating the key points. We will see how Volkswagen used its size to its advantage to draw attention; how Unilever used sexually valenced ads to promote its Axe fragrance; how Snickers, Kit Kat, and Campbell's managed to create top-of-mind awareness for their offerings; how winemakers redefined the category of fortified wines; how Sony used customer-friendly design to create the Walkman; and how McGraw-Hill was able to expand the advertiser base for its magazines.

Let's delve deeper into the factors that drive customer engagement and examine how behavioral science can assist managers in ensuring their offerings are considered by their target customers.

Thinking Fast and Slow

Thinking is a process of seeking and evaluating information. It directs people's actions and helps interpret the outcomes of these actions. The process of thinking is highly adaptable to the type of information available and the nature of the decision task. We will discuss the adaptive nature of thinking and the different ways in which people process information in more detail next.

The Two Systems of Thinking

Research in psychology and behavioral economics has shown that people engage in two types of information processing based on their level of involvement with what is being processed. At times, people evaluate available information in an automatic, shallow, heuristic, and mindless way; at other times, they engage in a controlled, deep, systematic, and more effortful evaluation. These two types of information processing—referred to as System 1 and System 2 processing—are most prominently articulated by Daniel Kahneman, one of the founders of modern behavioral science and a recipient of the Nobel Prize in Economics.[1]

System 1 and System 2 processing are different ways of taking in information and making decisions. System 1 operates automatically and quickly, requiring little or no effort. It is nonverbal, characterized by reduced vigilance, and focused on recognition rather than comparison. In contrast, System 2 is subject to conscious judgments, is slower, and requires much greater mental effort. It is intricately linked to language, is vigilant, and is focused on analysis and comparison rather than recognition. While System 1 is associative, heuristic-based, and relatively independent of an individual's working memory, System 2 is analytical, rule-based, and limited by working memory capacity (Figure 2).

Figure 2. The Two Systems of Thinking

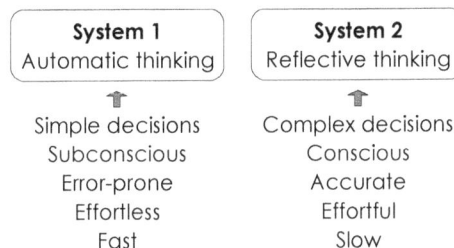

System 1 Automatic thinking	**System 2** Reflective thinking
⬆	⬆
Simple decisions	Complex decisions
Subconscious	Conscious
Error-prone	Accurate
Effortless	Effortful
Fast	Slow

The distinctive ways in which System 1 and System 2 process information have important implications for decision making. Individuals with a low level of involvement are more likely to rely on System 1 when evaluating the available information; they tend to employ *associative thinking*, relying on recognition and pattern matching, and focusing on the similarities of the available options. On the other hand, individuals who display a high degree of interest in the decision are more likely to rely on System 2 when evaluating the available information; they are more likely to employ *analytical thinking*, systematically comparing and contrasting both the similarities and differences of the available options.

The existence of two systems of thinking raises the question of when and how each system is activated when evaluating incoming information. A useful way to address this question is to think of it in terms of the effort–accuracy tradeoff. System 1 prioritizes low effort and speed at the expense of accuracy, whereas System 2 prioritizes accuracy at the expense of effort and speed. Even though people strive for accuracy, they have limited cognitive resources to thoroughly evaluate each piece of information. As a result, they must decide how to allocate cognitive resources and whether to use System 2 to carefully analyze the available information or to evaluate it on a subconscious level in a more superficial way by using System 1.

Two-system thinking reflects our brain's attempt to balance effort and accuracy. We rely on System 1 when making decisions that are not very important, such as buying paper towels; for repeated purchases, such as buying milk; and for decisions made under time pressure, such as when we are in a hurry. Conversely, we rely on System 2 when making consequential decisions, such as buying a car or a house and choosing a career or an educational institution. The extent of System 2's involvement in the decision process also depends on the nature of the object that is the focus of people's attention. For example, an ad depicting a delicious burger is likely to engage System 1 and elicit a visceral reaction that appeals to the sense of hunger. As a result, we process this ad in a very fast and intuitive fashion. In contrast, an ad that is heavy on verbal and numeric information requires relatively more complex processing and is likely to engage the more diligent and slow System 2.

Because System 1 has a much greater capacity to instantly evaluate vast amounts of information, virtually all information that reaches System 2 has already been processed by System 1. Thus, one important decision that System 1 must make when evaluating each piece of information is whether to pass it to System 2 for further evaluation or to keep it on a subconscious level and process it automatically. Given the myriad bits of information we are bombarded with every minute, only a small fraction of this information ever reaches System 2, with most of our thinking accomplished by System 1.

This reliance on System 1, however, comes at a cost. Consider the following problem: A bat and a ball cost $1.10 in total. The bat costs $1.00 more than the ball. How much does the ball cost? Our intuition tells us that if a bat and a ball cost $1.10 in total and the bat costs $1.00 more than the ball, then the ball costs $0.10. This seems like a simple problem that can be easily addressed by System 1 and, accordingly, it is often solved without the deliberate thinking characteristic of System 2. Recall, however, that one of the drawbacks of System 1 is that its ability to provide an instant, automatic, and effortless solution often comes at the cost of low accuracy. And this is exactly the case with the bat-and-ball example. The ball actually costs five cents, not ten cents.[2]

The above example raises the question: Why do we rely on System 1 if it is not very reliable? The problem is that we are cognitive misers. To preserve mental resources, we tend to outsource all relatively easy tasks to System 1 without engaging System 2. Because the bat-and-ball example seems relatively simple and appears to have a straightforward solution, we accept that solution without thinking too much about it.

System 1 not only influences the decisions we make, but it can also determine the way information is presented to System 2. Consider the following visual illusion of two tables in Figure 3, commonly referred to as Shepard tables, named after Stanford psychologist Roger Shepard.[3] How would you describe the shapes of the two tabletops?

Figure 3. The Shepard Illusion

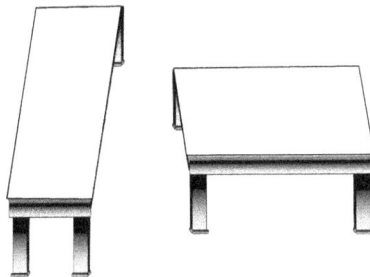

Chances are that you described the tabletop on the left as long and narrow and the one on the right as square-like. This, however, is incorrect. The two tabletops have exactly the same shape (this is not a typo; feel free to measure the tops of both tables for yourself). The two tabletops appear drastically different because our eyes perceive them according to principles of interpreting three-dimensional objects. What is particularly striking is that this pattern of perception is so strong that even after we know that the shapes of the two tabletops are identical, we still see them as very different.

The tabletop example demonstrates both the primacy and the power of System 1. Even when the analytical part of our brain, representing System 2, tells us that the tabletops are the same width and depth, it is powerless to diminish the magnitude of the illusion. System 1 manages to impose its own interpretation even in the presence of contradictory knowledge presented by System 2.

The Interplay Between System 1 and System 2

Even though System 1 and System 2 operate using different rules and processes, they do not function independently from each other. Instead, they are closely intertwined, complementing each other's strengths, and jointly maximizing the overall accuracy and efficiency of our mental processes. System 1 processes the incoming information, evaluates its relevance, and then either directly initiates a corresponding action or passes the information to System 2 for more detailed deliberation. System 1 is always turned on, even when we are not paying attention. In fact, it is System 1 that directs attention to things that might be important and merit consideration. One way System 1 determines what is worthy of conscious attention is by personal relevance.

The *cocktail party effect* is a prominent illustration of the way personal relevance guides the interaction between the two systems. This effect reflects our ability to focus our attention on a particular stimulus while filtering out a range of other stimuli. Imagine you are at a cocktail party chatting with friends when you suddenly hear your name from across the room. It is not because someone called out to you or said your name any louder. Rather, it is because the human brain is attuned to paying attention to things that have personal relevance, such as one's own name.[4]

The subconscious part of our brain, represented by System 1, processes most of the sensory input and monitors the conversations in the room, presenting them to System 2 as background noise. Once personally relevant information is detected, System 1 focuses attention on that information and, by doing so, activates System 2.

In addition to filtering the information that reaches System 2, System 1 can subconsciously influence the decisions made by System 2. Imagine you are in a store that offers a wide selection of wines from different parts of the world. The store is well lit, the wines are well organized, and French music is quietly playing in the background. You consider the available wines and select the one you like. A week later when you come back to the store, everything is the same except that the background music is German rather than French. Would the music influence your choice of wine?

A study done by a team of researchers from the United Kingdom suggests that the answer is yes. In the above example, most shoppers selected French wine when French music was playing and German wine when German music was playing. More important, when asked whether the music influenced their choice of wine, the overwhelming majority stated that music had no impact on their decision.[5]

The ability of System 1 to influence decisions made by System 2 goes well beyond the impact of music on purchase decisions. To illustrate, consider a survey in which college students in a romantic partnership were asked a series of questions that typically predict the strength of relationships: How much in love are you with your partner? How satisfied are you with the relationship? How long do you want to be in the relationship? The survey also included a few questions that probed their attention, such as how often they noticed and were distracted by good-looking members of the opposite sex. Several months later, participants were contacted again and asked about the current status of their relationship.

Surprisingly, the best indicator of a breakup was not the answers to questions about how respondents felt about their partner, satisfaction with the relationship, and how long they wanted it to last. It was their answer to the question asking about noticing and being distracted by attractive members of the opposite sex.[6] The subconscious mind represented by System 1 is a powerful force that can drive behavior unbeknownst to System 2.

The interplay between the two systems of thinking is not limited to the ability of System 1 to influence the decisions made by System 2. With System 1 responding automatically and intuitively, it falls to System 2 to weave a meaningful story to explain our actions and preferences. As System 2 tries to interpret the information from System 1 in a meaningful way, these interpretations are filtered through the prism of one's beliefs and experiences, which can lead to biases and inconsistencies.

The disconnect between the information furnished by System 1 and its interpretation by System 2 is often found in blind taste tests. When given unlabeled containers, many consumers are unable to pick their favorite beer out of a lineup based on taste alone. An important part of experiencing our favorite brand of beer is knowing that we are drinking that brand. Coca-Cola tastes better when Coke lovers know it is Coke than when they think it is Pepsi, and wine tastes better when we are told it is expensive than when told it is cheap. Even wine connoisseurs often fail to tell the difference between red wines and white wines when both are served in black glasses.[7] In the absence of cues that help infuse meaning into the information furnished by System 1, System 2 is not very effective.

Drawing Attention

Attention is selective. Because we receive more information than System 2 can consciously process, our brain must choose what information to pay attention to and what information to filter out. As a result, most information is processed by System 1 on a subconscious level and never enters the conscious mind. In fact, we are unaware of most things that happen around us unless System 1 deems them important. Attention determines what information will be processed and what will be ignored. The selective nature of attention allows us to focus on a particular object while filtering out irrelevant or distracting information.

We gather information from a variety of external sources, including reading product reviews, talking to friends, visiting company websites, and interrogating sales associates at retail outlets that sell the company's offerings. Alternatively, we might retrieve information from internal sources, such as accumulated memories of past experiences. We discuss the role of attention in these two ways of information processing in the following sections.

Gathering Information

Not all information is created equal. Certain things draw more attention than others. These attention magnets attract conscious thought to a particular piece of information. Identifying such attention magnets is key to engaging customers and directing their attention to a company's offerings. There are two main factors that determine the amount of attention paid to a particular object or event: its physical properties and its meaning.

Attention and the Physical Properties of Objects and Events

The physical properties of an object or event can have a significant impact on the attention they are likely to draw. Of the five basic human senses—sight, hearing, touch, smell, and taste—sight is by far the most important source of information. Because we receive most information through our eyes, the human brain is hardwired for visual information.

Visual properties of an object that draw attention include size, color, and movement. Color directs attention by helping to define the visual limits of objects and distinguishing one object from another. Objects that are red, orange, and yellow often draw the eye and usually get noticed first. These "warm" colors reflect light with the smallest frequency and longest wavelength, making them the most visible. Contrasting colors that differ significantly from the background or surrounding elements tend to be especially eye-catching.

Moving objects tend to attract more attention than static ones. There are evolutionary reasons for this attentional preference for motion: Natural selection likely removed any potential ancestors who did not immediately attend to predators rushing toward them. As a result, our eyes are naturally drawn to objects that are moving.

In addition to the visual properties of the object itself, the attention it draws also depends on how this object relates to its surroundings. The location of the object matters. Objects that are centered within the visual field tend to draw more attention than objects on the periphery. In a retail context, objects placed at or just below eye level will tend to be noticed more than objects on top or bottom shelves. Accordingly, retailers often adjust displays to match the eye levels of their target customers. A grocery store might place the wholesome Special K cereal on higher shelves, closer to the eye height of adults, and shelve Tony-the-Tiger-endorsed Frosted Flakes lower, closer to the eye height of children.

Another factor that defines the way an object relates to its surroundings is its distinctiveness. Objects that are visually distinct also draw attention. This tendency to notice and recall things that stand out is also referred to as the isolation effect—a term coined by German psychiatrist Hedwig von Restorff, who observed that people tend to pay more attention and better recall items that are distinct from others.[8]

For example, a word presented among a series of numbers is more likely to attract our attention and be remembered than the same word presented among a series of other words. A single daisy in a bouquet of red roses will surely be noticed first and hold attention longer than any of the roses. The unique shape of Method products makes them stand out from other cleaning products on store shelves. Likewise, free-standing objects tend to draw the eye more than objects surrounded by visual clutter. For instance, Volkswagen's famous "Think small" ad, featuring a small picture of a VW Beetle surrounded by mostly white space, was very effective in focusing readers' attention on the car.

Attention and the Meaning of Objects and Events

In addition to the physical properties of objects, attention is also guided by the meaning of these objects and their relevance to achieving active goals. This information is often processed by both System 1 and System 2, which focus our attention on goal-relevant information. Based on the type of active need, there are three main types of information likely to draw attention: information related to functional needs such as hunger and thirst, information related to emotional needs such as love and belonging, and information related to identity needs such as self-identification and self-expression.

Individuals with an unmet *functional* need tend to pay more attention to information that provides a faster, better, easier, or more efficient way to fulfill that need. For example, those trying to lose weight are more likely to pay attention to information related to dieting. Those considering buying a car are more likely to pay attention to car ads and perhaps even information about car insurance. Additionally, certain types of evolution-relevant information, such as sexually nuanced objects, tend to draw attention even without the corresponding needs being explicitly activated. For example, Unilever's ads promoting its Axe fragrance brand have capitalized for many years on the almost instant appeal of sexually laden imagery to its target audience, comprising mostly young men.

Individuals seeking *emotional* stimulation and looking for exciting experiences are likely to pay more attention to information that is emotionally rich and associated with things that are fun, memorable, and enjoyable. Those thinking about taking a break from the daily routine are more likely to pay attention to information related to a vacation in exotic destinations. Things that sound exciting—movies, sports events, and concerts—are more likely to draw the attention of individuals who feel bored. As with sexually nuanced objects, emotionally laden objects such as cute animals and babies tend to be universally relevant even in the absence of an active need for emotional stimulation.

Finally, individuals with a well-articulated system of values and beliefs tend to pay more attention to *identity-relevant* information that reflects these values and beliefs. Those passionate about a particular topic are likely to pay close attention to information related to that topic. Football fans are likely to pay close attention to information related to their teams. Those with strong political beliefs are likely to pay close attention to information related to these beliefs. And those insecure about their identity or who feel that their identity is being threatened are likely to pay attention to information that helps them to define, reassert, and express their identity.

In addition to these three types of information, another factor that can draw attention is *curiosity* — a motivational state characterized by a tendency to recognize and seek out novel and challenging information and experiences.[9] Curiosity is commonly recognized as an important motive that can influence behavior across virtually all human activities, including work, social interactions, leisure, education, sports, and decision making. Extant research has identified several factors that can arouse curiosity: complexity, novelty, uncertainty, and fear. These factors can act independently or in concert to arouse curiosity. Mainstream and social media often leverage these factors to spark curiosity and engage audiences. In the same vein, many companies use these factors in product packaging to capture customer interest and make their offerings stand out.

Recalling Information

As the newly gathered information is processed, some of it is encoded in memory to be retrieved in the future. Much of marketing communication, especially when it comes to brand building, aims to be encoded in memory and have a long-term impact on the target audience. This is why understanding the inner workings of memory and how people encode and recall information is important for designing user-friendly offerings and creating effective communication campaigns.

The Levels of Memory

We pay attention to only a small part of the information available to us, then store only a subset of this information in memory in a way that makes it readily retrievable. This processing and storing of information involve three types of memory: sensory memory, short-term memory, and long-term memory.

Sensory memory acts as a repository for information received through the senses of sight, hearing, smell, taste, and touch. Sensory memory requires no conscious attention and operates on a subconscious level. Information is stored in sensory memory only for a very brief period, typically less than a second, before it is either dismissed or sent to short-term memory.

Short-term memory, or working memory, serves as a temporary repository of information that is currently being processed. For example, we hold the beginning of a sentence we are listening to in short-term memory while attending to the rest of the sentence. Working memory has limited capacity, typically holding only around seven distinct words, numbers, or letters in an active, ready-to-process state. The length of time that short-term memory retains this information typically ranges from 10 to 15 seconds, depending on the information's relevance. Unless we actively retain this information, it dissipates and is no longer accessible. Transferring information from short-term to long-term memory is facilitated by rehearsal of the information and relating it to previously acquired knowledge.

The workings of short-term memory are also captured by the *Zeigarnik effect*, named after the psychologist who first reported it nearly a century ago. It states that an interrupted activity is easier to recall. The effect originated from an observation that waiters showed better memory for unpaid orders compared to those that were already paid. Moreover, once payments were made, they could no longer recall the order details. This pattern of memory is thought to occur because an initiated task creates mental tension, which enhances the recall of related information. This tension dissipates once the task is completed but remains for interrupted tasks, making the information more readily accessible and easier to remember.[10]

Long-term memory allows more permanent storage of information and has exponentially greater capacity than short-term memory. Long-term memory involves two core processes: encoding (memorizing), which involves storing the relevant information in memory, and retrieval (recalling), which involves evoking stored information from memory. Long-term memory can be thought of as an associative network of nodes representing units of information interconnected by links, with encoding and retrieving processes spreading information from node to node.

When an activated node encodes external information or retrieves internal information stored in long-term memory, it can also activate other nodes that are strongly associated with it. Thus, our ability to memorize and recall information is determined both by the information captured by different nodes and by the strength and organization of the associations among these nodes. The more attention we pay to the meaning of information when it is encoded, the stronger the resulting memory associations and the greater the likelihood of recalling the stored information.

Memory-Based Heuristics

Our judgments are often informed by our ability to recall relevant memories, especially when assessing the likelihood of certain events occurring. These judgments are crucial because many of our decisions, either implicitly or explicitly, involve probability estimates. For instance, deciding whether to buy travel insurance partly depends on estimating the likelihood of unexpected changes in travel plans. Similarly, choosing to invest in a new business opportunity relies on estimating the chances of its success. Even the decision to accept a dinner invitation can be influenced by the perceived likelihood of a first date blossoming into a relationship.

Generating probabilities and likelihood estimates is difficult. As a result, we often replace probability assessments with an evaluation of how difficult it is to remember or imagine instances of the event in question. For example, estimating the likelihood of last-minute changes to our travel plans is challenging. However, recalling past instances when our travel plans changed or imagining it happening in the future is relatively easy. Assessing likelihood by evaluating how easily we can recall previous instances or imagine them happening again is known as the *availability heuristic.*

To see the availability heuristic in action, try answering this question: Are there more words in English that start with the letter "K" or that have "K" as the fourth letter? Most people estimate that words starting with "K" are more prevalent than words with "K" in the fourth place. However, this assessment is incorrect. There are more words in English with "K" as the fourth letter. This error arises because it is much easier to generate instances of words that start with "K," since our memories are not indexed by the fourth letter in each word. Consider another example: Think of words that have "n" as the next to last letter. Now think of words that end in "-ing." Chances are you will find it easier to come up with examples in the latter case, even though there are more words that have "n" as the next to last letter than those ending in "-ing."

A classic illustration of the availability heuristic is the popular belief that airplanes are unsafe because of highly publicized plane crashes, even though flying is actually safer than driving. Consider this question: Which is a more likely cause of death, a shark attack or falling out of bed? If you answered that sharks kill more people, you would be wrong. There are about ten deaths from shark attacks per year, compared to over 400 deaths from falling out of bed, usually due to head and neck injuries.

Why do our probability assessments end up being so wrong? When we estimate the likelihood of an event, we rely on how easily we can envision that event. We ask ourselves: How easy is it to recall instances of each cause of death? Instances of shark attacks are well publicized and, therefore, more likely to be recalled. In contrast, there are rarely stories about someone dying by falling out of bed. As a result, we erroneously conclude that shark attacks are the more likely cause of death.

The availability heuristic has evolutionary origins. Our brains have been trained to assess probabilities based on the number of times we have encountered a particular object or event, with a greater number of past encounters indicating a higher likelihood of future occurrences. Unfortunately, this frequency-of-occurrence principle, which worked well in the past, is no longer valid. As we gain more information from various media sources, our assessments of how often we encounter a particular event no longer reflect its actual likelihood. Instead, our estimates are influenced by how frequently the media and marketing communications present this information. This is why the availability heuristic can lead to systematic biases in retrieving relevant information.

We often simplify our decisions by basing them on our memories of how much we liked a particular product or experience rather than on our memories of the actual attributes defining these products and experiences. This process, known as the *affect referral heuristic*, involves thinking and deciding based on how individuals feel about something rather than its actual performance. The affect referral heuristic is a mental shortcut that can greatly reduce the effort involved in encoding and retrieving relevant information. Instead of relying on large amounts of specific, difficult-to-recall information, we may consult a single affective judgment to guide our decisions.

Affect referral tends to return reasonably good results most of the time because products and experiences associated with positive emotions likely performed well in the past. However, since affect referral often trades accuracy for minimizing effort, it has its limitations. One such limitation is the misattribution of the affective response, which occurs when we associate the product with the positive affect stemming from unrelated factors. For example, the memory of liking a particular bottle of wine might stem from the celebratory occasion, the people with whom it was consumed, or the ambiance in which it was enjoyed. This is why relying solely on our memories of the product experience might not always accurately reflect the product's true qualities.

Focus, Primacy, and Fluency

Attention is the process of selectively focusing on distinct aspects of available information. This focus typically involves a tradeoff. Because our cognitive resources are limited, directing attention to one item means paying less attention to another. This tradeoff is captured in the very expression "paying attention": We pay the price for attending to something by ignoring something else. Paying attention is more than merely focusing on a particular item; it can also influence our beliefs about the relative importance of that item. We discuss the relationship between directing attention to specific information and its perceived importance in the following sections.

The Importance of Focus

Attention is selective, meaning we choose which information to process and which to ignore. Paying attention is not limited to consciously seeking information on a particular subject. More often than not, the way we direct our attention is determined subconsciously by System 1, which then alerts System 2 to concentrate on the incoming information. The mere fact that a particular piece of information has come to the attention of System 2 is then interpreted as an indication that this information is important. As a result, anything that draws attention to itself tends to appear more important.

The effect of attention on perceived importance is illustrated by a study in which students from the U.S. Midwest and Southern California were asked to evaluate either their own life satisfaction or the life satisfaction of a student in the other region. They were also asked to rate the importance of factors such as climate, social life, finances, and job prospects that were likely to contribute to these evaluations. Perhaps not surprisingly, both Californians and Midwesterners predicted Californians to be more satisfied with life and attributed this to the better climate.

The surprising part was that Midwesterners asked to evaluate their own life satisfaction were as happy as Californians. While Californians were indeed more satisfied with their climate than Midwesterners, the advantages of life in California were not reflected in the evaluations of overall life satisfaction. The distinct benefits of California (or drawbacks of the Midwest), such as climate, tend to be more pronounced when residents of one region explicitly thought about the quality of life in another. However, when they thought about their own life satisfaction, their attention was focused on other, more central aspects of life.[11]

Attention influences our thoughts and actions far more than we realize. Drawing attention to a particular object can increase its perceived importance even more than it deserves. This tendency to overweight the importance of things that are the focus of our attention is referred to as the *focusing illusion*, a term coined by Daniel Kahneman. His succinct description of the focusing illusion is: "Nothing in life is as important as you think it is when you are thinking about it."

When we focus on a specific attribute of a company's offering, we often exaggerate its true importance. For example, when customizing a car, buyers encouraged to think about how they will use a particular feature are likely to imagine this feature as being more important than it really is. Similarly, when food companies showcase a particular feature such as gluten-free, fat-free, or low-carb, they induce consumers to pay more attention to this feature, thereby increasing its perceived importance.

Focusing attention on a particular object not only can increase its perceived importance but also make it appear more attractive. This effect is illustrated by a study in which participants were asked to imagine entering a sweepstakes contest with a prize of an all-expenses-paid vacation to either Rome or Maui. Some participants were asked, "How more or less attractive to you is the trip to Rome?" while others were asked the same question about the trip to Maui. Thus, both groups of respondents were presented with the same information about the two vacation options; the only difference was the specific location—Rome or Maui—on which respondents focused their attention.

When asked to indicate which vacation option they would choose, participants' responses were markedly different. Those asked to evaluate the pros and cons of visiting Rome were more likely to ultimately choose it as their preferred vacation spot, whereas those asked to evaluate the pros and cons of going to Maui ultimately chose to visit Hawaii.[12]

Focusing attention on a specific option tends to bolster its attractiveness relative to the other options because it leads to placing greater weight on the attributes of this option than on the attributes of its rivals. When the focal option does not have major drawbacks, this focus can make its attractive features more prominent, increasing its overall attractiveness and the likelihood of it being chosen.

Consider, for example, the practice of asking customers to evaluate their experience with a company's offering with questions like "How are we doing?" Apart from gathering information about the specific customer experience, these questions might also end up bolstering customers' evaluation of the company and its offerings. Indeed, if the overall experience is positive, focusing customers' attention on the benefits of their experience with the company's offering without paying comparable attention to its competitors might enhance the perceived importance of this experience and further increase its value in customers' eyes.[13]

The Importance of Primacy

The discussion so far has focused on how explicitly directing attention to a particular object can increase its subjective importance. However, drawing attention does not have to be explicit to influence perceived importance. The mere sequence of presenting information can produce a similar outcome, with objects considered first likely to garner more attention and receive greater weight in subsequent decisions.

The impact of the order of presenting information on people's judgments can be illustrated with a study that asked participants to evaluate their satisfaction with life. College students were asked two questions: "How happy are you with your life in general?" and "How many dates did you have last month?" The correlation between the answers to these questions was essentially non-existent, indicating that general happiness and recent dating experience were unrelated.

However, when the order of these questions was reversed, with the dating question preceding the life happiness question, the outcome was markedly different. The answers to the two questions were highly correlated, indicating that starting with the dating experience significantly influenced participants' perception of life happiness. These findings were replicated when attention was first called to topics such as marriage and health. Asking a question about a specific aspect of one's life bolstered the subjective importance of that aspect, significantly impacting the subsequent evaluation of overall life satisfaction.[14]

The order of presenting information matters because people often pay more attention to the information considered first, which makes them regard this information as more important. This increased importance has two main consequences: Information considered first is given greater weight in forming overall evaluations of the items being considered. Additionally, the first piece of information can influence the evaluation of subsequently presented information, producing the so-called halo effect.

The *halo effect* is the tendency for an overall evaluation of a person or an object to influence evaluations of specific properties of that person or object in a way consistent with the overall evaluation. This effect dates back over a century to when psychologist Edward Thorndike observed that when evaluating others, people often believe that their individual traits—such as physical qualities, intelligence, leadership, and character—are highly correlated. For example, people tend to believe that those who score high on one dimension, such as character, are also likely to be better on others. Likewise, managers often rate individual qualities of their subordinates based on their overall evaluation of that person, and consumers often form evaluations of a product's performance on a particular attribute based on their overall impression of the product.[15]

The halo effect is aptly demonstrated by a study in which some participants were shown a video depicting the instructor as a warm, friendly person, whereas the others were shown a video picturing the instructor as a cold, distant person. The first group subsequently rated the professor more positively than the second group, not only in terms of his friendliness but also on unrelated dimensions such as physical appearance, mannerisms, and even accent.[16]

Another example of our tendency to pay more attention and assign greater importance to information considered first is a study conducted by psychologist Solomon Asch more than half a century ago. Participants in the study were presented with a list of characteristics describing a particular person and were subsequently asked to share their impression of the kind of person described. Some participants saw the following list: "intelligent, industrious, impulsive, critical, stubborn, envious," whereas others saw the same list but in reverse order: "envious, stubborn, critical, impulsive, industrious, intelligent." The only difference between the two lists was that the first set started with positive features and the second set started with negative ones.

Even though all participants were presented with the same information, the order of presenting the information made a big difference. Those who saw the list starting with positive features described the individual in positive terms, such as "A person who knows what he wants and goes after it. He is impatient with people who are less gifted, and ambitious with those who stand in his way. A forceful person with his own convictions, who is usually right about things." In contrast, those who saw the list starting with negative features described the individual in rather unflattering terms: "This person's good qualities such as industry and intelligence are bound to be restricted by jealousy and stubbornness. He is unsuccessful because he is weak and allows his bad points to cover up his good ones," and "He is maladjusted, envious, and impulsive."[17]

Because the information presented first tends to draw more attention, we are inclined to overemphasize its importance relative to the information that follows. As a result, anchoring the description with a positive attribute leads to a more positive overall evaluation, whereas descriptions that begin with a negative characteristic tend to produce a negative overall evaluation. Because the order of presenting information can play a key role in evaluating it, understanding primacy effects and accounting for their impact is essential in managing customers' impressions of a company's offerings.

The Importance of Fluency

In addition to alerting System 2 about relevant information, System 1 also informs System 2 about *processing fluency*—the ease with which information is evaluated. For example, text that is well organized, written in an easy-to-read font, and presented on a contrasting background is processed more fluently.[18] Consider the two phrases shown in Figure 4. Even though the text in both panels is identical, the panels vary dramatically in ease of reading: The phrase on the left is very easy to read, whereas most people will find the one on the right more challenging.

Figure 4. High and Low Processing Fluency

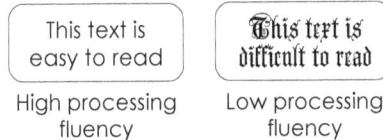

This text is easy to read	This text is difficult to read
High processing fluency	Low processing fluency

The impact of processing fluency is not limited to the perceptual properties of an object, such as font, organization, and contrast; it also involves the ease of processing the meaning of the information, a phenomenon referred to as *conceptual fluency*. The impact of conceptual fluency on preferences is illustrated with a study in which some participants were asked to list one reason to drive a BMW, whereas others were asked to list ten reasons. Later, both groups were asked to indicate their preference for BMW. One might expect that asking for ten reasons would have a more positive effect on the overall preference for the focal brand than asking for a single reason. After all, having more reasons is better than having a single reason.

However, just the opposite occurred: Those asked to list ten reasons indicated a weaker preference for BMW than those who had to come up with a single reason.[19] Because thinking of ten good reasons to support our preference for a brand is difficult, even for well-liked brands, our preference for these brands tends to diminish when the task becomes more challenging.

Processing fluency is also associated with the finding that repeated exposure to an object can make this object more likable — a phenomenon called the *mere exposure effect*. For example, encountering unfamiliar faces multiple times tends to make these faces more likable. Similarly, we tend to have more favorable attitudes toward brand names we have previously seen, even when we are unfamiliar with these brands and do not remember the initial exposure.[20]

A notable illustration of the mere exposure effect is the evolving perception of the Eiffel Tower. Originally erected as the entrance arch for the 1889 World's Fair, the Eiffel Tower was initially met with disdain by many Parisians, who considered it an eyesore and an unwelcome addition to the city's skyline. The French intellectual elite, including many renowned artists, writers, and architects, even penned a vehement public letter condemning the tower, labeling it as a "barbaric industrial object that even Americans wouldn't erect."

Over time, public opinion shifted and the Eiffel Tower, which was only intended to stand for 20 years, became an enduring symbol of Paris and France. A significant factor in this transformation was the mere exposure effect. As the tower was visible daily and loomed over everything else in Paris, Parisians gradually grew accustomed to its presence, which over time morphed into strong affection.

The positive effect of repetition on perceived attractiveness stems from the fact that processing fluency tends to create a sense of familiarity, which in turn makes objects more attractive. The relationship between familiarity with an object and its attractiveness has its roots in human history. From an evolutionary perspective, familiar objects tend to be perceived as less risky because if one has survived multiple encounters with the same object, it is likely that this object does not pose significant risk; hence, it is viewed as more attractive than an unfamiliar object.

In addition to increasing the attractiveness of the focal object, processing fluency can also increase the *credibility* of the communicated information, such that easy-to-process messages are perceived to be more credible. Processing fluency can boost credibility in three ways: by increasing its perceptual fluency, by repetition, and by rhyming.

First, making the perceptual fluency of a piece of information easier to process tends to make it more trustworthy and believable. For example, enhancing the visual characteristics of a message by using bright, easy-to-read colors against a contrasting background has been shown to significantly increase the perceived credibility and reliability of the information being presented.[21]

Repetition can further influence and enhance perceived credibility. When information is repeated, it becomes more familiar to the audience, thereby increasing its fluency and, as a result, its perceived trustworthiness. This effect is rooted in the way our brain processes repeated encounters with specific information. The more frequently we come across a piece of information, the more our brains tend to regard it as reliable and accurate.

This phenomenon is particularly powerful in shaping public opinion, as frequently repeated statements, whether true or false, are more likely to be accepted and believed by the public. This principle is widely utilized in advertising, where repeated messages are strategically employed to strengthen brand recognition, persuade consumers, and reinforce specific beliefs or attitudes within the target audience.

The credibility of a communicated message can also be increased by rhyming. Because rhyming enhances fluency, information that rhymes is perceived to be more credible. Compare the following two sets of phrases: "Caution and measure will win you riches" and "Woes unite enemies" with "Caution and measure will win you treasure" and "Woes unite foes." Even though both sets of phrases have the same meaning, the second set is typically rated as more credible. This rhyme-as-reason effect stems from our tendency to associate ease of processing with credibility, such that things that are easier to assimilate are also believed to be more credible.[22]

Repetition and rhyming are powerful tools to enhance the credibility of a message. A prominent illustration of the role of both rhyming and repetition was the murder trial of former football and movie star O.J. Simpson, often referred to as "the trial of the century." To proclaim Simpson's innocence, the lead defense lawyer repeatedly urged jurors to keep this in mind: "If it doesn't fit, you must acquit." The phrase referred to the fact that one of the key pieces of evidence against Simpson, the blood-covered gloves the killer was believed to have worn, appeared too small to fit Simpson's hand in an in-court demonstration. The rhyming phrase became highly associated with the trial and is often considered one of the key factors that contributed to the jury's decision to acquit Simpson of double-murder charges.

The Power of Associations

Mental associations are the connections between different concepts, events, or processes that exist in our minds. These associations are important because they form the foundation for creating and changing our beliefs. All our thoughts, beliefs, and emotional reactions follow from these associations. The only way to change existing thoughts, beliefs, and emotions is by creating meaningful new associations.[23]

Creating Meaningful Associations

Associations lie at the heart of how we form and change our beliefs. Striving to make sense of inbound information, the human brain instantly draws connections among different ideas, experiences, and feelings. The two routes for creating such associations and the role of selective attention and reactance in creating meaningful associations are addressed in more detail in the following sections.

The Two Routes for Creating Associations

According to one of the most prominent theories that explain how we process information—the Elaboration Likelihood Model—beliefs and associations can be created using two main routes: a central route that relies on direct, reason-based arguments and a peripheral route that relies on indirect, often subconscious arguments.[24]

The *central route* involves careful processing of relevant information. It is conscious in nature and relies heavily on System 2 processing. For example, a car manufacturer might advertise the performance and safety features of its automobiles, a food company might promote the taste and health benefits of its snacks, and a cosmetics company might tout the gentleness of its products. Because it appeals to our logic and reasoning, the central route can create associations that are meaningful, memorable, and impactful.

The central route, however, is not a universal solution for processing information. To be effective, it requires that the arguments in favor of the company's offering are strong and present sound reasoning for choosing it. More important, it calls for a relatively high level of involvement for the information to be thoroughly processed and internalized. In other words, this approach is most effective when the audience is in an analytical state of mind and is willing to engage in processing the available information.

The limitations on the effectiveness of the central route naturally raise the question of when it should be used. In general, we are more likely to use the central route when making decisions about more expensive purchases, purchases for which the sales cycle is long and involved, purchases that are of high personal relevance, and purchases that are not rushed or hasty. Because it requires high levels of involvement, we only use the central route when we have both the motivation and the resources—mental energy and time—to process that information.

The *peripheral route*, on the other hand, is often subconscious in nature and relies heavily on System 1 processing. Unlike the central route, which requires high levels of involvement, the peripheral route involves lateral thinking that does not require an analytical mindset or high levels of motivation. For example, a celebrity wearing a company's brand might encourage others to do so without explicitly enumerating its benefits. Because of its subtle nature, the peripheral route is particularly effective when we are not paying special attention to the available information. In fact, we may not even notice peripheral-route communications, as in the case of product placements where the company's offerings are embedded in a story, movie, or television show.

The peripheral route can be illustrated with a study in which participants were presented with a furniture store website and asked to choose between two sofas that varied in comfort and price. Participants were divided into two groups and shown the same two options. The only difference was the background on which these options were displayed—either fluffy clouds or pennies. Even though both groups of participants saw the same information, their responses were markedly different. Those who saw the fluffy-clouds background indicated a stronger preference for the more comfortable sofa and were willing to pay a higher price for it than those who saw a background featuring pennies. More important, when later asked whether the background had any effect on their choice, participants vehemently denied that they had been influenced in any way by the background.[25]

Another example of creating associations via the peripheral route is the use of colors. Because they have an almost immediate impact on the way we perceive objects, colors are commonly used as an indirect means of subtly conveying a wide range of associations. For example, warm colors such as yellow, orange, and red are often associated with activity and excitement, stimulating the senses, fostering aggression, and promoting risk-seeking behaviors. In contrast, cool colors such as purple, blue, and green tend to be associated with soothing and relaxation, calming the mind, and instilling a sense of tranquility.

Managing Involvement in Creating Associations

The two routes for creating associations vary in the level of involvement needed to process the available information: The central route requires a significantly higher level of involvement compared to the peripheral route. Accordingly, one might expect that if the target audience is paying attention, following the central route by providing logical arguments would be the most effective approach. This, however, is not necessarily the case. There are two conflicting theories on the role of involvement in creating associations: selective-attention theory and reactance theory.

Selective-attention theory argues that attention is crucial for forming meaningful associations. Focused attention enables us to concentrate on pertinent information while disregarding what is irrelevant or only marginally relevant to the decision at hand. Therefore, this theory suggests that communication is more effective when it captures greater attention. This implies that marketers would benefit from strategies designed to maximize the attention their messaging receives.

Reactance theory makes the opposite prediction. It argues that heightened scrutiny and the generation of counterarguments become more likely through the central route, particularly when there's suspicion of information being manipulated. This stems from a natural resistance to coercion; feeling forced into a decision typically prompts a negative reaction that diminishes the effectiveness of the message conveyed. Consequently, this theory suggests that an increased level of attention may detract from, rather than enhance, a company's persuasion efforts.

The potential disadvantages of drawing attention to a company's communications can be mitigated by trying to minimize recipients' reactance to persuasion attempts. Three prevalent strategies that achieve this balance include leveraging publicity, utilizing endorsers or influencers, and incorporating product placement.

Publicity is a valuable tool to mitigate reactance because it relies on information presented by a third party. When a message is conveyed through an independent medium such as a newspaper article or a national news report, it is generally met with less skepticism and fewer counterarguments than if the same message were delivered directly by the company as an advertisement. Therefore, shifting the source of the message to an independent entity can minimize the reactance that is elicited by overt marketing.

Reactance can also be overcome by using endorsers who lend their own credibility to the promoted offering. These endorsers can range from experts with professional knowledge relevant to the product to celebrities whose glamorous lifestyles are admired by consumers. This practice of leveraging high-profile endorsements has historical roots stretching back to the 18th century, when brands would often boost their appeal by associating with royalty. This tradition persists, exemplified by the issuance of royal warrants in the United Kingdom, allowing certain brands to declare "By Appointment to Her Majesty The Queen." Over time, the scope of lifestyle endorsements has broadened to encompass a diverse group of endorsers, including actors, athletes, musicians, models, and social media influencers.

Product placement is another approach to overcoming reactance. It works by leveraging the power of association: When a product is seen being used by a glamorous, heroic, or beautiful character in a film or television show, the positive qualities of this character can transfer to the product in the viewer's memory. Because the endorsement of the product is rather subtle and the information is delivered by an independent source, reactance does not stand in the way of creating relevant associations. Consequently, the product benefits form associations that enhance its appeal without directly confronting the consumers' defenses.

Creating Top-of-Mind Associations

A key factor influencing which options make it into a customer's consideration set is how readily these options come to mind as a means to fulfill an active need. Therefore, achieving top-of-mind status is crucial for any option to be considered, particularly when customers depend on their memory to come up with ways to satisfy their needs.

Top-of-mind awareness is one of the most valuable assets for a brand, significantly enhancing the likelihood that a brand's specific associations will come to mind when consumers seek solutions to fulfill their needs. To cultivate top-of-mind associations, managers can employ three main strategies: associate the offering with a frequently activated need, associate the offering with a frequent behavior, and associate the offering with a popular product category.

Associating an offering with a frequently activated need leverages the regular occurrence of certain needs to ensure the product is automatically considered as a solution. Some frequently occurring needs rooted in biological imperatives such as hunger, thirst, and sleep provide fertile ground for such associations. Additionally, needs that arise predictably at certain times of the day—like morning grooming routines or the late afternoon need for an energy boost—offer opportunities for creating top-of-mind associations. For instance, Mars has effectively positioned its Snickers candy bar as the go-to solution for between-meal hunger, aiming to be the first option consumers think of when they feel hungry before it's time for their next meal.

Associating the offering with a frequent behavior aims to ensure that every occurrence of a particular behavioral act brings to mind the company's offering. For example, Nestlé positioned its Kit Kat candy bar as a synonym for a break. To this end, Nestlé's ads cleverly tied together the way Kit Kats are typically consumed—broken into individual "fingers"—and the behavior of taking a break. As in the case of associating the offering with a frequently activated need, the company's goal here is to capitalize on the prominence of an already existing behavior and link its offering to that behavior so that it is considered at the time of the decision.

Associating the offering with a popular product category aims to ensure that thinking about the product brings the category to mind and thinking about the category similarly evokes the product. For example, Campbell's has created a strong association with the soup category such that when we see the brand, we think of soup, and when we think of soup, the first brand that comes to mind is Campbell's. The goal here is for the brand to short-circuit our decision process and get us to jump straight from a category-level decision, "I'd like some soup for dinner…" directly to the brand, "…so let's see which Campbell's soup looks good." A similar approach involved renaming fortified wines—a category of sweet wines produced by fortifying the wine with high-proof alcohol—as "dessert wines." By using a label associated with a frequent behavior—the consumption of a dessert after a meal—winemakers managed to increase top-of-mind awareness for these wines.

Associating the brand with a particular need, behavior, or product category can be supercharged by creating a single association that uniquely links the company's offering to something customers find meaningful. Lord Maurice Saatchi, the co-founder of the Saatchi & Saatchi agency, used the term "one word equity" to underscore the importance of having such a unique association. He writes: "Each brand can only own one word. Each word can only be owned by one brand. The future of advertising, whatever the technology, will be to associate each brand with one word. This is one word equity." The one-word-equity principle encapsulates top-of-mind awareness and ensures that the company's offering will always be a part of customers' consideration sets.[26]

Managing Customer Involvement

A key to engaging customers is understanding and managing their level of involvement with a company's products, services, and brands. The level of a customer's involvement is crucial, as it influences the amount of attention they will devote to learning about and interacting with these offerings. However, companies often misjudge their customers' actual level of involvement. In the following sections, we explore the disconnect between managers, who are deeply involved with the company's offerings, and their customers, who may not be as engaged.

The Involvement Gap

Managers devote considerable thought to their offerings. In doing so, they typically rely on System 2 to design, communicate, and deliver their products, services, and brands. In contrast, consumers rarely spend as much time thinking about the company and its offerings. They are usually less involved and evaluate offerings using System 1, preserving mental effort for more important decisions. This involvement gap—the disconnect between involved managers and uninvolved consumers—is the source of one of the most common marketing mistakes.

Marketing actions are often rooted in rigorous analysis, with teams of people refining ideas over weeks or months. Picture a scene from once-popular shows like *Mad Men*, with account executives in grey flannel suits and fedoras working early mornings and late nights to get every detail just perfect. Groups of executives sit around large boardroom tables, brows furrowed, while ideas are scrutinized and critiqued. This decision-making process involves teams of people applying System 2 thinking, scrutinizing actions from every angle. This is analytical thinking, checked and refined through even more analytical thinking.

Contrast this with the customer's experience in interacting with the output of that decision-making process. It is hard to imagine a context where consumers will spend as much time and effort thinking about their selection of a particular brand of toothpaste, paper towel, or cereal. These decisions typically involve System 1 thinking that is low involvement, association based, and intuition driven.

The distinct ways in which managers and consumers think about the company's offerings reflect how they balance the effort expended in making decisions and the accuracy of those decisions. The two mindsets representing the extremes in balancing effort and accuracy are referred to as maximizing and satisficing.

The *maximizing mindset* strives for perfect results. Maximizers tend to spend considerable time and effort to find the best available option. They try to gather and evaluate all available information, regardless of the time and energy this might take. Maximizers prioritize the benefits associated with accuracy over the costs associated with the extra effort required to achieve the best possible outcome. The maximizing mindset tends to be more analytical and relies heavily on System 2.

The *satisficing mindset*, on the other hand, is focused on achieving results that are merely good rather than perfect. The term "satisficing," coined by Nobel Prize-winning economist Herbert Simon, is derived from two adjectives: satisfying and sufficing. Satisficers are not searching for the best available option and are willing to settle for any option that meets their criteria. Because they are not holding out for the ideal outcome, satisficers do not feel the need to consider *all* the available information to make a decision. Their deliberations end the moment they come across an option that meets their criteria, even when they suspect that a better option might be available. Because of its focus on minimizing mental effort at the expense of accuracy, the satisficing mindset often relegates many of the decisions to the effort-efficient System 1.

How do these two mindsets contribute to the involvement gap? At the heart of the problem is that managers, with their analytical approach and focus on constantly improving their offerings, often end up being highly engaged maximizers. Because of this mindset, they often think of their customers as having a maximizer's willingness to invest the time and effort to assess the company's offering. This intuition, however, is often incorrect. Consumers approach most of their decisions with a satisficing mindset. Most of the time, they are unwilling to expend the extra time and effort to evaluate all aspects of all available options and, instead, are happy to settle for merely good-enough outcomes. This fundamental mismatch between the deeply involved managers and the uninvolved consumers creates a significant barrier to developing and communicating offerings that genuinely resonate with and create value for customers.

The challenges posed by the involvement gaps between managers and their customers beg the question: Why can't managers just step into their customers' shoes? Indeed, if managers can successfully see things from their customers' perspective, they should be able to sidestep the involvement gap. Unfortunately, that type of perspective-taking is challenging because of what psychologists call "the curse of knowledge." It is often difficult to impossible to take the perspective of someone who does not know the things you know. Feigned ignorance is never as thorough as actual ignorance.

One prominent example of the curse of knowledge involves a series of experiments in which some participants were asked to tap out the rhythms to well-known songs such as "Happy Birthday," while others were asked to guess the tapped song. The tappers wildly overestimated the likelihood that listeners would be able to figure out the tune, predicting that listeners would get it about fifty percent of the time, even though listeners were only able to guess accurately less than three percent of the time.

Versions of these experiments have been turned into party games in which one person hums a tune and another must guess the song. These games are popular because of how difficult it is for the listener to guess correctly and how shocked the tapper or hummer is that the listener does not get it immediately. When we already know a song, it is impossible for us to hear anything but the song when it is tapped out or hummed. It is also impossible for us to imagine how it would sound to someone who did not already know which song is involved.[27]

The magnitude of the involvement gap varies across different customers and purchase occasions. It is likely to be greatest in the case of lay consumers making non-essential decisions that do not require high levels of involvement, such as buying snacks, cleaning products, or basic office supplies. In contrast, the involvement gap is likely to be relatively small in cases of expert customers making important decisions. For example, consumers making big-ticket purchases such as a car as well as identity-relevant purchases such as designer handbags might thoroughly familiarize themselves with the available offerings and carefully consider their attributes. In addition, many business-to-business transactions involve purchasing agents that have the expertise and the willingness to carefully evaluate all available information. In such cases, the involvement gap is narrowed by the fact that both the customer and the manager share the same maximizing mindset.

Creating Value for the Uninvolved Customer

Given that most of the time customers are not very involved with the company's offering, how can a manager create value for these customers? What is the secret to designing offerings for uninvolved customers who are unlikely to pay much attention to these offerings? We address these questions in the following sections.

Designing Offerings for the Uninvolved Customer

Companies often overcomplicate their offerings, ignoring the fact that customers might not care about the extra functionality. Many product designers believe that more functionality is always better, as it has the potential to create additional customer value. From a customer's perspective, however, each additional function often ends up complicating the offering and making it more difficult to use.

As a result, products are often designed in ways that make perfect sense to the technologically minded and highly involved engineers who create them but resemble an unsolvable logic puzzle to the uninvolved consumers who end up using them. Even relatively simple functionality, such as the clocks on kitchen appliances, ends up demanding more time, effort, and skill than consumers have, resulting in their appliances displaying the default or some random time.

When balancing enhanced functionality and ease of use, a company should take into account several key factors. A primary consideration is that customers vary in their level of involvement with the company's products. Organizational theorist Geoffrey Moore argued that based on how they view technology people can be divided into two broad categories: technology enthusiasts and mainstream consumers.

Technology enthusiasts are fundamentally committed to new technologies and are willing to take advantage of the opportunities they afford. They appreciate advanced features and are eager to explore and utilize them. In contrast, mainstream consumers do not appreciate technology for its own sake and view technological innovation as a useful tool only insofar as it helps them optimize the efficiency and effectiveness of activities in their daily lives.[28]

The problem is that engineers often design offerings that appeal to like-minded technology enthusiasts. Moreover, because technology enthusiasts are usually among the early adopters of a company's products, the initial market performance can create the false impression that these products appeal to all customers and that it is just a matter of time until everyone adopts them. Most often, however, that's not what happens.

Rather than applauding the enhanced functionality—a key benefit for technology enthusiasts—mainstream customers view this functionality as an unnecessary complication that requires additional time and effort. This tendency of product designers to implicitly focus on the needs of technology enthusiasts while ignoring the needs of mainstream customers is one of the main hurdles that prevent technologically advanced offerings from gaining widespread acceptance.

To overcome the involvement gap, a company must prioritize simplicity and convenience over technological ingenuity. Sony's Walkman exemplifies a product built on the notion of simple and easy-to-use functionality. As the story goes, Akio Morita, the co-founder of Sony, noticed that people were listening to music all day long—in their homes, at work, in their cars, with some even carrying large stereos to the beach and the park. From his own experience, he also thought it would be nice to listen to music during transcontinental flights. Accordingly, he tasked engineers with developing a device that sounded like a high-end car stereo and yet was portable and easy to use.

The initial prototype developed by Sony's engineering department featured a recording function, as this was common for most stereo systems and could be achieved at a low cost. To their surprise, Morita vetoed the recording function, believing that the product should have a single benefit: playing music on the go. This clarity of purpose made what was a radically new technology for the time easier for customers to understand and use, ultimately helping make the Walkman an iconic, decades-long success.

Simple designs that prioritize ease of use over increased functionality have been key to the success of diverse company products such as Apple computers, tablets, and phones; Sonos wireless audio systems; and Breville higher end kitchen appliances. When it comes to product design, less can be more. The key is to balance the benefits and costs associated with increased functionality.

Advertising to the Uninvolved Customer

In addition to involvement gaps in designing the offering, a disconnect between the level of involvement of managers and their customers can occur in marketing communications. Advertising agencies often create complex messages that require high involvement, even when their audience is not invested in the company's messages and evaluates them in a very superficial manner. Guided by the misconception that their audience is as involved as their creative teams, agencies often develop complex stories that require a significant level of attention, motivation, and mental effort to comprehend. As a result, many consumers end up simply filtering out the company's message.

Customers' attention spans have dramatically evolved over the past several decades. In the early days of advertising, agencies would routinely produce print ads with paragraphs of dense text extolling the virtues of whatever was being sold. Television ads from the 1940s and 1950s were often long narrative affairs, with extensive exposition about the characteristics of the products or elaborate product trials. At that time, consumers had fewer distractions and were more likely to pay enough attention to follow the meandering plots of TV ads and more willing to read novel-length print ads.

Consider the iconic advertisement that later became known as the "Man in the Chair," created in 1958 for McGraw-Hill Magazines. The ad featured a stern-faced, middle-aged executive wearing a conservative brown suit, sitting in an office chair, hands clasped together, and looking intently at the reader. The body of the ad read: "I don't know who you are. I don't know your company. I don't know your product. I don't know what your company stands for. I don't know your company's customers. I don't know your company's record. I don't know your company's reputation. Now–what was it you wanted to sell me?" The ad copy concluded with, "Moral: Sales start *before* your salesman calls — with business publication advertising."

Very impactful at the time, the effectiveness of this ad depended entirely on the extent to which readers were willing to allocate the necessary mental effort to read the ad copy and ultimately grasp the point the ad was trying to make. It was a time when ads created by managers using System 2 thinking targeted consumers also willing to engage in System 2 thinking. This is no longer the case. The involvement gap has widened in the intervening decades. While communication campaigns are often still created with the same highly involved and analytical System 2 thinking, distracted and busy consumers are increasingly likely to ignore complex messages that require higher levels of involvement.

Having consumers ignore a company's communications is not the worst outcome. The communication campaign might also backfire, leading to negative rather than positive associations. This is often an issue with ads using contrast to highlight the benefits of the promoted offering, often by depicting less-than-desirable outcomes for customers who chose a competitor's offering. The problem with this approach is that contrast judgments require greater levels of involvement and mental effort. When customers' level of involvement is low, contrast judgments are replaced with similarity associations, meaning that customers associate — rather than contrast — the negative outcomes with the company's offering. As a result, distracted customers are likely to misconstrue the company's message and end up with negative associations regarding its offering.

The current age of attention deficit requires companies to view involvement as a scarce resource and a limiting factor in the consumption of information. Marketing communications must be designed to account for the fact that most people act like cognitive misers, nursing an increasingly narrow attention span. Companies must create stories that customers care about enough to engage with the offering. In the words of one of the pioneers of modern advertising, Howard Gossage, "Nobody reads advertising. People read what interests them; and sometimes it's an ad."

Summary

We think in different ways: fast and slow. Fast thinking (System 1) is subconscious, effortless, but also prone to errors. Slow thinking (System 2) is deliberate, more accurate, but more effortful. Most of the information is processed by System 1; only information deemed relevant by System 1 is processed by System 2. The two systems work together to allocate mental resources in the most efficient way. System 1 filters which information reaches System 2 and can also subconsciously influence the decisions made by System 2.

Attention is selective. Because we receive more information than we can process consciously, our brain must choose what information to pay attention to and what to filter out. Our brain detects information using two criteria: (a) the physical properties of the objects, such as color, imagery, size, location, motion, and distinctiveness; and (b) the meaning of the objects and their relevance to fulfilling active functional, emotional, and identity needs. We tend to rely on how easily instances of an event come to mind to assess the likelihood of that event (the availability heuristic) and how we feel about a particular offering to evaluate its performance (the affect referral heuristic).

Anything that draws attention to itself can make it seem more important than it actually is (the focusing illusion). Actively focusing attention on a particular object can increase its importance and make the object appear more attractive. Likewise, information considered first is likely to draw more attention and receive greater weight in subsequent decisions. Processing fluency reflects the ease with which information is interpreted by our minds, such that easy-to-process information is judged more positively and perceived as more credible. Common strategies to bolster message credibility involve increasing its perceptual fluency and using repetition and rhyming.

Mental associations are the foundation for creating and changing our beliefs: All thoughts, beliefs, and emotional reactions follow from these associations. Associations can be created using two main routes: a central route that relies on direct, reason-based arguments, and a peripheral route that relies on indirect, often subconscious arguments. Top-of-mind awareness is one of the most valuable assets a brand can possess. Common approaches to creating relevant top-of-mind associations include associating the offering with a frequently activated need, a frequent behavior, and a popular product category.

Managers tend to overestimate customers' interest in and involvement with their offerings. This disconnect between the level of involvement of managers and their customers is one of the most common marketing mistakes. The different ways in which managers and consumers think about the company's offerings reflect their distinct mindsets. Managers tend to have a maximizing mindset and are willing to expend considerable time and effort to design the perfect offering. In contrast, customers have a satisficing mindset, focused on achieving outcomes that are merely good rather than perfect. As a result, overly complicated product features and communication messages are often ignored and can even backfire, decreasing the attractiveness of the company's offering.

KEY TAKEAWAYS

People think fast and slow. Most of the information is processed automatically, without careful deliberation and reflection.

Attention is selective. Identifying the key attention drivers is crucial to customer engagement.

Attention drives importance. Things that draw attention are perceived as more important.

Associations create beliefs. Beliefs stem from meaningful mental associations; existing beliefs can be changed by creating new associations.

Design for low involvement. Managers tend to overestimate customers' level of involvement.

SPOTLIGHT: ENGAGING CUSTOMERS WITH STORYTELLING

A fundamental aspect of communication, learning, and persuasion is that the human brain is more adept at processing and remembering narratives than abstract logical arguments or data. In the words of cognitive psychologist Roger Schank, "Humans are not ideally set up to understand logic; they are ideally set up to understand stories." Several key factors underpin this statement, highlighting our natural inclination to understand narratives.

Cognitive Engagement. We are narrative thinkers, naturally wired to pay attention to and remember stories. Stories organize information in a coherent and easy-to-follow manner, making them more engaging than disjointed facts. Information presented as a story is easier to remember than the same information presented in a list or through abstract reasoning. This is because stories make it easier to connect new knowledge with existing memories. Stories can also simplify complex information by providing context and transforming abstract ideas into concrete, tangible elements that can be more readily visualized and understood. By contextualizing information and embedding it within a narrative framework, stories bridge the gap between abstract concepts and practical understanding, helping marketers more effectively communicate the benefits of their offerings.

Emotional Engagement. Stories have the unique ability to evoke emotions, making them more memorable and impactful than facts or figures. Emotional content enhances our ability to remember information by attaching emotional significance to it. While logic and data are important, they often lack the emotional component that makes a message compelling and memorable. Through stories, information becomes wrapped in an emotional context, rendering it more relatable and impactful. Stories often involve characters and situations that encourage the audience to put themselves in someone else's shoes. This process of empathy and perspective-taking is fundamental to social cognition and is more naturally elicited through narrative than through logical exposition.

Social Engagement. We are social beings who learn from and are influenced by others. Social engagement is a fundamental aspect of human nature: We innately seek connection, understanding, and validation through interactions with others. Stories, with their universal appeal and relatability, serve as a potent medium for these interactions, facilitating the sharing of insights, emotions, and experiences across diverse social networks. They possess a viral quality, enabling them to traverse communities and cultures, both in digital spaces like social media platforms and in face-to-face interactions. Historically, storytelling has been a primary means of passing knowledge, values, and experiences from one generation to the next, reflecting our natural predisposition to learn and communicate through stories.

In addition to effectively engaging the audience, storytelling helps navigate skepticism, which is particularly important in an environment where consumers are increasingly distrustful of overt advertising. By engaging audiences with compelling narratives that smoothly weave in the merits of a company's offering, storytelling transcends traditional advertising's direct approach. This subtlety is key because it shifts the focus from the offering itself to the story surrounding it, thereby lowering the barriers of skepticism and resistance. When the advertising message is embedded within an engaging story, it is perceived not as an intrusion but as an interesting narrative, increasing the audience's openness and receptiveness. Storytelling not only circumvents skepticism but also enhances the credibility and attractiveness of the brand message, fostering a more authentic connection between the company and its customers.

THE CX CANVAS: CREATING AWARENESS

Following the activation of relevant customer needs, a company must engage customers to ensure its offering becomes part of their consideration set. This step involves two key components: (1) analyzing the level of customers' awareness of the company's offering and (2) charting a course of action to ensure target customers consider this offering. These components of creating awareness are depicted in Figure 5 and detailed below.

Figure 5. Creating Awareness: The Big Picture

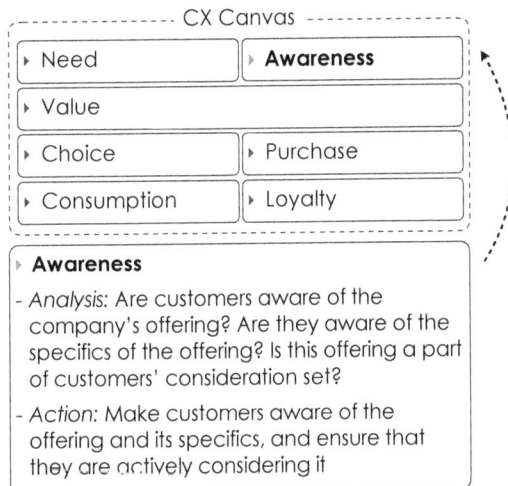

Analyzing customers' awareness aims to determine the degree to which target customers are aware of the existence of the offering and whether they are actively considering it as a means of fulfilling their active need. Here, a manager must ask the following questions:

- *Are customers aware of the company's offering?* This question seeks to establish whether customers have heard about the company's offering and can recognize it if confronted with it. This recognition can involve both verbal cues, such as the offering's brand name, and nonverbal cues, such as the offering's color and shape.

- *Are customers aware of the specifics of the offering?* This question aims to determine the extent of customers' awareness of the offering and, specifically, whether this awareness extends beyond general knowledge of its existence to familiarity with the distinct attributes of the offering.

- *Is this offering part of customers' consideration set?* This question aims to determine whether customers view the company's offering as a solution for fulfilling their active need. It is important because mere awareness of the specifics of the company's offering does not guarantee that customers will consider it when making a decision.

The ultimate purpose of assessing customers' knowledge and interest in the company's offerings is to develop an effective strategy to ensure that these offerings become part of the customers' consideration set. If customers differ in their awareness, they should be divided into groups based on their level of familiarity with the offering, and the company should develop tailored engagement strategies for each distinct segment.

Following the analysis of customers' awareness of the offering, a company must develop an action plan to engage target customers so the offering becomes part of their consideration set. The specific course of action depends on the level of customer awareness:

- *Lack of awareness.* Customers in this segment are unaware of the company's offering. Since awareness is necessary for consideration, the company's goal is to inform customers about the offering, its specifics, and its ability to meet their needs.

- *Limited awareness.* Customers in this segment are aware of the company's offering but know little about its specifics. Consequently, the company's goal is to educate customers about the offering's attributes. If customers hold incorrect views about the offering, the company must correct these misconceptions to reflect its true attributes.

- *Lack of consideration.* Customers in this segment are aware of the company's offering and its attributes but do not consider it relevant to their needs. The company's goal here is to create top-of-mind awareness of the offering so that it is considered when the relevant need becomes active.

The three customer segments and the corresponding company actions are summarized in Figure 6. Customers unaware of the offering tend to require greater effort from the company, whereas those who are aware of the offering and its specific attributes typically require less effort.

Figure 6. Creating Awareness: The Action Plan

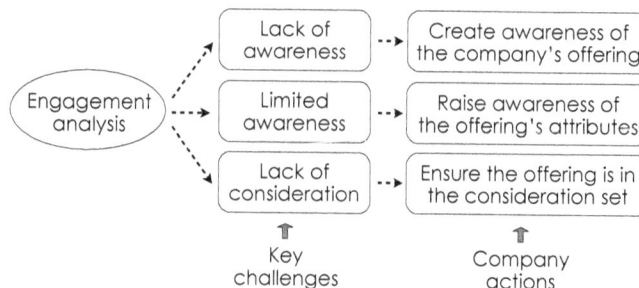

Imagine you are operating a 24-hour self-service carwash and want to increase the number of cars using your services. The carwash is in a high-traffic area, and many drivers could clearly benefit from having their cars washed. The challenge is how to get more of them to stop at your carwash.

To address this challenge, first consider whether drivers are even aware that your carwash exists. Next, determine if they know it is a self-service carwash that is open day and night. Finally, assess whether the key aspects of your carwash—location, hours of operation, and self-service—have caught drivers' attention enough for them to consider using it the next time they need a car wash.

Once you evaluate how much attention your carwash receives and identify factors that prevent drivers from using your service, the next step is to develop an action plan to address these issues. If many drivers are unaware of the carwash, make it more prominent, such as by painting it yellow—the most visible color and the first one the human eye notices. If drivers know about the carwash but mistakenly think it is a full-service facility with limited hours of operation, correct this impression with road signs highlighting that it is a self-serve, always-open facility. Finally, if drivers are aware of your carwash and its functionality but have never considered it for their car maintenance, you might benefit from offering promotions such as discounts for first-time customers.

CHAPTER FOUR

DESIGNING AND COMMUNICATING CUSTOMER VALUE

People don't want to buy a quarter-inch drill, they want a quarter-inch hole.

—Theodore Levitt, marketing professor,
former editor of *Harvard Business Review*

A ctivating a need and ensuring that customers are aware of a company's offering that can address this need is just the beginning of managing the customer experience. Once an offering enters a customer's consideration set, it is evaluated based on its ability to fulfill this need. This evaluation determines whether customers will ultimately choose and purchase the offering (Figure 1).

Figure 1. The Customer Experience Map: Evaluating the Offering

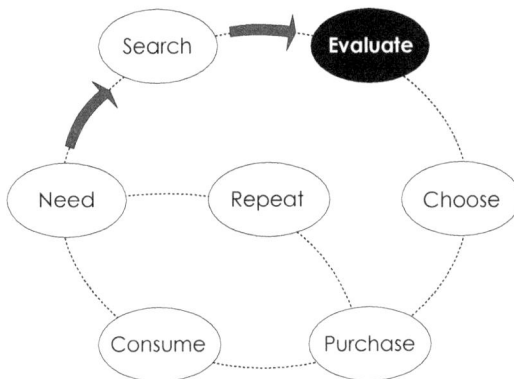

The value customers derive from an offering hinges on their evaluation of its benefits and costs. This evaluation is unique to each customer, shaped by their individual needs and preferences. The way customers evaluate the offering depends on various factors, such that even minor changes in the design and presentation can significantly impact how customers perceive its value. Consider the following scenarios:

- You oversee the development of a communication campaign for a new product. Should your message focus on the specific attributes of the product or on the benefits it creates for target customers? What factors do you need to consider when making this decision?

- You are advising a fashion retailer considering lowering its prices after research data shows that customers perceive its offerings as relatively expensive. Are there alternative ways to change customers' perceptions of this retailer's prices?

- The research and development team needs your guidance on whether to continue improving a product's performance on a particular attribute. What factors do you need to consider when making this decision?

- Market research shows that consumers are willing to pay only a small premium for a particular feature that comes standard on your product. You are considering removing this feature from future versions and lowering the price by the premium consumers are willing to pay to add this feature. Is this a good idea?

- You are in charge of Gillette's shaving division and note that your market share is declining. For decades, the company has focused its efforts on improving the performance of its razors and promoting functionality in its advertising. How would you recommend that Gillette position its razors in the future?

In this chapter, we will discuss the key principles of value creation. We start by examining the concept of customer value and the relationship between the attributes of a company's offering and the customer value created by these attributes. We then discuss the three key properties of the value function—reference dependence, loss aversion, and diminishing marginal value—and how offering attributes are translated into customer benefits and costs. We then delineate the three types of value—functional, psychological, and monetary—and show why focusing exclusively on a single type of value might backfire. Next, we examine customers' tendency to think in terms of categories such as good and bad and discuss how this categorization influences their evaluations. Finally, we address how customers make value judgments when some of the relevant information is not readily available and how inferential reasoning impacts this process.

The discussion of the conceptual issues involved in creating customer value is complemented with examples illustrating key points. We will discuss how Apple underscored the benefits of the iPod, how De Beers helped set the price for engagement rings, and how Coca-Cola Classic became an instant success. We will also explore how Tesla, Apple, and Warby Parker managed to create meaningful customer value propositions; how focusing on a single aspect of value caused Gillette to lose ground to Dollar Shave Club and Harry's; and how McDonald's value proposition helped make it the most popular restaurant chain in the world. Additionally, we will examine how the Belgian beer brand Stella Artois gained market share by touting its high price, how smoothing the corners of Cadbury Dairy Milk bars changed customers' perceptions of their taste, and how Volkswagen, Buckley's, and Listerine gained market share by advertising their shortcomings.

Now, let's explore the essence of customer value, the key aspects of the value function, the three domains of value creation, and the importance of categorical thinking and inference making in value judgments.

The Essence of Customer Value

Managing the customer experience is about creating customer value. Designing a meaningful customer experience is impossible without considering the value customers will derive from it. To create customer value, a manager must understand how customers form value judgments and the key principles of value creation.

Offering Attributes and Customer Value

Managers sometimes mistake the attributes of their offerings for the value these offerings create for customers. Attributes are objective aspects of a product or service and do not depend on customers' needs and preferences. In contrast, the value these products and services create is highly subjective, varying significantly with individual customer needs. Designing successful offerings requires understanding how customers evaluate their attributes and how they translate these attributes into benefits and costs.

The Essence of Customer Value

Customer value reflects the worth of an offering; it is a customer's assessment of the ability of a company's products and services to fulfill their needs (Figure 2). The value created by an offering is not absolute. It depends on the fit between an offering's attributes and the needs of its target customers. The closer the fit, the higher the value perceived by the customer.

Figure 2. Value as a Function of Customer Needs and Offering Attributes

The concept of customer value is closely intertwined with that of the customer experience. Designing customer experiences aims to generate customer value, making value creation a foundational element in managing these experiences. While closely linked, customer value and customer experience have distinct meanings. Customer value reflects customers' perception of the worth of an offering; it is a customer's overall assessment of the ability of this offering to fulfill their needs. The customer experience, on the other hand, is customers' perception of their interaction with an offering and the value they derive from this offering over time. Thus, the concept of customer experience introduces a temporal dimension to value creation and involves both the value customers derive from the offering and their interaction with it over time.

Two aspects of the process of creating customer value merit attention. First, because it is a customer's assessment of the worth of the company's offering, value is *intangible*. It does not physically exist in the market. Second, value is not something that inherently defines a company's offering; it is created when a customer interacts with this offering. Only when a customer considers an offering's ability to fulfill a particular need does the value created by the offering emerge.

Furthermore, because it reflects a customer's subjective assessment of the offering, value is *idiosyncratic*. This means the same offering can create different value for different customers. An offering that is appealing to one customer might be of little or no value to another. For example, a credit card offering travel perks can be attractive to a frequent traveler but of little interest to someone who rarely travels or whose travel expenses are covered by their company.

The key to designing a successful offering lies in aligning its benefits with the specific needs it aims to meet. Understanding what customers need and the benefits they expect from an offering is crucial, as these factors determine the value the offering will create. By identifying customer needs and anticipated benefits, a company can tailor its offering to meet these expectations and create customer value.

From Offering Attributes to Customer Benefits and Costs

A company's products and services are defined by specific attributes such as size, weight, power, and durability. These attributes are properties of the company's offerings, which customers interpret in terms of benefits and costs based on their needs and preferences. Unlike the customer-specific benefits and costs that define the subjective worth of the offering, the attributes defining the company's offerings are objective. They reflect what the offering *is* rather than what it means to customers.

Understanding the difference between attributes and benefits and costs is important because it highlights the contrast between how managers think about their offerings and how customers view them. Engineers, developers, and designers naturally focus on specific attributes that define the appearance and functionality of their offerings. In contrast, customers view offerings through the prism of the value they can create for them, focusing on the benefits and costs rather than the specific features.

To illustrate, when engineers design a car, they think about attributes such as engine specifications, interior and exterior dimensions, and the size of the fuel tank. In contrast, customers think about the value they can derive from using the car. They view the car in terms of benefits such as power, comfort, safety, and reliability, as well as costs such as price, fuel efficiency, and maintenance.

The notion that product development should start with identifying an unmet customer need rather than with a technological innovation is one of the primary drivers of Apple's success. Decades ago, Steve Jobs outlined Apple's approach to product development like this: "You've got to start with the customer experience and work backwards toward the technology. You can't start with the technology and then try to figure out where you're going to try to sell it. As we were trying to develop a strategy and a vision for Apple, we started with 'What incredible benefit can we give to the customer,' not with 'Let's sit down with the engineers and figure out what awesome technology we have and how we are going to market it.'"

The discrepancy between how engineers, developers, and designers think about an offering and how customers view it is the primary cause of many marketing failures. One of the most common marketing mistakes is that managers focus on the attributes of the offering rather than on the customer need the offering aims to fulfill. In the context of Theodore Levitt's quote at the beginning of this chapter, this means that managers should focus on the hole that customers need, not just on the attributes of the drill used to make it.

Attribute Evaluability and Customer Expertise

Customers evaluate a company's offering by comparing its attributes to their needs. The ease of assessing these attributes varies: Some are easy to evaluate, while others are more challenging. For instance, most consumers can readily decide whether they like the peppermint flavoring of a toothpaste but may struggle to assess the benefits of ingredients like stannous fluoride and sodium monofluorophosphate.

The ease of assessing the value of a given attribute, also referred to as attribute evaluability, hinges on two factors: individuals' ability to understand an attribute's meaning and their capacity to link the attribute's performance to their needs. As a result, attribute evaluability varies across customers. For example, while a layperson may not be familiar with the benefits of sodium monofluorophosphate, a dental professional would likely find it easier to assess this ingredient and weigh its pros and cons.

The disparity in how experts and lay consumers assess the benefits and costs of various attributes suggests that companies should adopt different strategies to communicate their offerings. Experts, familiar with specific attributes and able to weigh their pros and cons, typically prefer detailed attribute-specific information. They can easily evaluate how well the offering meets their needs based on their knowledge of both the product attributes and their own requirements. In contrast, lay consumers, who are unfamiliar with the offering's attributes, are better served by information about the offering's benefits.

Consider how Apple introduced the iPod. The newly minted iPod featured a 5GB hard drive, a specification that resonated with computer experts but did not mean much to the average consumer. In contrast, "1,000 songs in your pocket"—the more meaningful and evaluable equivalent of the 5GB hard drive—was something most consumers could easily understand and relate to. This skillful conversion of product attributes into relatable benefits was a key factor in the iPod's instant success.

Focusing on benefits for lay consumers is not without trade-offs. Since desired benefits can vary significantly across customers, the same attribute might deliver different benefits to different customers. Therefore, tailoring benefits to match the specific needs and preferences of individual customer segments is crucial. This often requires a multi-pronged approach, ensuring that different customers receive messages about the benefits most relevant to them. Precision in targeting is key, as any mismatch between the presented benefits and the actual needs of customers can be counterproductive.

The Value Function

Companies create customer value by designing the attributes of their offerings to match the needs of their target customers. This involves developing the product and service aspects of the offering, branding it with unique and meaningful associations, setting a price, running sales promotions, launching a communication campaign to inform target customers, and establishing a distribution network to deliver the offering to them.

Despite companies' efforts, the attributes defining their offerings do not always translate into value for customers. This potential mismatch raises the question: How does the performance of an offering's attributes translate into customer value? For instance, if a mobile phone's battery life is doubled, does this proportionally increase the value customers derive from it? If the offering's price is reduced by twenty percent, does its perceived value to customers increase by the same percentage? At the heart of these questions is understanding the relationship between an offering's attributes and the customer value they create. This relationship is defined by the value function.

The value function reveals the relationship between the performance of an offering's attributes and the value these attributes create for target customers. It reflects how customers translate the attributes of an offering into benefits and costs. Because it defines the value customers see in the company's offerings, understanding the nature of the value function helps managers focus on enhancing the attributes most likely to maximize customer value.

Research in psychology and behavioral science has identified three main properties of the value function: reference-point dependence, loss aversion, and diminishing marginal value. Reference-point dependence means that we evaluate objects not in isolation but relative to other objects or events. Loss aversion means that we view losses as more significant than equivalent gains. Finally, diminishing marginal value suggests that improving performance on a given attribute results in progressively smaller increases in value.[1]

The key properties of the value function are depicted in Figure 3. The reference point reflects the standard that a person uses to evaluate an offering. Based on whether the offering presents an improvement or a deterioration relative to the reference point, its value is framed as either a gain or a loss. The value function is not symmetrical with respect to gains and losses: It is steeper for losses than for gains. This asymmetrical nature of the value function, referred to as loss aversion, reflects the fact that people tend to be much more sensitive to losses than to gains of the same magnitude.

Figure 3. The Value Function

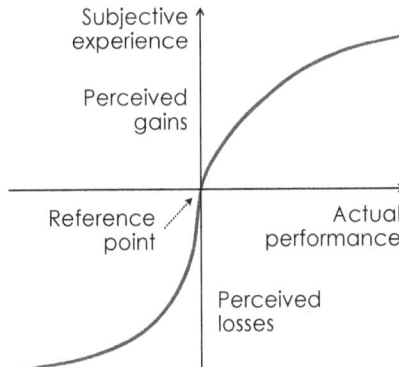

The relationship between the actual performance of the offering and the value it creates for customers is not linear; rather, it is concave in the domain of gains and convex in the domain of losses. This relationship reflects the principle of diminishing marginal value, which states that the impact of an additional improvement in an offering's performance tends to decline as the offering's overall performance improves. Conversely, the impact of further deterioration in performance tends to decrease as the overall performance of the offering deteriorates.

The three properties of the value function depicted stem from prospect theory, which describes the mental processes involved in choosing among uncertain prospects. Developed by behavioral science pioneers Amos Tversky and Daniel Kahneman, prospect theory has profoundly influenced managerial decision making in virtually all aspects of business life. We address the three properties of the value function in more detail in the following sections.

Reference-Point Dependence

Value is relative rather than absolute. People assess the benefits and costs of an offering relative to a reference point that typically has a known value. In this section, we discuss how reference points serve as evaluation benchmarks and explore the anchoring bias that arises from relying on these reference points.

Reference Points as Evaluation Benchmarks

Consider the following scenario. An automobile manufacturer is testing the performance of its new midsize sedan and is interested in consumers' reactions after test-driving the car. The results reveal a bimodal pattern: Some of the drivers found the car very agile and responsive, whereas others found it a bit sluggish and detached from the road. What might have caused such a different reaction from consumers who drove the same car?

One possible account for this discrepancy is drivers' reference points, defined by the type of car they currently drive. Those driving a sports car were likely to experience the new sedan as not very responsive. In contrast, those downsizing from a larger sedan or an SUV might have had the opposite experience and viewed the new car as fast and nimble. The difference in reference points can dramatically change the way we experience and evaluate objects we encounter.

Reference-point dependence reflects the fact that we assess the value of objects not in absolute terms but relative to other objects that serve as reference points. This principle suggests that we evaluate objects in terms of gains and losses relative to the reference point (Figure 4). When the current experience is superior to the reference point, such as a similar experience in the past, it is considered a gain. Conversely, when the current experience is inferior to the reference point, it is considered a loss. In the example above, the performance of the new car is likely to be evaluated as an improvement, or a gain, by drivers used to a less agile car and as a downgrade, or a loss, by drivers used to a sports car.

Figure 4. Reference-Point Dependence

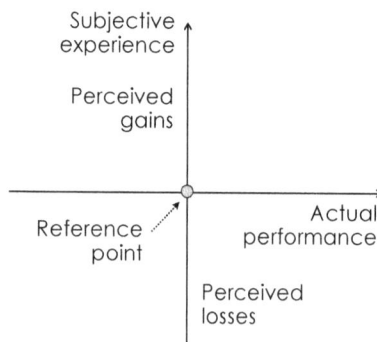

Reference dependence—reliance on reference points to form judgments—is a fundamental aspect of how our minds operate. It applies not only to complex judgments but also to trivial ones. Consider the following simple demonstration: Put three jars in front of you—one with ice-cold water, one with room-temperature water, and one with hot water. Place one finger in the cold water and one in the hot water. A few seconds later, put both fingers in the room-temperature water. Even though you know both fingers should sense the same temperature, the sensation is different. This is because our brain uses the previous state as a reference point to define the current experience.

Reference points can also guide the assessment of more complex experiences and emotional states. Consider how athletes evaluate outcomes of sports events. Intuition suggests that gold medal winners should be happier than silver medal winners, who, in turn, should be happier than bronze medal winners. However, this is not always the case. A study examining the happiness of Olympic medalists by evaluating photographs of athletes on the victory podium and their post-competition audio interviews found that bronze medal winners are often happier than silver medalists. This counterintuitive finding can be explained by the fact that silver and bronze medalists use different reference points. Silver medal winners compare themselves to the athletes who won gold and experience a sense of loss. In contrast, bronze medalists compare themselves to those who did not win a medal at all, leading to a sense of accomplishment and happiness.[2]

The impact of reference points can also be observed in evaluating the monetary value of an offering. Imagine you are in a store, about to buy a new watch that costs $70. The same watch is available at another store two blocks away for $40. Both stores have equally good levels of service and reputation. Would you travel two blocks to save $30? Now, imagine you are in a store about to buy a new camera that costs $800. The same camera is available at another store two blocks away for $770. Both stores have equally good levels of service and reputation. Would you travel two blocks to save $30?

Studies show that people are more likely to choose to go to the other store in the former case rather than in the latter. Strictly speaking, this choice is not rational, as in both cases the outcome is the same: You spend extra time and effort to save $30. The reason you are more likely to travel the two blocks for the watch is that the $30 savings seems more significant in the context of a $70 purchase than when compared to an $800 purchase. The purchase price—$70 or $800—serves as a reference point against which the value of the $30 savings is assessed.[3]

The principle of reference-point dependence is frequently used in retail pricing when shoppers are given both the regular and sale prices of an item. Shoppers who do not have the expertise to objectively assess the value of the offering tend to focus on the difference between the regular price and the sale price—rather than on the actual benefits provided by the offering—when making a choice. This principle is a crucial aspect of the pricing model for many retailers, who use higher prices—the regular price of an offering or its pricing by competitors—to create favorable reference points that customers can use to evaluate their offerings.

Reference points can be very impactful when we are uncertain about the real value of an offering. Consider how De Beers, which for many years controlled the diamond supply, managed to convince the American public to spend a significant portion of their income on diamond rings. With its iconic advertising suggesting, "How can you make two months' salary last forever?" De Beers managed to define buyers' expectations of the price they would have to pay for a ring. By setting a high reference price and extensively promoting it to the public, De Beers turned this price into an implicit norm that consumers felt compelled to follow to express their appreciation for a loved one.

Reference-Point Effects and the Anchoring Bias

The anchoring bias is a reference-point effect that occurs in sequential judgments. It is the tendency for the first piece of information to serve as an anchor and influence subsequent judgments toward this anchor. This bias is often subconscious and can occur automatically without us realizing its impact. Moreover, the reference point does not need to be relevant; even unrelated information can serve as a reference point and influence subsequent judgments.

The anchoring bias was most prominently demonstrated nearly half a century ago in an experiment where participants observed a roulette wheel with numbers between 0 and 100, predetermined to stop at either 10 or 65. After spinning the wheel, participants were asked whether they thought the percentage of African nations in the United Nations was higher or lower than the number at which the wheel stopped (10 or 65). Next, they were asked to provide their best estimate of the actual percentage of African nations in the United Nations. Surprisingly, the results showed that participants' estimates were significantly influenced by the number on the wheel: Those for whom the wheel stopped at 10 estimated on average that the number of African nations in the United Nations was 25%, compared to 45% for those for whom the wheel stopped at 65. This outcome is particularly striking because participants perceived these numbers to be random and unrelated to the question they were asked to answer.[4]

Multiple studies have shown that arbitrary numbers can lead participants to make incorrect estimates skewed toward the initial number. For example, asking people to write down the last two digits of their social security number had a significant impact on how much they were subsequently willing to pay for items whose value they did not know, such as wine, chocolate, and computer equipment. Individuals whose social security numbers ended with higher two-digit numbers were willing to pay significantly more—sometimes even twice as much—than those whose social security numbers ended in lower digits. Reference points matter even when they are clearly irrelevant to the evaluated object.[5]

What drives the anchoring bias? One popular explanation is that when faced with a decision involving a high degree of uncertainty, we use the information contained in the anchor as a starting point and then adjust from it to arrive at our final answer. The problem, however, is that we adjust insufficiently, resulting in an answer that is closer to the anchor than it would otherwise be. This anchoring-and-adjustment account for the anchoring bias can be illustrated with the following example.

Imagine that two groups of people are asked to compute, within five seconds, the product of the numbers one through eight, either as $1 \times 2 \times 3 \times 4 \times 5 \times 6 \times 7 \times 8$ or reversed as $8 \times 7 \times 6 \times 5 \times 4 \times 3 \times 2 \times 1$. Would both groups come up with the same answer? One study showed that the median estimate in the first case was 512, whereas in the second case it was 2,250 (the correct answer is 40,320). The discrepancy in estimates stems from the lack of time to accurately calculate the final answer, leading participants to make a guess after the first few multiplications, using their last multiplication result as a starting point. Because the initial calculation of the first group was lower than that of the second group, their overall answers were also lower.[6]

Since reference points provide a benchmark for determining the value of an object, they can play a key role in decision making and choice. Whether they are products that have been purchased before, alternative options in the consideration set, or even random numbers encountered prior to making the decision, reference points can provide a frame of reference for determining an object's value. In the words of William Shakespeare, "There is nothing either good or bad, but thinking makes it so."[7]

Loss Aversion

Very few decision options are perfect; most have both advantages and disadvantages. As a result, when making a choice, we must trade off these pros and cons to identify the option with the highest value. In doing so, we do not place the same weight on benefits we have to give up as we do on benefits we have an opportunity to gain. Instead, we display loss aversion, attaching greater significance to things we must forgo compared to things of equivalent value we stand to gain. We discuss the principle of loss aversion and the endowment effect in more detail in the following sections.

The Principle of Loss Aversion

Loss aversion refers to our tendency to asymmetrically weigh positive (gains) and negative (losses) deviations from a reference point, placing more weight on losses than gains. Simply put, the pain of losing is psychologically more powerful than the pleasure of gaining. As a result, we tend to favor avoiding losses to acquiring equivalent gains.

Consider making the following bet: Heads you win $X, tails you lose $100. How much does X have to be for you to take the bet? For many people, X is around $200, suggesting that the pain of losing is twice as powerful as the pleasure of gaining. In this case, the $100 premium they demand to take the bet reflects loss aversion. While the subjective pain from a loss is not always twice as large as the pleasure from a corresponding gain, the basic principle is surprisingly robust: Losses loom larger than corresponding gains. The loss felt from parting with money or any other object of value feels worse than gaining the same amount of money or the same object.[8]

The asymmetric nature of the value associated with gains and losses can be visually represented as shown in Figure 5. Here the horizontal axis represents the actual change in an offering's performance, and the vertical axis represents the subjective experience of that change. Loss aversion is captured by the fact that the value function has a steeper slope for losses than for gains—a pattern implying that the subjective experience of losses is exaggerated relative to that of corresponding gains.

Figure 5. Loss Aversion

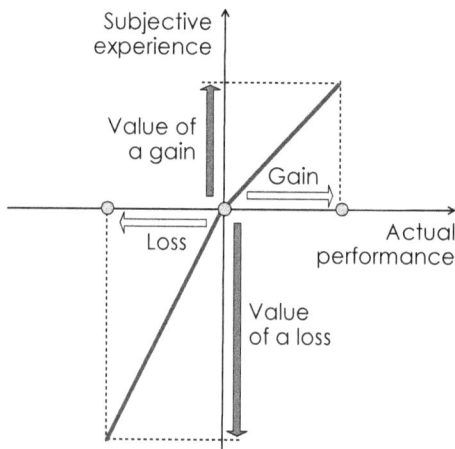

Loss aversion is readily apparent when we compare the subjective valuation of a change in the performance of an offering with a change of the same magnitude in the opposite direction—an improvement, or gain, in one case and a detraction, or loss, in the other. The subjective experience of this change varies depending on the direction—enhancement or detraction—such that losses loom larger than gains of the same magnitude.

Loss aversion is particularly prominent in cases involving monetary exchanges. Consider, for example, investors' reactions to fluctuations in the stock market: A loss of $10,000 hurts more than the satisfaction derived from a gain of $10,000. Similarly, we tend to react more strongly to surcharges than to discounts of the same magnitude. Imagine you are about to purchase a painting from an art gallery. The art dealer tells you the price of the painting is $150 if you use a credit card but that there is a $10 discount for cash payments. Would you pay with a credit card or cash? Now, imagine that in the same scenario the art dealer told you the price of the painting is $140 if you pay cash but that there is a $10 surcharge if you use a credit card. Would you pay with a credit card or cash?

Although the ultimate price for the painting in both scenarios is the same, buyers are more likely to pay cash in the latter scenario than in the former. This is because we view surcharges as losses and discounts as gains. The loss aversion principle dictates that the subjective experience of a surcharge is greater—in absolute terms—than the subjective experience of a discount. This discrepancy guides our preferences toward the payment method associated with greater perceived value and lesser pain. As a result, we are less likely to pay with a credit card in the scenario involving a surcharge, even though the actual price we end up paying is the same.

Loss aversion extends beyond price evaluations and willingness to pay; it permeates all aspects of our lives. A notable example demonstrating loss aversion is an experiment published a quarter of a century ago involving a decision task related to a disease expected to kill 600 people—a scenario eerily reminiscent of the COVID-19 pandemic. Some participants were presented with options in a gain frame: "If program A is adopted, 200 people will be saved. If program B is adopted, there is a one-third chance that 600 people will be saved and a two-thirds chance that no one will be saved." The rest of the participants faced a loss frame: "If program C is adopted, 400 people will die. If program D is adopted, there is a one-third chance that no one will die and a two-thirds chance that 600 people will die."[9]

Even though both scenarios present choices with objectively equivalent outcomes—programs A and C depict outcomes that are objectively equivalent to programs B and D—respondents' preferences differed significantly. In the gain-framed scenario, a majority (72%) preferred program A over program B (28%). Conversely, in the loss-framed scenario, preferences flipped, with a majority (78%) favoring program D over program C (22%). This response pattern indicates that we tend to be risk-averse when choices are framed as gains, preferring to secure these gains. However, when choices are framed as losses, we become more inclined to take risks to avoid these losses. This shift from risk aversion in gain frames to risk-taking in loss frames highlights a broader trend in decision making under uncertainty, which has been demonstrated across various fields such as economics, medicine, and social behavior.

Loss aversion is also clearly seen in customers' responses to companies discontinuing products to introduce new ones. Even though customers might recognize the benefits of new products, the displeasure from giving up the benefits of a familiar product often surpasses the appeal of the new product, even when the latter is objectively better. In one of the most publicized product launch fiascoes, Coca-Cola replaced its regular Coke with New Coke. Many consumers gained new appreciation for the value of the original product, forcing the company to quickly reverse its decision and bring back the "old" Coke rebranded as Coca-Cola Classic. The subsequent success of Coca-Cola Classic underscores the insight of English writer G. K. Chesterton: "The way to love anything is to realize that it might be lost."

Loss Aversion and the Value of Consistency

The principle of loss aversion has been the cornerstone of many business models. Consider McDonald's, for instance. What makes McDonald's the most popular restaurant chain in the world? It does not offer the most spectacular culinary experience. What it does offer is consistency: Even though the quality is average, it remains the same across individual experiences. The Big Mac with fries tastes the same whether it is served in

New York, Beijing, or Sydney. Additionally, the customer experience has not changed much over time. Consistency is the real key to McDonald's success.

Consistency is a crucial element of customer experience because loss aversion leads us to highly value uniformity. When making decisions, we aim not just to maximize potential benefits but also to mitigate risk and minimize the possibility of negative outcomes. When selecting a fast-food restaurant, our priority often is not to seek the best culinary experience but to ensure predictable quality of service and food. We might bypass a lesser known restaurant that could potentially offer a superior burger to avoid the risk of a disappointing meal. Because we tend to avoid risk, McDonald's often presents an easy choice. This pattern of behavior becomes especially noticeable when traveling abroad. Faced with the uncertainty associated with unfamiliar local restaurants, many prefer the familiar McDonald's experience, valuing the predictability of knowing exactly what to expect over the adventure of trying something new.

This preference for consistency is not limited to McDonald's or the food industry; it is a widespread pattern of consumer behavior. Well-known brands like Apple, Samsung, and LG command a premium not just because they offer the best specifications but because they provide a predictable level of quality and user experience. Consistency is equally critical in service sectors such as banking and hospitality. Customers often favor banks with a reputation for dependable service over newer ones offering more attractive rates or fewer fees. Hospitality chains like Marriott and Hilton draw guests not just with amenities but with the reliable level of service and experience they guarantee. The trust built on consistent service delivery positions these brands as safe choices, enabling consumers to minimize risk and avoid the potential disappointment associated with unpredictable outcomes.

Our willingness to sacrifice a potentially superior experience for the consistency of a familiar offering reflects a type of thinking commonly referred to as defensive decision making.[10] This mindset prioritizes minimizing potential losses over maximizing possible gains. From an evolutionary perspective, defensive decision making is well justified: To survive in a world full of threats, the human brain had to devise strategies to minimize risk and ensure survival. The same survival instinct operates in the business world. By choosing the option that offers consistent performance, managers might not achieve the best outcome, but they also avoid the fallout of a poor decision.

The Endowment Effect

Loss aversion is closely related to our tendency to place greater value on an object we own than on the same object when we consider acquiring it. This asymmetry in valuation based on ownership is referred to as the endowment effect.[11] The essence of this effect was eloquently summarized by Aristotle, "For most things are differently valued by those who have them and by those who wish to get them: What belongs to us, and what we give away, always seems very precious to us."[12]

A classic illustration of the endowment effect involved a study in which participants were divided into three groups. One group was given a coffee mug and later offered the chance to trade it for a Swiss chocolate bar. Another group received the chocolate bar first, with a later offer to exchange it for the mug. A third (control) group was simply asked to choose between the two items, with no prior endowment. Without the endowment effect, all groups should have displayed similar preferences. However, this was not the case. The control group showed no strong preference for either item. Yet, those initially given a mug overwhelmingly chose to keep it instead of trading it; the same response was seen in those given a chocolate bar. Giving up the mug or chocolate bar participants were endowed with incurred a sense of loss that was greater than the gain from obtaining another item of objectively equal value.[13]

The endowment effect is a key factor behind many retailers' no-questions-asked return policies. Shoppers compare the benefits that they can gain by acquiring a given item against the loss of the financial resources they will use to pay for it. When perceived benefits and costs are balanced, shoppers might be indifferent about making the purchase. However, a lenient return policy can encourage them to proceed, offering a safety net to reconsider the decision. Once customers own an item, their reference point shifts, and ownership of the item becomes the reference point in subsequent decisions. Consequently, the perception of gains and losses reverses: Returning the item is now seen as a loss, while the refund is considered a gain. Due to loss aversion, customers are more likely to value what they would lose by returning the item over what they would gain, thereby decreasing the likelihood of returning items they were initially unsure about.

Diminishing Marginal Value

When designing their offerings, companies are frequently faced with the question of how an improvement on a particular attribute translates into customer value. For example, would doubling the battery life of a mobile device also double the value customers receive from this improvement? Would increasing the speed of the internet connection by fifty percent also increase the value customers derive from the higher speed by the same amount? What would be the impact on sales revenues of lowering the price by ten percent? More generally, how does product performance translate into customer value? The relationship between the magnitude of changing an offering's performance and the corresponding change in customer value is discussed below.

The Principle of Diminishing Marginal Value

When developing new offerings or modifying existing ones, some managers assume that technological improvements create customer value at a constant rate. In other words, they believe a particular level of improvement in an offering's performance will translate into the same improvement in customer benefits. This assumption implies a linear relationship between the actual performance of the offering and the customer benefit it creates (Figure 6). A manager who subscribes to this assumption will likely continue to invest in improving an offering's performance on a given attribute regardless of the offering's current performance on this attribute.

Figure 6. Linear Value Function

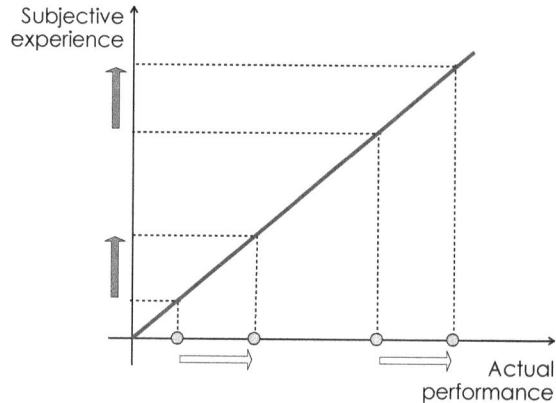

The belief that improving an attribute is independent of the level of performance already achieved leads to a perpetual improvement fallacy. Managers focus on constantly enhancing an offering's performance without realizing that as performance gets better, customers care less about further improvements. The relationship between an offering's actual performance and the value it creates for its customers is not linear. Rather, it is subject to diminishing marginal value: The higher the current level of performance, the less marginal value is created by further improving that attribute.

The notion of diminishing marginal value was introduced by Daniel Bernoulli more than two centuries ago. He argued that value is determined not by the objective properties of things but by the subjective experience of these properties, and that this experience depends on the current state of the decision maker. In his words: "A gain of one thousand gold coins is more significant to a pauper than to a rich man even though both gain the same amount." The more people have of something, the less a further improvement means to them.[14]

Consider how the improvement in the single-charge driving distance of an electric car influences the value a buyer derives from this enhancement. When the driving distance is relatively low, even small increases in distance have a significant impact. As the driving distance improves, the same increase in driving distance that used to produce a large increase in customer value now has much less impact. Increasing the driving distance by 100 miles will have a greater impact when the current driving distance is 100 miles than when it is 1,000 miles.

The principle of diminishing marginal returns is illustrated in Figure 7. Unlike the scenario with the linear value function shown in Figure 6, in this case performance improvements do not lead to proportional increases in customer value. Rather, the value function is concave, meaning that improving the offering's performance generates most value at lower levels of performance. As the performance of the offering improves, any further enhancements result in a progressively smaller impact on customer value.

Figure 7. Diminishing Marginal Value Function

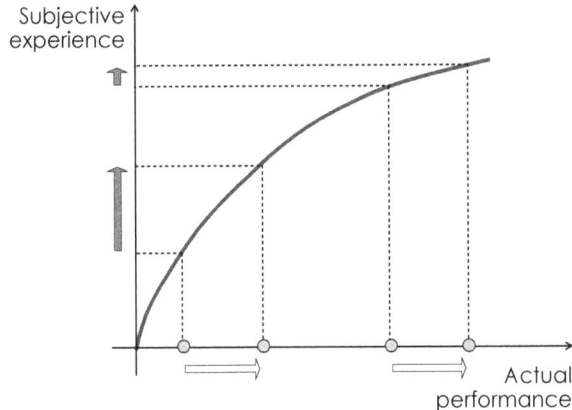

The diminishing marginal value effect is clearly illustrated by comparing the subjective valuations of changes in an offering's performance, as shown on the horizontal axis in Figure 7. Improvement on a given attribute delivers greater value when starting from a lower baseline than from a higher one. Once an offering reaches a certain level of performance on a given attribute, further improvements in performance on this attribute are seen as less valuable.

The tendency of marginal benefits to decrease as an attribute's performance improves prompts a strategic question: What should a company do when its offering approaches an optimal performance level for a given attribute? The diminishing marginal value principle indicates that at this point managers should reassess the overall performance of the offering to pinpoint where enhancements could deliver the most benefits to customers. This may involve focusing on improving areas where the offering is lacking rather than further refining attributes on which it already excels.

The Marginal Value of Combined Experiences

Imagine you are an investment advisor who has just executed three very profitable trades for a client. How should you communicate the financial gain? Would it be better to send a single email summarizing the total gain, or should you send individual emails for each successful trade? Now, consider the opposite scenario where your trades have resulted in a substantial loss. Would you relay this information in one comprehensive message or with separate messages for each trade? The broader question here is whether outcomes should be combined or segregated when communicated, and how the nature of the outcome — whether it is a gain or a loss — might influence this decision.

The decision to separate or combine performance outcomes partly depends on whether the outcomes are gains or losses. The principle of diminishing marginal value suggests that separating gains can enhance perceived customer value. For instance, if a customer makes three trades, each earning a $1,000 profit, the total gain is $3,000. Due to diminishing marginal value, the customer will derive more enjoyment from three separate gains of $1,000 each than from a single combined gain of $3,000, even though the total monetary gain is identical in both scenarios. Because each additional "unit" of performance offers progressively smaller increases in value, combining these experiences can lead to a perception of lower overall value compared to the sum of individual experiences. This logic is illustrated in Figure 8.

Figure 8. Combining and Separating Positive Outcomes

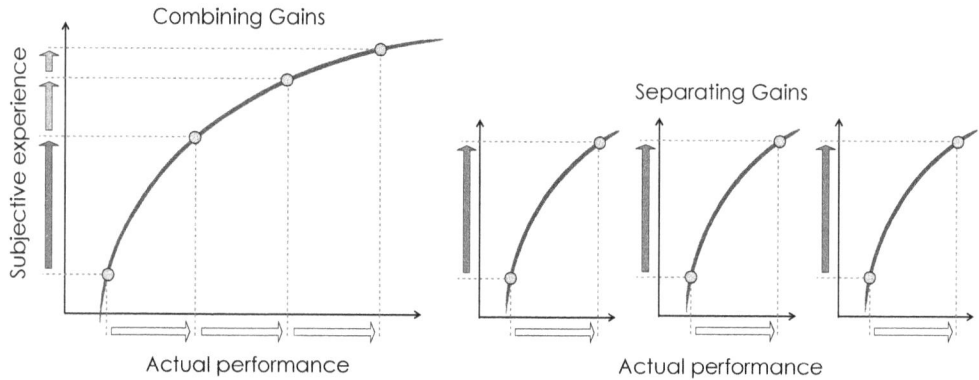

The principle of combining experiences applies to losses as well as gains: The perceived value of combined losses, in absolute terms, is lower than the sum of individual losses. However, since these experiences are negative, reducing the absolute perceived magnitude of the loss translates to greater utility (or, strictly speaking, less disutility) for customers. Therefore, unlike with gains, combining losses into a single experience tends to yield greater subjective value than separating them. This concept is illustrated in Figure 9.

Figure 9. Combining and Separating Negative Outcomes

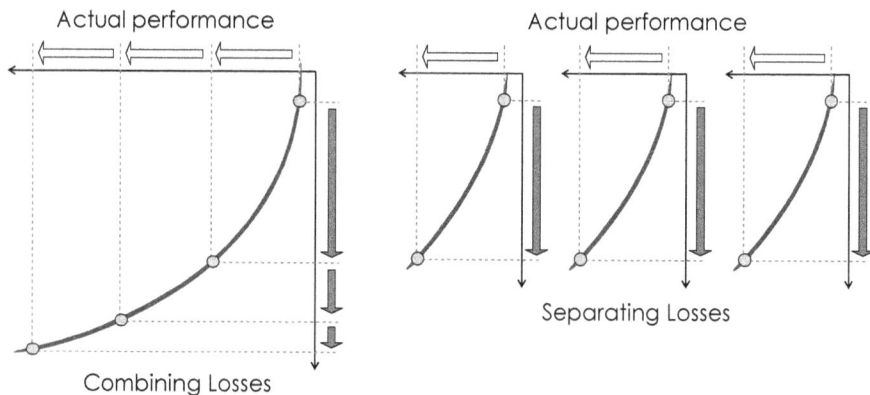

The strategy of aggregating losses, often likened to "ripping off the bandage," is based on the idea that enduring a single painful experience is generally preferred over facing several smaller painful incidents. For example, an investment adviser might find that presenting a client with a single $3,000 loss causes less psychological discomfort than reporting three separate losses of $1,000 each. Therefore, unlike with positive outcomes, combining negative outcomes can effectively reduce the perceived magnitude of loss, thereby improving the customer's overall experience.

Understanding the psychological impact of combining and segregating individual experiences is important because it helps managers maximize the value customers derive from the overall experience. While both gains and losses are subject to diminishing marginal value, combining and segregating individual experiences can lead to directionally opposite outcomes, depending on whether they are perceived as enhancements or detractions relative to a reference point. Of course, the logic of combining outcomes is not a universal rule applicable in every situation. Rather, it reflects the ways people experience a series of gains or losses, which, in turn, influences the overall value they derive from the experience.

Functional, Psychological, and Monetary Value

So far, we have discussed value primarily in terms of benefits and costs, treating it as a unidimensional construct where all benefits and costs align on a single dimension of customer value. However, value is more complex, encompassing three distinct dimensions: functional, psychological, and monetary. The following sections will explore these dimensions of value and their role in crafting superior customer experiences.

The Three Dimensions of Customer Value

Consider the value drivers derive from an electric car like Tesla. Functionally, Tesla offers numerous benefits such as speed, power, acceleration, extended driving range without recharging, comfort, trunk size, reliability, and safety. Beyond functionality, it offers important psychological benefits. For instance, some owners might value the advanced technological features, the car's ability to self-update its software, and the sense of being at the forefront of automotive technology. Others may take pride in driving an electric vehicle for its environmental benefit of being eco-friendly. Owning a Tesla can also signal a tech-savvy image and convey high socioeconomic status. The value customers derive from owning a Tesla also involves a significant monetary dimension. This includes the purchase price, which is offset by various financial incentives and savings, such as government tax credits, savings from using electricity rather than gasoline, and lower maintenance costs.

The Tesla example demonstrates how an offering can generate value for customers across three key dimensions: functional, psychological, and monetary. These three dimensions of value are illustrated in Figure 10 and discussed in more detail below.

Figure 10. The Three Domains of Customer Value

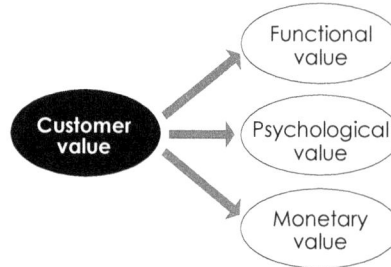

- *Functional value* reflects the benefits and costs directly related to an offering's performance. The functional value of an offering is typically assessed by answering the question: Does the offering's performance create value for target customers? Take, for example, the Apple Watch. Its functional value includes its ability to tell time, run different apps, and seamlessly connect to other mobile devices such as phones and tablets. Attributes that create functional value include performance, reliability, durability, compatibility, ease of use, size, portability, and packaging. For offerings that are mostly utilitarian, such as office supplies and industrial equipment, functionality is usually the key source of value.

- *Psychological value* reflects the psychological benefits and costs customers derive from the offering. It extends beyond mere functional benefits, tapping into customers' emotions and self-identity. The psychological value of an offering is typically assessed by answering the questions: How do target customers feel about the offering? What does the offering say about their identity? For instance, the Apple Watch caters to psychological needs by keeping users connected and reducing anxiety over missed appointments. In some developing countries, it may even symbolize the owner's socioeconomic status. For luxury and fashion offerings, where customers seek emotional and self-expressive benefits, the psychological value conveyed by the offering is of primary importance.

- *Monetary value* reflects the financial costs and benefits associated with the offering, such as its price, discounts, and fees, as well as the monetary costs associated with using and disposing of the offering. In addition to costs, an offering can also have monetary benefits in the form of cash-back offers, prizes, and financial rewards. The monetary value of an offering is determined by answering the question: What are the monetary costs and benefits of the company's offering? For example, the monetary value of the Apple Watch is defined by its purchase price, adjusted for any promotional discounts. In markets with commoditized products, where functional and psychological differences are minimal, monetary value often becomes the decisive factor.

Even though they represent different dimensions of customer value, the functional, psychological, and monetary domains are interconnected. Take Warby Parker, for instance, a direct-to-consumer brand offering high-quality, stylish eyeglasses at prices below those of traditional brands. The functional value comes from its trendy, durable eyewear, the convenience of trying on five frames at home, and a straightforward return policy. The psychological value is derived from wearing fashionable glasses that express the wearer's personality as well as the moral satisfaction from supporting Warby Parker's charitable program, which donates a pair of glasses for every pair sold. The monetary value, meanwhile, is highlighted by the brand's competitive pricing, offering significant savings compared to conventional designer eyewear.

The value created across different dimensions is not always positive. This is because value encapsulates both benefits and costs, and in certain cases, costs may overshadow the benefits in a specific dimension. Functional and psychological values are generally positive, reflecting the benefits customers seek and appreciate in an offering. Conversely, monetary value is typically negative, representing the cost or price paid for the offering. For instance, a person may value the functional advantages and psychological appeal of a luxury car but perceive negative monetary value due to the car's high price. For an offering to create customer value, its cumulative benefits across functional, psychological, and monetary dimensions must surpass the associated costs.

Managing Value Across Domains

A common mistake that managers make is allocating most of their resources to improve the performance of their offerings in just one of the three value domains. While prioritizing a domain that customers care about is logical, it should not come at the expense of neglecting opportunities for creating value in the other domains. Overfocusing on a single area of value not only yields diminishing returns in customer benefits over time but also exposes the company to competitive threats in the underdeveloped areas.

Consider Gillette's plight. Since King Gillette introduced the first safety razor in 1903, the company has focused on improving the functionality of its razors. Initially, Gillette emphasized the safety benefit of its razor and promoted it as the "Gillette safety razor" to differentiate it from traditional straight razors that required skill to avoid nicks and cuts. Later, when razors using disposable blades became commonplace and nicks and cuts were no longer an issue in shaving, Gillette focused its efforts on improving the closeness of the shave. In doing so, it increasingly promoted its technological innovations to convince customers of the advantages of its razors.

Of course, promoting functional benefits is important, especially for a product that must perform well to be viable. The problem is that Gillette focused only on the functional aspect of value, neglecting the monetary and psychological aspects. To make matters worse, Gillette's razors had already reached the point of diminishing marginal returns, meaning that most of its customers were already satisfied with its products and placed little importance on further improvements in the shaving experience. Despite this, the company gradually raised prices, believing that consumers would fully appreciate the benefits created by the new technological developments.

Gillette's missteps in managing its customer value proposition caught the competition's attention, creating an opening for two companies that reached billion-dollar valuations in under five years: Dollar Shave Club and Harry's. Dollar Shave Club emphasized its low price, directly comparing itself to Gillette and making it appear vastly overpriced. Harry's, on the other hand, focused on building a brand that resonated deeply with younger consumers. It anthropomorphized its brand, giving razors human names like Truman and Winston.

Harry's razors featured a variety of bright colors while its packaging was environmentally friendly and easy to open—in stark contrast to Gillette's subdued colors and plastic packaging that required scissors to open. Even though Harry's also used price to differentiate itself from Gillette, it was positioned to provide its customers with a means to express their identity by choosing a razor aligned with their personality and value system. Dollar Shave Club's and Harry's strategies were so successful that they forced Gillette to slash its prices after losing significant market share.

Gillette's example shows that a company must have a holistic view of the customer experience and consider *all* dimensions of customer value. This does not necessarily mean that an offering should excel on all three value dimensions—a task that is out of reach for most companies. Rather, companies should allocate resources in a way that maximizes customer benefits across these three domains. After gaining superiority and reaching a point of diminishing returns on one attribute, a company might benefit from shifting some of its resources to the other domains of value in which its offering underperforms.

Thinking in Categories

The value function discussed earlier in this chapter assumes that when evaluating a company's offerings, people quantify their benefits and costs and think about them in numerical terms. Although this assumption is useful for illustrating the key properties of the value function, it rarely reflects the way most people make decisions. Thinking in numbers can be difficult, as it demands significant mental effort and knowledge of how to assign specific numeric values to an offering's attributes. Consequently, people tend to adopt a qualitative approach, favoring reasons over equations to weigh the benefits and costs associated with a company's offerings.

Reasoning typically involves qualitative thinking, a process where we classify options into distinct categories. This approach translates the quantitative characteristics of options—like speed, power, and reliability—into discrete evaluations that are then used to generate reasons for or against choosing the options. Such translations are crucial because the reasons we use to make decisions are inherently qualitative rather than numeric. In the sections below, we delve deeper into the role of categorization in evaluating offerings and examine how categorical thinking can introduce decision biases.

Categorization and Stereotyping

Categorization is a fundamental cognitive process of sorting, organizing, and classifying information into groups based on shared characteristics. It simplifies and organizes complex information, helping us make sense of our surroundings. This process leans heavily on qualitative thinking, allowing us to classify objects into distinct categories rather than quantitatively evaluating each attribute. For instance, we often categorize objects into binary groups such as good and bad, vice and virtue, expensive and inexpensive, before and after, large and small, and safe and risky.

One common instance of categorization is *stereotyping*, which involves generalizing toward a prototype—the most prominent example of a given category. Stereotyping is often used in social contexts, where people attribute a set of generalized characteristics to others based solely on their group membership, often relying on limited information. Social stereotyping can encompass a variety of factors, including race, gender, age, nationality, religion, occupation, and social class. While streamlining decision processes, stereotyping oversimplifies the rich individuality and complexity of people within these groups, leading to broad generalizations that fail to recognize personal distinctions. Consequently, stereotypes often result in biases, especially when individuals do not conform to the characteristics attributed to their group.

The preference for qualitative over quantitative thinking significantly influences how we evaluate objects, leading to categorizations that often result in polarized evaluations. For instance, we tend to consider the difference in the perceived magnitude between prices such as $7.95 and $8.05 as greater than that between $7.85 and $7.95, despite the actual differences being identical. This is because the different left digits place the prices into distinct mental categories, creating the perception that prices within the same category are more alike than prices in different categories. Similarly, lines of the same length are perceived as different if they are labeled differently, and temperature changes across days are perceived to be greater if those days fall in different months. By grouping individual items together and treating everything within these groups as identical, categorization and stereotyping frequently distort our perceptions, resulting in a biased view of reality.

One of the most common types of categorization involves classifying objects into virtues and vices based on their perceived "goodness." This vice–virtue categorization reflects our judgment of an item as good or bad. In the realm of food, virtues refer to foods deemed beneficial for health and weight management, though they may not always be the most enjoyable to eat. Examples include fruits like apples and berries, vegetables such as broccoli and spinach, as well as foods labeled organic, light, fat-free, and low-fat. In contrast, vices are indulgent foods that offer immediate gratification but are deemed "bad" for long-term health. Typical vices include chocolate cake and ice cream, as well as foods described as rich, creamy, and decadent.[15]

The vice–virtue categorization influences how many Americans perceive their meals, with studies indicating that nearly half believe most foods can be classified as either good or bad for health.[16] This dichotomy also forms the basis of many nutritional guidelines and popular diets such as South Beach and Atkins, which advocate the consumption of certain food groups while advising against others. Despite variations in specific recommendations, the underlying principle of distinguishing between virtues and vices remains a common thread across most dietary advice.

A notable drawback of the vice–virtue categorization is its tendency to overlook the extent to which objects possess specific characteristics. This oversight can result in paradoxical outcomes, especially when evaluating offerings that comprise both virtues and vices. Stories abound about dieters trying to "balance" their meal by ordering a Diet Coke to go along with their double bacon cheeseburger and super-sized fries. While many consumers are amused by those who think that a low-calorie drink can offset a high-calorie meal, they often make similar choices themselves without even realizing it.

The pitfalls of vice–virtue categorization are vividly demonstrated in a study where participants were asked to estimate the calorie content of a fast-food meal. One group was shown just a cheeseburger, while another group saw the same cheeseburger accompanied by a green side salad. When asked to estimate the calorie content of their respective meals, the results were striking. Those presented with only the cheeseburger estimated its calorie content to be higher than the group shown the cheeseburger with a salad. Paradoxically, the addition of a salad reduced the perceived calorie content of the entire meal. This phenomenon was not limited to just cheeseburgers and salads; similar outcomes were noted across various vice–virtue meal combinations, underscoring the widespread misconception that adding a healthy item to a meal somehow reduces its overall calorie count.[17]

The paradoxical outcome observed in vice–virtue evaluations is one of many examples of how categorization deeply affects our perception and judgment of the world. Although these mental shortcuts simplify complex information, they frequently lead us to overlook the nuanced details of the objects being considered. Therefore, recognizing the constraints of categorical thinking is essential—whether in social contexts, dietary choices, or other areas—for understanding how customers think and behave.

Categorizing events by their timing is another prevalent mental shortcut. We convert the continuous flow of time into discrete intervals, like years, days, and hours, to make it more manageable. However, this fragmentation leads us to perceive these intervals as fundamentally different from one another. For instance, the start of a new year prompts many to set resolutions, treating the upcoming year as qualitatively distinct from the previous one, despite the continuity of time. This categorization obscures the fact that the transition from December 31 to January 1 is no different in temporal distance than the transition from December 30 to December 31 or from January 1 to January 2. Similarly, we tend to overestimate the actual distance between events, making those scheduled for the next day, week, or month seem farther away than they truly are.

The categorization of time is also evident in the common practice of segmenting life into decades—"the 20s," "the 30s," "the 40s," and so on—as if significant aging and development occur only upon crossing these rather arbitrary thresholds. This perspective prompts those approaching a new decade to reevaluate their lives and pursue goals reflective of lifelong aspirations. This phenomenon of "decade transition" prompts individuals to evaluate their personal and professional achievements, leading to significant life changes, renewed goals, or even a shift in values and priorities.

This tendency to partition time into categories is supported by research indicating a surge in behaviors, such as running a marathon, as people reach an age ending in 9. Specifically, 29-year-old individuals are nearly twice as likely to run their first marathon as those aged 28 or 30. This trend declines in the early 40s but sees a dramatic increase at age 49, with 49-year-olds being three times more likely to run a marathon than those a year older. Across different age groups, first-time marathon runners whose age ends in 9 are overrepresented by nearly fifty percent.[18]

This pattern of behavior supports the notion that despite the continuous nature of time and aging, we think of time in categorical terms, thereby accentuating the perceived differences between adjacent time periods placed into separate categories.

Unit Bias

One important consequence of categorization is that it makes us more sensitive to changes in price than to changes in quantity. To illustrate, consider a choice between two snacks: Snack A is offered at $5.99 for a 4-oz package, while Snack B is also priced at $5.99 but for a 3.5-oz package. Now imagine that Snack A is still priced at $5.99 for a 4-oz package, but Snack B is priced at $6.79 for a 4-oz package. In which scenario are most people more likely to choose Snack B? Contrary to predictions made by classical economic theories, most of us are more likely to choose Snack B in the first scenario than in the second, despite Snack B being slightly more expensive per ounce in the first scenario.

Consumers' tendency to pay more attention to price than quantity has not remained unnoticed by companies seeking to improve their profit margins without raising prices. During the past several decades many companies have shrunk the size of their offerings to improve their bottom line—a phenomenon referred to as shrinkflation.

Notable examples include Dreyer's Grand Ice Cream, which reduced its package size from 1.75 to 1.5 quarts; Frito-Lay, which decreased the quantity of chips in bags from 12 to 10 ounces; and Henkel Corporation, which downsized its Dial soap bars from 4.5 to 4 ounces. Similarly, PepsiCo introduced an 89-oz bottle of Tropicana orange juice to replace the previous 96-oz jug, while Procter & Gamble reduced the count of paper towels in its Bounty brand from 60 to 52. Likewise, Kellogg's reduced the sizes of several cereals, including Froot Loops and Cocoa Krispies, by an average of 2.4 ounces, and Walmart decreased its Great Value paper towels from 168 to 120 sheets per roll. Unilever followed suit by reducing Hellmann's mayonnaise jars from 32 to 30 ounces, shrinking Skippy Peanut Butter from 18 to 16.3 ounces, and downsizing Shedd's Country Crock Spread from 48 to 45 ounces.[19]

The shift by companies toward reducing product quantity instead of increasing prices stems from people's tendency to focus more on changes in price than changes in quantity, a phenomenon known as unit bias. This bias is especially pronounced with packaged goods, where we think in terms of units—like a can of soda, a box of cereal, or a container of orange juice—rather than the actual volume or weight. As a result, we tend to overlook small reductions in quantity, focusing more on the price tag. In line with this pattern of thinking, Chewy.com, an online retailer of pet food, justified its decision to reduce the size of some of its products, saying: "The cans remained the same price, as the difference in amount of product is not significant and rarely impacts the number of cans being fed to the cat."[20]

Unit bias stems from two main factors. First, when purchasing packaged goods, most of us are unaware of the exact quantity we need to buy, leaving us oblivious to changes in product size. Even when we notice these changes, their impact may be negligible because the desired consumption quantity is not well defined. Most of us do not need to buy exactly 96 ounces of orange juice, 168 paper towels, or 1.75 quarts of ice cream. As a result, we are willing to go along with relatively minor changes in package size. The fungible nature of our thinking is well captured in the words of famed American baseball player and manager Yogi Berra: "You better cut the pizza in four pieces because I'm not hungry enough to eat six."

The second, and arguably more critical, reason we tend to emphasize price over quantity stems from the fundamentally different ways in which we process price-related and quantity-related information. Price, as a universal measure of value, is typically evaluated quantitatively. We engage in monetary transactions daily, encountering a range of prices across different product categories. This frequent exposure makes even slight price differences prominent. Conversely, product quantity is often assessed qualitatively. We think in terms of units purchased or consumed—such as a can of Coke, a jar of mayonnaise, or a box of cereal—rather than the specific quantity these units represent. Therefore, unless the size of a purchased unit markedly diverges from what we expect, we are likely to overlook minor variations in quantity, focusing instead on the price of the unit.

Unit bias influences not just perceptions of price and quantity but also consumption patterns. For instance, dividing a larger quantity into separate units can change how we perceive the amount we consume, thereby influencing our behavior. This effect is demonstrated in a study where participants were given containers of potato chips to eat while watching a movie. Some participants received containers with uniformly colored chips, while others had containers with red chips interspersed at regular intervals. The introduction of the colored chips, which served as visual cues of the quantity consumed, led to a marked reduction in the amount of chips eaten: Participants with the visual cues consumed less than half the amount of chips eaten by those not given such cues. Partitioning the quantity into a series of smaller units significantly changed the way people viewed consumption quantity and, ultimately, their behavior.[21]

Drawing Inferences

Most decisions involve evaluating offerings without access to all the relevant information. In such cases, individuals rely on the available information to infer what is not directly observable. Depending on whether the evaluations are consistent with or directionally opposite to the available information, these inferences fall into two categories: halo-based and compensatory.

Halo-Based Inferences

The halo effect refers to the tendency of a specific characteristic of an object or person to influence the overall evaluation of that object or person, as well as its performance on specific attributes that are not readily observable (this effect is discussed in more detail in Chapter 3). For instance, studies have shown that individuals perceived as attractive are often also judged to possess more positive personality traits, to be more sociable, mentally healthier, and more intelligent compared to those of average appearance. The halo effect can also lead to judgments about the relationship between specific attributes. Thus, positive evaluations of observable attributes often result in positive assumptions about unobservable ones, while negative evaluations usually lead to negative assumptions.[22]

A common example of halo-based inferences is the perceived relationship between price and quality. In the absence of direct information about a product's quality, consumers often rely on its price to gauge performance, assuming that higher-priced offerings are of superior quality. This perception spans categories: More expensive household appliances are seen as more durable, high-priced hotels are expected to offer better service, and premium-priced wines are believed to provide a superior sensory experience. Some companies even use price–quality inferences to promote the quality of their products. For over two decades, the Belgian beer brand Stella Artois promoted its quality with the slogan "reassuringly expensive," suggesting its use of the finest ingredients.

Price–quality inferences can influence not only expectations but also the actual consumption experience. Research demonstrates that in blind taste tests, the same wine was perceived as more enjoyable and its taste more intense when it was associated with a higher price compared to a lower one. This price–quality inference was not limited to just perception; it also changed the way consumers experienced the wine, such that higher priced wine resulted in increased activity in parts of the brain associated with pleasant experiences.[23]

In addition to price–quality inferences, the halo effect can also be observed among nonprice attributes. For example, it has been shown that people often inappropriately generalize health and nutrition claims on food packages, creating a "health halo" effect. This leads them to believe that products with such claims have other positive health attributes not explicitly mentioned. For example, foods labeled as low in cholesterol are often assumed to be low in fat, and vice versa. Similarly, "low fat" labels can significantly lower the perceived calorie content of foods, regardless of their actual calorie count.[24]

The halo effect can also be related to the physical properties of an object. For example, round shapes are often associated with sweetness, while angular shapes are linked to bitterness. When Cadbury smoothed the corners of its Dairy Milk bars—arguably to reduce the amount of chocolate in each bar—it faced numerous complaints from consumers expressing displeasure that the company had sweetened the taste of the iconic chocolate. In reality, however, the Dairy Milk recipe remained unchanged; the perceived difference in taste resulted from the halo effect of the rounder shape of the bar.[25]

Similarly, many consumers believe that the flaked crystals in Folgers instant coffee make it more enjoyable, even though the shape of the coffee crystals has no impact on the actual taste. While the size and shape of particles are important for ground coffee because they influence the amount of flavor extracted in the brewing process, in the case of instant coffee, the size and surface area are irrelevant because the entire crystal dissolves.[26]

Another common source of inference is brand-based halos, where a brand's reputation influences perceptions of attributes that are not observable at the time of purchase. For instance, customers cannot readily assess the mineral purity of Fiji water, the durability of Michelin tires, the reliability of Sub-Zero appliances, or the longevity of DieHard batteries. Instead, they rely on the brand to infer these unobservable qualities. This reliance on the brand is more pronounced for attributes that are less visible and difficult to evaluate prior to consumption. Brands use the power of the halo effect to make the invisible visible.[27]

The impact of brands on consumer beliefs and behavior is prominently documented in a study where participants were offered a cocktail of fruit juice, vodka, and Red Bull, labeled either as a "Vodka–Red Bull cocktail" or simply a "Vodka cocktail." Even though both groups of participants consumed identical drinks, those who had the cocktail emphasizing the energy drink reported feeling more intoxicated, took more risks, and were more sexually self-confident compared to those who consumed the same drink without the Red Bull brand mention.[28]

Halo-based inferences can also stem from a company's corporate social responsibility activities. In a revealing study, participants were asked to rate the taste of wine, with some told that the winery donates a percentage of its revenues to the American Heart Association. Despite all participants tasting the same wine, novice wine drinkers who were aware of the company's charitable contributions rated the wine more favorably than those who were not informed of the contributions. This benevolent halo effect has been shown to influence product evaluations across different consumption domains, including cosmetics, household products, and productivity software.[29]

Compensatory Inferences

Compensatory inferences reflect the belief that an advantage on one dimension is offset by a disadvantage on another, and vice versa. Consider Volkswagen's long-running ad campaign that glorified the flaws of the Beetle with taglines like "Lemon," "Ugly. Slow. Noisy. Expensive.," "It's ugly but it gets you there," and "The 1970 VW will stay ugly longer." Rather than following the conventional approach of emphasizing the car's advantages, VW focused on its most obvious disadvantages, believing that highlighting the car's deficiencies would underscore its advantages on more important attributes. VW's promote-the-flaws approach worked, and a few years after the launch of the campaign, VW sold more cars than any other imported brand had ever sold.

Compensatory inferences stem from the zero-sum heuristic, which reflects the belief that things are universally balanced, such that losses in one domain are offset by gains in another. Accordingly, when consumers are presented with an option that seemingly outperforms the others, they may suspect an unseen flaw in the dominant option, expecting a balance in overall performance. This discrepancy prompts inferences about missing attributes that could level the playing field. For example, when one of two equally priced wireless service plans appears superior in all observable aspects, consumers might speculate about hidden drawbacks in areas like customer service, reliability, or undisclosed fees in the seemingly better plan.[30]

In addition to arising from people's belief that market offerings tend to be balanced in their overall attractiveness, compensatory inferences often stem from general beliefs about attribute-specific relationships. A common example is the unhealthy-tasty heuristic, where people tend to believe that taste and health benefits are inversely related, such that tasty foods are unlikely to be healthy and vice versa.[31]

This unhealthy-tasty heuristic is not limited to food items. For example, to promote the effectiveness of its cough syrup, the Canadian brand Buckley's capitalized on consumers' healthy-not tasty intuition with taglines like "It tastes awful. And it works.," "Tastes like a horror. Works like a wonder.," and "Got a cough? Trade it for a gag." Buckley's also encouraged consumers to post their disgusted faces online. Similarly, Listerine argues that its unattractive taste is an indication of the effectiveness of its mouthwash: "If it did not taste so strong, it would not be working. Listerine has the taste people hate." By emphasizing the drawbacks of their products, Buckley's and Listerine were able to reinforce the effectiveness of their offerings and make their advertising messages more credible.

Buckley's and Listerine's strategy exemplifies how positioning a product as inferior on a particular, often insignificant, attribute can be effective. Following this approach, Smucker's leverages its unique name to assert product quality, suggesting that "With a name like Smucker's, it has to be good." Similarly, the NO-AD sunscreen brand implies that by foregoing advertising, it offers better value to consumers. Avis used its second-place status in the car rental industry to highlight its commitment to service with the slogan: "When you're only number two, you try harder. Or else." This marketing approach is underpinned by the compensatory belief that a product's perceived disadvantage in one area is offset by its advantages in more critical areas.

In addition to reinforcing the effectiveness of its products, highlighting a drawback of a company's own products can offer an extra benefit: Consumers may perceive the company's advertising messages as more credible. After all, it is difficult to counter-argue a company's admission that its product is inferior in a particular attribute. Such transparency can lead consumers to view the brand as more honest and trustworthy, further enhancing its appeal. By setting realistic expectations about the performance of their offerings, companies can also reduce disappointment and increase customer satisfaction, turning perceived weaknesses into strengths.

Compensatory inferences also influence how consumers evaluate specialized versus all-in-one products. For instance, a toothpaste marketed solely for its cavity prevention may be viewed as more effective in this area than one advertised as also providing tartar protection. The underlying belief is that being a "jack of all trades" comes at the cost of inferior performance on specific attributes. This perception becomes more pronounced during direct comparisons of specialized and all-in-one options, typically resulting in the all-in-one products being seen as underperforming on specific attributes, thereby enhancing the value of the specialized products in consumers' eyes.[32]

SUMMARY

A company creates customer value by developing offerings defined by specific *attributes*. Unlike benefits, which reflect the subjective value of the offering for customers, the attributes defining the company's offerings are objective; they reflect what the offering is rather than what it means to customers. The degree to which a particular attribute is meaningful to customers depends on whether they have the necessary knowledge to interpret its meaning. Experts, who can evaluate the pros and cons of the offering's attributes, generally prefer attribute-specific information, whereas lay consumers, unfamiliar with the offering's detailed attributes, are better served by information that highlights the benefits of the offering.

The *value function* reveals the relationship between the attributes of an offering and the value they create for target customers; it reflects how customers translate the attributes of an offering into benefits and costs. The value function is characterized by three key properties: reference-point dependence, loss aversion, and diminishing marginal value.

The principle of *reference-point dependence* states that people assess the value of objects not in absolute terms but in comparison to other objects that serve as reference points. Relative to these reference points, advantages are perceived as gains and disadvantages are perceived as losses. The anchoring bias, a specific manifestation of reference-point effects in sequential judgments, demonstrates how the initial piece of information acts as an anchor, pulling subsequent evaluations toward itself.

The principle of *loss aversion* refers to people's tendency to asymmetrically evaluate gains and losses relative to a reference point, with a stronger emphasis on avoiding losses than on achieving equivalent gains. This bias stems from the psychological impact of loss being greater than that of gain, leading people to prioritize loss avoidance over the acquisition of equivalent gains. The endowment effect further illustrates this principle, showing that individuals value objects they own more highly than identical objects they do not own.

The principle of *diminishing marginal value* refers to the tendency for each additional unit of gain to result in an ever-smaller increase in subjective value. Because the benefits from improving an offering's performance do not increase linearly, focusing on improving areas where an offering is lacking rather than on areas where it already excels can create greater customer value. The decision to combine or segregate individual experiences is contingent on the nature of these experiences: Segregating positive experiences and consolidating negative ones can increase perceived customer value.

Value comprises *three domains*: functional, which reflects the benefits and costs directly related to an offering's performance; psychological, which reflects the psychological benefits and costs customers derive from the offering by tapping into their emotions and self-identity; and monetary, which reflects the financial costs and benefits associated with the offering, such as its price, discounts, and fees. These dimensions of value are interrelated, meaning an offering can excel in multiple areas simultaneously. Focusing exclusively on creating value in one domain can make the company vulnerable to competition in other domains. After gaining superiority on one value dimension, a company could benefit from shifting resources to the dimension(s) on which it underperforms.

Evaluations often employ *categorical thinking* where individuals abstract from the specifics of the considered objects and assign them to more general categories. This process simplifies information by organizing objects into distinct groups, such as good and bad, expensive and inexpensive, and safe and risky. An important limitation of categorization is that it does not fully account for the degree to which an option possesses a particular attribute. One important consequence of categorization is that people often display greater sensitivity to changes in price than changes in quantity, a phenomenon referred to as *unit bias*.

When all relevant information is not readily available, people draw *inferences* about unobservable attributes describing the choice options. These inferences can be classified into two types: halo-based and compensatory. Halo-based inferences reflect the tendency of a specific aspect of an object or person to influence the overall evaluation of this object or person, as well as its performance on specific attributes that are not readily observable. In contrast, compensatory inferences reflect individuals' tendency to balance an option's shortcomings on one dimension by presuming excellence on another.

KEY TAKEAWAYS

Focus on benefits. Translate product attributes into benefits following the value function.

Reference points define benefits. Value is relative: It is defined in relation to a reference point.

Beware of loss aversion. Losses loom larger than equivalent gains: An item is valued more when viewed as a loss than as a gain.

Account for diminishing marginal value. The marginal benefit from improving an attribute decreases as the overall level of benefits on this attribute increases.

Manage value across the three domains. Value is created on three domains: functional, psychological, and monetary; focusing on a single domain can open doors to competition in the other domains.

Keep in mind that people think in categories, not numbers. Value judgments typically involve qualitative thinking that classifies objects into distinct categories.

Inferences matter. People spontaneously draw halo-based and compensatory inferences that can influence the perceived value of the offering.

SPOTLIGHT: CREATING VALUE IN BUSINESS MARKETS

A distinct challenge in business markets is that buying decisions are frequently made by purchasing departments that are focused on monetary benefits. This bias stems from the compatibility principle in psychology, which suggests that people prioritize information that aligns with their goals and the format of the decision criteria—quantitative or qualitative—used in the decision. Consequently, in decisions framed in quantitative terms—such as evaluating the prices of competing offerings—numerical attributes are often given more importance than qualitative ones.[33]

This focus on readily quantifiable monetary benefits can lead to the oversight of crucial nonmonetary benefits such as reliability, durability, and warranty coverage. This is problematic because many nonmonetary benefits, though lacking a specific dollar value at the time of purchase, can significantly impact the total value ultimately created by the offering.

To effectively communicate the real value of its offerings to financially oriented managers, a company must express the functional benefits of these offerings in monetary terms—a process commonly referred to as *economic value analysis.* This approach quantifies nonmonetary benefits by estimating their financial impact, thereby presenting a more comprehensive assessment of an offering's value. Because of its focus on the total value created by an offering, economic value analysis is frequently used by companies to justify premium prices for their high-value, high-price offerings.

Consider the following example: A construction equipment manufacturer prices its offering at $2 million, which is half a million higher than the competitive offerings. At first glance, the company's equipment appears overpriced, suggesting a need to lower prices to stay competitive. An alternative approach to competing on price is to quantify all benefits and costs associated with the company's offering and compare this overall value to competitors' offerings.

Suppose the value analysis identifies several attributes of strategic importance to buyers: durability, reliability, warranty, and service speed. Further analysis assesses that the company's equipment offers superior durability, extending its usage by an additional three years; higher reliability, resulting in four fewer breakdowns per year; an extended warranty covering an extra year; and faster repair services, averaging four hours quicker than competitors. Using this analysis, a company might demonstrate that its offering is actually underpriced, providing greater value than its competitors. This logic is illustrated in Figure 11.

Figure 11. Creating Value in a Competitive Context

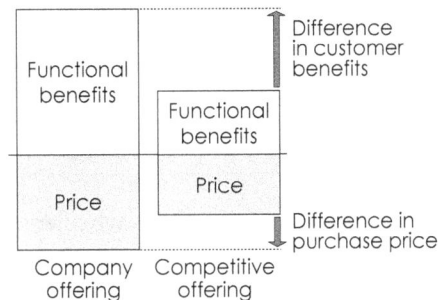

Calculating the monetary value of functional benefits quantifies the competitive edge of a company's offering, encompassing both its monetary and nonmonetary advantages. This calculation helps financially oriented members of the management team grasp the full value of the offering, demonstrating its superiority over cheaper alternatives. Translating functional benefits into monetary terms also facilitates informed decision making and strategic pricing that reflects the total value of the company's offering.

THE CX CANVAS: DESIGNING AND COMMUNICATING CUSTOMER VALUE

Designing and communicating a company's offering aims to ensure that it creates superior value for customers and that they clearly see its benefits outweigh its costs. This process involves two key components: (1) analyzing the value created by the company's offering and customers' perception of its benefits and costs, and (2) developing a course of action to ensure that the company's offering creates customer value and that customers understand this value (Figure 12).

Figure 12. Designing and Communicating Customer Value: The Big Picture

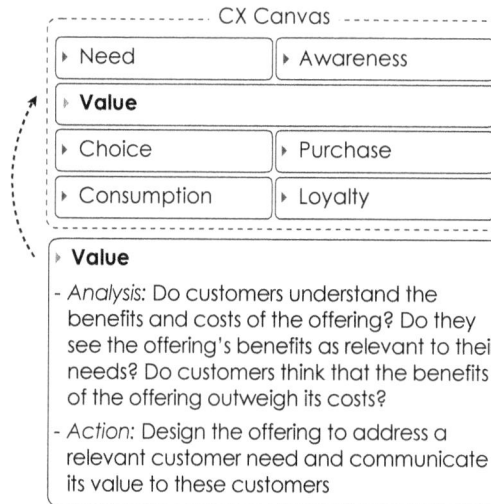

```
------------- CX Canvas -------------
  ▸ Need              ▸ Awareness
  ▸ Value
  ▸ Choice            ▸ Purchase
  ▸ Consumption       ▸ Loyalty
------------------------------------

  ▸ Value
  - Analysis: Do customers understand the
    benefits and costs of the offering? Do they
    see the offering's benefits as relevant to their
    needs? Do customers think that the benefits
    of the offering outweigh its costs?
  - Action: Design the offering to address a
    relevant customer need and communicate
    its value to these customers
```

The customer value analysis aims to assess whether customers understand the benefits and costs associated with the company's offering, whether they see the benefits as relevant to their needs, and, ultimately, whether they think that the offering's benefits justify its costs. Here, the manager must ask the following questions:

- *Do customers understand the benefits and costs of the offering?* This question goes beyond assessing whether customers are aware of the attributes of the offering to determine whether they understand the potential value created by these attributes.

- *Do customers see the benefits of the offering as relevant to their needs?* This is important because customers might understand the potential benefits of the offering and believe that it could create value for others but may not see the offering as personally relevant to their own needs.

- *Do customers think that the benefits of the offering outweigh its costs?* This is important because even if customers appreciate the benefits of the offering, they might consider its costs too high and reject the offering because it does not create sufficient value.

The ultimate purpose of customer value analysis is to determine whether the company's offering fulfills customer needs and is perceived as such by the customers. This analysis helps the company develop an action plan to ensure that its offering creates value for target customers and that these customers understand and appreciate its benefits. Accordingly, there are three potential challenges, each requiring a distinct approach:

- *Customers misunderstand the benefits and costs of the offering.* Although customers might be aware of the offering's attributes, they might not accurately translate these attributes into benefits and costs. The company's goal here is to articulate the value of the offering by clearly explaining the meaning of each of its attributes.

- *Customers do not see the benefits of the offering as personally relevant.* Customers might understand the potential benefits of the offering but not consider these benefits applicable to their needs. The company's goal here is to demonstrate the personal relevance of the offering's benefits and explain how it can address customers' needs.

- *Customers think that the offering's costs outweigh its benefits.* Customers might understand the benefits and costs of the offering and consider the benefits relevant to their needs but find the costs associated with the offering—such as time, money, and effort—exceeding its benefits. The company's goal here is to demonstrate the value of its offering and, if necessary, redesign it so that its benefits clearly exceed its costs.

The above challenges of creating customer value and the corresponding company actions are summarized in Figure 13. When customers cannot translate the attributes of the offering into specific benefits, cannot relate these benefits to their own needs, or believe the costs outweigh the benefits, the company should focus on improving customer communication. In the latter case, the company might also consider redesigning the offering to better align its benefits with customers' needs and expectations.

Figure 13. Designing and Communicating Customer Value: The Action Plan

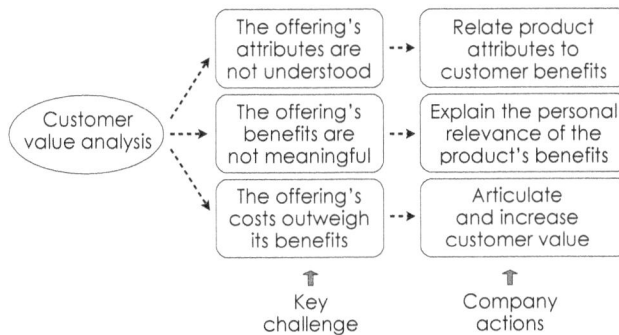

Imagine you are launching a new credit card targeting frequent travelers. Marketing research shows that after considering the card your target customers do not apply for it. To address this problem, you must first determine whether your target customers understand the benefits associated with the card. For example, some customers might misunderstand the value of the airline miles earned, such as how much they need to spend to qualify for a free ticket. Others might find the car rental insurance coverage offered by the card irrelevant to their needs. Additionally, some might understand the benefits offered by the card but view them as insufficient to justify the card's annual fee.

Once the factors deterring customer adoption have been identified, you must develop a course of action to address these issues. If the main problem is that customers do not understand the value of frequent flyer miles, a communication campaign with practical illustrations could be helpful. If customers do not see the additional coverage as relevant to their needs, you might identify scenarios where these benefits are valuable. Finally, if the main barrier is that customers do not find the benefits meaningful enough to offset the card's fees, you might consider enhancing the existing benefits, adding new ones, or adjusting the card's annual fee.

CHAPTER FIVE

CRAFTING THE CHOICE ARCHITECTURE

Give me a lever long enough and a fulcrum
on which to place it, and I shall move the world.

—Archimedes

C hoice reveals preferences by indicating the outcome of the deliberation process. It typically follows customers' realization of an unmet need, their consideration of the available options, and their evaluation of the benefits and costs of these options (Figure 1). The question then is how customers select a particular option. Do they always evaluate all available options to select the most attractive one? Would the way in which the decision options are presented influence their choice? What factors influence their choices?

Figure 1. The Customer Experience Map: Making a Choice

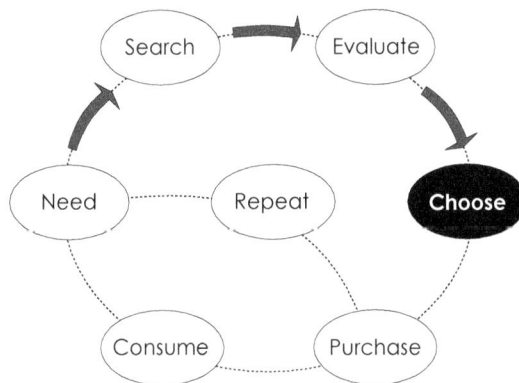

Customers' choices are determined not only by their inherent preferences but also by the context in which they make decisions. The importance of the decision context in determining choice outcomes underscores the role of *choice architecture*—a term used to describe the different ways in which choice options can be presented to decision makers. Understanding the impact of choice architecture on customer decisions is important because it can dramatically change the way customers approach the choice process and, ultimately, the option they select. Consider the following scenarios:

- You are the manager of an established cereal brand and are considering promoting your cereal using endcap displays. Placing your cereal at the end of an aisle can increase its visibility to shoppers, but it would also incur additional costs to secure the endcap space. What factors should you consider when making this decision?

- You oversee a popular brand of beef jerky and are facing an increase in the cost of beef. You are considering raising the price but are concerned about how consumers will react. What options, other than increasing the price, might you consider to deal with rising costs?

- You are advising a manufacturer of small kitchen appliances facing challenges with the introduction of a new bread-making machine. Despite a strong brand reputation, sales of the new machine have been slow to take off. What options should your client consider?

- You are managing a toothpaste brand and considering extending your product line. The argument for increasing the available assortment is that offering more options will make it more likely for consumers to find one that best matches their preferences. Are there any additional factors you need to consider when making this decision?

- You are designing an online configurator for a major car manufacturer and are deciding whether to offer a stripped-down model so that buyers can add the features they like, or a model loaded with premium features that allows buyers to easily remove the features they do not want. Would both options lead to the same outcome?

In this chapter, we address these questions while delving into how people make choices, the forces that guide their decisions, and the importance of choice architecture. We start by discussing how people make choices, focusing on the decision heuristics they use. We then examine the role reasons play in choice and their ability to influence decision outcomes. Next, we address the role of the choice context in guiding the decision process, why offering too many options can be counterproductive, and how decision fatigue can influence choice by depleting mental resources. Finally, we discuss how default options influence choice and their role in the decision process.

The discussion of the conceptual issues involved in crafting the choice architecture is complemented by examples of managerial decisions that illustrate key points. Specifically, we will discuss how companies like Frito-Lay, Henkel, Procter & Gamble, Unilever, and Walmart managed to raise the per-unit price of their offerings while minimizing consumer pushback; how Williams-Sonoma increased the sales of one of its offerings by adding a functionally superior product; why many infomercials promoting impulse-buy novelty products air late at night; and why Google pays Apple billions of dollars every year to be the default search engine on Apple's devices.

Now, let's examine how people make choices, the factors influencing decision making, and how choice architecture can enhance the likelihood of an offering being selected.

Thinking and Deciding

Making a choice involves assessing the attractiveness of the available alternatives and selecting the one that best fits the decision maker's needs. Two main theories explain how people make choices, one from economics and the other from psychology. Economists assume that people systematically evaluate the available options to choose the one that will bring them the highest utility. Psychologists, on the other hand, argue that to minimize mental effort, individuals often use decision shortcuts, or heuristics, which are inconsistent with the rational model of choice advanced by economic theory. These two approaches—the rational model of choice and the heuristics-based model of choice—are discussed in the following sections.

The Rational View of Choice

The rational model assumes that we carefully and deliberately consider the available offerings and then choose the one that offers us the highest value. This model further assumes that we have clear and consistent preferences, enabling us to readily select the best option.

According to the rational-choice model, decision makers evaluate the performance of all available options and then select the one with the highest level of performance. This process involves multiple stages. First, individuals must identify all relevant attributes describing the choice options and determine how important each of these attributes is to them. Next, they assess how well each choice alternative performs on each attribute, ultimately deriving an overall evaluation of each alternative. Once the value of each available option has been defined, decision makers select the one with the highest overall value.

For example, when choosing a box of cereal, a consumer might consider attributes such as nutrition content, taste, calorie count, and amount of carbohydrates. These attributes might vary in importance, with nutrition and taste being of utmost importance, and calorie count and amount of carbs being of least importance. Next, the consumer will evaluate each option under consideration on each attribute, assess the overall attractiveness of each option, and select the cereal with the highest overall valuation. The valuation process implied by the rational model of choice can be represented by the following equation:

$$V_A = w_1 \cdot a_1 + w_2 \cdot a_2 + w_3 \cdot a_3 + \ldots + w_n \cdot a_n$$

Here, V_A is the value of offering A, i is an index denoting the specific attribute being evaluated, w_i is the importance of that attribute, a_i is the offering's performance on that attribute, and n is the total number of attributes describing the offering. Because the valuation of an offering is represented as a sum of weighted attribute-level assessments of an offering's performance, this approach is commonly referred to as the *weighted-additive model*. To make a choice, individuals compare their valuations of the available options (e.g., V_A versus V_B versus V_C) and select the one with the highest value.

Suppose the consumer in the above example is using a 10-point scale to evaluate the importance of each attribute of a cereal, rating nutrition as 7, taste as 5, calorie count as 4, and carb count as 3. Next, the consumer evaluates how well the first cereal performs on each of these attributes. Let's say the consumer determines that it scores 6 on nutrition, 7 on taste, 6 on calories, and 3 on carbs. The consumer then adds up these scores, adjusted for the importance assigned to the corresponding attributes. In this case, the overall evaluation of the first cereal would be $7 \times 6 + 5 \times 7 + 4 \times 6 + 3 \times 3 = 110$. Following the same procedure, the consumer must evaluate the other options (e.g., V_B and V_C) and ultimately select the one with the highest value.

Despite its popularity among economists, the rational model of choice has an important limitation: It assumes that people have unlimited cognitive resources and time and always evaluate the available information systematically. This model further assumes that people have perfect information about the available options, have stable preferences that do not change over time, assign numeric values to each option based on its performance, have infinite mental capacity, and are willing to allocate the necessary effort to make the best choice. Many of these assumptions are so unrealistic that Richard Thaler, a recipient of the 2017 Nobel Prize in Economics, described them as applying to "econs" — mythical creatures that exist only in economic textbooks — rather than to humans who live in the real world.[1]

Heuristics and Biases

Decision makers rarely sort through offerings in the diligent and unbiased fashion formalized by the rational-choice model. Instead, they tend to use *heuristics* — decision shortcuts based on a limited subset of the available information. These heuristics are akin to rules of thumb that aim to reduce mental effort, often at the expense of decision accuracy.

When making a choice, we pursue two conflicting goals. On the one hand, we try to make an accurate decision by selecting the option that best fits our needs. On the other hand, we aim to minimize the mental effort involved in the decision. As a result, we do not always engage in the thorough analysis prescribed by the rational-choice model. Instead, we are guided by the principle of *bounded rationality*, whereby the accuracy of our decision process is limited by the amount of mental effort we are willing to allocate to a particular decision task.[2]

The tradeoff between accuracy and effort is a key principle guiding our choices. These tradeoffs occur when gaining one benefit involves giving up another. The closer choice options are in overall attractiveness while offering distinct benefits, the more difficult the decision. The role of tradeoffs in choice is often illustrated with the so-called Buridan's Paradox, named after 14th century French philosopher Jean Buridan. It describes a hypothetical situation of a donkey that is equally hungry and thirsty and is placed precisely midway between a stack of hay and a bucket of water.

The paradox is that despite the abundance of both hay and water, the donkey, unable to choose between the two, dies of thirst and hunger. Buridan's donkey would have survived had it not succumbed to the line of thinking suggested by economics and instead employed a decision heuristic, such as going immediately to the option it saw first. Indeed, either the water or the food would have been sufficient to meet one of the donkey's pressing needs had it chosen either option instead of trying to decide which option was the best one.

Heuristics are ubiquitous because, on many occasions, we are willing to sacrifice accuracy to minimize the time and effort involved in making less important choices, allowing us to be more diligent with more significant decisions. As a result, rather than evaluating the available options systematically until one option becomes clearly superior, we use heuristics that enable us to make decisions relatively quickly and efficiently, albeit not always with the highest accuracy.

One common approach to minimize decision effort involves reliance on the *satisficing heuristic*, a term derived by combining "satisfy" and "suffice." This heuristic entails evaluating the available options until an acceptable option is found, at which point that option is selected and further evaluation is halted, even if this means potentially forgoing a better option. Thus, rather than considering all available options, the satisficing heuristic calls for selecting the first option that meets an individual's decision criteria. For example, consumers might put the first cereal that meets their preferences in their shopping cart without considering the other available options, even though expending greater effort might have yielded a cereal they like better or one that is on sale.

Selecting the first "good enough" option simplifies the decision process by eliminating the need to consider all available options since the goal is not to choose the best option but one that is merely acceptable. Because the decision process stops once an acceptable option is found, the order in which options are evaluated matters. This is one reason why point-of-purchase displays can significantly impact shoppers' decisions and are often used by retailers to "push" products they believe will yield higher profitability.

Another way decision makers can simplify their choices is by focusing only on the most important attribute describing the available options and selecting the option with the highest value on that attribute—without considering the other attributes. For example, when choosing a cereal, shoppers might focus only on the attribute that is most important to them (say, taste) and select the best-tasting cereal, even though it might not have the highest score across all attributes.

Focusing exclusively on the most important attribute simplifies the decision in two ways. First, it makes it easy to decide: Because there is only one attribute to consider, there is no need to make tradeoffs across different attributes. Second, it makes it easy to rationalize the decision, as choosing the option that is best on the most important attribute is easy to justify to oneself and others. For example, a consumer might say, "I chose this cereal because taste is most important to me, and this is the best-tasting cereal." Like the satisficing heuristic, this approach, also referred to as the *lexicographic heuristic*, can save time and effort but can impair choice accuracy.

Our reliance on heuristics to make decisions matters because different heuristics can lead to different outcomes. Consider a consumer choosing among three different brands in the cereal example discussed earlier. Let's say this consumer cares most about nutrition (rating it as 7), followed by taste (5), calories (4), and carbs (3). The performance ratings of each brand on these attributes are as follows: Cereal A scores 6 on nutrition, 7 on taste, 6 on calories, and 3 on carbs. Cereal B scores 7 on nutrition, 6 on taste, 5 on calories, and 3 on carbs. Cereal C scores 4 on nutrition, 6 on taste, 6 on calories, and 5 on carbs.

Using the "rational" model (which calls for adding the cereal's ratings on different attributes, adjusted for the importance of each attribute) results in the following overall evaluation scores: Cereal A - 110 points, Cereal B - 108 points, Cereal C - 97 points. Accordingly, the consumer will choose Cereal A because it has the highest score. Using the lexicographic heuristic, however, will result in choosing Cereal B because it has the highest score (7) on the most important attribute (nutrition) for this consumer.

Finally, using the satisficing heuristic and a decision criterion that any cereal will do if it has a rating of 3 or higher, this consumer could choose any of these three options. Because all options meet the decision criterion, the consumer's choice in this case will depend on which option is encountered first. As this example shows, the use of heuristics that imply different decision rules can dramatically impact choice outcomes.

Mental Accounting

Mental accounting, a term coined by behavioral economist Richard Thaler, describes how we categorize and perceive money. Even though money is fungible—meaning it is made up of units that are all the same and indistinguishable from one another—we often compartmentalize our funds into "mental accounts," treating money differently based on these categories. Such mental accounting contradicts a fundamental economic principle: Money serves as a uniform medium of exchange and should be considered interchangeable without labels. Theoretically, a dollar holds the same value regardless of its origin or intended use. In practice, however, we frequently assign subjective value to money, rendering it less fungible than it really is.[3]

Like most decisions, mental accounting is not without its pitfalls and often leads to irrational outcomes. Consider, for example, a person who admires a very expensive cashmere sweater but declines to buy it, feeling it is too extravagant. A couple of weeks later, he receives the same sweater as a gift from his wife. He is thrilled to get the sweater, despite the fact that he and his wife share joint bank accounts. Although the two outcomes have the same financial consequence, the way they are experienced is quite different.[4]

There are two common types of mental accounts: one based on the origin of the money and the other on its intended use. Windfall gains, such as unexpected lottery winnings or inheritances, serve as a prime example. Despite no rational basis for differentiation, we often treat this money distinctly from our regular income, indulging in purchases we would usually avoid. For instance, finding a $100 bill on the street might lead us to splurge on a gourmet dinner, even if we have pressing financial obligations like credit card debt or a savings goal for a major purchase. This decision reflects the perception of the found money as somehow special, warranting discretionary spending that deviates from our usual financial behavior.

In addition to being categorized by its origin, money is often allocated based on its intended use. Imagine someone saving for a new car while only making minimum payments on their credit card debt. Logically, paying off the high-interest credit card debt first makes more financial sense. However, it is common to pay a premium—through higher interest charges—for the privilege of saving, prioritizing the satisfaction of reaching a savings goal over the rational prioritization of debt reduction.

Allocating money based on its intended use can be further illustrated with the following scenario. Imagine you have decided to see a movie and have already paid $10 for a ticket. Upon entering the theater, you realize you've lost the ticket. Would you be willing to spend another $10 to buy a new one? Now, consider a different situation where, upon arriving at the theater intending to buy a ticket, you discover you've lost a $10 bill. Would you still proceed to pay $10 for the movie ticket? Even though both scenarios have identical monetary outcomes—the need to pay $10 to watch the movie—nearly twice as many respondents presented with the second scenario indicated they would buy the ticket compared to those presented with the first scenario. Mental accounting makes people think about money differently based on its designated usage.[5]

The ubiquity of mental accounting stems from three main factors. First, it conserves mental energy and simplifies future decisions by pre-allocating money to specific categories like housing, food, or vacations. Second, mental accounting serves as a self-regulation tool, aiding in the achievement of financial goals, optimizing expenditures, and warding off impulse buys. Finally, by creating specific savings and spending categories, mental accounting helps justify our actions, thus reducing both anticipated and post-decision regret.

Choice Based on Reasons

The discussion so far has implicitly assumed that when making decisions we form numerical evaluations of the available options and use these evaluations to select the best alternative. However, on most occasions this is not what happens. Rather than deriving quantifiable assessments of the available options, we typically generate reasons for and against each alternative.

Reasons as Drivers of Choice

When making a choice, we rarely think in terms of numerical assessments of the benefits and costs of the available options. Instead, we tend to consider the reasons for and against each option. Generating numeric estimates can be difficult and effortful because we are not evolutionarily adapted to think in numbers. Our minds are better suited to generating reasons that articulate arguments for and against a particular course of action. Consequently, when presented with a choice among different options, we often select the one supported by the strongest reasons (Figure 2).[6]

Figure 2. Reasons as Drivers of Choice

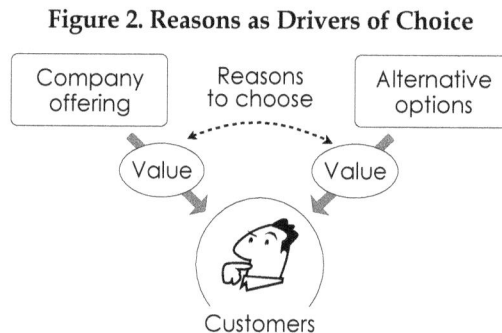

Reasons are key drivers of human thinking and behavior. Even the weakest reason can be better than not having a reason at all. The importance of reasons in guiding people's actions is illustrated by a classic study in which participants waiting to use a copy machine were asked by the experimenter to let them cut in line. When the experimenter did not provide a reason for the request, simply stating, "Excuse me, I have five pages. May I use the copy machine?," around 60% of those waiting in line agreed. However, when the experimenter provided a reason, stating, "Excuse me, I have five pages. May I use the copy machine because I'm in a rush?," this number neared 95%. Surprisingly, the same high percentage of participants was willing to let the experimenter cut in line when the provided reason was superficial: "Excuse me, I have five pages. May I use the copy machine because I have to make copies?"[7]

Reason-based choices can lead to outcomes that differ from those predicted by rational choice models. For example, rational choice models predict that adding sales promotions with little or no value for some buyers can only increase—but never decrease—the attractiveness of an offering. Buyers who find the sales promotion attractive will be more likely to purchase the offering, while those who do not care about the sales promotion will not be affected. However, this is not always the case.

Even when they do not diminish an offering's benefits, undesirable promotional incentives might make it less likely that shoppers will purchase the offering. For example, adding a sweepstakes promotion making buyers eligible to purchase a limited-edition item they did not care about halved their interest in making a purchase. This occurred even though the promotion was optional and could be easily ignored.[8] Buyers who found the prospect of winning the sweepstakes unattractive used that as a reason to decide against purchasing the promoted product.

The above logic applies not only to benefits that consumers find unattractive but also to those that are relatively small compared to the overall value of the offering. For example, a minor monetary benefit, such as a $5 discount on a $1,000 purchase, can be viewed as a weak reason for purchase, thereby lessening the appeal of the promoted option. By diluting the overall impact of the offering, benefits perceived as minor or irrelevant can detract from the overall attractiveness of the considered option.

People's reasons for making choices can be broadly categorized into three main types, each corresponding to one of the three dimensions of value discussed in Chapter 4: functional, psychological, and monetary (Figure 3). Functional reasons focus on utility and effectiveness, often summed up in the decision maker's mind as "I prefer this option because it is better." Psychological reasons relate to emotional gratification or self-identification, reflected in statements like "I prefer this option because it makes me feel good" or "I prefer this option because it reflects my identity." Finally, monetary reasons concentrate on the financial aspects of the available options, with the underlying rationale being "I prefer this option because it is cheap(er)."

Figure 3. The Three Main Reasons in Choice

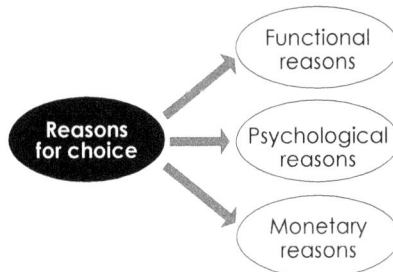

When making a choice, buyers often have multiple reasons for and against purchasing the available options. While affirmative reasons tend to facilitate choice and negative reasons tend to impede it, this is not always the case. Sometimes, an additional reason for choosing a particular option can make it less attractive. This occurs because different types of reasons might negate one another's impact, even though each reason considered in isolation supports the choice of that option. For example, the motivation for engaging in an intrinsically rewarding activity, such as donating blood, can be weakened by offering monetary compensation.[9]

The Essence of Choice Architecture

One of the key findings in decision research is that people do not have well-articulated, hardwired preferences. Instead, our preferences are formed on a case-by-case basis and are influenced by the decision environment. As a result, factors defining the decision context — such as the number of options to choose from, the characteristics of these options, and even the time available for making the decision — inform our choices.

Imagine you are thinking about subscribing to a magazine and are given two options: a print edition for $59 and a print+digital edition for $125. Now, imagine you are given a third option: a digital-only subscription for $125 (the same price as print+digital). Would the presence of the third option change your initial preference? Common sense suggests it should not; the third option is clearly irrelevant since it is inferior to the print+digital offer. Yet, research suggests otherwise. When choosing between the print and print+digital options, 68% of study participants opted for the print+digital subscription. However, when the digital-only option was added, the number of people who chose the print+digital subscription jumped to 84%.[10]

Why are our decisions influenced by irrelevant factors, such as the presence of a clearly inferior option that is unlikely to be chosen? This occurs because we often do not have a clear sense of which option is best for us and decide by comparing the available options. In the example above, adding the digital-only option creates a reference point, making the print+digital option appear like a bargain since we are effectively getting the print version for free.

Because the decision context influences how we perceive and evaluate options, altering this context can shift our preferences — a principle central to choice architecture. Coined by Richard Thaler and Cass Sunstein, *choice architecture* refers to the way decision-making environments are organized.[11] It operates on the premise that decisions are inherently shaped by their context and that modifying this context can steer choices. By strategically designing these environments, choice architects aim to guide decisions without restricting freedom of choice. This approach allows marketers to subtly direct buyers toward behaviors or selections that serve business goals by optimizing how products, prices, and information are presented.

For example, the layout and design of a supermarket serve as deliberate applications of choice architecture aimed at guiding consumer behavior. Products placed at eye level on shelves are more likely to be noticed and chosen than those placed on higher or lower shelves. Similarly, the strategic placement of impulse buys — like candy and magazines — near the checkout counter leverages the consumer's momentary waiting time to encourage spontaneous purchases. These carefully considered placements are designed to increase the desirability and visibility of certain products, subtly influencing shopping behaviors while preserving the shopper's freedom to choose.

E-commerce is another illustration of choice architecture in action. By deliberately designing website layouts, orchestrating the information sequence, and setting default options, online retailers can significantly influence consumer decisions. For instance, highlighting "bestseller" or "most popular" products can guide consumers toward these options, subtly suggesting that they are the preferred choices among peers. This social-proof approach leverages the consumer's tendency to conform to perceived norms, nudging them toward products they might not have otherwise considered.

Choice architecture is ubiquitous. Just as every building, no matter how simple, follows an architectural plan, every decision we face is shaped by an underlying choice architecture. This architecture is defined by numerous factors: the array and number of options presented, the order in which they're shown, the details provided about each option, and the time frame given for making a choice. These elements collectively determine the context in which decisions are made, serving as the unseen framework of our choices and subtly guiding outcomes.

Because every choice task involves a series of decisions about how this task is presented to decision makers, everyone posing a choice for others effectively acts as a choice architect. Retailers deciding on product assortments, marketers emphasizing certain features when promoting their offerings, mortgage brokers detailing loan options, human resource administrators structuring benefit plans, officials organizing ballots, and even parents deciding how to offer dinner choices to their children are just a few examples of choice architects.[12]

Grasping the fundamentals of choice architecture empowers managers to tailor decision environments that resonate with how people think and decide, thus helping their customers make better choices. Understanding how the specifics of the decision context influence choice enables managers to nudge customers toward decisions believed to be in their best interest while still preserving their freedom to choose otherwise. We discuss some of these "nudge" strategies later in this chapter.

The Invisible Influence of Choice Context

Up to this point, our discussion has focused on the role decision context plays in our decisions without examining the specific factors that influence these decisions. Accordingly, in this section, we will examine the pivotal role of decision context in choice and some common context effects, including the role of decision frames; the nature of the decoy, similarity, attraction, and compromise effects; and the power of social proof.

Framing the Decision

Why do some see a glass as half full while others see it as half empty? It depends on how the question is framed and the perspective we take. Framing defines how information is presented, often by setting a reference point used to evaluate this information. The same information can lead to different outcomes depending on the reference points embedded in the decision context. This highlights the pivotal role of context in decision making, demonstrating that the way information is framed can significantly alter an individual's response to it.

Framing can influence a wide range of decisions, from simple perceptual biases to complex problems with consequential outcomes. Take, for instance, the Ebbinghaus illusion, a classic demonstration of context's impact on perception. This illusion presents two identically sized circles placed close to each other, with one encircled by larger circles and the other by smaller ones (Figure 4).

Figure 4. The Role of Decision Context: The Ebbinghaus Illusion

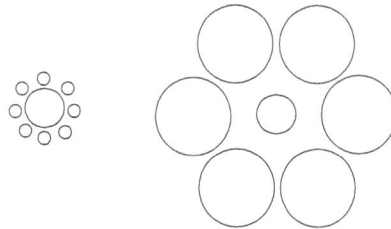

Due to the contrasting contexts, the central circle surrounded by larger circles appears smaller than its counterpart encircled by smaller circles. Removing the surrounding circles clarifies that the central circles are indeed the same size. However, the true testament to the influence of context is that even with this knowledge, the initial illusion persists when the surrounding circles are reintroduced. This enduring perception, despite contrary evidence, highlights the pervasive power of context in shaping our perceptions.

The impact of framing is vividly demonstrated in a study by University of Iowa researchers Irwin Levin and Gary Gaeth, who explored how different descriptions of the same product influence perception. Participants were asked to evaluate ground beef labeled as either "75% lean" or "25% fat." Both descriptions are equivalent, of course: Beef that is 75% lean has 25% fat. Yet, framing the beef's content as a virtue ("lean") rather than a vice ("fat") led to a significant disparity in perceptions. Across all measures, the beef framed as 75% lean was rated more favorably: It was perceived as leaner, less greasy, and of higher quality.

Simply switching the decision frame nearly doubled the perceived leanness rating of the beef—a powerful effect given that the only difference was the way the meat was described. Even more remarkable is that this pattern of ratings persisted after participants sampled the freshly cooked meat. Following the taste test, they were still convinced that the meat described as three-quarters lean was indeed much leaner than the same meat described as one-quarter fat.[13]

The power of frames is further illustrated by the success of Ivory soap—the American icon of purity and cleanliness. Its century-old slogan—99 44/100% pure—originated from a chemical lab analysis of the soap's composition.[14] However, this slogan is not a direct quote from the lab report, which stated that the soap contained only 0.56% impurities. Strictly speaking, both descriptions—99 44/100% pure and containing 0.56% impurities—are equivalent. But that is not how our brains process this information. Which soap are you more likely to buy: one that is 99 44/100% pure or one that contains 0.56% impurities? Even though the two labels have the same meaning, the first one is much more compelling. This positive framing made Ivory soap, introduced in 1879, one of the most successful global consumer brands ever.

Framing effects extend beyond our evaluation of offerings' performance; they also shape our perception of the value of offerings consumed over time. Imagine being tasked with promoting Grand Vividus, the premium offering of the Swedish mattress company Hästens. Touted as the pinnacle of luxury sleeping experiences, the mattress is meticulously hand-assembled and stitched by skilled artisans, who dedicate over 600 hours to its creation. Hästens further elevates the experience by offering up to three visits annually for thirty years by a team of experts to adjust and maintain the bed, including flipping, massaging, and even altering its firmness to accommodate changes in the owner's weight. Given the craftsmanship and service, one might assume the Grand Vividus sells itself. However, there is a problem: It comes with a $400,000 price tag.[15] How would you present this offering to potential customers?

To address this challenge, imagine engaging buyers with the question, "How much is a good night's sleep worth to you?" This approach shifts the conversation from the initial shock of the sticker price to the benefits the mattress provides over time. By breaking down the cost over the mattress's warrantied 25-year lifespan, the nightly cost comes to about $45. While still a premium, this framing helps potential buyers see the expenditure not just as a one-time cost but as a long-term investment in personal well-being, making the substantial price tag more digestible.

Another notable example of the impact of framing on evaluating offerings consumed over time is Dollar Shave Club's (DSC) approach to pricing their razor cartridges. Unlike its main competitor, Gillette, which sells cartridges through a variety of retail outlets on a per-unit basis, DSC adopted a direct-to-consumer monthly subscription model. Its prices range from $1 per month for five basic two-bladed cartridges to $9 per month for three premium cartridges. These prices resonated with consumers, many of whom find DSC's monthly fee more palatable than Gillette's $16 price tag for a 4-pack of top-tier cartridges—even if Gillette's cartridges are arguably of higher quality and last longer.

By shifting consumer focus from the immediate cost per cartridge to the value of a good shave each month, DSC managed to change how consumers thought about the cost of shaving. The success of DSC's dollar-a-month framing underscores a key insight: For products perceived as relatively expensive—whether a $400,000 bed or a box of razor cartridges—usage-based pricing can be more appealing than conventional unit pricing.

Context Effects in Choice

Context effects describe the influence of the choice set's composition on decision outcomes. These effects underscore the psychological impact of the decision environment, demonstrating how subtle changes can significantly sway judgment and choice. Context effects are typically associated with shifts in individuals' preferences based on the nature of the options in the choice set and the way these options are presented to decision makers. Some common context effects—the decoy effect, the attraction effect, the similarity effect, and the compromise effect—are outlined below.

The *decoy effect* describes the increase in preference for an option in the presence of an inferior option. This effect can be illustrated with an example from high-end kitchenware retailer Williams-Sonoma. One of the products it offered was a bread-making machine priced at $275. Initially, the demand for the product was not great until the company introduced a second, functionally identical but slightly larger bread-making machine at a significantly higher price. Following the addition of the new machine, sales of the original bread maker almost doubled. Although the new, more expensive machine did not sell particularly well, its presence made the original machine appear as a more appealing bargain. The more expensive machine served as a decoy, highlighting the value of the original machine by comparison and thus boosting its sales.[16]

A slightly more complex version of the decoy effect is the *attraction effect*, in which the decoy option is added to a set consisting of two options rather than one. The magazine subscription example discussed earlier in this chapter illustrates the attraction effect. In that case, adding the digital-only subscription, priced the same as the print+digital option, to the original choice set ended up increasing, rather than decreasing, the share of the print+digital option.

Another illustration of the attraction effect is offered by a study in which moviegoers were presented with two popcorn options: a small popcorn for $3 and a large popcorn for $7. Almost everyone chose the $3 option, with many mentioning the high cost of the large size. On a different day, the concession stand added a third option: a medium popcorn for $6.50. Presented with the three options—a small popcorn for $3, a medium popcorn for $6.50, and a large popcorn for $7—significantly more people ended up buying the large popcorn. The addition of a closely priced but inferior option suddenly made the price of the large popcorn seem like a comparative bargain.[17]

Both the decoy and attraction effects run counter to normative economic theories, which predict that adding an option to a choice set cannot increase the choice share of either of the available options. According to these theories, adding an option can only detract from the share of the existing alternatives since there are now more options to choose from. However, these effects demonstrate that adding an inferior option can increase, rather than decrease, the share of one of the existing alternatives.

Related to the attraction and decoy effects is the *similarity effect*, which states that adding an option to a choice set hurts similar alternatives more than dissimilar ones.[18] In this context, similarity means not only that the alternatives have similar attribute values but also that they are similar in overall attractiveness. Thus, a person confronted with choosing between two equally attractive options is likely to face a more difficult choice and is more likely to decide to postpone the decision compared to a person confronted with two options, one of which is more attractive than the other.

The *compromise effect* highlights our tendency to choose the middle option in a set of alternatives, regardless of the option's specific attributes or performance. This effect stems from our inclination to avoid extremes and is more pronounced for those who do not have clearly articulated preferences or are unsure about the value of the available options. In such scenarios, the middle option emerges as a seemingly safer choice—perceived as less extreme and thus less subject to regret or criticism.[19]

The compromise effect can be illustrated by a study in which participants were asked to choose from a set of soft drink sizes at a fast-food restaurant. The study divided participants into three groups, each presented with different size options: The first group was given a choice of 12-, 16-, and 21-ounce drinks; the second group was offered 16-, 21-, and 32-ounce drinks; and the third group could choose from 21-, 32-, and 44-ounce drinks. The results consistently showed a strong compromise effect across all groups. The 16-ounce drink was more frequently selected when it was the middle option rather than the smallest or largest option. Similarly, the 21- and 32-ounce options were chosen more often when they served as the middle option in their respective sets. Across all scenarios, participants showed a strong preference for the soft drink that appeared as the middle option, regardless of its actual size.[20]

The decoy, attraction, similarity, and compromise effects are just a handful of the myriad context effects that influence human decision making. These phenomena illustrate the remarkable malleability of human preferences, revealing how choices can be swayed by the decision context in which they are presented. These effects also underscore the power that choice architects possess in shaping individuals' decisions. Understanding and applying these phenomena helps choice architects design decision environments that subtly guide people toward mutually beneficial outcomes.

The Power of Social Proof

Framing and context effects discussed so far stem from how relevant information is presented to decision makers. Another factor that can influence our decisions is the social environment in which these decisions are made. This includes the influence of peers, cultural norms, and societal expectations, which can subtly or overtly sway choices and preferences. The social influence, also referred to as *social proof*, creates a complex landscape for decision making, where we navigate not only the facts at hand but also the social implications of our choices.

The role of social influence on our decisions is demonstrated in a series of now-classic experiments by renowned psychologist Solomon Asch. Participants in his "vision test" studies were seated in a room and asked to estimate the length of different lines shown to them (Figure 5). Each person had to loudly announce their answer to each question in turn. The catch was that there was only one actual participant; the rest were "confederates" (or "double agents") who were part of the experiment. They were seated in such a way that they always provided their answers before the "real" participant, and their answers were deliberately wrong. To illustrate, in the example below, confederates unanimously declared that the length of the line on the left matched the length of line B on the right (the correct answer, of course, is C).[21]

Figure 5. The Power of Social Proof: Solomon Asch's Experiment

Remarkably, the answers voiced by others had a dramatic impact on the lone participant's choice. When surrounded by individuals all declaring the same incorrect answer, the average participant concurred with the confederates' wrong answer for as many as one-third of all questions. In contrast, when no confederates were present, the error rate was negligible, indicating that without social pressure the correct answer was rather evident. Interestingly, when the correct answers were revealed, most participants attributed their performance to their own misjudgment and "poor eyesight" rather than to social influence.

As a psychological phenomenon, social proof stems from our tendency to look to the behavior and actions of others to determine our own. This tendency is based on the principle that when uncertain about a decision or action, we often look to others and mimic what they do, assuming their actions are reflective of the correct behavior. For example, research indicates that highlighting how the energy usage of an individual household compares with that of its neighbors can lead to a decrease in energy consumption.[22] Similarly, hotel guests are more inclined to participate in programs aimed at conserving resources — like reusing towels — if they are informed that previous guests in their room have done so.[23]

Social proof is a powerful marketing tool that leverages the influence of others to persuade potential customers to purchase products, adopt new behaviors, and engage in social activities. It reflects the human need to conform to the expectations of others and make choices that are perceived as correct or popular within a social context. By highlighting widespread acceptance and approval, social proof amplifies the perceived value and desirability of offerings, subtly guiding buyers toward decisions they perceive as endorsed by others.

Choice Overload and Decision Fatigue

An important decision that choice architects face is determining the size of the choice set — that is, how many options to present to customers. The challenge lies in striking the right balance between providing sufficient variety to meet customers' diverse preferences and minimizing the effort required from customers to identify their preferred choice. A larger set of options, while offering breadth, is often associated with increased effort and can lead to decision fatigue, whereas a smaller set runs the risk of not meeting the needs of some customers. The nuanced ways in which the choice set size influences decision outcomes and the impact of decision fatigue on consumers' ability to make choices are discussed in the following sections.

The Paradox of Choice

Conventional wisdom suggests that having more options to choose from is always better. Following this logic, Coca-Cola has expanded its product line from a single "secret" formula to "freestyle" vending machines offering over 100 different ways to customize a soda. Coca-Cola is not alone in expanding its product assortment. Crest and Colgate each offer over 25 varieties of toothpaste, and Campbell's offers more than 50 varieties of condensed soup. This proliferation of products and product variations raises the question: Is there a downside to offering an extensive assortment of options?

Most economic theories of choice argue that from a customer's perspective, having more options is always better. Their rationale is straightforward: The greater the variety of options, the higher the chance that each customer will find an option that fits their preferences. Indeed, if one assumes that decision makers know exactly what they want and are willing to invest time and effort to find the option that best matches their preferences, having more alternatives can only benefit choice. Yet, on many occasions, this assumption does not hold, and large assortments can be detrimental to choice, leading to a phenomenon referred to as *choice overload*.

A classic study documenting choice overload involves choosing different types of jam in a grocery store. On different days, shoppers were shown two different assortments, one containing 24 varieties of jam and one containing only six varieties. The display with 24 options tempted 60% of the shoppers to stop and examine it, while the display with six options attracted the attention of only 40% of shoppers. The fact that a larger display is more likely to draw attention than a smaller display is not unusual. What was surprising was the impact of the size of the display on shoppers' purchase behavior. Only 3% of shoppers who stopped to examine the larger assortment ended up making a purchase; in contrast, 30% of the shoppers who stopped to examine the smaller assortment ended up purchasing at least one of the jams. This stark difference highlighted a counterintuitive insight: Having too many options can be overwhelming and potentially hinder decision making, leading to lower purchase rates.[24]

The negative impact of assortment size on choice extends well beyond the realm of jams: It has been replicated across multiple product categories in different industries. For example, it has been shown that as the number of funds offered in retirement plans increases, the likelihood that employees will choose an investment fund (rather than keeping their savings in a money market account) tends to decline. Retirement plans offering just two investment options garnered around 75% participation, whereas those offering 60 or more funds had a significantly lower level of participation, around 60%.[25] Similar effects have been shown across a variety of consumer packaged goods, holiday destinations, and even online dating sites.

This is the *paradox of choice*: We value the freedom of choice and prefer to have more options, yet when it comes to making the actual choice, having more options can be counterproductive. This abundance often leads to a greater likelihood of delaying the choice decision and lower levels of satisfaction with the chosen option. Ironically, the overabundance of options stemming from our obsession with choice and companies' often misguided efforts to expand their product lines has become an obstacle to choice, impeding rather than facilitating our decision making.

The paradox of choice stems from the interplay of two opposing forces, one favoring larger assortments and the other favoring assortments comprising a smaller set of options. On the one hand, having more options to choose from facilitates choice by increasing the chance that the available offerings will match an individual's preferences. Having more options also creates the feeling of freedom of choice, thus providing an additional psychological benefit that helps increase decision confidence and choice satisfaction.

At the same time, having more options to choose from can be detrimental by complicating the decision process. There are three main reasons for this. First, having more options to consider inevitably leads to greater effort in evaluating these options. Additionally, a larger choice set amplifies the complexity of decisions due to the need to evaluate and make tradeoffs between a greater number of options, each with its own set of benefits to consider. As the number of options in the choice set increases, so does the number of decisions that involve giving up certain benefits to obtain others. Finally, the presence of more options intensifies the potential for regret, as choosing one option inherently means forgoing others, potentially leading to greater anticipated discomfort from having to pass up the additional options.

Factors influencing choice overload are illustrated in Figure 6. The positive impact of assortment size follows the rule of diminishing returns: Increasing the size of the choice set initially benefits decision makers, but the magnitude of this impact tapers off as the assortment becomes sufficiently large. The negative impact of assortment size, on the other hand, follows the opposite pattern: It is negligible when the choice set involves only a few options and increases as the assortment gets larger. The cumulative effect of benefits and costs reflecting the impact of assortment size on choice follows an inverted-U pattern. Too few options, as well as too many options, are likely to complicate choice, with the optimal assortment size somewhere in the middle.[26]

Figure 6. Drivers of Choice Overload

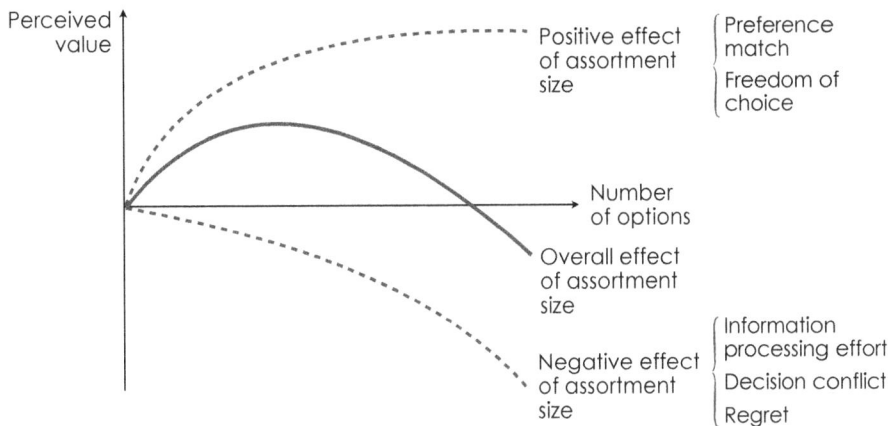

The complex nature of the impact of assortment size on choice prompts the question: What is the optimal number of options that provides customers with the needed variety without the negative consequences of choice overload? The reality is that there is no universal "ideal" assortment size. Choice complexity—and thus, overload—is not solely determined by the number of options. It also depends on factors such as the options' relative appeal, the amount of information provided for each option, the way these options are presented to decision makers, the time frame for making a choice, and the importance of the decision. Therefore, determining the optimal assortment size requires examining the specific context in which the decision is made.[27]

The possibility of overloading customers with too many options presents managers with the challenge of designing assortments that offer customers a sufficient variety of options while minimizing the possibility of choice overload. Several strategies can help reduce decision complexity.

The most intuitive solution is to *reduce the number of options*. Following this approach, many brick-and-mortar retailers curate their assortments by providing a limited set of options that best matches the preferences of the majority of their customers. For example, a Costco store carries around 4,000 different items, about 30 times fewer than the number of items carried by a Walmart store. Online retailers and service providers like Amazon, Netflix, and Google utilize sophisticated algorithms to curate and prioritize options based on individual user preferences, ensuring a tailored experience that simplifies decision making.

An alternative approach to combating choice overload is to *streamline the decision process* by providing customers with a simple criterion for choice, thus reducing decision complexity to a single key attribute that defines the options. Consider how winemakers tackled the challenge of convincing the American public to drink wine. Unlike "old world" countries such as France, Italy, and Spain, which have established wine-making traditions and strong wine cultures, wine is not the first drink of choice for many Americans.

One particular challenge was that choosing a wine could be an intimidating process, overwhelming buyers with a variety of options from difficult-to-remember brands. This complexity was further exacerbated by wine labels, which featured a plethora of information, including the name of the producer, the estate and region where the grapes were grown, the grape varietal, the vintage year, and the alcohol content. Adding to this complexity was the fact that many "old world" wines were blended, combining multiple wine varietals.

To address this challenge, in the 1960s, winemaker Robert Mondavi started promoting the concept of varietal labeling, where wines are named after the predominant grape used in their production, such as Cabernet Sauvignon, Merlot, Pinot Noir, and Chardonnay. Although blended wines can create more complex and flavorful profiles, single-varietal labeling had the benefit of making wine selection easier by helping customers develop easily remembered preferences. This simplification strategy contributed to the growth of U.S. wine consumption as many consumers were able to name their preferred wine varietal and were less intimidated by having to make their wine selection.

Beyond reducing the number of options and streamlining the decision, mitigating choice overload can also be achieved by helping customers *articulate their preferences* prior to making a choice. The rationale for this approach is that decision makers face two distinct tasks when choosing. First, they must decide which benefits are important to them and prioritize these benefits. Then, they must select the option that best aligns with these priorities.

The challenge here is that simultaneously deciding which criteria are important and choosing the option that is superior on these criteria is a very complex task. Therefore, helping customers articulate their preferences prior to making a choice can greatly facilitate the decision process. This approach explains why skilled salespeople often engage with customers to identify the key benefits they are looking for and the compromises they are willing to make before introducing them to the available options. Once buyers know what they want, a larger assortment can facilitate rather than impede choice.[28]

Providing a *default option* is another common approach to alleviate choice overload. Because they offer an easy way to decide—essentially allowing individuals to make a choice by not making one—default options are a powerful tool against choice overload. For example, in the case of retirement plans, studies have shown that as the number of available funds increased, employees were more likely to stick with the fund designated as the default. The presence of a default option, which automatically becomes the selected choice if the decision maker does not make an alternative selection, helps overcome the detrimental effects of choice overload. The ways in which default options influence choice are explored in more detail later in this chapter.

The Pitfalls of Decision Fatigue

Decision fatigue refers to a mental state characterized by depleted cognitive resources and a feeling of tiredness, which can hinder decision making. A striking demonstration of the impact of decision fatigue on choice involves a study of more than 1,100 parole decisions over the course of a year, examining how the time of day when the prisoner appeared in front of the parole board affected the outcomes.

The study found that the proportion of rulings in favor of the prisoners varied dramatically based on when their cases were heard. Although judges approved parole in about a third of the cases, the probability of being paroled fluctuated significantly throughout the day. The percentage of favorable rulings started at about 65%, dropping to virtually zero at the end of each session, only to go back up to 65% after each break. As the judges became more tired, they were more likely to revert to the default option, which was to deny parole.[29]

Decision fatigue shares similarities with choice overload, as both can impede the process of making choices. For instance, the task of selecting a paint color from Benjamin Moore's 3,500 options can lead to both choice overload and decision fatigue. However, these concepts diverge on three key aspects.

First, choice overload typically emerges from a single decision involving a vast array of options, whereas decision fatigue is often the result of facing a series of challenging decisions, which may not always include large assortments. Moreover, choice overload is merely one of many contributors to decision fatigue, which can also arise from the cumulative burden of making multiple sequential decisions. Finally, while choice overload results in diminished satisfaction and confidence in the selected option and an impaired ability to tackle tough decisions, decision fatigue can extend beyond these outcomes and lead to compromised self-regulation in areas unrelated to the initial choice.

The impact of decision fatigue on an individual's self-control can be illustrated by a study in which some participants were asked to memorize a seven-digit number (a difficult task), while others were asked to memorize a two-digit number (an easier task). After this memorization task, both groups were presented with a choice between a chocolate cake and a fruit salad as a reward.

The findings revealed that those tasked with the more difficult memorization task were more likely to choose the chocolate cake over the fruit salad, indicating a reduction in self-control. This pattern suggests that people possess a finite pool of cognitive energy that can be utilized for various mental activities. Consequently, a difficult mental task that leads to decision fatigue can deplete the energy available for maintaining self-control in other domains.[30]

In another study, after participants were given either an easy or a difficult decision task, they were assigned a seemingly unrelated self-control task: holding their hand in ice water for as long as they could. Interestingly, the group faced with the difficult decision task showed less endurance, keeping their hand in the ice-cold water for about 25 seconds, significantly shorter than the roughly 70 seconds managed by those who had completed the easier task.[31]

Similar results were obtained when some participants were given an easy cognitive task—thinking about anything they wished—while others were given a more challenging task: thinking about anything except a white bear. The difficulty of the latter task stems from the paradox that trying not to think about something often makes that thought more persistent; the moment you try not to think about a white bear, it immediately pops up in your mind. Participants in both groups were then given money to spend in a convenience store that carried a variety of indulgent, impulse-buy products such as gum and candy. The findings showed that those assigned the more difficult task of not thinking about a white bear exhibited lower self-control, spending more money on indulgent items.[32]

In addition to being caused by effortful choice tasks, decision fatigue can also arise from our internal clock, which orchestrates our daily activities through circadian rhythms. These rhythms, marking physical, mental, and behavioral changes over a 24-hour cycle, govern functions like sleep patterns, body temperature, and eating habits. Circadian rhythms can vary from person to person, defining an individual's chronotype, or personal circadian rhythm. At the same time, because circadian rhythms are primarily responsive to light and darkness, they exhibit universal patterns across different individuals.

This universal aspect of circadian rhythms is highlighted by a study analyzing the emotional tone of over 500 million tweets. It found that positive affect—reflected through emotions such as enthusiasm, confidence, and alertness — tends to increase in the morning, decrease in the afternoon, and rise again in the early evening. This bimodal daily pattern of positive affect is further supported by data from studies of self-reported levels of enjoyment and happiness.[33]

The role of decision fatigue in shaping our choices becomes particularly evident when considering why many infomercials promoting impulse-buy products air late at night. By the end of the day, our mental resources are largely depleted, significantly lowering our capacity to regulate impulses. This reduction in self-regulation, together with diminished decision-making abilities, creates an ideal setup for advertisers to persuade viewers to buy their offerings. This is why understanding how decision fatigue influences people's choices is important not only for companies promoting their offerings but also for policymakers who aim to ensure that consumers are not swayed in a way detrimental to their interests.

The Power of Defaults

Defaults are pre-set courses of action that automatically take effect unless the decision maker specifies an alternative. The presence of a default option relieves the decision maker from having to make an active choice: Failing to make an active selection results in the acceptance of the default as the chosen outcome. In the sections that follow, we delve into the nuances of how default options serve as cognitive shortcuts and the psychological underpinnings that make them effective tools in guiding decision outcomes.

Defaults as Drivers of Choice

A striking example of the power of defaults is the discrepancy in organ donation rates among different European countries. For instance, in Germany, only 12% of citizens have opted to be organ donors, compared to nearly 100% of citizens in neighboring Austria. Similarly, in the U.K. and Denmark, less than 20% of the population has consented to be organ donors, compared to nearly 100% in France and Portugal (Figure 7).

Figure 7. Organ Donation Rates Across Countries

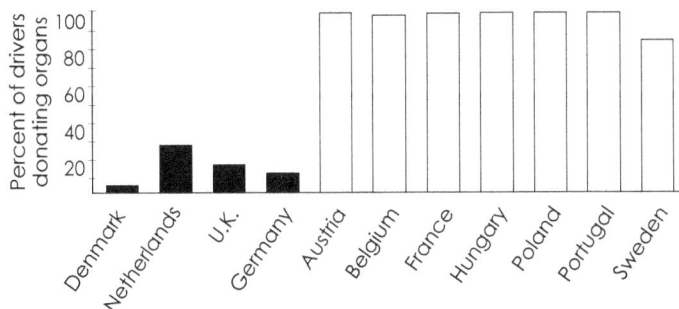

All these countries are fairly similar in many aspects of their social life and moral standards — a fact that makes it difficult to account for such a huge discrepancy in organ donation rates. Instead, the difference in donation rates stems from something so minor that one might not have expected it to make such a big impact: the default option on their driver's license application. Countries with a lower percentage of organ donations are those in which the driver's license default is not to be an organ donor, and drivers need to opt in to become donors. In contrast, countries with high donation rates are those in which drivers agree to become donors by default and have to opt out if they do not wish to participate in organ donation.[34]

The impact of defaults can be seen in virtually all aspects of our lives. For example, participation in employer retirement savings plans tends to be significantly greater in companies where employees are automatically enrolled (with the ability to opt out) compared to companies where employees are not enrolled by default and must opt in. It has been shown that participation in employer retirement savings plans nearly doubled in companies where employees were automatically enrolled.[35] Other areas in which defaults have been shown to influence people's behavior include giving consent to be contacted by companies for promotional purposes, agreeing to allow browser cookies to collect personal data, choosing among different energy providers, and even deciding which food to eat.

Based on the action required from decision makers, defaults can be categorized into "hard defaults" and "soft defaults." *Hard defaults* entail a pre-selected option that remains in effect unless an alternative is actively chosen. Hard defaults can be opt-out or opt-in. Opt-out defaults automatically enroll individuals, necessitating an active decision to unenroll. For instance, subscription-based services like magazines, gyms, and online streaming platforms tend to renew automatically, placing the onus on customers to cancel if they wish to opt out. Conversely, opt-in defaults require individuals to take an active step to enroll. For example, many investment brokerage firms by default deposit dividends into money market accounts, and to have them reinvested, customers must make an active choice.

Unlike hard defaults, which necessitate an active choice only if the decision maker opts for an alternative, *soft defaults* simply endorse a particular option but still require the decision maker to make an active selection. An everyday example of this is how many online companies handle browser cookies, asking users to actively accept or reject them. A striking historical example of a soft default is the ballot design in the 1938 referendum on the annexation of Austria by Germany, where the "Yes" vote option was emphasized by a significantly larger circle placed centrally on the ballot, compared to the smaller, off-center "No" option. Not surprisingly, 99.7% of the Austrian population voted in favor of the annexation. Other, less nefarious examples of soft defaults include product recommendations labeled as "you might also like," film and TV show recommendations marked as "editor's pick," and items marked as "customer favorites" by retailers.

Soft defaults do not necessarily have to be explicit. For example, a study conducted at Subway sandwich shops showed that using a menu highlighting low-calorie options made customers nearly 50% more likely to choose a low-calorie sandwich than those given a menu with a mix of low-calorie and high-calorie options. In contrast, those who were given a menu highlighting the highest calorie sandwiches were about 50% less likely to choose a low-calorie sandwich.[36] These findings suggest that placing healthy options, such as fruits and vegetables, up front rather than in their usual place toward the end of the cafeteria line can make them act like a default option, thus increasing their consumption.

How Defaults Work

Why are we so sensitive to the presence of default options? One reason is the path of least resistance: Accepting the default often requires *less effort*, be it physical or cognitive, than making an active decision. Consequently, for decisions deemed less important, we tend to conserve our mental energy by adhering to the default. For example, most of us stick with the default search engine on our mobile device. Even though changing it is relatively easy, very few invest the time and effort to switch to an alternative search engine. Our inertia is one of the reasons why Google pays Apple billions of dollars every year in exchange for being the default search engine on Apple's devices.

The effort to make an active choice is not limited to physical actions; it often involves considerable mental exertion, particularly with complex or emotionally charged decisions. As a result, when faced with decisions about organ donation or selecting between medical procedures with uncertain outcomes, we often opt for the default choice, sidestepping the need to actively engage with the decision. Yet, despite helping make decisions easier, defaults do not exempt us from making a choice. As American philosopher and psychologist William James pointed out, "When you have to make a choice and don't make it, that is in itself a choice."

Our preference for default options is partly due to our inherent tendency to value potential losses more than potential gains, a concept known as loss aversion (discussed extensively in Chapter 4). Defaults take advantage of loss aversion by establishing a reference point from which all other options are evaluated. As a result, the perceived cost of deviating from a default often appears greater than the potential benefits of alternative choices. When the default option is seen as the status quo and no other options clearly outperform it, any change involves tradeoffs—sacrificing one benefit to gain another. Due to loss aversion, the perceived losses from moving away from the default often feel more significant than the potential gains.

Consider the process of selecting features when ordering a new car. When the default option is a basic model, buyers are less likely to upgrade to features like designer paint colors, leather upholstery, and entertainment systems. However, if the default is a car loaded with features and buyers must exclude the ones they do not want, they are more likely to retain additional features.[37] This behavior illustrates how reference points and loss aversion influence the way a default option can steer our preferences and decisions.

When faced with significant decisions, we often gravitate toward the default option to sidestep the *regret* that might come from rejecting it in favor of an uncertain alternative, particularly if we are unsure which benefits matter most to us. This anticipated regret is the regret we imagine we might feel in the future about choices we are currently contemplating. The anticipation of remorse, should the decision's outcome fall short of our expectations, can sway our choices toward the path that seems most likely to avoid future negative feelings. Default options help reduce this regret because they typically require no action, and regret is more intense for outcomes resulting from our actions than from inaction.[38] The role of action-driven regret is explored further in the next chapter.

Defaults can shape decisions because they act as an *implicit endorsement*, leading us to believe that the default option was chosen for its merit. This belief is based on the assumption that if a company has selected a particular option as the default, there must be a good reason for it. This applies to both universal defaults, such as organ donor status on a driver's license application or highlighting a menu item in a restaurant, and personalized defaults, such as recommendations from online platforms suggesting an option best suited to an individual's preferences. The impact of defaults is particularly strong when we are uncertain about our choices or lack comprehensive information about the options available. In these situations, we are more inclined to trust the company's implicit recommendation rather than make our own decision.

Finally, defaults can benefit from being viewed as *social norms*. If we believe that companies set defaults to reflect the preferences of the majority, we might see these defaults as de facto social norms that dictate expected behavior. For instance, when presented with a restaurant bill suggesting an 18% tip, we are likely to leave a larger tip than if the bill suggested a 15% tip, as we tend to adhere to what we believe is a social norm. Thus, when we lack well-defined preferences or when straying from the default could lead to social embarrassment or other adverse consequences, we are more inclined to rely on these perceived social norms and stick with the default option.

All these factors contribute to defaults' ability to sway our decisions. Many decision scientists argue that defaults are the most potent and universal tool at the disposal of choice architects. Whether we like it or not, our judgments are invariably shaped by the presence of defaults, which in turn determine how we decide. Because of their ubiquity, defaults should be used judiciously and in a way that benefits not only the company but also its customers and society at large. Companies that successfully navigate the delicate balance between pursuing their strategic interests and upholding customers' and societal welfare will likely be rewarded with greater customer loyalty and trust.

Summary

The rational model of choice assumes that people have well-articulated preferences and meticulously evaluate every option to select the one with the highest value. In reality, this is not the case. People often use decision shortcuts, or *heuristics*, to reduce mental effort, often at the expense of decision accuracy. One such shortcut is the satisficing heuristic, which involves choosing the first option that meets an individual's decision criteria without considering all available options. Another shortcut focuses only on the most important attribute of an option, ignoring the other attributes. Because different heuristics rely on different decision rules, they can lead to different choice outcomes.

When making a choice, we think in terms of *reasons* for and against each option rather than numerically expressed values. Faced with conflicting reasons for choosing among competing options, we must reconcile these conflicts and develop a convincing rationale to justify our choice to ourselves and others.

Choice architecture defines the ways in which options are presented to decision makers. The basic premise of choice architecture is that decisions are defined by their context; therefore, by changing the context, it is possible to influence choice outcomes. Choice architecture involves factors such as the number of available options, the selection of options in the choice set, the sequence in which these options are presented, the number of attributes describing each option, the choice of specific attributes describing each option, and the time frame for making the decision.

Framing defines the way in which information is presented, typically by setting a reference point for evaluating this information. The same information can lead to different outcomes depending on the reference points embedded in the decision context. Framing can influence a wide range of decisions, from relatively simple perceptual tasks to more complex problems involving consequential choices. *Context effects* define the impact of the composition of the decision set on choice. Decoy and attraction effects reflect the increased preference for an option when an inferior option is present. The similarity effect reflects the decrease in preference for an option in the presence of a similar option. The compromise effect is the tendency to favor the middle, less extreme option regardless of its actual performance.

The *choice paradox* is the discrepancy between our desire for more options and our inability to make optimal decisions when presented with a large set of alternatives. While having more choices can increase the likelihood of finding the "ideal" option and create a feeling of freedom, it can also impair decision making. This impairment can stem from the increased effort required to process information, the greater number of tradeoffs to consider, and the heightened potential for regret over the options not chosen.

Decision fatigue involves a depletion of cognitive resources and a sense of tiredness. Since we have a limited pool of energy shared across different mental activities, engaging in mentally challenging tasks reduces the resources available for self-control in other areas. Choice overload and decision fatigue can be reduced by decreasing the number of available options, providing customers with a simple criterion for choice, helping them articulate their preferences before making a choice, and offering a default option.

Default options are pre-set courses of action that take effect unless the decision maker specifies an alternative. There are two types of defaults: hard defaults, where an option is automatically chosen unless an alternative is selected, and soft defaults, which suggest a preferred option but require the decision maker to make an active selection. Defaults influence decision making in several ways: They reduce the effort required to make a choice, attenuate loss aversion, minimize anticipated regret, and signal social norms. Due to these influences, defaults are among the most potent and versatile tools for shaping people's decisions.

KEY TAKEAWAYS

Choices rely on heuristics. People's decisions are often based on simplified decision rules that do not follow the normative economic models.

Reasons guide decisions. People tend to think in terms of reasons rather than in terms of numerically expressed utilities.

The decision context matters. Because most choices are influenced by the decision context, choice architecture can shape the decision outcome.

Less can be more. Having too many choices can backfire when consumers lack well-defined preferences. Making a series of difficult choices can lead to decision avoidance and impaired self-regulation.

Defaults can guide choice. Defaults are a powerful tool that can steer the decision-making process and shape choice outcomes.

SPOTLIGHT: DECISION MAKING IN BUSINESS MARKETS

Business managers and individual consumers, while sharing many similarities, exhibit notable differences in their decision-making processes. One key difference is that business decisions are typically made by a *decision-making unit* rather than by a single individual. This unit typically comprises representatives from different departments or functional areas within an organization, including senior management; product, service, and brand managers; and representatives from research and development, finance, accounting, legal, purchasing, marketing, sales, and information technology departments.

In addition to varying in their department affiliation, members of a business decision-making unit can play several different roles. Initiators originate the buying process by identifying an unmet need or a problem that needs solving. Influencers impact the decision process by expressing relevant preferences and recommendations. Gatekeepers influence the decision process by imposing certain restrictions on the options being considered. Deciders make the ultimate selection of what, why, and when to buy. Buyers negotiate the specifics of the purchase, such as the final price, delivery, and guarantees, and execute the purchase transaction. Finally, end users utilize the purchased product or service (Figure 8).[39]

Figure 8. The Composition of a Business Decision-Making Unit

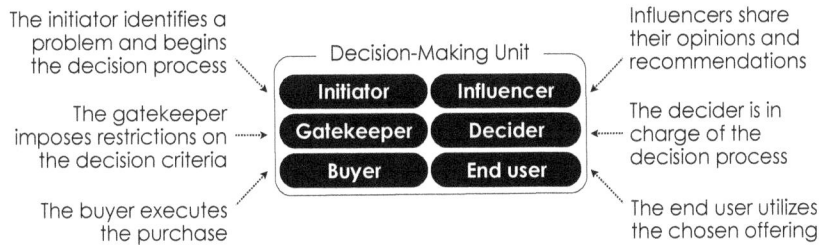

The initiator identifies a problem and begins the decision process

Influencers share their opinions and recommendations

Decision-Making Unit

Initiator	Influencer
Gatekeeper	Decider
Buyer	End user

The gatekeeper imposes restrictions on the decision criteria

The decider is in charge of the decision process

The buyer executes the purchase

The end user utilizes the chosen offering

The roles of initiator, influencer, gatekeeper, decider, buyer, and end user represent decision-making functions that can be assumed by individual managers or teams within a business. Consequently, a single role may be shared among several managers, and conversely, one individual may fulfill multiple decision roles throughout the buying process.

For instance, the buying process could be initiated by the marketing department, which might also be the end user of the product or service. Gatekeeping functions might be distributed across legal, accounting, and information technology departments to manage information flow and compliance. Decision-making authority often rests with senior management, while the task of executing the purchase may be designated to a purchasing manager. Finally, all of the above entities have the potential to exert influence over the decision-making process.

Consider the process of purchasing customer relationship management (CRM) software. Given the significant investment, multiple entities are likely involved, including C-suite executives, marketing and sales teams, IT engineers, and the purchasing department. This decision might also involve external consultants hired to assist with the selection and integration of the software with the company's legacy systems. In this scenario, the marketing and sales teams are the users of the service, consultants might initiate and influence the decision, the IT department acts as the gatekeeper, C-suite executives are the ultimate deciders, and the purchasing department is the actual buyer.

Throughout the entire process, the buying decision is influenced by various entities, each contributing unique insights, expertise, and attitudes toward the offering. Consequently, focusing solely on the needs and preferences of the actual buyer represents a significant oversight that many businesses encounter. To avoid this myopic view of the customer, managers must thoroughly understand the composition of the decision-making unit and the specific roles its members play.

Recognizing and addressing the distinct needs and preferences of all entities involved is essential for the success of the company's offering. Adopting such a holistic approach not only shifts the focus beyond the immediate buyer but also increases the likelihood that the offering will satisfy the broader requirements of the entire decision-making unit.

THE CX CANVAS: CRAFTING THE CHOICE ARCHITECTURE

Not all offerings that create value are chosen by customers. For an offering to be chosen, it must clearly surpass other alternatives that fulfill the same need. Therefore, a company must not only emphasize the benefits of its offering but also ensure that it stands out from the competition. To achieve this, a manager must (1) analyze the context in which customers make their choices and (2) provide customers with a compelling reason to choose their offering. These two aspects of crafting the choice architecture are depicted in Figure 9 and discussed in more detail below.

Figure 9. Crafting the Choice Architecture: The Big Picture

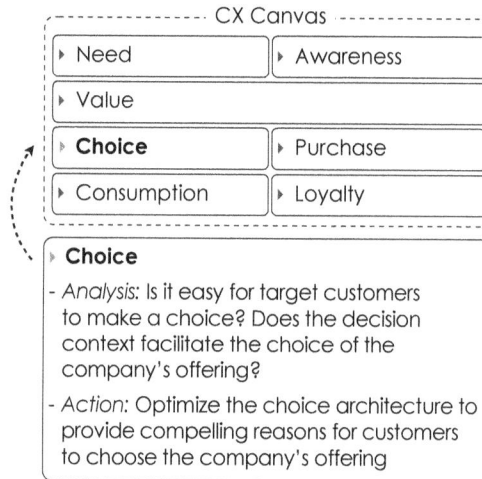

The first step in crafting the choice architecture is to examine the context in which customers make decisions. This involves identifying the available options, articulating reasons why customers might choose the company's offering over other alternatives, and pinpointing any significant impediments to selecting the company's offering. To achieve this, a company must consider the following questions:

- *Is it easy for customers to make a choice?* This question seeks to identify factors influencing customers' choices, such as the number of available alternatives, their benefits and costs, and the decision time frame. It also aims to determine if any factors, like choice overload or decision fatigue, might prevent customers from choosing any of the available options.

- *Does the decision context facilitate the choice of a particular option?* This question aims to determine whether customers' valuation of the company's offering translates into reasons for selecting it over alternatives that fulfill the same need. This is important because an option that is viewed as attractive in isolation could be rejected in favor of another option with stronger reasons for purchase.

The ultimate purpose of analyzing the decision context is to identify factors that can both facilitate and impede the choice of the company's offering. This analysis helps the company develop an action plan to increase the likelihood that target customers choose its offering. Here, companies often face two common challenges, each requiring a distinct course of action:

- *Poorly designed decision context.* This challenge arises when the decision context prevents customers from choosing any of the available options. The company's goal here is to redefine the decision-making context to simplify the choice process. This can include reducing the number of available options, adjusting the sequence in which customers evaluate these options, and extending the time frame for making the decision.

- *Insufficient reasons for choice.* This challenge occurs when customers, despite appreciating the offering's benefits, lack sufficient reasons to choose it over other available options. The company's goal in this case is to help customers formulate compelling reasons for choosing its offering and rejecting the alternative options.

These challenges and the corresponding company actions are summarized in Figure 10. The two actions are interconnected: Optimizing the decision context can involve articulating reasons for choosing the company's offering, and highlighting the offering's benefits can help streamline the decision-making process.

Figure 10. Crafting the Choice Architecture: The Action Plan

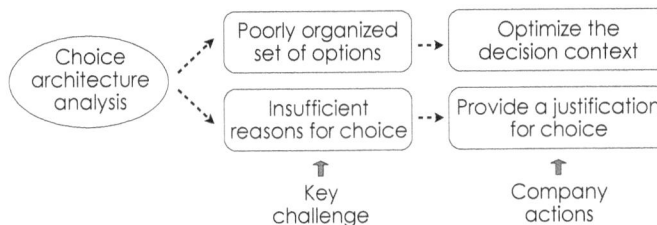

Retailers like Amazon, Target, and Walmart face significant challenges when deciding what products to carry and how to present them to their customers. First, they must ensure that shoppers can readily locate products they are looking for and easily identify the product that best fits their needs. Without this, shoppers might delay purchases or choose a different retailer that makes their choice easier. Beyond ensuring that shoppers make a purchase from their store, retailers might also benefit from guiding shoppers toward a particular option, either because they believe it better fits customers' needs or because it is more profitable for the retailer.

After identifying the challenges faced by their customers, retailers must develop a course of action to address these challenges. For example, if shoppers find it difficult to navigate the available options or feel overwhelmed by the number of choices, retailers might curate their assortments to include only the most relevant offerings, eliminating marginally attractive options. Alternatively, retailers might deliberately include an inferior option in their assortment to enhance the perceived benefits of another option, leveraging the decoy and attraction effects. Retailers might also organize the available options in a way that guides customers to products that best meet both the customers' needs and the retailer's goals.

CHAPTER SIX

BEHAVIORAL NUDGING

Gravity explains the motions of the planets,
but it cannot explain who sets the planets in motion.

—Isaac Newton

Once customers have evaluated the available options and chosen their preferred one, the next step is to acquire that option (Figure 1). However, selecting an option does not necessarily lead to an immediate purchase. Sometimes, there is a delay between choosing an option and making the purchase. In such cases, a company must focus not only on ensuring that its offerings are selected by target customers but also on converting these selections into actual sales.

Figure 1. The Customer Experience Map: Making the Purchase

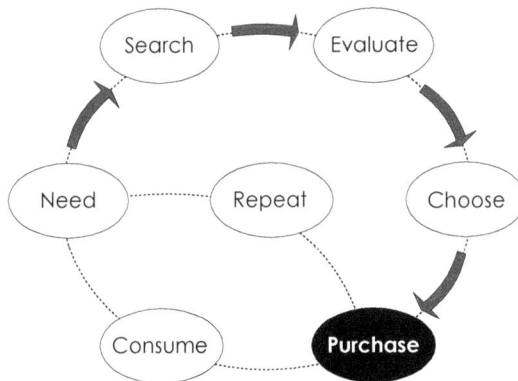

At times, a bit of judicious nudging is necessary to encourage customers to convert a choice into a purchase. Nudging plays a crucial role because buyers often procrastinate, putting off purchasing their chosen offering, and in some cases, never following through on their decision. Nudging seeks to give an extra push to buyers to act on their choices and to eliminate any barriers that may prevent them from completing the purchase. Consider the following scenarios:

- You oversee the marketing campaign for the 911—Porsche's iconic sports car. The data analytics team suggests that based on the buyer profile and the

$100,000+ price of the car, your advertising activities should focus exclusively on financially well-off consumers in their late 40s and early 50s. Would you follow their recommendation? Why?

- You are a retail manager responsible for the canned soup category. The store has recently stocked quantities of several varieties of soup that you are trying to move to free up inventory space. You are considering offering a 2-for-1 volume discount with no limit on the purchase quantity. Is this a good idea? Why?

- A real estate agent just had her clients—first-time home buyers—sign a contract on a new house. She is considering following up with the buyers later that evening; however, she is concerned that she might end up bothering them and that it might be a better idea to follow up a week or so later to advise them about the specifics of closing on the house. What would you advise?

- You are a campaign manager for a political candidate who has a chance to win the election in a race that polls show is very close. Your research team tells you that your candidate enjoys strong support among younger voters. The challenge is that when election day comes, many of these voters fail to cast a vote. What can you do to ensure larger participation from this demographic?

In this chapter, we address these questions and explore how behavioral nudging can help turn customer choices into actual purchases. First, we examine the gap between choosing and buying, discussing strategies managers can use to bridge this gap. We then identify three main cognitive barriers that can prevent action: performance uncertainty, preference uncertainty, and choice uncertainty. Next, we address emotional barriers to action, focusing on anticipated regret. Finally, we examine implementational barriers to action, focusing on implementation uncertainty and implementation viability, and how these can prevent decisions from becoming actions.

The discussion of the conceptual issues involved in behavioral nudging is complemented with examples of companies using relevant behavioral insights. Specifically, we will explore what the McRib, a pumpkin latte, and the Disney Vault have in common; how Genentech encouraged physicians to adopt its new asthma drug by educating them on the way it should be administered; how a cafeteria manager can encourage students to make healthier choices; how a political campaign can encourage voters to show up at the polls; and how changing one button on a company's website increased sales by $300 million.

Now, let's delve deeper into the gap between choice and purchase, the types of action drivers, and the three main barriers—cognitive, emotional, and implementational—that can impede purchases.

From Choice to Purchase

Purchase decisions do not invariably result in immediate transactions. Often, there is a delay between the selection of an offering and its actual purchase. In some instances, these decisions do not culminate in a purchase at all. This reality underscores the importance of making the transition from choice to purchase a key aspect of managing the customer experience. In the following sections, we explore the nature of the gap between choice and purchase and the various obstacles that can prevent a purchase.

The Gap Between Choice and Purchase

The decision to buy a product or service and the actual act of purchasing can unfold simultaneously. An impulsive purchase, like an item bought at the cash register while waiting in line, is one example of a contemporaneous choice and purchase decision. However, the journey from choice to purchase is not always straightforward. Often, there is a temporal gap between these two events. For instance, after deciding to upgrade their mobile phone, a person may not immediately visit a store to make the purchase. Similarly, a person planning a vacation might research and decide on a destination months in advance but delay booking flights and accommodations until a later date.

The gap between choice and purchase can range from a few minutes to years or, in some cases, decades. Consider, for example, the decision process of a customer who ultimately purchases Porsche's flagship sports car, the 911 Carrera. According to Porsche, the typical 911 buyer in the United States is over 50 years old. Most of these buyers, however, did not develop an affinity for this car just before making the purchase. Instead, many current Porsche owners made the decision to buy the car when they were teenagers but were unable to do so due to budgetary constraints and family considerations.

Various elements can intervene, subtly steering the shopper toward a different choice than initially intended. For instance, a consumer might have their heart set on buying a specific brand of sneakers. Yet, upon entering the store or browsing online, this consumer might encounter a plethora of alternatives. Factors such as special deals, new arrivals, or limited-edition models can act as distractions or enticements, making the shopper reconsider the chosen option.

Advertising and marketing strategies can significantly influence buyer behavior. Buyers set on a particular item might change their minds after seeing a compelling advertisement for an alternative. This advertisement could highlight features buyers had not considered, presenting the alternative as a better fit for their needs or desires. In such scenarios, the power of suggestion and the appeal of something presented as new or improved can easily sway the buyers' decision.

Social influences, such as recommendations from friends, family, and online reviews, can introduce doubt or conviction into the buyer's mind. For example, a person determined to buy a specific smartphone might shift their preference after hearing about a friend's positive experience with another brand. Social media platforms amplify this effect, with users frequently sharing their purchases, reviews, and endorsements. The fear of missing out on a popular or highly recommended product can drive consumers to abandon their initial choice in favor of what seems to be the crowd favorite.

The context in which a purchase is made can also have a considerable impact. Economic factors such as price changes, discounts, and financial incentives can make alternatives more attractive. A buyer intent on purchasing an affordable item might opt for a more expensive option if a sale or discount is offered at the right time. Similarly, the urgency of the need or the purpose of the purchase can lead to decision changes. A buyer needing an item immediately may settle for a readily available alternative rather than wait for their preferred choice to be in stock.

Personal factors such as changes in taste, lifestyle, or financial situation can lead to shifts in buying behavior. A consumer might begin shopping with a specific product in mind but end up choosing something that better aligns with their current priorities or values. For example, an increased interest in sustainability can prompt a buyer to opt for eco-friendly products over their usual choices. Similarly, a change in financial circumstances might cause consumers to prioritize cost over brand loyalty.

Nudging to Action

Various factors can influence whether and when customers purchase a chosen offering, and most of these factors are beyond a company's control. A company cannot stop competitors from developing superior products, nor can it ensure that its target customers will always have the time, money, or energy to make a purchase. However, a company can increase the likelihood of customers purchasing its offerings by guiding their thoughts and actions to facilitate the transition from choice to purchase. This process of encouraging individuals to think and act in a particular way is the essence of nudging.

The term "nudging" is used in two different contexts. *Decision nudging* describes activities that guide individuals' mental processes toward a specific decision. For example, placing healthier foods at eye level in a cafeteria can naturally encourage people to choose these over less healthy alternatives. This arrangement does not prevent customers from choosing less healthy options; rather, it subtly encourages healthier choices by making them more visually prominent and accessible. As this example illustrates, nudges are usually implicit, meaning they are subtly integrated into the decision-making environment, guiding individuals without making them feel coerced or that their range of options is limited.

Choice architecture is a prime example of nudging that influences the selection process by encouraging individuals to choose a particular option without restricting their freedom of choice. For instance, a grocery store might use nudging by placing fruits and vegetables in more accessible locations while positioning sugary snacks on higher or lower shelves. This arrangement allows customers to purchase whatever they desire but promotes healthier choices by making fruits and vegetables more visually and physically prominent.

Menu design in restaurants is another example of decision nudging. Having a separate dessert menu can reduce the likelihood that guests will skip the appetizer after seeing an appealing dessert. Including an overly expensive "decoy" item on the menu makes other pricey items seem more reasonable by comparison. Placing a wine as the second cheapest option on the list can increase the likelihood of it being chosen because it occupies a sweet spot for customers who want to avoid the cheapest option, which might be perceived as lower quality, while also seeking to avoid overspending on pricier options.

In addition to shaping decision makers' choices, nudging can play a crucial role in prompting them to act once a preferred option has been selected. This type of nudging is referred to as *behavioral nudging*. Unlike decision nudging, which aims to guide individuals toward choosing a particular option, behavioral nudging focuses on encouraging individuals to take a specific action. For example, after a person has decided to purchase an item and placed it in the shopping cart, a behavioral nudge might be a reminder to complete the purchase. Thus, behavioral nudging complements decision nudging by ensuring that individuals act promptly on their choices, helping to close the choice–purchase gap.

Action Drivers and Action Barriers

Behavioral nudging can occur in two different ways, each with its unique mechanism and implications. These two approaches to nudging can be illustrated with the following analogy: Imagine trying to push a heavy concrete block to a new location. Despite your efforts, the block moves sluggishly, resisting your attempts to shift it. How can you accelerate its movement? One option is to increase the force with which you push the block. Alternatively, you could reduce the friction by inserting sliding pads or applying a surface lubricant beneath the block.

Behavioral nudging is also similar to how aircraft engineers improve the speed and fuel efficiency of an airplane. To make airplanes faster and more efficient, they use a two-pronged approach: increasing the power of the aircraft engine and making the aircraft more aerodynamic to reduce wind resistance.

As with moving a concrete block or improving the performance of an aircraft, there are two ways to nudge people to act: by increasing the forces that motivate them to make a purchase and by removing barriers to purchase. In the first case, a company might make its offering more attractive by enhancing its benefits—for example, by offering sales promotions. Alternatively, a company might reduce the impediments that prevent buyers from purchasing the chosen option — for example, by alleviating buyers' concerns about the performance of its offerings. We address these two approaches, adding action drivers and removing action barriers, in the following sections.

Action Drivers

Action drivers aim to further motivate individuals to purchase the chosen offering in two ways: by making customers' unmet needs more prominent and by making the chosen option more attractive (Figure 2).

Figure 2. Action Drivers

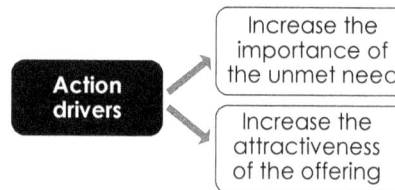

Increasing the Importance of the Unmet Need

One common reason buyers delay purchasing a chosen offering is the lack of urgent need for its benefits. When buyers are reasonably satisfied with the status quo, they might not rush to purchase because the immediate benefit is unclear. In such cases, buyers might wait for an opportune moment or delay the purchase in anticipation of a better price. For example, a person who has decided to upgrade to a new mobile phone might not purchase it immediately because their current phone meets their needs reasonably well, and there is no urgency to replace it.

The intensity with which people act on their choices is determined by their need state. Based on the degree to which a given need is prominent in their minds, there are four main need states: *delight*, where the need is fully satisfied; *indifference*, a state in which the need is reasonably met but still leaves room for enhancement; *discomfort*, where individuals recognize an unmet need but have yet to take action to fulfill it; and *problem*, indicating a significant unmet need that individuals are actively seeking to resolve (these need states are discussed in Chapter 2).

Individuals facing a well-defined problem are more inclined to actively seek solutions for their unmet needs, identifying these issues as critical pain points. Conversely, those who are delighted with their current offering are less motivated to act. Given this variance in individuals' motivations, a company can benefit from focusing its efforts on amplifying the importance of needs among customers who are largely satisfied with the status quo or who recognize an unmet need but lack a plan of action. One such strategy involves repositioning offerings from being perceived merely as "nice-to-have" enhancements to "must-have" essentials, capable of significantly improving an individual's situation.

Note that nudging those who are already actively seeking a solution might not be the most effective way to allocate resources, as these customers are already motivated to act. Similarly, nudging those who are delighted with their current offering is unlikely to produce results since these customers lack an active need to guide their behavior. To incite action, a company must first elevate customer motivation by transforming a state of indifference into a perceived problem that demands resolution.

Increasing the Attractiveness of the Company's Offering

Another approach to narrowing the choice–purchase gap is to increase the value customers expect to receive from the company's offering. Unlike amplifying the prominence of the underlying need, which broadly targets customer motivation without tying it directly to a specific offering, the value-enhancement strategy focuses squarely on the offering itself. Enhancing the appeal of the offering can be accomplished in two ways: by reducing costs to customers and by increasing customer benefits.

Perhaps the most common tool to stimulate purchases by reducing customers' costs are monetary incentives such as coupons, rebates, volume discounts, and price reductions. These incentives often incorporate a temporal element, such as an expiration date, making them particularly effective in nudging customers to make a timely purchase to take advantage of the promotion.

An alternative approach to enhancing the attractiveness of an offering is to increase customers' benefits. This is often achieved through nonmonetary promotions such as premiums, prizes, contests, sweepstakes, and games. For example, to encourage frequent visits, McDonald's includes toys with its Happy Meals, distributing close to a billion toys per year. Similarly, to boost sales, Pepsi's "Twist and Win" promotion on specially marked products offered instant awards ranging from cash to free gas, drinks, and movie tickets, all imprinted under the bottle cap.

In addition to using incentives that increase the actual benefits of the offering, another approach to amplifying its value is to enhance its *perceived* benefits. This is often achieved by creating a sense of scarcity. Scarcity can work in two ways. First, it can bolster our perceptions of the intrinsic value of the offering. We often interpret scarcity as an indication of the offering's appeal, based on the notion that opportunities seem more valuable when they are less available. Besides increasing the perceived attractiveness of the offering, scarcity can also involve an emotional component, such as the fear of missing out (FOMO). In this case, scarcity creates anxiety from the belief that we might miss a unique opportunity by not purchasing the offering.

The impact of scarcity on purchase decisions has been documented in numerous studies. Data collected across multiple product categories show that imposing a quantity limit on sales promotions can boost the likelihood of purchase. For instance, research involving end-aisle displays for canned soups found that introducing a purchase limit of twelve cans increased the average number of cans bought from three to seven.[1]

This outcome challenges traditional economic theories suggesting that sales should decrease when quantity is restricted, as it prevents customers from buying in larger quantities. Contrary to these theories, the observed effect of scarcity shows that the perceived value of a product can increase as its availability decreases, illustrating that scarcity can enhance the desirability of an offering.

Scarcity has been used by many companies to bolster the desirability of their offerings. For example, after introducing the McRib in 1981, McDonald's removed it from the permanent menu and only occasionally brings it back—a tactic that has made the McRib one of the company's most anticipated offerings.[2] Starbucks followed a similar, albeit more systematic, strategy by introducing seasonal items such as its Pumpkin Spice Latte in the fall. The use of scarcity to drive sales is not limited to the food industry. Walt Disney Studios frequently limits the availability of home video releases for some of its feature films, making them available only for a limited time before placing them in the "Disney Vault" until a future re-release.

Scarcity impacts not only everyday choices but also important decisions. Consider the allure of investing with Wall Street financier Bernie Madoff, who orchestrated the largest Ponzi scheme in history. Madoff expertly crafted a sense of scarcity and exclusivity around his investments, portraying them as privileged options not accessible to the general public. This exclusivity amplified the appeal of investing with him, transforming the investment into a status symbol indicative of insider access. The psychology behind this phenomenon is that scarcity tends to increase the perceived value of an item, leading people to believe it represents superior quality or a unique opportunity.

Action Barriers

Nudging customers to act can lead to an interesting paradox: Companies often invest most of their resources in designing and managing action drivers like sales promotions and bonus offerings. However, better results can often be achieved by removing impediments to action. Eliminating obstacles that prevent buyers from acting on their decisions can be more effective than simply increasing the force to push them toward action.

The influence of action barriers on individuals' decisions and behavior can be likened to the concept of friction in physics. Friction is the resistance to motion between two objects. There are two primary types of friction: static and dynamic. Static friction occurs between objects that are not moving relative to one another, while dynamic friction occurs between objects in motion. To ensure greater movement, it is essential to minimize both types of friction.

In marketing, both static and dynamic friction can hinder customer actions. Static friction is more significant at the beginning of the purchase process, potentially preventing a customer from taking the first steps toward acquiring a selected offering. This might include hesitancy to visit a store—whether brick-and-mortar or online—to make the purchase. Dynamic friction, on the other hand, becomes relevant once the purchase process has started and encompasses obstacles encountered during the transaction, such as additional steps required to complete a purchase.

Generally, static friction is stronger than dynamic friction, mirroring the physical principle that initiating motion requires more force than maintaining it. This principle holds true for customer behavior as well: Often, more effort is required to motivate customers to initiate an action than to continue an action they have already started.

Action barriers can be divided into two types: situational and psychological (Figure 3). *Situational barriers* to action typically arise from changes in the value provided by the company's offering and the business environment in which the company operates. Specifically, there are three main types of situational impediments that might force individuals to delay or even reverse their selections: changes in a company's offering, changes in competitive offerings, and changes in the context in which the purchase is made.

Figure 3. Barriers to Action

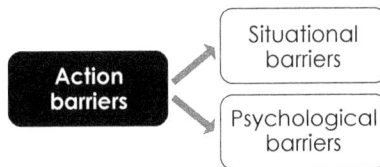

Offering-specific barriers to purchase involve modifications made by the company. These changes can lead customers to discover new information about the performance, price, or availability of their preferred option, potentially making it less attractive and prompting them to reconsider their initial choice. The three most common purchase impediments resulting from adjustments to a company's offering are a reduction in benefits, an escalation in monetary cost, and increased difficulty in obtaining the offering.

One common reason for a decrease in the benefits of an offering is a company's decision to reformulate the offering to reduce costs. This type of decision typically results from the erroneous assumption that the cost reduction will bolster the company's profitability without impacting sales. The decrease in benefits might also be caused by a company's unsuccessful attempts to improve the offering, as well as by an increase in its price after the customer has decided to purchase it.

In addition to changes in the value of an offering, defined by its benefits and costs, purchases might be delayed by changes in the offering's availability. For example, the chosen offering might be sold out, as often happens with many of Apple's newly launched mobile devices. As a result, a consumer who decided to buy Apple's newest iPhone immediately upon its release may end up delaying the purchase due to its limited availability. The intent to purchase the chosen offering might also be swayed by an increase in the time and effort required to acquire it. For instance, a customer who has decided to purchase a bulky item from a warehouse store like Costco might reconsider after discovering that the store does not offer delivery service.

In addition to changes in a company's own offerings, another impediment to purchase involves changes in the competitive landscape. A customer may initially select a particular product but later choose an alternative after discovering a new option not previously considered or after learning more about the initially rejected options. Since the perceived value of an offering is often judged in comparison to other available alternatives, an increase in the attractiveness of competing options—either new or improved—diminishes the likelihood that customers will follow through with their initial choice.

Purchase decisions can also be hindered by idiosyncratic factors unique to an individual's circumstances. These typically include changes in the resources—time, money, and physical and mental energy—needed to acquire the chosen offering. For instance, a customer with limited time may opt for an offering that requires less time to purchase. Financial constraints, such as unexpected economic hardship or the lack of readily available payment methods—cash, credit card, or a payment app—also serve as significant barriers. Additionally, purchases might be impeded by restricted access to the offering, such as distance from physical stores or a reluctance to make purchases online.

Beyond situational factors, buyers' decisions are also influenced by psychological barriers that stem from their perceptions and actions toward an offering. These barriers can be categorized into three groups: (1) cognitive barriers, related to uncertainty about the offering and its value; (2) emotional barriers, which include negative feelings associated with the offering; and (3) implementational barriers posing logistical challenges in acquiring the offering (Figure 4).

Figure 4. Psychological Barriers to Action

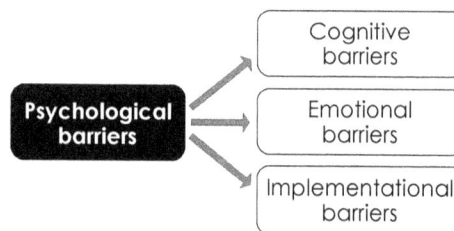

Cognitive barriers arise from uncertainties buyers may have about their decisions, such as: "Will the chosen offering perform as expected?" "Do I really need the benefits of this offering?" "Did I make the right choice among the available options?" Emotional barriers, on the other hand, are rooted in concerns about the decision maker's affective state following the decision: "Will I regret my choice after making the purchase?" Implementational barriers revolve around the practicalities of making the purchase: "How do I make my choice a reality?" "Is the chosen offering worth the resources required to acquire it?" These three categories of barriers to action are explored in greater depth in the following sections.

Cognitive Barriers

Cognitive barriers stem from uncertainties concerning the functional aspects of the offering. There are three main types of cognitive barriers: performance-uncertainty barriers, which involve a lack of clarity about how the product or service works; preference-uncertainty barriers, which arise from uncertainty about one's own needs and desires; and decision-uncertainty barriers, which reflect the decision maker's confidence in having made a good choice. We discuss these three types of uncertainty barriers and strategies to overcome them in more detail below.

Performance Uncertainty

Performance uncertainty reflects buyers' doubts about whether the chosen offering will perform as expected. The key question buyers might ask is: "Will the chosen offering perform as expected?" The answer to this question largely hinges on how visible the benefits and costs of the offering are to these buyers.

Performance uncertainty can be a key barrier to purchase because not all aspects of a company's offering are immediately observable to customers. Certain attributes carry more uncertainty, making their benefits harder to evaluate compared to attributes that are relatively transparent. Based on the observability of their benefits, attributes can be divided into three categories: search, experience, and credence (Figure 5).[3]

Figure 5. Performance Uncertainty as a Function of the Observability of Benefits

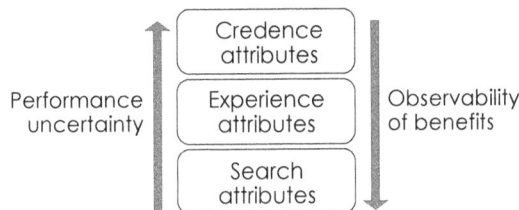

- *Search attributes* are associated with the least amount of uncertainty and are typically identifiable through inspection before purchase. For example, the size of a toothpaste tube, the color of a car, and the location of a restaurant are search attributes.

- *Experience* attributes involve higher uncertainty and are usually discovered through consumption. For instance, the flavor of a toothpaste, the comfort of a car, and the taste of a restaurant meal are considered experience attributes because their quality cannot be determined just by observing them.

- *Credence* attributes have the highest level of uncertainty as their true performance remains unknown even after consumption. Examples include the cavity prevention benefits of a toothpaste, the safety of a car, and the potential side effects of a drug. These are credence attributes because customers cannot objectively assess their performance, even after use.

The distinction among these three types of attributes is crucial due to the varying levels of uncertainty they present to buyers. Search attributes are transparent and carry the least uncertainty. In contrast, experience attributes are harder to communicate because informing buyers about the benefits is not sufficient; they need to use the product to fully understand its advantages. Therefore, for products characterized by experience attributes, performance uncertainty can be reduced by offering buyers firsthand experiences to appreciate the company's offering. Common tools for providing such experiences include product samples and free trials.

Finally, credence attributes carry the highest level of performance uncertainty because their benefits cannot be directly observed or compared. Evaluating these attributes requires significant consumer trust. This trust can be cultivated by developing a strong brand that supports the company's claims about the performance of its offerings. Additionally, trust can be reinforced by providing guarantees and warranties that back up the promised performance of the offering on these unobservable attributes.

Performance uncertainty is often heightened by the mental shortcuts customers use when making decisions. For example, customers tend to focus on search attributes because they are immediately observable, while they might overlook experience and credence attributes due to their less obvious or intangible nature. To counteract this, an effective strategy involves using storytelling combined with social proof, such as credible testimonials endorsing the product's performance. This approach not only clarifies the benefits of the offering but also engages the customer's imagination, fostering a deeper understanding and appreciation of its advantages.

Preference Uncertainty

Preference uncertainty indicates how confident individuals are that they will appreciate the benefits of their chosen option. The key question they might consider is "Do I really need the benefits of this offering?" The answer largely depends on how well-defined their preferences are.

Unlike performance uncertainty, which arises from the possibility that the offering might not fulfill its promise, preference uncertainty reflects customers' difficulty in determining how relevant the benefits of the offering are to them. Thus, even if they were reasonably confident at the time of purchase, their preferences could change over time, making the value of the offering less clear. One reason for this shift in perceived attractiveness is the focusing illusion: When making decisions, we concentrate on the benefits of the chosen option and greatly exaggerate the difference it might make to our quality of life. As a result, we often overstate the future value we expect from the benefits of the chosen option (a detailed discussion on the focusing illusion can be found in Chapter 3).

The problem with overestimating the importance of the offering's benefits is that this perception does not last. Once we make our selection, our attention inevitably shifts elsewhere, diminishing the perceived importance of the benefits associated with the chosen offering. Additionally, while the act of choosing primarily focuses on acquiring the offering and tends to highlight its benefits over its costs, once the choice is made, the costs—whether in terms of time, money, or effort—may become more prominent. This increased visibility of the costs, combined with the decreased emphasis on the benefits, can lead us to question the wisdom of our choice.

Preference uncertainty may also arise from a diminished emphasis on certain needs that were more prominent at the time of choice. This reassessment is particularly common following impulsive decisions, where the benefits of the chosen option were not thoroughly weighed against its costs. As time passes, the initial appeal of the benefits may fade, making the overlooked costs more apparent and significant, raising doubts about the wisdom of the choice.

Consider the purchase of a vacation ownership after a persuasive sales presentation at a resort in an exotic location. Consumers might initially be captivated by the allure of having a wonderful vacation spot every year, neglecting to fully consider the associated costs. However, as the initial excitement about vacationing in that exotic locale wanes, the reality of various costs—such as the opportunity cost of the initial investment, annual maintenance fees, and the necessity to plan vacations well in advance—becomes apparent, leading to second thoughts about the purchase decision. This is why many salespeople try to close the purchase while buyers are still excited about the prospect of owning a timeshare.

Choice Uncertainty

Choice uncertainty reflects the level of confidence buyers have in their decision, specifically whether they have selected the best option among all available alternatives. The key question on their minds at this point is "Did I make the right choice?"

Choice uncertainty is similar to preference uncertainty in that it reflects individuals' assessment of their ability to choose an option that meets their needs. However, it diverges from preference uncertainty in its focus. While preference uncertainty concerns how much individuals feel they need the benefits provided by their chosen option, choice uncertainty revolves around their confidence in having made the best selection among the available options. Therefore, choice uncertainty does not question the importance of the need the chosen offering fulfills but rather focuses on whether the selected option is the most suitable among all alternatives.

Choice uncertainty is closely tied to cognitive dissonance, a psychological discomfort that arises when making compromises during decision making. The theory of cognitive dissonance, introduced in the 1950s by American psychologist Leon Festinger, suggests that individuals are motivated to maintain harmony among their beliefs, attitudes, and behaviors. Inconsistencies among these elements result in *cognitive dissonance*, a state of psychological discomfort experienced when a person holds conflicting beliefs, ideas, or values simultaneously. Consequently, individuals seek to reduce this discomfort and restore cognitive consistency.[4]

A classic example of cognitive dissonance can be seen in individuals who continue to smoke, fully aware of the health risks associated with smoking. There is a clear conflict between individuals' awareness of the evidence linking smoking to serious health issues and their persistence in this behavior. To ease the discomfort caused by this dissonance, smokers may resort to a range of justifications or rationalizations. For instance, a smoker might minimize the risks associated with smoking ("It won't happen to me"), highlight the difficulty of quitting due to addiction ("I've tried quitting, but I can't"), or focus on the perceived benefits of smoking, such as stress relief or social advantages ("It helps me relax" or "All my friends smoke").

Choice often leads to cognitive dissonance because most options have both pros and cons, making it uncommon to find a clear best choice. As a result, once buyers have made a decision, they must reconcile the drawbacks of their chosen option while also recognizing the benefits they missed by not selecting the alternatives. This awareness can lead to post-decision dissonance, as buyers wrestle with the imperfections of their choice, and the appeal of the options they passed over. This dissonance can create uncertainty, raising doubts about whether they made the best decision. Consequently, buyers may delay their purchase, reconsider their choice, or even select a different option.

There are three primary strategies for resolving cognitive dissonance. The first is to change one of the conflicting beliefs, attitudes, or behaviors. For example, a smoker who understands the health risks of smoking might decide to quit. The second strategy is to acquire new information that reduces the dissonance. For instance, a smoker might focus on studies suggesting potential weight loss benefits from smoking or find articles that question the strong link between smoking and cancer, thereby easing their discomfort. The third approach is to downplay the importance of the conflicting beliefs or behaviors. A smoker might rationalize their habit by thinking that life is short and should be enjoyed, or by believing that smoking just one cigarette a day isn't a serious health risk.

Cognitive dissonance can vary in intensity, primarily depending on two factors. The first is the relative attractiveness of the options: The closer the options are in desirability, the stronger the dissonance experienced. When we face choices that are similarly appealing and involve trade-offs between benefits and costs, we are more likely to experience post-decision conflict due to the benefits of the rejected options. For example, choosing an SUV over a convertible might lead to discomfort from missing out on the pleasure of driving with the top down.

The second factor influencing the strength of cognitive dissonance is the importance of the decision. The more important the decision, the greater the dissonance. This is because the consequences of making the wrong choice are more severe, intensifying the discomfort of missing out on the advantages of the unchosen options. In contrast, for less critical choices like selecting a type of chewing gum, snack, or soft drink, the consequences of a less-than-ideal choice are minimal, as is the resulting dissonance.

Emotional Barriers

In addition to cognitive barriers, the gap between choice and purchase can also be influenced by emotional factors. These emotional barriers, often stemming from negative feelings associated with the offering, can either amplify cognitive barriers—such as performance, preference, and choice uncertainty—or exist independently of them. The most potent emotional barrier to action is anticipated regret.

Anticipated Regret as a Barrier to Action

Anticipated regret is a forward-looking emotion that reflects the regret we expect to feel in the future based on the decisions we make today. It represents our predictions about our future emotional responses to our current choices, asking "How will I feel about this decision in the future?"

Anticipated regret is distinct from the traditional form of post-decision regret commonly known as buyer's remorse. While post-decision regret is a backward-looking emotion tied to decisions that have led to unfavorable outcomes and a sense of personal responsibility for these outcomes, anticipated regret is forward looking. It involves buyers predicting the regret they might feel in the future as a result of their current decisions. This form of regret reflects how buyers *expect to feel* once they acquire the offering. In this context, anticipated regret is often described as a "prospective emotion about the future past."[5]

Anticipated regret is closely tied to our tendency for counterfactual thinking, which involves imagining scenarios contrary to what has actually occurred. This type of thinking envisions a past that never happened by considering alternative outcomes to events that have already taken place. Rooted in the concept of "what might have been," counterfactual thinking contrasts imagined possibilities with the actual state of affairs.[6]

Counterfactual thoughts are inherently evaluative rather than merely speculative. These imagined alternatives are judged as either superior (upward counterfactuals) or inferior (downward counterfactuals) to what actually occurred. Upward counterfactuals, where we envision better scenarios than the actual outcomes, are more common, especially after decisions that result in negative consequences. This tendency often triggers "what if...?" scenarios that imagine the absence of the unfavorable outcome. When these upward counterfactuals are directly related to our own choices, they can lead to negative emotions such as regret, guilt, and blame.

Regret often arises from counterfactual thinking, typically occurring when we encounter an undesirable outcome and start wondering what could have been done differently to achieve a better result. While counterfactual thinking involves "what if...?"

scenarios, regret shifts this to "if only..." considerations, adding a wishful-thinking element to the counterfactual interpretation of reality. Although counterfactual thinking usually looks backward, generating alternatives to past events, it can also apply to future situations. These forward-looking scenarios, known as anticipatory counterfactuals, or "prefactuals," fuel anticipated regret, which can play a significant role in holding us back from taking action.

Action as a Source of Anticipated Regret

Imagine driving to work along your usual route and getting into a car accident. Now, picture deciding to take a new route that day and getting into an accident. In which scenario would you likely experience greater regret? Most people would feel more regret in the second scenario.

This example highlights the general principle that actions often lead to greater regret than inactions. Choosing a new route—an action—deviates from the status quo, which tends to amplify feelings of regret. Similarly, an investor who chooses not to switch from one mutual fund to another will likely feel less regret upon learning that the other fund performed better than an investor who made the switch, only to discover later that the original fund outperformed the new one.[7]

The tendency for actions to evoke greater regret than inactions is closely linked to our inclination to generate counterfactual scenarios. Inaction is associated with a single, well-defined outcome—maintaining the status quo—making it relatively easy to imagine and more likely to serve as a reference point in counterfactual thinking. On the other hand, taking action and diverging from the status quo can lead to multiple potential outcomes, making it harder to identify a specific alternative action to consider when generating counterfactual thoughts.[8]

Following this logic, adverse outcomes where the alternative is easy to imagine are more likely to evoke counterfactual thinking than those where the alternative is harder to envision. For instance, a driver who has an accident after taking an alternative route can readily imagine a different course of action: sticking to the usual route. In contrast, a driver who gets into an accident while following their regular route might find it challenging to spontaneously come up with an alternative because multiple other routes exist.

The differences in how we generate counterfactual thoughts for actions versus inactions directly correlate with the level of regret we experience. Unfavorable outcomes resulting from a departure from usual behavior tend to be more regrettable than those that occur due to inaction and sticking to the status quo. The intensity of regret is influenced by both the disparity between the ideal counterfactual outcome and the actual result, and by how easily the counterfactual outcome comes to mind.[9]

Because we engage in counterfactual thinking about both past and future events, we can also experience regret for our anticipated future actions. This anticipated regret can act as a barrier to taking those actions. Given our general preference for maximizing positive outcomes and minimizing negative emotions, we may avoid actions likely to lead to regret over an undesirable outcome. Therefore, understanding and managing the anticipated regret associated with our choices is crucial for bridging the gap between making a decision and acting on it.

Implementational Barriers

In addition to cognitive and emotional factors, a third set of factors that can impede action involves the practicalities of implementing a decision. These implementational barriers make it difficult to translate a decision into action. Specifically, there are two key types of implementational barriers: implementation uncertainty and implementation viability. We discuss these two barriers to action in the following sections.

Implementation Uncertainty

Implementation uncertainty arises from a lack of clarity about the logistics required to execute a decision that has already been made. At this stage, the key question becomes "How do I make my choice a reality?" When making a choice, the focus is typically on the value of different options and their relative benefits and costs. However, once the decision is made, attention shifts to the practical steps needed to bring that choice to life. For instance, the decision to see a particular movie must be followed by specific actions such as finding a nearby theater where the movie is playing, purchasing tickets, and driving to the theater.

Implementing a decision can become a barrier to action when there is no clear path to translate that choice into a specific set of actions. This implementation uncertainty is further complicated by the challenge of integrating new behavioral intentions into our established habits and daily routines. Consequently, even relatively minor implementation challenges can act as surprisingly strong inhibitors, preventing us from taking the necessary steps to follow through on our decisions.

Consider Genentech's experience in promoting its new drug Xolair. Clinical studies demonstrated that Xolair was highly effective in preventing asthma attacks, and the drug was well regarded by both medical professionals and industry experts. Confident in the drug's potential, Genentech invested millions in promoting Xolair's health benefits to physicians. However, despite the clear medical advantages and the company's extensive advertising efforts, adoption rates remained low.

An analysis of the situation revealed an unexpected challenge. The problem wasn't that doctors were unaware of Xolair's benefits; they understood them quite well. The real challenge was that Xolair required a different delivery method. Unlike the more common pills or inhalers, Xolair was administered via an intravenous drip—a process unfamiliar to many physicians who would be responsible for administering it in their offices. Once this barrier was identified, the solution became clear: Instead of continuing to emphasize the drug's health benefits, Genentech shifted its focus to educating doctors on how to administer it.[10]

The critical role that implementation uncertainty plays in impeding action highlights the need to identify strategies for streamlining the implementation of a chosen course of action. One effective approach is to raise awareness of the specific steps required to achieve the desired outcome. This is precisely what Genentech did once it recognized the true barrier to Xolair's adoption. Numerous studies have shown that clearly outlining implementation steps can be more effective than simply highlighting the benefits of the outcome itself.

For example, in one study, students at a large university were asked to report what they ate at the university cafeteria over a two-week period. Midway through the study, they were shown a slogan promoting the consumption of healthy options like fruits and vegetables. One group saw a general slogan advocating for a healthy lifestyle: "Live the healthy way, eat five fruits and veggies a day." The other group was presented with a more specific action-oriented slogan: "Each and every dining hall tray needs five fruits and veggies a day." Surprisingly, while participants found the first slogan more appealing, it did nothing to increase fruit and vegetable consumption. In contrast, the second slogan led to a significant increase in the consumption of healthy options.[11]

In addition to raising awareness of the specific actions needed to achieve a desired outcome, implementation uncertainty can be reduced by developing an explicit implementation plan. Research has shown that taking small initial steps, known as "channel factors," can effectively guide behavior toward acting on a decision. The term "channel factors," coined by psychologist Kurt Lewin, refers to these initial actions that create a pathway (or channel) for implementing a particular behavior. Much like the path a river carves as snow melts in the spring, channel factors act as a catalyst, directing and focusing actions in a specific direction.[12]

The Folgers campaign launched in the early '80s, featuring the tagline "The Best Part of Waking Up Is Folgers in Your Cup," is a prime example of forming implementation intentions in advertising. This campaign became one of the most recognizable in American culture, not only for creating top-of-mind awareness about Folgers but also for how it seamlessly integrated the brand into consumers' daily routines. By linking the everyday activity of waking up with the brand-specific action of enjoying a cup of Folgers coffee, the campaign transformed a simple morning habit into a memorable ritual for many households. This strategic association between an everyday event and a specific brand action embedded Folgers into the daily lives of consumers, illustrating the power of connecting brand messaging with daily habits and rituals.

The impact of forming implementation intentions is further illustrated by a study conducted during the Democratic presidential primary. In this study, a large sample of voters was divided into three groups, each receiving different information before election day. The first group received a standard message, "Get out the vote!," reminding them of the election and their civic duty to vote. The second group received the same message but was also asked, "Do you intend to vote?" The third group received the same message as the second group, along with three follow-up questions designed to help them develop an implementation plan: "What time do you expect to head to the polls?" "Where do you expect to be coming from?" and "What do you think you'll be doing before you head out?"[13]

The results showed that the standard reminder had virtually no effect on voter turnout; in fact, it led to a 0.7% decrease. The second message, which asked voters about their intention to vote, resulted in a 1.1% increase in turnout—demonstrating a self-prophecy effect, where asking people about their intentions can increase the likelihood of them following through.[14] The third message, which encouraged voters to form implementation intentions by planning their voting-related activities in advance, had the most significant impact, increasing turnout by 9.1%—a substantial effect that could meaningfully influence an election's outcome.[15]

The results from this and many other studies show that people are more likely to act on their decisions if they create explicit implementation intentions. Articulating the *when*, *where*, and *how* of following through on a specific decision helps create mental links between a future situation and the intended behavior.[16] These mental links are often represented as "if situation X, then action Y." However, forming implementation intentions does not, by itself, motivate people to act. Rather, these intentions aim to reduce the uncertainty associated with their future actions and help fit the desired behavior into their daily routine. Creating implementation plans can facilitate making decisions a reality and close the choice–purchase gap.

Implementation Viability

Beyond the uncertainty involved in executing a decision, buyers' actions can be complicated by unexpected obstacles encountered during the purchase process. These challenges can introduce doubts about the viability of the initial choice, potentially leading to delays or even a reversal of the decision. At this stage, individuals might find themselves asking a critical question: "Is the required action worth the resources I have to expend?"

Implementation viability refers to the extent to which the resources needed to acquire an offering are justified by its benefits. Any unexpected increase in the effort, time, or money needed to obtain the chosen product or service can lead to a delay or even a cancellation of the purchase. Therefore, a key challenge for companies is to streamline the purchase process, eliminating any friction that buyers might encounter during the transaction.

One source of friction during the purchase process is companies' desire to collect as much information as possible from customers before they make a purchase. Managers often justify this approach by arguing that contacting customers after the purchase is logistically more complex and likely to yield lower response rates. However, what many companies overlook is that this unexpected requirement to complete a purchase can backfire, leading customers to postpone or reconsider their decision altogether.

Consider the customer shopping experience at Harry's, one of the largest online companies selling shaving products. The purchase process is quite simple, requiring shoppers to answer just three questions: (a) How often do you shave? (with 3 options), (b) Would you like to add grooming products? (with 2 offerings), and (c) Choose your razor color (from 4 colors). After answering these questions, shoppers can immediately place an order for their chosen razor and a set of blades, typically priced around $5. This streamlined approach is designed to minimize friction, making the purchase process quick and easy.

Now compare this with the approach used by Unilever's Dollar Shave Club, which presents shoppers with a more detailed set of questions: (a) What do you shave? (8 options), (b) How often do you shave? (4 options), (c) Any problems when you shave? (7 options), (d) Do you have or are you worried about any of these issues on your face? (8 options), (e) Describe the hair on your head (5 options), (f) Do you use a body wash or bar soap to get clean? (4 options), and (g) What type of deodorant do you use? (4 options). After answering these seven questions, shoppers are given the option to place an order for a six-item bundle, typically priced at over $40.

Unilever's decision to gather extensive information about shoppers' shaving behavior significantly complicates the purchase process. First, shoppers must navigate through seven questions, each offering a wide range of options, which can feel overwhelming. Additionally, the personal nature of some questions may cause discomfort, particularly for first-time customers. Furthermore, the initial expectation set by the company's name—implying affordability and setting one dollar as a reference point—stands in stark contrast to the reality of being presented with a much pricier bundle at the end of this lengthy and complex process.

Complicating the purchase process often results in the abandoned shopping cart problem. Many companies discover that shoppers fill their carts with desired products only to abandon them before completing the purchase. In brick-and-mortar stores, a common reason for this is the long wait at the cashier or the realization that the total cost is higher than expected. While online retailers don't face the issue of checkout lines, one might assume that the purchase process would be more streamlined. However, the reality is quite the opposite: The abandoned shopping cart problem tends to be more prevalent among online retailers.

Two main factors contribute to the common occurrence of shoppers not finalizing their purchases with online retailers. First, the minimal effort required to add an item to a virtual shopping cart often leads to a lower commitment to complete the purchase. The second, and perhaps more significant, reason is the tendency of some companies to complicate the buying process in an effort to collect more information about their customers. While this approach is intended to inform marketing strategies, it can be shortsighted and counterproductive. By making excessive demands for personal information, companies risk deterring potential buyers from completing their purchases.

A powerful example illustrating the abandoned shopping cart problem, its cause, and solution involves a large electronics retailer (think of Best Buy).[17] The company noticed that after adding items to their cart, a rather large number of their customers never completed the purchase. At first glance, the problem did not seem to be the complexity of the checkout form. After all, it involved only two fields, two buttons, and a link. The fields were Email Address and Password; the buttons were Login and Register, and the link was Forgot Password. With such a simple setup, how could there be a problem?

To understand the problem, put yourself in a customer's shoes. You have just filled your cart with items you like, and after pressing the checkout button, you arrive at the checkout form. Since this is your first experience with the company, you're still unsure whether you will make another purchase from this retailer. All you want to do is pay for the items in your cart. Instead, you are confronted with a form that requires you to provide personal information and register with the company, as if you are already committed to becoming a loyal customer.

Naturally, this situation led to frustration among many shoppers who had no intention of forming a long-term relationship with the company at that moment. Ironically, the issue was not that shoppers were unwilling to provide personal information; after all, they still needed to provide their name, shipping address, and credit card details to complete the purchase. Many did not even mind sharing their email address, as it helped them track the delivery of their order.

The real problem was the requirement to create a password at the very beginning of the checkout process. Some shoppers could not remember if it was their first time on the site, while others grew increasingly frustrated after repeatedly failing to match the correct email and password combination. The company's data revealed that 45% of all customers had multiple registrations, with some having as many as ten. Additionally, around 160,000 shoppers requested new passwords daily, but 75% of them never attempted to complete their purchase after making the request. This unnecessary friction at checkout was a significant factor in the high rate of abandoned shopping carts.[18]

Once the problem was identified, the solution was surprisingly simple. The company replaced the Register button with a Continue button and added a message: "You do not need to create an account to make purchases on our site. Simply click Continue to proceed to checkout. To make your future purchases even faster, you can create an account during checkout." This change made registration optional rather than a barrier to purchase. After entering all the necessary information to complete the purchase, the only extra step needed to register was to enter a password. At this point, shoppers could consider the benefits of registering, with little downside. Moreover, having just completed a purchase, they were likely to feel more committed to the company, making them more thoughtful in choosing a password they would remember.

The redesign was highly effective, leading to a 45% increase in the number of customers completing their purchases and a $300 million boost in online revenues. And all it took was changing one button. Of course, not every problem has such a straightforward solution; some issues require more complex efforts. However, to arrive at the simplest and most effective solution, a company must first clearly identify the problem and its root cause. Without knowing the cause of a problem, it is virtually impossible to design an effective solution. By identifying and addressing implementational barriers that disrupt the buying process, companies can better ensure that customer choices lead to actual purchases.

SUMMARY

Many purchase decisions are not immediately followed by action; some involve a delay between the decision and the actual purchase, while others never lead to a purchase at all. Behavioral nudging seeks to encourage action and close the gap between choosing and buying.

Nudging can prompt decision makers to act on their choices through two main strategies: enhancing the motivations that drive customers toward making a purchase and eliminating the obstacles that prevent them from acquiring their chosen option. These two nudging strategies—creating action drivers and removing action barriers—along with their key components are illustrated in Figure 6.

Figure 6. Action Drivers and Action Barriers

Action drivers motivate individuals to purchase the chosen offering. There are two basic ways to incite action: by highlighting the unmet need and by making the chosen option more attractive. Prominence is increased by turning indifference into a problem that needs to be addressed, often through monetary incentives such as coupons, discounts, and price reductions. Attractiveness is enhanced by increasing perceived benefits, often via sales promotions such as premiums, prizes, and contests, as well as by creating a sense of scarcity about the offering.

Action barriers are obstacles that prevent buyers from acting on their decisions and purchasing the chosen offering. There are two types of action barriers: *situational barriers*, which involve changes in a company's offering, competitive offerings, or the context in which the purchase is made; and *psychological barriers*, which deal with how individuals think about and act toward the offering. Psychological barriers, in turn, can be divided into three main categories: cognitive, emotional, and implementational.

Cognitive barriers arise from uncertainty associated with an offering and can be categorized into three main types. *Performance uncertainty* refers to the degree of confidence individuals have that the chosen option will meet their expectations. Performance uncertainty depends on the type of attributes describing the choice options—search, experience, and credence. *Preference uncertainty* reflects how convinced people are that they will enjoy the benefits of their choice in the future. *Choice uncertainty* involves the confidence individuals have in selecting the best option among alternatives. It is closely related to cognitive dissonance—a state of unease arising from the trade-offs made to reach a decision. The closer the options are in their attractiveness and the more consequential the decision, the greater the dissonance.

Emotional barriers are tied to the negative feelings associated with an action or decision. One of the strongest emotional barriers is anticipated regret, a forward-looking emotion where people imagine the regret they might feel in the future about the decisions they are currently making. Anticipated regret is closely linked to counterfactual thinking, where individuals mentally create alternative outcomes for events that have already occurred. Undesirable outcomes that arise from straying from a normal course of behavior are often more regretted than those that result from inaction and sticking with the status quo. The intensity of regret depends on how large the gap is between the desired alternative outcome and what actually happened, as well as how easily the alternative outcome comes to mind.

Implementational barriers stem from the logistical challenges of acquiring a product or service and can be divided into two main types: implementation uncertainty and implementation viability. *Implementation uncertainty* refers to the difficulty of finding a clear path to turn a decision into action, often compounded by the need to integrate the purchase into existing behavioral habits. This uncertainty can be reduced by creating a detailed implementation plan that specifies when, where, and how to follow through on the decision. *Implementation viability*, on the other hand, concerns whether the resources required—such as effort, time, and money—are justified by the offering's benefits. Any unexpected increase in these resources can lead to delays or a decision not to purchase at all. The key to reducing implementation friction is streamlining the buying process to provide the path of least resistance for individuals to act on their choices.

KEY TAKEAWAYS

Mind the choice–purchase gap. Choices do not always result in an instant purchase.

Identify the key action drivers and barriers to action. The choice–purchase gap can be closed by both creating a push and removing friction.

Reduce uncertainty. Preference uncertainty, performance uncertainty, and decision uncertainty are common barriers to action.

Minimize regret. Anticipated regret is a powerful emotional state that can derail the purchase process.

Formulate an implementation plan. People are more likely to follow up on their choices if they have a clear path to implementing their decisions.

SPOTLIGHT: THE PSYCHOLOGY OF PERSUASION

The psychology of persuasion explores how people are influenced to alter their attitudes, beliefs, and behaviors through social interactions. At the heart of this field are key insights into social influence and persuasive techniques. Drawing from this knowledge, Robert Cialdini, author of the bestselling book *Influence*, identifies six fundamental principles of persuasive communication.[19] These principles, often termed "weapons of influence," include reciprocity, consistency, social proof, liking, authority, and scarcity.

Reciprocity. The principle of reciprocity suggests that we naturally feel compelled to return favors or gifts, a concept well documented in social psychology. For example, one study found that diners are more likely to leave a larger tip if the waiter includes a small gift — such as a mint, candy, or fortune cookie — with the bill. Moreover, the tipping behavior scaled with the size of the gift: Offering two candies instead of one more than doubled the tip left by diners.[20] Receiving a gift creates a sense of obligation to reciprocate. The more personal and unexpected the gift, the stronger the desire to return the favor. This principle is one reason companies give out free samples; beyond simply allowing customers to experience their product, it often creates a subtle pressure to make a purchase in return. Reciprocity also plays a role in the exchange of favors, as seen in the "door-in-the-face" technique, where a large request is followed by a smaller one after the initial request is declined. This strategy is effective because concessions are perceived as favors that need to be reciprocated, thereby increasing the likelihood that the smaller request will be granted.

Consistency. The principle of consistency highlights a fundamental human tendency to act in ways that align with our prior commitments, reflecting a deep-seated desire for consistency in our actions. Psychologists have identified this drive for consistency as a key motivator in human behavior, indicating that we are more likely to agree to a significant request if we have already consented to a smaller, related one. For example, a study found that people who agreed to place a small postcard in their front window supporting a "Drive Safely" campaign were four times more likely to later agree to erect a large wooden sign on their lawn for the same cause. This phenomenon is effectively used in the "foot-in-the-door" technique, where agreeing to a minor request sets the stage for compliance with a more substantial, related request.

Consensus. The consensus principle, also known as the *social proof* principle, suggests that when we are uncertain about how to act, we often look to others for cues on how to respond. This behavior stems from our need to make decisions that are validated by the choices of our peers, using their actions as a heuristic, or shortcut, to navigate ambiguity. Social proof is particularly influential when the observed behaviors come from people who are perceived as similar to us. We are more likely to imitate the actions of those we identify with, as their behavior seems more relevant to our own situation. In marketing, the consensus principle is frequently applied by promoting products as "bestselling," "most popular," or "highest in customer satisfaction." Such endorsements serve as powerful social proof, signaling to potential buyers that a product is a good choice by leveraging their natural inclination to conform to the group's consensus.

Liking. The principle of liking is based on the idea that people are more likely to agree with and say "yes" to individuals they like. This preference is influenced by our tendency to like those who are similar to us, those who compliment us, and those who share common goals and cooperate with us. For example, research shows that people who discover commonalities with one another are nearly twice as likely to reach an agreement in negotiations compared to those who do not explore their similarities. Additional studies also suggest that we are more inclined to help those who resemble us, whether in appearance, attire, or behavior. This principle is closely linked to the "halo effect," where a positive impression in one area leads to positive assumptions in other areas. For instance, physically attractive individuals are often perceived as having other favorable qualities, such as kindness, intelligence, and honesty. Similarly, when we find someone likable—whether due to shared interests, compliments, or collaborative efforts—we tend to develop an overall positive impression of them, making us more inclined to agree with their requests or opinions.

Authority. The authority principle is rooted in the idea that we tend to trust credible experts and are inclined to follow the directives of authority figures with little question. This predisposition to obey authority is essential for maintaining societal order. For example, a request from someone in a uniform or business attire is typically met with greater compliance than one from a person dressed casually. Medical professionals can boost patient adherence to treatment plans by visibly displaying their qualifications, such as diplomas, in their offices. Even luxury items like designer clothing, extravagant cars, and fine jewelry can convey a sense of authority, using social cues to influence behavior.

Scarcity. The scarcity principle is based on the idea that items perceived as rare or in limited supply are often more valued than those that are abundant. This principle operates on the belief that the possibility of missing out on an opportunity increases our desire for it. Emphasizing the exclusivity and limited availability of a product or service can significantly heighten its attractiveness. One common application of this principle is the "limited quantity" approach, where buyers are informed that a particular item is in short supply and may not be available for long. Another tactic involves telling potential buyers that a sought-after item has just sold out, but they might still be able to secure one if they promptly commit to the purchase.

THE CX CANVAS: NUDGING CUSTOMERS TO ACT

When there is a delay between a customer's choice and their purchase, a company may need to encourage them to act. Designing such a "nudge" strategy involves two key steps: (1) analyzing the factors that could either promote or hinder the purchase, and (2) developing a strategy to motivate customers to make the purchase (Figure 7).

Figure 7. Nudging Customers to Act: The Big Picture

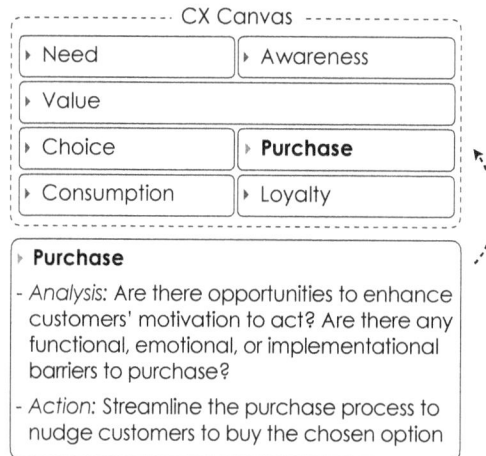

The development of a nudge strategy starts with identifying the key factors that influence customers' actions, including those that facilitate and those that act as barriers to purchase. Here, a manager should ask the following questions:

- *Are there opportunities to enhance customers' motivation to act?* This question aims to establish whether there are unexplored action drivers that could motivate customers to move forward with the purchase.

- *Are there cognitive barriers to purchase?* This question assesses customers' level of uncertainty regarding the functional aspects of the offering, including uncertainty about its performance, their own preferences, and the wisdom of their choice.

- *Are there emotional barriers to purchase?* This question evaluates customer emotions related to the choice process and the chosen option, particularly sources of negative affect, such as anticipated regret, that can impede purchase.

- *Are there implementational barriers to purchase?* This question identifies logistical factors that hinder translating choice into action. Key barriers here include implementation uncertainty, reflecting a lack of clarity about the logistics of purchasing the chosen offering, and implementation viability, arising from unexpected obstacles in the purchase process.

The purpose of this analysis is to determine the cause(s) of a potential choice–purchase gap and develop an action plan to nudge customers toward purchasing the chosen option. There are four potential impediments to purchase, each requiring a distinct course of action:

- *Insufficient motivation to act*. Despite choosing an option, customers may not act on their decision due to a lack of sufficient incentive to break from the status quo. The company's goal here is to motivate customers to purchase the chosen offering by making their unmet need more prominent and increasing the attractiveness of the chosen option.

- *Cognitive barriers to purchase*. Customers' desire to acquire the chosen offering can be impeded by uncertainty about its functional aspects, uncertainty about their own preferences, and uncertainty about whether they have selected the best possible option. The company's goal here is to reduce these cognitive barriers by minimizing customers' uncertainty and affirming their choice.

- *Emotional barriers to purchase*. Customers can experience negative emotions related to how they expect to feel after purchasing the chosen offering. The company's goal is to reduce this negative affect, typically by minimizing the regret customers anticipate experiencing after making the purchase.

- *Implementational barriers to purchase*. Unexpected obstacles can emerge while customers try to purchase the chosen option. These obstacles often involve uncertainty about how to acquire the chosen option and unforeseen impediments that complicate the purchase. To remove these barriers, a company must streamline the purchase process, making it intuitive and minimizing the effort required to acquire the offering.

The four challenges to purchasing the chosen offering and the corresponding company actions are summarized in Figure 8. The first challenge—insufficient motivation to act—often requires providing additional incentives to overcome the inertia of the status quo and encourage customers to follow through with their purchase decision. The remaining three challenges, which involve cognitive, emotional, and implementation barriers, necessitate identifying and removing various sources of friction that customers might encounter when attempting to turn their choices into reality.

Figure 8. Nudging Customers to Act: The Action Plan

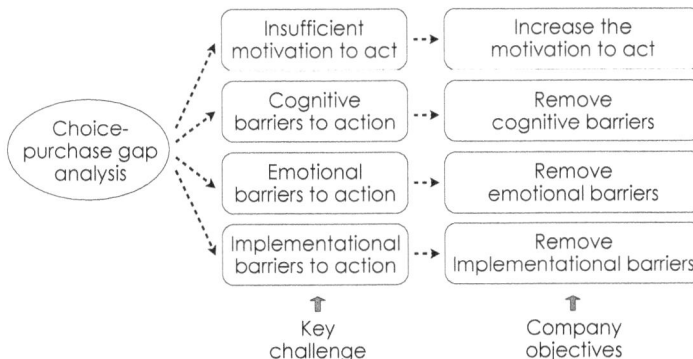

Consider the challenges that mobile phone manufacturers like Apple, Samsung, and Xiaomi face when trying to convince customers to upgrade to the latest version of their devices. One key challenge is that some customers who have already decided to upgrade are slow to act on their decision. An analysis of customer intent might reveal that some procrastinate because they are satisfied with their current phone and do not feel a pressing need to upgrade. Others may have second thoughts about whether the new model offers significant improvements over their current one, whether it will meet their future needs, or whether they have overlooked a potentially better option. Additionally, some consumers might delay their purchase out of fear that they will regret it if the price of the chosen phone drops in the future. Finally, some may have attempted to buy the phone but were deterred by long lines at the retail store.

After identifying the reasons for this delay, the next step is to nudge customers toward completing their purchase. The strategy should address the specific barriers to action. For customers who delay because they do not see an immediate benefit in upgrading, the company could offer time-limited incentives to encourage prompt action. For those concerned about the phone's performance, featuring testimonials from other customers or endorsements from celebrities could provide reassurance. For customers worried about securing the best price, a low-price guarantee could alleviate their concerns by promising to refund the difference if the price drops. Finally, for those who are delayed by logistical issues, the company should streamline the purchase process, making it fast, easy, and perhaps even enjoyable.

CHAPTER SEVEN

ORCHESTRATING THE CONSUMPTION EXPERIENCE

When we use price, product, placement, and promotion techniques, people call it marketing. When we orchestrate a consumer experience that delights, people call it magic.

—Steve Jobs

The consumption experience is the culmination of a customer's interaction with a company's offering. This journey begins when customers identify a need and start searching for ways to fulfill it. They explore the available options, assess the benefits and costs, and choose the most appealing one to purchase. The next phase is the actual consumption of the product or service, where customers experience its benefits firsthand (Figure 1). This experience is crucial in shaping the value customers derive from the offering and their overall satisfaction with it.

Figure 1. The Customer Experience Map: Consuming the Offering

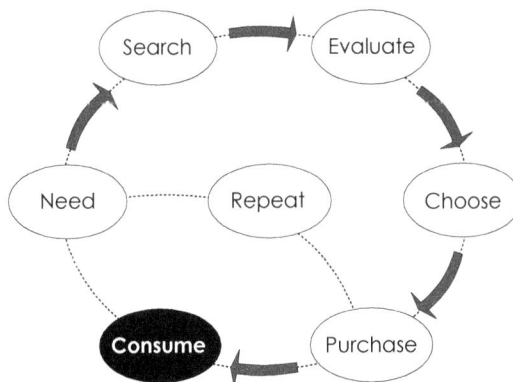

Early models of buyer behavior treated the purchase of an offering as the endpoint of the customer experience. Even today, some companies develop their market strategies with the primary focus on selling their offerings, without adequately considering how customers will interact with and experience those offerings after the purchase.

This narrow view of creating customer value overlooks the significant impact that the consumption experience has on customer satisfaction and, ultimately, on the company's ability to cultivate a loyal customer base.

Designing meaningful consumption experiences is the key ingredient in creating customer value. To achieve this, a company must understand how customers interact with its offering and how these interactions provide customer benefits. Consider the following questions:

- You are in charge of the marketing activities for a major Hollywood studio and need to develop a communication plan for the release of a new movie, which you hope will be a blockbuster. The movie is still in the early stages of filming and is expected to be ready for release in two years. Would you invest resources in promoting the movie well in advance, or focus your entire budget on promoting the movie during the weeks leading up to its theater release?

- You are managing a popular soft drink brand and are charged with increasing sales volume. Internal company research shows that most of your target customers are aware of your product and like it. What are the different ways in which you can encourage your customers to consume more of it?

- You are advising a real estate developer who specializes in building custom, high-end single-family homes. The developer wants to make the interior spaces of the houses more appealing to buyers. What should the developer do to make their designs more attractive to customers?

- You are the founder of a video game startup, and your goal is to ensure that the game your team is working on is "sticky" and keeps players engaged over time. What guidance would you offer to the game's software engineers to achieve this? Why are these recommendations crucial for long-term player engagement?

- You are advising a medical device company that is developing a new device to break down kidney stones. The company is deciding between two options that produce identical medical outcomes but differ in how patients experience the procedure. The first option lasts about 20 minutes and involves a pain level of 8 on a 10-point scale, while the second option lasts about 40 minutes and involves a pain level of 8 for the first 35 minutes and a pain level of 6 for the last five minutes. Which of the two options is more likely to be perceived by patients as less painful?

In this chapter, we will explore these questions as we delve into the science of designing a meaningful consumption experience. We begin by examining the key elements of the consumption experience, which include the anticipation of using the offering, the actual usage, and the disposal at the end of its lifecycle. We will then consider the two critical consumption decisions that customers face: when to consume the offering and how much to consume on each occasion. Next, we will discuss habituation—

why the allure of new experiences often fades over time—and what strategies a company can employ to counteract this effect. We will then highlight the importance of engaging customers on an emotional level and outline different methods for creating emotionally engaging experiences. Finally, we will discuss the role of retrospective evaluations in shaping the customer experience and identify strategies for creating truly memorable experiences.

This discussion on the conceptual challenges of creating impactful experiences is enhanced by examples from companies that have successfully applied relevant behavioral insights. We will explore how companies like Apple, Marvel, and Bloomsbury create anticipation when launching new products; how Amazon's frustration-free packaging improves the customer experience; the strategies used by Michelob, Korbel, and Grey Poupon to define different usage occasions for their products; how Pepsi, Heinz, and Procter & Gamble encourage faster consumption of their products; how Hollywood studios structure their films to maintain viewer engagement; how car manufacturers like Porsche and BMW keep customers connected to their vehicles long after the initial excitement fades; how video game companies such as Tetris, Minecraft, and Candy Crush captivate players and keep them hooked; how companies like Harley-Davidson and Fiskars build subcultures around their brands; and how medical device companies can enhance the overall customer experience by managing patient discomfort.

Let's explore the key aspects of the consumption experience, the critical challenges in managing it, the significance of managing habituation and fostering emotional engagement, and the role of the peak–end rule in shaping retrospective evaluations

Consumption as an Experience

Managing the consumption experience involves creating value at every stage of the consumption process. The core experience begins with the customer's initial interaction with the product or service, including delivery, unpacking, and setup, and continues through its use and eventual disposal or service termination. In some cases, value can also be generated before these direct interactions by building a sense of anticipation. This pre-experience anticipation, combined with the various stages of the core experience, shapes the overall consumption experience and customer satisfaction. We discuss the two main components of the consumption experience—*anticipation* and *core consumption*—in the following sections.

The Power of Anticipation

Anticipation is a crucial, yet frequently underestimated, facet of the consumption experience. Leveraged strategically, anticipation can greatly increase the value that customers gain from an offering. By cultivating excitement about its products or services, a company can engage customers even before they begin interacting with the offering.

This proactive approach not only enriches the overall consumption experience but also extends its perceived timeline, beginning the subjective experience long before the actual product or service is encountered.

For example, Apple announces its new products months in advance, a strategy that generates extensive media coverage and creates anticipation among millions of customers. Similarly, Hollywood studios frequently start promoting blockbuster movies months, or even years, ahead of their release to build awareness and heighten audience anticipation. Bloomsbury, the publisher of the Harry Potter series, effectively created anticipation by announcing the release dates of new books well in advance. The excitement generated among Harry Potter fans translated directly into sales. For instance, the seventh and final book in the series sold nearly all 12 million initial print copies on the first day of its release.

The power of anticipation was first prominently documented over a century ago by Russian physiologist Ivan Pavlov. In his classic experiment, Pavlov observed that dogs began to salivate not only when food was placed in front of them but also when they heard the footsteps of his assistant bringing the food. He termed this a conditioned reflex—a type of automatic learning where an individual (or dog) learns to associate unrelated objects or events. Through this experiment, Pavlov demonstrated the power of anticipation by showing that merely expecting an event can trigger both physiological and psychological responses.

People not only anticipate future events, but they also derive value from that anticipation. Whether it is looking forward to dinner plans or feeling excited about an upcoming movie premiere, the anticipation itself can be a significant source of enjoyment. In fact, the value generated by anticipation can be so profound that we might even delay consumption to extend the experience.

Imagine you could receive a kiss from your favorite movie star. How much would you pay to receive that kiss immediately? Now consider how much you would be willing to pay if the kiss happened in three hours, 24 hours, three days, a year, or even three years. The principle of temporal discounting suggests that we perceive future outcomes as less valuable than those available in the present. As a result, we are likely to pay a premium for immediate rewards while undervaluing future experiences. This bias toward instant gratification means our willingness to pay for that kiss will be highest if it happens right away, rather than a week, a month, or a year from now.[1]

However, this is not what happened when participants in a study were asked to state their willingness to pay for a kiss from their favorite movie star.[2] Contrary to the conventional wisdom that future benefits are valued less than immediate ones, participants were willing to pay more to receive the kiss in three hours than to receive it immediately. The value of the kiss, as indicated by participants' willingness to pay, followed an inverted U-shape, peaking with about a three-day delay. Surprisingly, participants were even willing to pay more to receive the kiss in a year than to have it immediately. This pattern suggests that we derive enjoyment not just from the experience itself but also from anticipating it, which can prolong and perhaps even enhance the overall consumption experience.

The Core Experience

The core consumption experience encompasses the customer's direct interaction with the offering. It begins with the initial contact, continues through the actual use of the product or service, and concludes with the disposal of the product or the disconnection of the service. We discuss these experiences — *first touch*, *usage*, and *disposal* — in the following sections.

First Touch

After the anticipation phase, the consumption experience moves to the moment when the customer first interacts directly with the offering. This initial interaction is crucial, as it sets the tone for the entire experience — underscoring the adage, "you only get one chance to make a first impression." This first impression serves as an anchor, significantly shaping the customer's subsequent evaluation of the overall experience.

The first experience usually involves several key components: delivery, unboxing, setup, and first use. Many companies have built and maintained their market positions by providing exceptional value during these first interactions. For instance, retailers selling products that require assembly — such as home appliances, furniture, and sports equipment — often offer "white-glove" delivery services. These services go beyond standard doorstep delivery by setting up the product and helping customers get started with it more easily.

When it comes to unboxing, Amazon enhances the consumption experience with its "frustration-free" packaging, designed to prevent the "wrap rage" often caused by hard-to-open plastic casings. This packaging not only makes it easier for customers to access their products but also appeals to eco conscious consumers by being environmentally friendly.

Sonos, a developer of multi-room audio systems, owes much of its success to the simplicity of its product setup. Their high-end home surround-sound systems are among the easiest to install, appealing to customers who seek a quality audio experience without the usual complexity. Similarly, Breville stands out in the premium kitchen appliance market. The company has earned numerous accolades for its simple and intuitive interfaces, which minimize the need for frequent consultations with the product manual. This thoughtful design ensures that, from the very first moment, customers can enjoy a seamless and satisfying interaction with their appliances.

Apple is widely recognized as an expert in designing offerings that instantly create unique sensory experiences. Apple's packaging is as visually appealing as its products, featuring a clean and simple design that draws attention to the product inside. To achieve this, Apple employs a dedicated team solely focused on packaging design. For Apple, design extends far beyond visual appeal; the packaging must also be functional and easy to open and use. This approach reflects Apple's overarching design philosophy, encapsulated by Steve Jobs' words: "Design is not just about how it looks; it's about how it works."

Usage

Following the initial interaction with the offering comes the ongoing usage phase, where customers fully engage with and consume the benefits of the product or service. The usage experience is shaped by two types of benefits: utilitarian and hedonic. Utilitarian benefits pertain to the functional aspects of the offering, such as power, speed, and reliability, while hedonic benefits relate to the customer's subjective experiences, like the enjoyment derived from using the product.

The way customers experience these two types of benefits—utilitarian and hedonic—evolves over time. Familiarity with the functional benefits typically increases as customers progress along the learning curve. As they become more accustomed to the offering, they gain a better understanding of its features and find it easier to use. Enjoyment of the offering, on the other hand, tends to decrease over time due to habituation. As customers grow accustomed to the benefits of the offering, the intensity of the emotional experience associated with it tends to diminish (Figure 2).

Figure 2. The Dynamics of Familiarity with and Enjoyment of Using the Offering

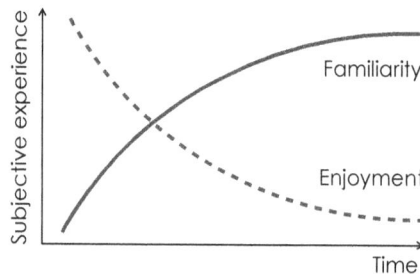

The different patterns of subjective experience with utilitarian and hedonic benefits suggest that distinct strategies are necessary for managing consumption. To maximize customer value from utilitarian attributes, a company should streamline the process of familiarizing customers with the functional aspects of the offering, ensuring it is easy and quick. Conversely, to enhance the hedonic benefits, the company should focus on providing sustained enjoyment over time. In this context, to successfully manage the consumption experience, a company should *make new things familiar and familiar things new*. We will explore the various aspects of the consumption experience and the impact of habituation in more detail later in this chapter.

Disposal

Using the offering is often not the final step in the customer experience. Once customers have consumed the benefits of the offering, they frequently need to dispose of the product or disconnect the service. While disposal may not be a major concern for some offerings, it can be an important aspect of the overall experience for others, presenting several challenges at the end of the consumption cycle.

The first challenge is the actual disposal of the product, which involves getting rid of items that are no longer in use. This challenge is particularly significant for bulky items or those containing hazardous materials. Some companies have turned this challenge into an opportunity to create customer value. For instance, Best Buy offers the removal of old household appliances with the delivery of new ones, while Office Depot provides a recycling program for products containing hazardous materials, such as rechargeable batteries and mobile phones.

Another challenge customers face is capturing the residual value of products they no longer need. For example, someone upgrading to a new mobile phone may want to monetize the old one. To address this, many mobile phone manufacturers and service providers offer trade-in options for old devices when purchasing new ones. This approach is also used by automotive dealerships, musical instrument stores, and consumer electronics retailers. Offering trade-in options not only allows customers to recoup some monetary value from their unwanted items but also provides the satisfaction of contributing to waste reduction.

For environmentally conscious customers, disposing of unwanted products in a sustainable way can be challenging. As climate change increasingly impacts our lives, more people are considering the sustainability of their consumption behaviors. In response, companies are investing in helping customers dispose of products responsibly. For example, Nespresso provides free prepaid recycling bags for returning used capsules and has partnered with the Swedish lifestyle bike company Vélosophy to create a fashionable bicycle made from recycled aluminum capsules, motivating customers to recycle their capsules.

Managing Consumption

Designing a superior customer experience requires understanding the key consumption decisions customers must make. Broadly, these decisions fall into two categories: deciding *when* to consume the offering and determining *how much* (and how often) to consume it. The key elements of these decisions—defining *usage occasions* and *managing usage quantity*—are discussed in the following sections.

Defining Consumption Occasions

One of the first decisions a customer must make after purchasing an offering is when to use it. The choice of usage occasion is significant because it can shape how customers perceive the offering and influence the rate at which they consume it. Since the same offering can be consumed on different occasions, a company's actions can play a crucial role in positioning the offering by associating it with specific consumption circumstances.

The evolution of Michelob's advertising illustrates how different positioning strategies can suggest alternative usage occasions. The company's original positioning in the 1960s focused on quality rather than a specific usage occasion, branding itself as a premium beer with the tagline, "In beer, going first class is Michelob. Period." This approach positioned Michelob as a beer for special occasions, leaving it up to customers to decide which moments warranted Michelob's first-class quality.

One challenge with this premium positioning was its association with special occasions, naturally limiting the frequency of consumption. To address this, Michelob attempted to refresh its image to make the brand more relevant to consumers' everyday lives. However, the new positioning—"Where you are going is Michelob"—was too vague and failed to resonate with consumers. Recognizing this, Michelob repositioned the brand again, this time with the more specific tagline "Weekends were made for Michelob." While this positioning identified a clear usage occasion, it had a strategic flaw: It targeted only two days of the week, ignoring drinking occasions during the rest of the week, such as happy hours.

Given the limitations of its most recent repositioning, Michelob adjusted its messaging to "Put a little weekend in your week," aiming to extend its appeal to everyday use. However, this approach lacked a compelling reason for consumers to choose Michelob over other brands on a daily basis. Realizing the shortcomings of this broad positioning, Michelob tried yet another repositioning with "The night belongs to Michelob," focusing on evening consumption. Unfortunately, this strategy also overlooked a key beer-drinking occasion: the happy hour.

Michelob's numerous repositioning efforts highlight the challenges companies face in identifying the optimal usage occasions for their products. It also emphasizes the importance of establishing meaningful associations in customers' minds and the need to maintain consistency in these associations. Frequent brand repositioning can be counterproductive, as it risks diluting the brand's identity and confusing consumers.

The choice of a usage occasion can significantly influence how frequently customers use an offering and the likelihood of it becoming a habit. This is because offerings associated with frequent occasions are more likely to create habits quickly than those linked to rare events. For instance, Korbel—a California champagne brand—launched an advertising campaign aimed at making Korbel the go-to champagne for New Year's celebrations. The campaign featured commercials showing festivities disrupted when someone realized, "The champagne is not Korbel." Despite the substantial investment in this campaign, it failed to establish a habit of drinking Korbel every New Year's Eve.

The challenge with Korbel's approach was that habit formation requires many repetitions, which is difficult to achieve with an occasion that occurs only once a year. Additionally, many consumers had already developed loyalty to a particular champagne brand and were using that brand for *all* special occasions—a pattern of behavior that was difficult to modify by a brand associated with a single usage occasion.

Another example of how an offering's positioning can influence the choice of usage occasion involves Grey Poupon, a Dijon mustard brand that gained prominence in the U.S. during the 1980s. A series of advertisements positioned Grey Poupon as a premium product consumed in luxurious settings. One iconic commercial featured a Rolls-Royce pulling up next to another, with a passenger asking, "Pardon me, would you have any Grey Poupon?" The other passenger replies, "But of course!" This campaign resonated with consumers, leading to a significant increase in sales.

However, after the initial surge, sales began to decline. The problem was that many consumers saw Grey Poupon as a luxury item reserved for special occasions. As a result, even though they had a jar of Grey Poupon in their refrigerator, they typically opted for popular mustard brands like French's for everyday meals, considering them a more practical choice. Recognizing this challenge, Grey Poupon shifted its strategy by downplaying the brand's luxury image. The company introduced a squeezable bottle to replace some of its elegant glass jars, launched a bright-yellow version of the mustard, and began encouraging daily use with taglines like "Meets your daily requirement of yellow."

Managing Consumption Quantity

In addition to deciding *when* to consume an offering, customers often need to determine *how much* to consume on each occasion. This decision is particularly relevant for products designed to be used over time. For instance, when using liquid laundry detergent, we must decide how much detergent to use per load. When pouring cereal into a bowl in the morning, we gauge how much cereal will make us feel satisfied. And when adding ketchup to a burger at lunch, we must decide on the right amount to enhance the flavor without overwhelming it.

The need to decide how much of an offering to use raises the question of how these decisions are made. Research shows that when unsure of the appropriate amount to consume, we often use the size of the offering as a reference point, with larger sizes encouraging greater consumption. For example, studies have found that we tend to eat more from a large popcorn bucket than from a small one. Furthermore, because the size of the offering serves as a reference point, we often feel compelled to consume it all. In one study, for instance, moviegoers given a large bucket of popcorn felt compelled to finish it, even when the popcorn was stale.[3]

Understanding the relationship between the size of the offering and the quantity consumed allowed Pepsi to gain market share by subtly encouraging its customers to drink more soda. The story goes that John Sculley, then a vice president at Pepsi (who later became the CEO of Apple and famously fired Steve Jobs), decided that the best way to compete with Coca-Cola was not by designing a fancier bottle, but by creating a bigger one. This strategy was based on a simple observation: The more soda people have at home, the more they will consume. This insight led to the introduction of the two-liter plastic bottle in the 1970s—a packaging innovation that was soon adopted by Coca-Cola and other soda manufacturers.

The size of the offering is just one factor that determines how much we consume. Product design also plays a significant role in influencing consumption quantity. Take, for example, the different strategies Heinz employed to encourage consumers to use more ketchup. The bottleneck of ketchup consumption was quite literally the neck of the bottle, which made it difficult to get the second half of the ketchup out. To solve this problem, Heinz redesigned the bottle by increasing its size, making it squeezable, and, most important, turning it upside down so that ketchup is always ready to be squeezed out. The easier it is to squeeze out ketchup, the more we tend to use.

In addition to increasing the size of the offering and redesigning its packaging, another way to influence consumption quantity is by educating customers on how to use the product and helping them determine the appropriate amount for each occasion. For instance, Heinz once educated consumers on how to get more ketchup out of its traditional glass bottle by explaining that tapping the neck (rather than the bottom) makes the ketchup flow more easily.

Perhaps the most famous example of a company increasing consumption by changing how customers use its product is Procter & Gamble's decision in the 1950s to add the word "repeat" to the usage directions on its shampoo bottles. The phrase "Lather–Rinse–Repeat" has since become synonymous with the strategy of boosting sales by encouraging customers to increase the amount they use on each occasion.

So far, we have discussed scenarios where customers must decide how much of a product to use, which is relevant for items like liquid laundry detergent, cereal, and milk, where customers determine portion size. However, not all products allow customers this flexibility. Certain products, such as printer cartridges, water filters, and razor blades, come in single units designed for use across multiple occasions. For these products, consumption quantity is determined by the length of time a customer uses each unit, which is reflected in how frequently they replace it.

For example, a common challenge for companies making water filters is that customers often forget to replace the filter, using it much longer than recommended. This is counterproductive for customers, who no longer receive the desired level of water filtration, and for the company, whose sales suffer due to lower filter replacements. Similarly, when shaving, consumers must decide how long to use the same cartridge before replacing it. Replacing the cartridge too soon wastes money, while using it too long can lead to a subpar shave.

To help customers determine the optimal replacement frequency, many companies incorporate usage markers into their products. Water filters often include timing devices, shaving cartridges have indicator strips that change color when it is time for a replacement, and toothbrushes feature colored bristles that fade as they wear out. While these markers are helpful, they are not always sufficient on their own. For them to be effective, customers need to develop a habit of paying attention to them and adjusting their behavior accordingly.

For instance, many consumers are unaware that the colored strip on razor cartridges is meant to indicate blade sharpness, and even those who know about it may ignore it, believing they can get a few more shaves from the cartridge. Thus, both strategies—adding usage markers and educating customers to pay attention to them—are essential for ensuring optimal replacement frequency.

Overcoming Habituation

Many consumption experiences are prone to habituation—a phenomenon where the intensity of experiences diminishes over time. Habituation occurs because objects and events that initially have a strong subjective impact gradually become less relevant as time passes. The essence of habituation as a psychological process, along with strategies to disrupt the habituation pattern, are discussed in the following sections.

The Essence of Habituation

Habituation is similar to the principle of diminishing marginal value, which suggests that each additional unit of an offering provides a progressively smaller increase in perceived value. For example, increasing the number of blades from one to two has much greater impact on the shaving experience than increasing the blades from four to five, even though in both cases a single blade was added. This principle also applies to consumption experiences: The more we engage with an offering, the less enjoyment we derive from its future use.

The key distinction between diminishing marginal value and habituation lies in their scope. Diminishing marginal value typically describes how we value objects and events at a specific point in time, while habituation explains how our evaluations evolve throughout the consumption experience.

Take, for example, the experience of owning a new car. In the first month, everything about the new car is thrilling—you enjoy the "new car" smell, explore the car's features, and feel a proud sense of ownership. A month later, the car is still enjoyable, but the initial excitement has begun to wane. By the third month, you still appreciate the car, but your focus shifts to other aspects of your life. By the fourth month, the initial thrill has faded, and driving the car becomes just part of your daily routine (Figure 3). This is the essence of habituation: Initially strong experiences gradually diminish in intensity over time.

Figure 3. The Impact of Habituation on the Consumption Experience

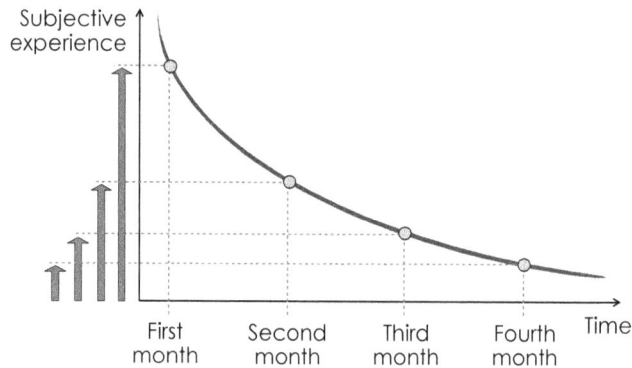

The impact of habituation on the consumption experience is similar to sensory adaptation in psychophysics, where our sensory receptors become less sensitive to a stimulus after continuous exposure. For instance, our visual system adjusts to the intensity of light in the environment. When you first turn off the lights, your vision is limited, but as your pupils dilate and your retina receives more light, you gradually start to see objects in the dark. Similarly, we adapt to temperature changes. The water in a swimming pool might initially feel very cold, but after a few minutes, it feels comfortable—not because the water temperature has changed, but because our bodies have adapted. We also adapt to noise. For example, after initially being bothered by it, we eventually stop noticing background sounds like automobile traffic or the hum of an air conditioner. In fact, all of our sensory inputs are adaptive, meaning that the intensity of sensations tends to diminish with continued exposure.

Habituation is closely tied to how our brain regulates both positive and negative experiences. When we engage in a rewarding activity, dopamine neurons are activated, increasing dopamine levels in the nucleus accumbens—the brain's "reward center" responsible for controlling hedonic experiences. A similar increase in dopamine occurs when we experience something negative. With repeated exposure to the same experience, the amount of dopamine released gradually decreases, leading to lower stimulation and, ultimately, habituation.

Habituation has an evolutionary basis and arises from the limitations of our mental faculties. Our brains are designed to focus on changes in the environment, while ignoring constant, unchanging stimuli. By adapting to stable aspects of the environment that are unlikely to pose new threats, we can conserve mental resources and redirect our attention to changes that might present new risks or opportunities. In this way, habituation allows us to adapt efficiently, filtering out information that has become irrelevant and freeing up mental capacity to process new and potentially significant aspects of our environment.

Breaking the Habituation Pattern

Even though habituation is common, it is not insurmountable. One effective strategy to mitigate its effects is by dividing the consumption experience into distinct episodes. This approach can keep each experience feeling fresh, countering habituation by introducing variety into the process. The impact of partitioning on habituation is linked to the orienting reflex—our instinctive response to changes in the environment. While habituation reduces our sensitivity to stimuli that remain constant over time, the orienting reflex heightens our attention to new changes. As we become familiar with a new environment, the orienting reflex diminishes, and habituation takes over.

Consider the consumption experience depicted in Figure 3. Because of habituation, the intensity of the subjective experience decreases over time. Now imagine that the experience is restarted every month by creating a sense of novelty that makes us look at the offering with a fresh pair of eyes. This can reset the consumption experience, potentially making it as intense as it was during the very first interaction with the offering (Figure 4). For example, Tesla keeps its customers engaged with their vehicles by continuously updating the software to add new functionality, thereby reinvigorating the customer experience and reducing habituation.

Figure 4. Managing Habituation through Partitioning

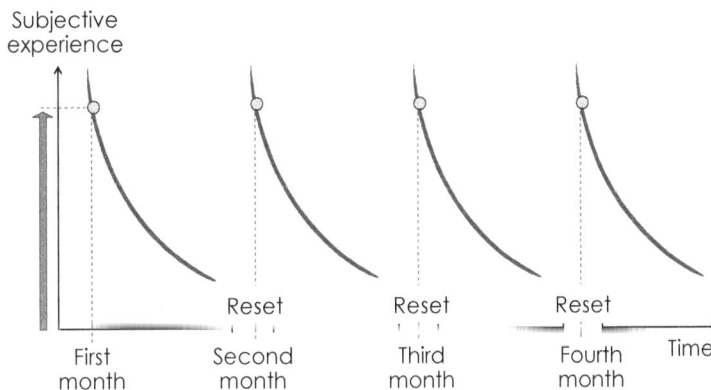

The role of partitioning in shaping the overall consumption experience can be illustrated by examining how commercial interruptions affect the enjoyment of television programming. Conventional wisdom suggests that commercial breaks make movies less enjoyable to watch. Indeed, most viewers see commercials as a necessary evil—the price to pay for watching a movie for free. However, in some cases, commercial breaks might actually increase the enjoyment derived from watching television programming.

Consider an experiment where participants were asked whether they would enjoy a movie more with or without commercial interruptions. Unsurprisingly, most participants believed they would enjoy the movie more without interruptions. However, after actually watching the movie—some with commercials and others without—their reactions told a different story. Those who watched the movie with commercial breaks enjoyed it more than those who watched it without commercials. The insertion of an otherwise undesirable experience ended up enhancing overall enjoyment by partitioning the movie consumption, with the resulting variety re-energizing their experience.[4] While commercial breaks are unlikely to improve every viewing experience, introducing variety can enhance the customer experience by counteracting habituation.

Partitioning is a fundamental principle in the movie industry, employed to keep viewers engaged through the strategic use of shots and cuts. Shots are the individual segments captured from specific camera angles, forming the backbone of the movie experience. Cuts are the transitions between these shots—such as close-ups or changes in angle—that serve to reinvigorate the viewer's engagement and prepare them for the next segment. This technique of combining shots with cuts not only mitigates habituation but also directs the viewer's attention to crucial narrative elements. The refreshed focus following each cut increases the likelihood that viewers will absorb subsequent information more effectively. Similarly, commercials use cuts and transitions to emphasize the most important parts of their messages, taking advantage of the viewer's heightened post-cut attention to reinforce the advertisement's key points.[5]

The concept of partitioning to reduce habituation is vividly illustrated in the architectural designs of Frank Lloyd Wright, one of the 20th century's most renowned architects. Wright employed a straightforward yet powerful formula for managing habituation: compress, expand, and repeat. Unlike traditional methods that design buildings from the "outside in"—focusing on maximizing the external footprint and cramming in as many standard-sized rooms as possible—Wright designed from the "inside out." He began by imagining the experiences of the building's future occupants, then shaped the structure and its interior spaces to create a dynamic and engaging experience for those moving through the house.

To enhance the dramatic effect of his designs, Wright deliberately crafted smaller spaces leading into larger ones, creating a temporary sense of tension followed by a feeling of release. This architectural technique was examined in a study that analyzed the spatial dynamics of one of Wright's buildings from the perspective of someone approaching and entering the house. As one approaches the house, there is an initial feeling of compression, which persists up to the porch door. Entering the larger porch area then brings a sense of release. This cycle repeats upon entering the main door, where the sense of compression returns. Finally, after navigating through a narrow hallway, one enters the expansive living room with its high ceilings and large windows, experiencing a profound sense of release. By partitioning spaces, altering perspectives, and creating a sense of variety, Wright's buildings reduce habituation and inject a renewed sense of excitement into everyday experiences.[6]

So far, we have discussed how partitioning the consumption experience can help reduce habituation. In addition to partitioning, another effective strategy for mitigating the impact of habituation involves fostering emotional engagement. We examine the role of emotional engagement in managing habituation in the following section.

Fostering Emotional Engagement

Emotional engagement can counteract habituation by energizing customers with interactive experiences that generate excitement about the offering. This type of engagement strengthens customer connections through experiences that are both relevant and meaningful. Emotional engagement is primarily driven by two types of emotions: experience-based and identity-based. In the following sections, we will explore the nuances and impact of engagement associated with these two types of emotions.

Managing Experience-Based Emotions

Experience-based emotions reflect the emotional responses customers have during their interactions with an offering. These emotions go beyond cognitive evaluations of the functional aspects, capturing the affective responses generated through the use of a company's products and services. Two common strategies for engaging customers through emotionally charged experiences are generating arousal and creating flow.

Generating Arousal

One approach to avoiding habituation and keeping customers engaged over time is by generating a sense of excitement about the offering. This excitement, also known as arousal, refers to a state of heightened physiological and psychological stimulation, which ultimately influences the intensity of the emotional response to the offering. The higher the level of arousal, the stronger an individual's emotional reaction to the company's offering.

Arousal is a crucial component of our emotional response to the environment. Emotions can be defined along two key dimensions: valence and arousal. *Valence* reflects whether an emotion is positive or negative. For example, happiness, love, gratitude, and amusement have positive valence, while emotions like anger, hate, envy, and fear have negative valence. *Arousal*, on the other hand, indicates the intensity of the emotional response. High-arousal emotions include happiness, anger, frustration, and hate, while low-arousal emotions encompass calmness, relaxation, and contentment.

Research has shown that higher arousal levels are often linked to increased engagement, a fact that many companies have leveraged to counteract habituation and sustain customer interest over time.[7] To inject more excitement into their offerings, an increasing number of companies have redesigned their products to include more interactive experiences.

For example, car manufacturers are shifting from simply highlighting the functional features of their vehicles to emphasizing the emotional benefits that resonate with how customers feel while driving. Porsche has introduced an experience center—a high-performance driving facility where customers and car enthusiasts can rent various Porsche models and drive them on the company's track. BMW has taken this concept further by offering performance driving clinics led by professional instructors and updating its motto from "The Ultimate Driving Machine" to "Sheer Driving Pleasure." Similarly, when Akio Toyoda became Toyota's CEO, he issued a company-wide mandate: "Stop making boring cars! Start creating exciting cars that evoke an emotional response."[8]

The impact of arousal on customer engagement extends beyond just positive emotions. Research has shown that negative emotions can evoke even stronger affective responses than positive ones. This suggests that eliciting negative emotions that can agitate customers may effectively trigger more intense emotional reactions, thereby increasing social interactions.[9] This tendency for individuals to be more engaged with content that contains high levels of negativity and arousal presents an ethical challenge for social media platforms like Facebook, YouTube, and Instagram.

On one hand, social media companies have found that content likely to provoke higher levels of negativity and arousal—such as divisive topics—tends to drive greater customer engagement, which often translates into increased profitability. To capitalize on this, these companies frequently use algorithms to assess the expected engagement rate of each post, including clicks, reactions, comments, and shares. This approach inherently prioritizes content that generates strong negative emotions, as these emotions are more likely to foster high levels of engagement and go viral.

On the other hand, promoting divisive topics that fuel strong negative emotions can be detrimental to society, fostering animosity and division. This creates a conflict between societal well-being and the financial goals of media companies that curate content for their users. Such scenarios highlight how scientific advancements can be used not only for the benefit but also to the detriment of customers. Therefore, when leveraging emotions to boost customer engagement, companies must carefully balance their own interests with the welfare of their customers and society at large. This ethical consideration is crucial to ensuring that business practices contribute positively to the social fabric.

Creating a State of Flow

Engaging customers on an emotional level can also be achieved by designing interactive activities that align with their skill level. The match of tasks and skills creates "flow," a state of mind that drives sustained motivation, or being "in the zone." Flow is the mental state in which a person is fully immersed in an activity and derives great enjoyment from it. This state is associated with hyperfocus and tunnel vision on a single activity. Psychologist Mihaly Csikszentmihalyi, who first identified this phenomenon, describes flow as a state of "heightened focus and blissful immersion." When in flow, individuals become so engrossed in the activity that external distractions fade away; nothing else seems to matter, and the experience itself is so enjoyable that they revel in it, even at great cost, for the sheer joy derived from the activity.[10]

Flow and arousal share similarities, as both involve heightened mental engagement and can elicit strong emotional responses that might overshadow rational thinking. However, arousal is a more generalized state that does not necessarily center on a specific activity and isn't dependent on an individual's skill level. In contrast, flow is closely associated with specific activities that demand intense focus and a corresponding level of skill.

Flow can also be linked to partitioning, a concept discussed earlier in this chapter, with both playing crucial roles in enhancing an individual's engagement with a company's offering. The key difference lies in how they achieve this engagement. Partitioning fosters engagement by breaking up the consumption experience into distinct episodes, thereby creating a sense of disruption and re-engagement. Flow, on the other hand, is the opposite of partitioning. Instead of fragmenting the experience, flow aims to integrate these episodes, creating a seamless and immersive experience.

In marketing, the state of flow is often achieved by designing interactive consumption experiences that match individuals' skill levels with the right degree of complexity. The entire video game industry is built on this principle: It creates a sense of progress toward goals that continually increase in difficulty. Consider Tetris—one of the earliest video games responsible for countless hours of lost productivity, as players found themselves unable to step away. Although Tetris is a relatively simple game, involving just seven different shapes of building blocks, it captivates players with its visual and intellectual challenge. Crucially, the game's complexity increases as players develop the skills needed to tackle the next level, keeping it challenging yet achievable.

Flow explains why video games like Tetris are so addictive: They provide clear goals, immediate feedback, and a sense of progress. This combination is the perfect formula for preventing habituation; just as players become comfortable with one level, they move on to a new one that demands greater attention. This principle underpins the success of games like Super Mario Bros., Grand Theft Auto, Minecraft, and Candy Crush Saga.

Candy Crush Saga, for example, has become one of the most successful video games ever, with over three billion downloads. What is remarkable is that it can be played for free, while allowing players to pay for more challenging experiences. Despite the option to play for free, the game was generating over a billion dollars per year at its peak. It became so addictive that it began to interfere with the daily lives of some players, leading to the emergence of Candy Crush addiction clinics around the world. This extraordinary level of engagement was achieved by adhering to the principle of flow, designing the game to create an immersive experience with a sense of progress toward increasingly difficult goals.

Managing Identity-Based Emotions

In addition to evoking experience-based emotions, engagement can also be nurtured through emotions that resonate with the personal relevance of a company's offerings to its customers. Unlike experience-based emotions, which are often detached from a customer's self-image, identity-based emotions are deeply tied to how customers perceive themselves. Engaging customers through identity-based emotions can be accomplished in two ways: by signaling self-identity and by fostering a sense of belonging.

Signaling Self-Identity

One approach to creating emotional engagement is to tailor offerings to reflect a customer's identity. This strategy is highly effective because identity-related needs—such as self-expression and self-fulfillment—are fundamental drivers of human behavior. As discussed in Chapter 2, these needs are often positioned at the top of the hierarchy of human needs, emphasizing their importance. Consequently, offerings that cater to these self-expressive needs not only capture attention but also significantly enhance engagement by aligning with benefits that customers deeply value.

Self-expressive offerings often involve brands that embody the self-image customers aspire to create. These self-expressive brands can be categorized along three basic dimensions: status, personality, and expertise.

Status brands symbolize membership within specific socioeconomic classes. These brands are typically sought after for their ability to signal social status, wealth, and income (see the discussion of the Veblen effect in Chapter 2). Status brands tend to thrive in environments characterized by new wealth creation and social mobility, such as the emergence of upper and middle classes in developing nations. Examples of status brands include luxury names like Rolls-Royce, Bugatti, Louis Vuitton, and Cartier.

Personality brands appeal to individuals' self-image by enabling them to express their unique values, preferences, and tastes. Unlike status brands, which emphasize wealth, status, and power, personality brands reflect a person's distinct beliefs, preferences, and values. Additionally, while status brands are often exclusive and priced beyond the reach of the broader market, personality brands are typically not defined by their price, making them accessible to a wider range of buyers. Examples of personality brands include Lululemon, Warby Parker, Abercrombie & Fitch, and Quiksilver.

Finally, *professional brands* convey an individual's expertise in a particular area. These brands are usually highly specialized and recognized for their superior functional performance in their respective fields. For example, DeWalt is known for its professional-grade tools, which enhance the perceived expertise of construction workers. Other examples include CAT for construction equipment, Hilti for power tools, Montblanc for executive accessories, and Paul Mitchell for hair care, each underscoring professional proficiency in their respective domains.

An important aspect of self-expressive brands is their heightened resilience to habituation. This resilience arises from their use in socially rich contexts, where frequent personal interactions allow individuals to continually showcase their social status, personality, and expertise. For example, a Rolls-Royce may not provide the most exhilarating driving experience, but its enduring appeal as a status symbol helps prevent it from becoming monotonous. Similarly, luxury accessories like Hermès Birkin and Kelly handbags keep consumers engaged by serving as ongoing expressions of their owners' social standing in every social encounter.

Fostering a Sense of Belonging

A related approach to engaging customers taps into their need for belonging. This need reflects the desire to be an accepted member of a group and to feel part of something larger than oneself. It stems from an inherent drive to connect with others and gain social acceptance. Alongside the need for self-actualization, the desire for belonging occupies the uppermost tier of Maslow's hierarchy of needs, highlighting its significance as a higher level human need.

The need for belonging goes beyond simply having acquaintances; it involves gaining acceptance, attention, and support from others. This need has deep evolutionary roots, as it has historically played a crucial role in human survival. In the face of existential challenges like escaping predators, finding food and shelter, or reproducing, individuals who were part of a group were more likely to survive than those who faced these challenges alone. Consequently, evolution has favored individuals with a stronger need for belonging, reinforcing its role as a key driver of human behavior.

In marketing, the need for belonging is a powerful tool for creating engaging experiences. This is often achieved by offering participatory experiences that foster emotional engagement through the creation of social connections. By cultivating a sense of belonging and emotionally engaging customers, these experiences help mitigate the habituation that might otherwise set in after acquiring the company's offerings.

A prime example of customer engagement driven by the need for belonging is the Harley Owners Group (HOG). Established in 1983, HOG was designed to build enduring connections between Harley-Davidson, its dealerships, and its customers. Membership in HOG goes beyond simply owning a loud, customized motorcycle; it represents being part of a community. HOG's community-building efforts encompass a wide range of activities, from group rides, competitions, rallies, and weekend excursions to non-riding events like charity fundraisers and social gatherings. Through HOG, Harley-Davidson has cultivated a consumption subculture rooted in a shared allegiance to the brand and the lifestyle it represents. The primary goal of HOG is not merely to sell motorcycles but to celebrate and promote the Harley-Davidson lifestyle.[11]

Engaging customers by creating a sense of belonging doesn't necessarily require a self-expressive product like a motorcycle. A sense of belonging can be fostered even in seemingly mundane product categories. Take Fiskars, the Finnish company known for products ranging from axes to kitchen knives, and especially for its iconic crafting scissors with the distinctive orange handles. To make its products more exciting and to build an emotional connection with customers, Fiskars hired several passionate crafters as brand ambassadors. These ambassadors actively engaged with the crafting community by blogging, attending conventions and events, and creating online gathering spaces. Through their efforts, they cultivated a dedicated community of brand-loyal enthusiasts, known as "Fiskateers," that grew to thousands of members. These Fiskateers eagerly sought out product information, wrote reviews and recommendations, and played a key role in expanding the Fiskateer community.

Creating Memories

Creating impactful experiences starts with understanding how customers evaluate them. This raises an important question: What has a greater influence on how customers assess their experience with a company's offering—the emotions they feel during the experience or the memories they form afterward? The following sections explore the answer to this question and outline the key principles for crafting memorable experiences.

The Power of Retrospective Evaluations

Consumption experiences can be evaluated in two distinct ways. First, we can make instant assessments of experiences as they happen. These assessments typically reflect our moment-to-moment reactions and are then combined to form an overall evaluation. Alternatively, we can make retrospective assessments, which are based on how we remember those experiences later. Instead of evaluating each moment individually, we form an overall judgment based on our reflection of past events.

In general, people can be thought of as having two selves: the *experiencing self* and the *remembering self*. The experiencing self evaluates experiences in real-time, focusing on the momentary experiences and the affective reaction these experiences evoke at the time of their occurrence. In contrast, the remembering self focuses on the memories of the actual experiences and evaluates them as they are remembered at a later point in time (Figure 5).[12]

Figure 5. Instant and Retrospective Evaluations

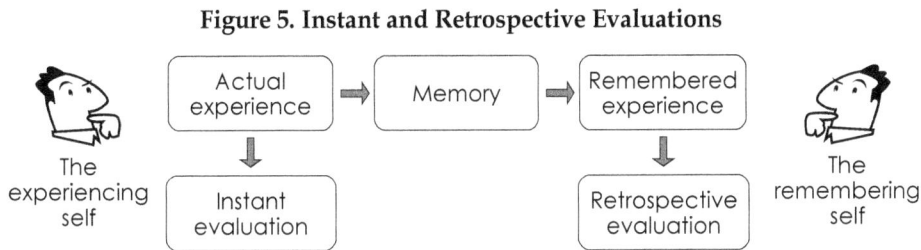

The existence of instant and retrospective evaluations raises an important question: Which one has a more significant impact on how we assess our experiences? It might seem logical to assume that instant evaluations, being more immediate and vivid, would have a stronger influence on our overall assessment. This assumption aligns with the idea that instant gratification drives much of human behavior, suggesting that our immediate emotional responses are paramount in evaluating experiences. However, this is not always the case.

Consider a thought experiment where you were offered a chance to go on a highly enjoyable trip, with one condition: You cannot take photos, and all your memories of the trip will be erased afterward. Would you still go? Surprisingly, many people would choose to decline such a vacation. This reaction aligns with research showing that our evaluations of experiences are often retrospective. In other words, we frequently make decisions based on the anticipation of creating enjoyable memories rather than focusing solely on the moment. This suggests that the "remembering self," rather than the "experiencing self," plays a more significant role in shaping future decisions.[13]

The fact that we tend to evaluate our experiences retrospectively leads to another important question: What aspects of the experience do we focus on and consider most significant? A key finding in memory research is that the duration of an experience has little impact on how we remember it. This phenomenon is often referred to as *duration neglect*.

Multiple studies have shown that the pleasantness and intensity of an experience have a much greater influence on its retrospective evaluation than its actual length. For example, in one study, participants watched video clips that varied in pleasantness, intensity, and duration. After viewing each clip, they rated their immediate emotional response and, at the end of the task, provided an overall evaluation of the emotional impact of each clip. The findings revealed that the duration of the video had virtually no impact on their retrospective evaluation, which was almost entirely shaped by the pleasantness and intensity of the experience.[14]

Duration neglect occurs because we struggle to think of time as an independent dimension and we tend to overlook the duration of events when making retrospective judgments.[15] Since the length of an event does not significantly influence how we remember it, it is important to identify the factors that drive retrospective evaluations. Two of these factors are captured in the so-called peak–end rule.

The Peak–End Rule

We do not remember every detail of an experience; instead, we tend to focus on specific moments that define it. These defining moments are not randomly selected from the overall experience but follow a consistent pattern known as the *peak–end rule*. According to this rule, our retrospective evaluations are primarily influenced by two key factors: the most intense positive or negative moments (the "peaks") and the final moments of the experience (the "end"). This tendency to give greater weight to the peaks and the end of the overall experience in evaluating past events is discussed next.

Actual and Remembered Experiences: Peaks and Valleys

Our memories of experiences are significantly shaped by their most extreme moments. Take driving, for example. If you live in a major city, much of your time in the car is likely spent sitting in traffic. However, when reflecting on your driving experience, you most likely do not dwell on those tedious hours. Instead, you focus on the most exciting moments—like the thrill of rapid acceleration as you pass another car or the sharp, responsive handling on winding roads. These extreme moments do not always have to be positive. Along with exhilarating driving experiences, we also tend to recall negative moments, such as receiving a speeding ticket or dealing with a car breakdown.

Regardless of whether the extreme experience was positive or negative, we tend to remember the exciting moments (the "peaks") and forget the mundane experiences (the "valleys").[16] The impact of peak experiences on overall evaluations is illustrated in Figure 6, which depicts a series of unremarkable everyday experiences and a single exciting positive moment. If we simply average these episodes when forming an overall evaluation of the experience, the combined experience would be slightly higher than the average everyday experience, given that there are many ordinary moments and only one peak experience. However, in reality, we tend to clearly recall the peak experience while only vaguely remembering the uneventful daily experiences.

Figure 6. The Impact of Positive Peak Experiences on Retrospective Evaluations

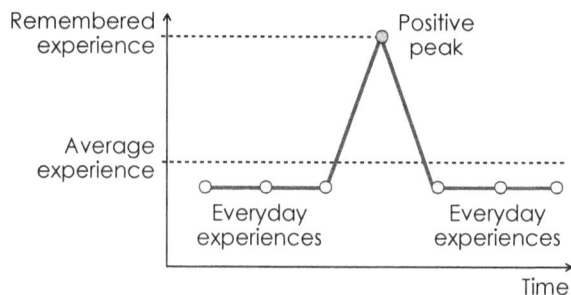

The same *peak rule* applies to extremely negative experiences. Imagine a scenario where your days are filled with mostly unremarkable, everyday moments, but there is one extremely unpleasant event. If we were to average these episodes to form an overall evaluation, the combined experience might appear only slightly worse than the average daily experience. However, in reality, we are more likely to vividly remember the peak negative experience while forgetting most of the mundane daily moments (Figure 7).

Figure 7. The Impact of Negative Peak Experiences on Retrospective Evaluations

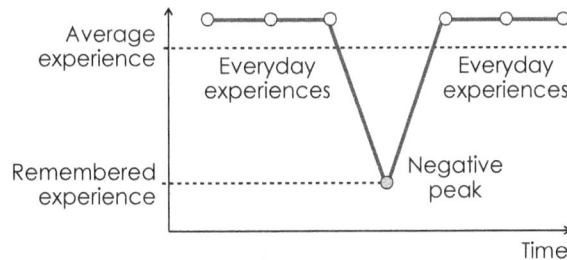

Our tendency to prioritize extreme moments over everyday experiences, and to overlook the duration of individual events, suggests that companies can gain a significant advantage by intentionally creating special moments that define the retrospective evaluation of an experience. Nevertheless, many companies focus solely on day-to-day satisfaction, neglecting the creation of these impactful, defining moments that linger in customers' memories. The problem with this approach is that it overlooks the opportunity to create memorable experiences. By deliberately crafting memorable peaks in the customer experience, companies can ensure that these moments stand out, transforming an otherwise forgettable experience into something truly unforgettable. Just a few carefully designed notable moments can shape the entire memory of an experience, leading customers to associate the brand and its offerings with positive emotions.

The crucial role that peak moments play in shaping the consumption experience raises an interesting question: Is it possible to create experiences composed entirely of peak moments? Beyond the complexity and cost of designing such experiences, there is also a behavioral challenge to consider: Peaks are always relative. An experience is extraordinary only when contrasted with ordinary ones. This is why everyday experiences are important: They serve as reference points that make the extraordinary moments stand out.

The importance of reference points in defining extraordinary moments was eloquently articulated by French writer Alexandre Dumas in *The Count of Monte Cristo*: "Those born to wealth, and who have the means of gratifying every wish, know not what is the real happiness of life, just as those who have been tossed on the stormy waters of the ocean on a few frail planks can alone realize the blessings of fair weather."[17] Simply put, there are no peaks without valleys.

Actual and Remembered Experiences: The Ending

So far, we have explored the first aspect of the peak–end rule: the role of extreme experiences in shaping retrospective evaluations. Another crucial factor in defining an experience is its final moment. Numerous studies have demonstrated that endpoints can have a disproportionately large impact on the overall experience, often shaping how the entire experience is remembered.

A classic study illustrating the importance of endpoints in evaluating an experience involved tracking the real-time pain intensity of patients undergoing colonoscopy and lithotripsy (a non-invasive procedure for breaking down kidney stones) and then comparing these real-time assessments with the patients' retrospective evaluations of the pain. Despite significant variations in the duration of these procedures, longer experiences were not necessarily remembered as more painful. Instead, patients' overall judgments of pain were strongly influenced by two key factors: the peak intensity of pain and the intensity of pain during the last three minutes of the procedure. In other words, the worst part of the experience and the final moments played a decisive role in shaping how the entire experience was remembered (Figure 8).[18]

Figure 8. The Ending Can Change the Overall Evaluation of an Experience

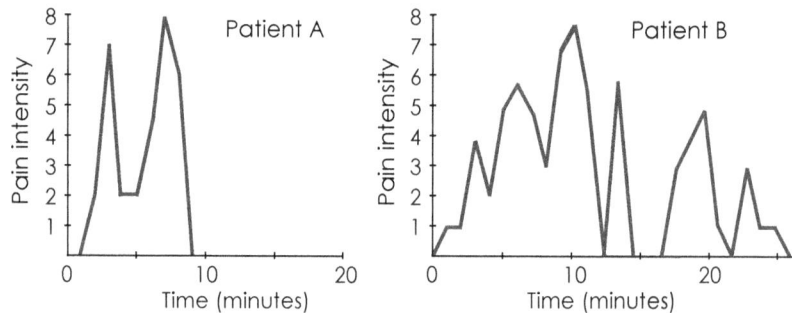

Our tendency to focus on endpoints when evaluating past experiences is vividly illustrated in a study where participants were asked to hold their hand in a tub of cold water on two separate occasions. Unbeknown to them, the two scenarios differed in both duration and water temperature. In the first scenario, participants kept their hand in water cooled to 14°C (about 57°F) for 60 seconds. In the second scenario, they kept their hand in the 14°C water for 90 seconds, but during the last 30 seconds, the water was gradually warmed by 1°C to 15°C.

When asked to evaluate each experience, participants reported less pain in the 90-second condition and described it as less unpleasant than the 60-second one. Furthermore, when given the choice of which trial to repeat, most participants chose the 90-second condition, despite the longer exposure to uncomfortable temperatures. Thus, extending a negative experience can paradoxically improve its retrospective evaluation, as long as the additional time contributes to a more positive ending.[19]

Endpoints of an experience can influence not only how it is evaluated but also future behaviors. For example, in one study students were asked to keep diaries and record daily evaluations of their experiences during spring break. At the end of the vacation, students also rated their overall experience and indicated whether they would like to repeat the vacation they just had. The results show that the intention to repeat the vacation was almost entirely determined by the evaluation of their final moments, regardless of the quality of the daily experiences recorded in their diaries.[20] As this study shows, the end of an experience can overshadow everyday moments, not only shaping how the entire experience is remembered but also influencing future decisions and behaviors.

SUMMARY

Designing meaningful consumption experiences is essential for creating customer value. To design such experiences, a company must understand how customers engage with its offerings and how these interactions deliver customer benefits. The process starts by defining the key stages of the customer experience and identifying opportunities to create value at each stage. This can be done by building anticipation before customers receive the offering, optimizing their first interaction with it, orchestrating the actual usage experience, and simplifying the end-of-life disposal of the product.

Creating an exceptional consumption experience requires understanding how customers decide when to use an offering and how much of it to use. When uncertain about how much to consume, customers often rely on the available quantity as a reference point. Consequently, larger product sizes can increase consumption volume and speed up the rate of consumption. For products used over time, a company can optimize consumption quantity and enhance the overall experience by incorporating usage indicators and educating customers on optimal usage and replacement frequency.

Habituation is the tendency for the impact of experiences to diminish over time: Objects and events that initially have a strong subjective impact gradually become less engaging. This pattern mirrors sensory adaptation in psychophysics, where continuous exposure to a stimulus leads to decreased sensitivity. An effective way to counteract habituation is to partition the consumption experience into distinct episodes, making each one feel fresh and rejuvenating interest.

Habituation can also be mitigated by fostering *emotional engagement*, which can arise from two types of emotions: experience-based and identity-based. Experience-based emotions are tied to how customers feel during their interaction with the offering. These emotions can be enhanced by inducing arousal—a state of heightened physical and psychological activity that intensifies emotional responses—and by facilitating flow, where customers become fully immersed in activities that match their skills. Identity-based emotions, on the other hand, are linked to the personal relevance and meaning of a company's offerings and are directly related to an individual's self-image. These emotions can be cultivated by affirming self-identity and fostering a sense of belonging.

Our evaluations of experiences are often retrospective, driven more by our memories than by the actual events. When making these evaluations, we tend to overlook the duration of the experience and instead focus on specific moments that define it. These defining moments are not randomly selected but follow a consistent pattern known as the peak–end rule. This rule suggests that our retrospective evaluations are shaped by the most intense positive or negative moments (the "peaks") and the final moments (the "end") of the experience. These key moments influence how we remember everyday experiences, shape our behavioral intentions, and determine our future actions.

KEY TAKEAWAYS

Define the consumption experience. Create value by managing anticipation, first impressions, actual consumption, and the disposal of the offering.

Identify the key consumption drivers. Manage usage occasions, frequency, and quantity to define when customers use the offering and how much they consume.

Beware of habituation. Break the habituation pattern by partitioning the consumer experience and infusing variety.

Generate excitement. Engage customers emotionally through interactive experiences.

Create memories. Follow the peak–end rule to craft memorable experiences.

SPOTLIGHT: IDENTIFYING SERVICE GAPS

Designing and managing customer experience can be significantly improved by identifying and preventing service failures. A widely used approach in service management is the gap model of service quality. This model outlines the service delivery processes, key interactions that define these processes, and the discrepancies (gaps) in a company's efforts to deliver customer value (Figure 9).[21]

Figure 9. The Service-Gap Model[22]

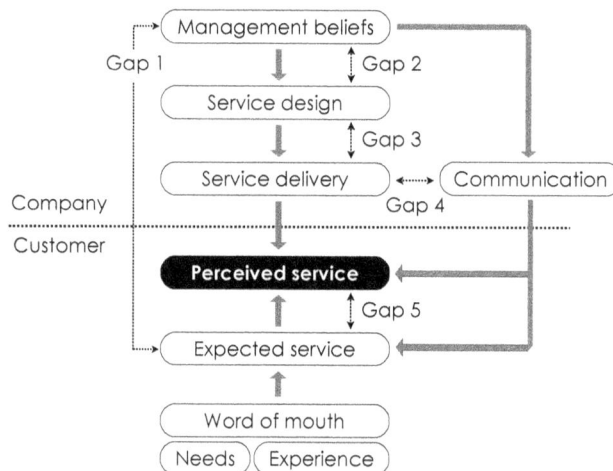

According to the service-gap model, customers' evaluations of a service experience are shaped by their perceptions of the actual service provided by the company and their expectations of what the service should be. These expectations are influenced by factors such as company communications, word-of-mouth information about the service from different sources, the specific needs customers seek to fulfill with the service, and their prior experiences with the company's service. The actual service delivered by the company is determined by the beliefs held by management about the level of service the company should provide to its customers as well as how this service should be implemented.

Identifying and preventing these breakdowns is crucial for creating a superior customer experience. The five commonly encountered service gaps are detailed below.

- The *market-insight gap* (Gap 1) arises when there is a mismatch between customer expectations and management's understanding of what constitutes good service. For instance, the management of a fast-food chain might believe that customers most value a large menu selection, while customers actually prioritize quick service. This gap often results from poorly conducted customer research, misinterpretation of research findings, or a flawed market strategy that targets customers with diverse and sometimes conflicting needs and expectations.

- The *service-design gap* (Gap 2) reflects a discrepancy between management's understanding of customer needs and the translation of those needs into concrete service specifications. For example, even if managers know that speed of service is crucial, they might fail to establish clear policies to guide front-line employees. Service-design gaps frequently stem from management's failure to convert insights about specific customer needs into standardized, actionable service policies. These gaps can also occur when a company cannot align supply with demand, leading to insufficient resources to meet customer needs and maintain service quality.

- The *service-delivery gap* (Gap 3) reflects a discrepancy between service-quality specifications and the actual service provided. For instance, even with well-defined guidelines and policies, employees may fall short of meeting management's standards due to a lack of willingness or ability. This gap often arises from deficiencies in employee recruitment, training, motivation, and supervision. Since service delivery is interactive, it also depends on how customers respond to the service. Service quality can suffer if customers fail to communicate their needs accurately, do not follow standard communication norms, or otherwise hinder the service-delivery process.

- The *service-communication gap* (Gap 4) occurs when there is a mismatch between what is communicated about the service and what is actually delivered. This gap emerges when the company's communications—through advertising, public relations, or personal selling—misrepresent the service that customers eventually receive. For example, a fast-food chain might advertise quick and friendly service but fail to meet these expectations in practice. Service-communication gaps typically result from a disconnect between the company's desire to promote its services to generate demand and its actual ability to deliver superior service. These gaps can range from minor overpromising and slightly exaggerating service benefits to major misrepresentations, with little alignment between what is promised and what is delivered.

- The *service-expectation gap* (Gap 5) reflects a discrepancy between what customers expect and their perception of what they receive. Customer expectations play a key role in shaping their service experiences, leading individuals with different expectations to perceive the same service encounter differently. Several factors influence these expectations, including customers' needs and preferences, their previous experiences with the company's services, communications from third-party sources like friends, family, media, and competitors, as well as the company's own communications.

Because it highlights the essential elements of delivering effective service, the gap model is often used to conduct service quality audits within organizations. To do this, a company starts by mapping out the key steps in its service process, identifying potential areas where service discrepancies could occur, testing for the presence of actual service gaps, and, when needed, developing an action plan to close these gaps and enhance service delivery. By systematically addressing these gaps, a company can significantly improve the consistency and quality of its service offerings, ultimately leading to higher customer satisfaction and loyalty.

THE CX CANVAS: ORCHESTRATING THE CONSUMPTION EXPERIENCE

Because consumption is often the most critical aspect of a customer's experience with a company's offering, it is essential to develop a strategy that maximizes the value derived from this experience. Crafting such a strategy involves two key elements: (1) analyzing customers' interactions with the company's products and services, and (2) developing a course of action to enhance the value customers gain from these interactions. These two components of creating impactful experiences are illustrated in Figure 10 and are discussed in detail next.

Figure 10. Orchestrating the Consumption Experience: The Big Picture

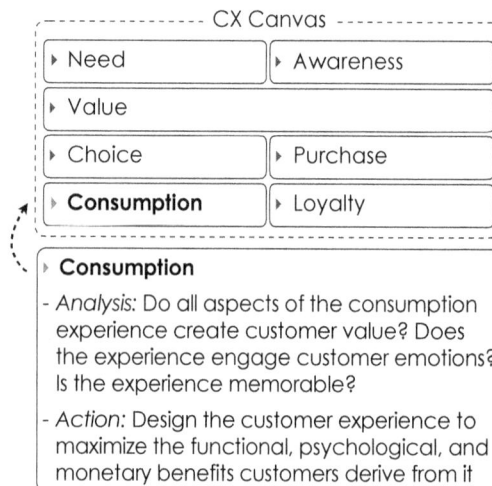

Orchestrating a meaningful consumption experience starts with evaluating whether customers' interactions with the company's offerings create value throughout the entire experience, engage customers emotionally, and create lasting memories. This analysis can be guided by the following questions:

- *Do all aspects of the consumption experience create customer value?* This question aims to identify all components of the customer experience, assess the value created across these components, and identify areas where the experience can be enhanced. This ensures that the company does not inadvertently overlook relevant aspects of the customer experience, thus missing an opportunity to create value for both customers and the company.

- *Does the experience engage customer emotions?* The goal is to determine the level of customers' emotional engagement with the offering and identify ways to enhance this engagement. This is crucial because emotions can have a greater impact on customers' experiences than the functional aspects of the offering.

- *Does the experience create meaningful memories?* This question seeks to establish whether the consumption experience is both impactful and memorable. This is important because customers tend to seek and value experiences that create meaningful memories and often prioritize these experiences over those that offer only transient gratification.

The primary goal of this analysis is to examine how customers interact with the company's products and services to uncover opportunities for enhancing the overall consumption experience and maximizing its value. In this context, three main challenges can be identified, each necessitating a distinct course of action:

- *Certain aspects of the experience do not create customer value.* Pinpointing deficiencies in the consumption experience helps uncover opportunities for enhancement. This can be achieved by augmenting all relevant elements of the experience—from anticipating the experience, to customers' first interaction with and usage of the offering, to ultimately disposing of the offering—in a way that maximizes customer value.

- *The experience is not emotionally engaging.* This challenge stems from a missed opportunity to connect with customers on an emotional level. A company's goal in this case is to deepen customers' emotional bond with the offering, thereby creating a more impactful consumption experience. This can be achieved by providing interactive experiences that generate excitement and evoke emotions tied to the personal relevance of the company's offerings to its customers.

- *The experience does not create meaningful memories.* Although customers may have a satisfactory experience, it might not be memorable. The goal is to enhance the experience to leave a lasting impression on customers. This can be achieved by creating exceptional moments that stand out in their memories and ensuring the experience concludes on a high note.

The three challenges to delivering a meaningful consumption experience, along with the relevant actions, are summarized in Figure 11. These challenges are interconnected: Each has the potential to profoundly impact the overall consumption experience. The ultimate goal of the action plan is to help the company uncover new ways to enhance the consumption experience, engage customers on an emotional level, and create a memorable and meaningful journey.

Figure 11. Orchestrating the Consumption Experience: The Action Plan

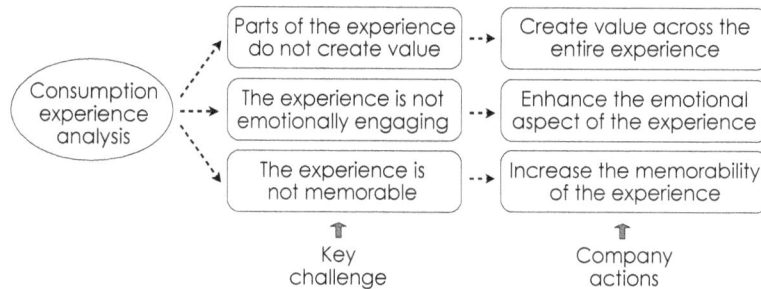

Imagine you are managing a restaurant and want to enhance your customers' dining experience. You might start by identifying aspects that fall short of customers' expectations and detract from the overall experience. A practical approach is to create a flowchart outlining the entire dining experience from a customer's perspective—including parking, coat checking, wait time to be seated, placing an order, and receiving the food—to pinpoint potential trouble spots.

Next, evaluate the experience in terms of its ability to engage customers by appealing to their feelings. Consider factors such as the restaurant's ambiance, the staff's attitude, and how the meals are assembled and presented to diners. Finally, assess how memorable the experience is, focusing on whether it has peak moments and a positive endpoint.

Once the problematic areas have been identified, the next step is to address these challenges. The resulting actions should reflect the identified deficiencies in the customer experience. For example, if excessive wait time between ordering and receiving meals detracts from the experience, consider speeding up service, offering a complimentary amuse-bouche between courses, or providing entertainment to make the wait more engaging.

If the experience meets customers' expectations but is not emotionally engaging, consider ways to connect with customers on a deeper level. For instance, you could ask patrons if they are celebrating a special occasion and incorporate this into the dining experience. If the experience is satisfactory but uneventful, consider adding special peak moments, such as flambéing a dessert tableside.

And if the ending of the experience is not particularly positive or memorable, consider reimagining the final moments. For example, instead of concluding with payment—a potentially unpleasant experience—you might offer a prepaid set menu so that the last thing diners experience is the joy of eating dessert. Alternatively, you could offer a "surprise" dessert or a parting gift after the bill has been paid to leave a lasting positive impression.

CHAPTER EIGHT

MANAGING CUSTOMER LOYALTY

I'll take fifty percent efficiency to get one hundred percent loyalty.

—Samuel Goldwyn, American film producer,
co-founder of MGM Studios

Customers often have recurring needs, leading to an iterative interaction with a company's offerings that involves repeated purchase decisions. There are several ways customers can make these decisions. They might restart the decision-making process by seeking new information about available options, forming a new consideration set, and making a choice that may or may not include the previously purchased option.

Alternatively, customers might adjust their consideration set without actively seeking new information. For example, they could expand the set by including new options or narrow it by excluding some previously considered options. Customers might also choose a different option from the initial consideration set. Finally, they might simply repurchase the same offering without exploring other options (Figure 1).

Figure 1. The Customer Experience Map: Managing Loyalty

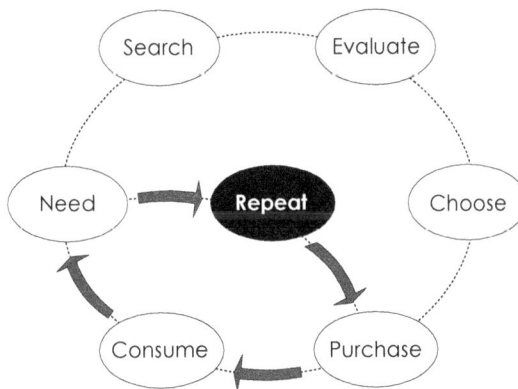

Clearly, the latter scenario — straight repurchase — is the most desirable outcome for the company whose products or services were initially chosen by the customer. The likelihood of this behavior largely depends on how satisfied customers are with the company's offering and the extent of their loyalty to the company, its products, and its brands. To encourage repurchase, a company must identify the drivers of customer loyalty and develop strategies to build and maintain a loyal customer base. The challenge lies in creating actionable strategies that effectively promote customer loyalty. Consider the following scenarios:

- You are advising a large grocery retailer on managing the inventory of different yogurt flavors it carries. Your client hired a marketing research company to conduct an experiment where participants were presented with five different yogurt flavors and asked to imagine buying single-serve yogurt containers for an entire week. The retailer is considering setting inventory levels for different yogurt flavors based on the experiment's results. What would you advise?

- You are designing a loyalty program for a large hotel chain with resorts in various exotic destinations. One of the key decisions is determining the nature of the rewards customers will receive for each stay: cash or points redeemable for future stays. What factors should you consider when making this decision?

- The product development team is seeking your guidance on the formulation of a new odor-removal product. The question is whether to add a particular scent or leave the product fragrance-free. The team is inclined to keep the product unscented, believing that its primary benefit—removing odors— is in itself a sufficient reason for customers to buy and use the product. They are also concerned that not everyone will like the same scent and adding one might make the product less attractive to some potential buyers. What would you recommend?

- You are advising a major sports team on their loyalty program. The program offers members early access to seats for major games and season tickets, as well as free visits to some team training sessions. One challenge is how to attract customers to grow the program and maintain their interest. What would you advise?

- You are advising a pharmaceutical company that has developed a new drug to be taken in weekly cycles—every day for six days, followed by skipping the seventh day. The concern is that patients might forget to skip the drug after six days or forget to resume taking it after the day off. What steps should the company take to ensure patients comply with the prescribed medication schedule?

This chapter addresses the scenarios above by delving into the crucial elements of customer loyalty and the science behind cultivating a loyal customer base. We begin by exploring the benefits of loyalty for both companies and their customers, identifying four primary drivers of loyalty. Next, we examine functional loyalty, emphasizing the role of satisfaction in fostering loyal customers and discussing the core principles of designing effective reward programs. We then highlight the importance of emotional loyalty, illustrating how connecting with customers on an emotional level can help build lasting loyalty. Following this, we explore identity-based loyalty, focusing on the need for self-expression as a driver of loyalty and the role of brands in fostering this connection. Finally, we investigate the key drivers of behavioral loyalty and the critical role of habit formation in designing customer experiences.

The discussion of the conceptual issues involved in creating customer loyalty is enhanced with examples of managerial decisions that illustrate the key points. Specifically, we look at how Procter & Gamble repositioned Febreze to become a billion-dollar brand, how the advertising agency Goodby, Silverstein & Partners got consumers excited about drinking milk, how Southwest Airlines made the flight experience enjoyable and memorable, how Johnnie Walker inspired people around the world, why Real Madrid continues to be one of the world's most widely supported football teams, how Dove created a loyal customer base by becoming an identity-relevant brand, and how Oil of Olay rejuvenated its brand to increase its loyal customer base.

Now, let's delve deeper into how loyalty influences customer behavior and examine the roles of the four main types of loyalty—functional, emotional, identity, and behavioral—in driving customer actions.

Understanding Customer Loyalty

Successful companies carefully cultivate their relationship with customers to foster long-term loyalty. Loyalty is important because it influences many decisions that customers make, helping a company solidify its market position by increasing the value it creates and captures from its customers. Customer loyalty does not just happen. It requires a deep understanding of how loyalty impacts customer behavior and a strategic, sustained effort by the company to build a loyal customer base.

Loyalty as a Driver of Customer Behavior

Imagine a company launching a new product, such as toothpaste. Market tests show that customers like the product and indicate they are likely to buy it. Despite this promising start, the product launch results in a lukewarm customer response and fails to gain market share. While several factors could drive this outcome, one commonly overlooked by managers is the fact that many customers already have established preferences and loyalties to other brands. As a result, when these customers need to buy toothpaste, they often ignore other options and continue purchasing the brand they have trusted for years.

Loyalty is a key source of value for a company, offering several important benefits. First, retaining existing customers saves resources that would otherwise be spent acquiring new customers to compensate for attrition. Additionally, serving existing customers often incurs lower costs since they are already familiar with the company's offerings. Loyal customers are also more likely to become advocates for the company, attracting new customers and strengthening the loyalty of current ones.

Not only do companies seek loyal customers, but customers themselves often prefer to be loyal. This preference is rooted in a desire for consistency: If customers have a positive experience, they are likely to stick with the same offering. Loyalty simplifies decision making, allowing customers to repurchase their current product without going through the time-consuming process of seeking, evaluating, and selecting another option that meets their needs. Loyalty also streamlines the consumption experience, as customers familiar with the company's offering tend to find it easier to use and better utilize its features. And for some, loyalty serves as a means of self-identification: They choose lifestyle brands such as Harley-Davidson, Ralph Lauren, and Diesel to express their preferences and values to others.

Customer loyalty can be generally divided into two main types: psychological loyalty and behavioral loyalty.

Psychological loyalty reflects the way customers think and feel about a company and its offerings. Because it reflects a customer's state of mind, psychological loyalty cannot be readily observed; it can only be inferred from customers' behavior. Psychological loyalty is not binary but spans a spectrum of preferences that vary in strength. On one end are customers with little affinity for the company's offerings who are open to considering other options if they are competitively priced and easily accessible. At the opposite end are those who are completely loyal and are willing to pay a premium, exert extra effort, and wait to get the company's offering.

Behavioral loyalty reflects the way customers act with respect to an offering, such as how frequently they repurchase the offering, whether they also purchase competitors' offerings, and if they actively advocate for the company's offering. Unlike psychological loyalty, which is not readily observable by the company, behavioral loyalty can be readily observed and measured. Behavioral loyalty varies in intensity and can involve different levels of commitment to the company's offering. For example, some customers may split their loyalty between two brands, choosing the company's products only half the time, while others may be exclusively loyal, consistently purchasing only from the company and ignoring all other brands.

To highlight the difference between these two types of loyalty, consider a customer who exclusively buys Harley-Davidson motorcycles due to a strong emotional attachment to the brand, versus a customer who uses Uber's ride-share service simply out of habit or because there are no better alternatives. Both customers display behavioral loyalty by repeatedly choosing the company's offerings, but their motivations differ. As a result, their responses to changes in the market are likely to vary. The Harley-Davidson customer is more likely to stay loyal even when new competitors emerge, while the Uber customer might switch as soon as a comparable alternative becomes available.

True loyalty encompasses both psychological and behavioral elements. Behavioral loyalty is crucial because psychological loyalty must translate into actual market actions to have an impact. Conversely, psychological loyalty is vital because without a strong connection to the company's offerings, customer behavior can easily shift in response to more attractive alternatives or challenges like stock-outs and temporary price increases. Ultimately, customer actions are driven by their beliefs and feelings toward the market options available to them. Without a psychological attachment, customers will eventually move away from the options they currently use. For behavioral loyalty to endure, it must be grounded in psychological commitment.

Loyalty Barriers and Loyalty Drivers

Customer loyalty is difficult to acquire and challenging to sustain. This is somewhat paradoxical given that loyalty benefits both companies and their customers. If companies seek loyal customers and customers derive value from being loyal, why is customer loyalty not ubiquitous? To answer this question, it is important to consider both the barriers that hinder customer loyalty and the strategies to cultivate it.

Barriers to Loyalty

Although customers recognize the benefits of being loyal to a company's offerings, various obstacles can hinder their willingness to become and remain loyal. Identifying these barriers is crucial for a company aiming to build a loyal customer base. Broadly speaking, there are three main barriers to loyalty: a decrease in the attractiveness of the company's offering, a change in customer preferences, and variety-seeking behavior.

A *decrease in the attractiveness* of the company's offering can arise from several factors. First, it might be due to a decrease in the offering's benefits. For instance, a company could alter its product's formulation to cut costs, inadvertently making it less appealing to customers. Additionally, increasing the cost to buyers—such as raising prices or maintenance expenses—can diminish the offering's appeal. Availability issues, like stock-outs or extended delivery times, can also reduce an offering's attractiveness.

The decline in the relative attractiveness of a company's offering can also result from competitors enhancing their offerings. For example, competitors might introduce superior technology, improve service, permanently lower prices, or launch aggressive sales promotions. To illustrate, Amazon has successfully drawn many customers away from traditional retail stores by offering a broader product assortment and greater convenience at competitive prices.

In addition to a decrease in the attractiveness of a company's offering, another barrier to loyalty is a *change in customer preferences*, which often involves a heightened focus on reducing costs or the pursuit of different benefits. Various factors can drive customers to reduce costs or minimize the time and effort required to obtain an offering. For example, their financial situation might have deteriorated, forcing them to seek lower priced options. Alternatively, changes in their life circumstances, such as a busier schedule, could limit their ability to invest time and effort in obtaining a product, leading them to choose a more convenient option. Customer preferences can also evolve, prompting them to seek different benefits. For example, a promotion at work might inspire a customer to upgrade from a mid-size sedan to a luxury sports car, only for them to later switch to a larger SUV to accommodate a growing family.

Another important barrier to loyalty is customers' desire for *variety* in their consumption experiences. Over time, people often become bored with the offerings they routinely choose due to habituation and seek novelty for its own sake. Beyond simple boredom, the desire for variety can also be driven by the fear of missing out. In this case, curiosity about other available options and the concern that they might be missing out on something better can motivate customers to explore alternatives. For example, imagine being faced with a selection of yogurt flavors: strawberry, raspberry, blueberry, peach, and vanilla. While strawberry may be your favorite, you might occasionally choose other flavors to satisfy a craving for variety or to discover a new flavor that could surpass strawberry as your top choice.

Research on variety-seeking behavior has revealed an intriguing pattern: Purchases intended for future consumption usually involve a greater variety than those intended for immediate consumption. For example, when buying yogurt for the week, we might choose one of each flavor we enjoy. Yet, when purchasing for immediate consumption, we have a much lower inclination toward variety. For instance, if our preferred flavor is strawberry, we are likely to end up choosing it on most days. This behavior suggests that people tend to overestimate their need for variety—a phenomenon known as the diversification bias.[1]

The Four Paths to Loyalty

Building loyalty starts with understanding the underlying reasons why customers remain loyal to a company and its products or services. In this context, there are four primary drivers of customer loyalty: functional, emotional, identity, and behavioral loyalty. These drivers correspond to how customers think (the mind), how they feel (the heart), who they are (the self), and how they habitually act (the hand). The four drivers of customer loyalty are illustrated in Figure 2 and discussed in more detail below.

Figure 2. The Four Drivers of Loyalty

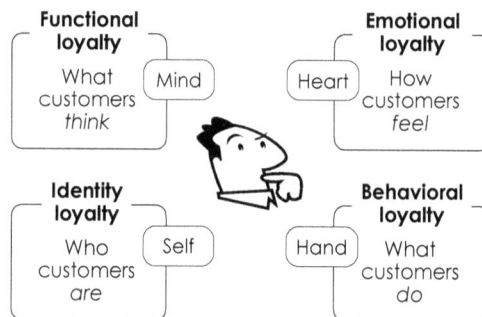

- *Functional loyalty* is rooted in the customer's *mind*, reflecting what customers *think* about the functional benefits of the offering. Here, customers might justify their preference by saying: "I use it because it is the best." Functional loyalty typically arises from satisfaction with the utilitarian aspects of the offering.

- *Emotional loyalty* originates from the customer's *heart*, highlighting how customers *feel* when engaging with the offering. Here, customers might justify their preference by saying: "I use it because it brings me joy." This type of loyalty stems from creating an affective connection with customers by tapping into their feelings.

- *Identity loyalty* arises from the customer's *self-image* and mirrors who customers *are* and how they perceive themselves. Here, to justify their preference customers might say: "I use this because it is me." This form of loyalty is typically associated with offerings that align with customers' values, enhance their self-image, and are seen as integral to their identity.

- *Behavioral loyalty* stems from the customer's habitual actions and reflects how they *act*, such as when their hand grabs a product off the shelf without much thought. Here, to justify their preference, customers might say: "I use this because this is what I usually do." This type of loyalty is typically associated with routine, low-involvement purchases that require little mental deliberation.

The first three types of loyalty—functional, emotional, and identity—align with the core human needs that a company aims to satisfy with its offerings (as discussed in Chapter 2). Functional loyalty arises from meeting customers' functional needs, emotional loyalty from addressing their affective needs, and identity loyalty from catering to their need for self-expression. Behavioral loyalty, on the other hand, may originate from any of these three types of needs and develops from habits formed over time while fulfilling these needs. Next, we explore these four types of loyalty in greater depth.

Functional Loyalty

Functional loyalty stems from satisfaction with the performance aspects of a product or service. Delivering customer satisfaction is the key to cultivating a loyal customer base. Satisfied customers are more likely to stay with the company longer, increase their purchases, recommend the company to others, and ultimately create more value for the business. We explore how satisfaction drives loyalty and examine the critical elements of designing effective reward programs in the following sections.

Satisfaction as a Driver of Loyalty

Customer satisfaction reflects how effectively a company's products and services meet or exceed a customer's needs and expectations. Needs are fundamental drivers of behavior and play a crucial role in determining customer satisfaction. However, they are not the only factors customers consider when evaluating their experience with a company's offerings. Customers often have expectations regarding a product's performance, and they use these expectations as a benchmark to assess their satisfaction with the actual experience.

To achieve customer satisfaction, both needs and expectations must be met. Even if an offering satisfies a customer's needs, it may still result in dissatisfaction if it falls short of their expectations. Conversely, when customers have low expectations—such as when choosing from less desirable options—an offering that merely meets those expectations might not lead to satisfaction.

To deliver customer satisfaction, a company must recognize that customers have varying needs, and the same product or service may result in different satisfaction levels. Some customers might prioritize performance, while others may value reliability or convenience above all else. For example, for courier companies such as FedEx and DHL, speed is often the key attribute on which they need to deliver to stay competitive. In contrast, for container shipping companies such as Maersk and MSC, on-time delivery is often more important than speed as their customers need to coordinate logistics—arranging off-loading equipment, trucking, and storage—to handle shipments efficiently. Therefore, to foster customer satisfaction, a company must tailor its offerings to align with the diverse values of its customers.

Comparing needs and expectations with actual experiences typically leads to one of four outcomes. Customers are *satisfied* when their needs are met and their expectations are confirmed, meaning their actual experience aligns with both. Customers are *dissatisfied* when their needs are unmet, and the actual experience falls short of their expectations. Customers are *delighted* when their needs are met, their expectations are surpassed, and they feel that no further improvement is necessary or possible. And customers are *indifferent* when the offering largely meets their needs, and they are content with it, even if they believe a superior option might be available.

Given the crucial role that expectations play in evaluating the customer experience, satisfaction is often defined by the confirmation or disconfirmation of these expectations, which serve as a reference point (Figure 3). The expectancy–disconfirmation model has become the dominant method for assessing customer satisfaction. According to this model, satisfaction occurs when expectations are met, while dissatisfaction arises when the actual performance falls short of expectations, a scenario known as negative disconfirmation. Conversely, delight is experienced when actual performance exceeds expectations, a scenario known as positive disconfirmation.[2]

Figure 3. Expectations Drive Satisfaction

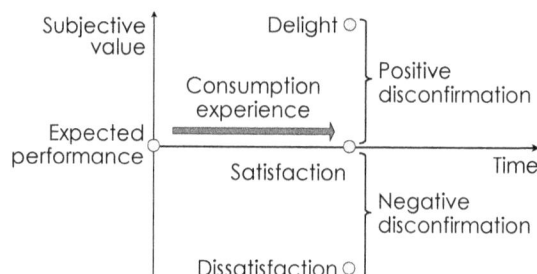

Expectations are shaped by several factors, including customers' needs, their previous experiences with the same or similar products, the brand image, and communications related to the offering. For instance, a consumer looking to upgrade her phone may have high expectations for a company's new product because of her positive experience with her current phone, the company's reputation, its advertisements, recommendations from the salesperson, positive product ratings, and advice from friends.

In addition to serving as a reference point for evaluating a customer's experience, expectations can also influence the experience itself. Reference points can impact customers' perceptions in two ways. One possibility is that the expectations create a halo effect, where high expectations lead to increased satisfaction. Such a halo effect often occurs when the actual experience is ambiguous and difficult to evaluate objectively. For example, novice wine drinkers tasting an expensive but average-quality wine might perceive it as exceptional, believing that a high price indicates superior taste.

Alternatively, instead of aligning their perception of the experience with their expectations, customers might focus on the gap between what they expected and what they actually experienced. In such cases, high expectations can lead to lower satisfaction if the actual experience falls short. This typically occurs when the actual experience significantly differs from what customers anticipated, especially when the quality of the experience can be readily assessed. For example, a wine connoisseur tasting an expensive wine may feel extremely dissatisfied if the wine turns out to be merely average.

The comparison of needs and expectations with the actual experience has an asymmetrical impact on satisfaction: The negative effect of unmet expectations is much stronger than the positive effect of exceeding them. This phenomenon aligns with the principle of loss aversion, discussed in Chapter 4, where negative deviations from the reference point (losses) are given more weight than positive deviations (gains). This asymmetry also extends to customers' willingness to share their experiences: Dissatisfied customers tend to be more vocal and more likely to criticize the company than satisfied customers are to praise it.

The asymmetrical way in which customers assess positive and negative experiences underscores the importance of managing customer expectations. While nearly every company strives to prevent negative experiences, the perception of an experience can vary greatly depending on customers' expectations. The same experience might be viewed as positive when expectations are low and as negative when expectations are high. This reliance on meeting expectations calls into question the strategy of some companies that promise not only to meet but also to exceed customer expectations.

Promising to exceed expectations is a double-edged sword: While striving to surpass expectations can attract new customers, failing to deliver on this promise can lead to disappointment, even if the actual experience is positive. Moreover, even when a company succeeds in surpassing the high expectations it has set, this can raise future expectations to levels that may become increasingly difficult to meet. Setting realistic expectations that a company can consistently fulfill is often a more effective strategy than setting lofty expectations that may not always be realistic.

Reward Programs as a Driver of Loyalty

Reward programs, also known as loyalty programs, are designed to build and sustain customer loyalty by offering rewards for ongoing patronage. These programs can increase the frequency of customer engagement with the company's offerings, retain current customers, and attract new customers who value the benefits provided by the loyalty program. Popular examples of reward programs include airlines' frequent flyer programs, hotels' frequent stay programs, and credit card companies' spending-based reward programs.

Rooted in the idea that behaviors followed by a reward are more likely to be repeated, rewards have become a cornerstone of nearly all loyalty programs. By offering incentives for purchasing and using their products or services, companies seek to foster ongoing loyalty and boost consumption. For these programs to succeed, it is crucial that customers view the rewards as both attainable and desirable.

Based on their type, the benefits provided by reward programs fall into two main categories: hard benefits and soft benefits. Hard benefits include rewards like money, points, and miles that can be accumulated and redeemed for the company's products and services. Soft benefits, on the other hand, offer exclusive privileges such as priority treatment and dedicated service centers, designed to enhance the customer experience and make them feel valued by the company.

When deciding on the *hard benefits* of reward programs, companies face an important decision: Should the rewards be monetary, such as cashback, or nonmonetary, like loyalty points? Economic theories suggest that customers would naturally prefer monetary rewards over nonmonetary rewards of equivalent value, given the fungibility of money and the flexibility it offers in purchasing desired items. However, this is not always the case, especially with rewards involving hedonic experiences geared toward self-indulgence. One reason for this preference is that nonmonetary rewards alleviate the so-called "pain of paying," which can spoil the enjoyment derived from consumption or discourage the purchase altogether.

Research shows that purchases involving monetary transactions often trigger negative emotions associated with spending money. This pain of paying tends to be more intense for hedonic experiences, such as vacations, fine dining, and fashion accessories, which are harder to justify since they are not necessities. Spending on such experiences can also evoke guilt, particularly when individuals consider more practical uses for their money.[3] This reaction partly stems from the fact that frugality is considered a virtue in many cultures, while self-indulgence often conflicts with prevailing social norms.

In contrast, nonmonetary rewards, such as frequent flyer miles and hotel stays, often bypass the tradeoffs associated with monetary transactions. These rewards are typically not fungible and cannot easily be used to pay for necessities. Instead, customers tend to place these rewards in a separate mental account designated for hedonic experiences (see Chapter 5 for more detail on mental accounting). Once these rewards are allocated to the "fun" mental account reserved for enjoyable activities, individuals feel less pressure to justify their indulgences and are less likely to experience guilt for choosing self-gratifying options. Moreover, since earning loyalty perks usually requires some effort, customers may feel that they have earned the right to indulge, viewing these rewards as a deserved benefit for their loyalty.

When determining *soft benefits*, a key decision for a company involves deciding whether to implement multiple levels of benefits and how many premium service levels to offer. Introducing different levels of benefits means categorizing customers into tiers, with higher tiers receiving more substantial rewards. This tiered structure can significantly influence customers' perception of their status within the program. A sense of status is critical because it can provide customers with a feeling of achievement that reflects their level of loyalty to the company. It can also offer a sense of elevated social standing compared to customers in lower loyalty tiers.

Customers' perceptions of their status within a loyalty program are shaped not only by the benefits of their tier but also by the number of tiers—both above and below their own—as well as the relative size of each tier. Status is inherently relative, and its evaluation depends on the social standing of other customers, who act as reference points. Consequently, the exclusivity of attaining a privileged status enhances customers' perceived superiority. Introducing additional tiers below a particular customer's tier can increase their perceived status, while adding tiers above can decrease it. This relative perception underscores the importance of thoughtfully designing and managing the various status levels within a loyalty program.[4]

Reward programs not only help companies retain their existing customers but also encourage more frequent engagement with their products or services. This is because the criteria for earning rewards often serve as implicit goals that drive customer behavior. The closer a customer gets to reaching a reward, the more likely they are to take actions to achieve it. This phenomenon, known as the *goal-gradient effect*, was first observed in the 1930s by psychologist Clark Hull, who found that rats navigated mazes faster as they approached food. Subsequent studies confirmed that humans exhibit a similar pattern: Our motivation to achieve a goal intensifies as we get closer to it.

To explore the goal-gradient effect in reward programs, researchers at Columbia University examined how purchase frequency changed as customers neared a reward. The study focused on a coffee shop that used punch cards to reward loyal customers, offering a free drink after every ten purchases—a typical loyalty program at the time. To test whether customers speed up their purchases as they approach the reward, the researchers compared the time between the first and second purchases with the time between the ninth and tenth. The results showed that the time between the ninth and tenth purchases was about 20% shorter than between the first and second. This indicates that as customers got closer to earning the free drink, they increased their rate of consumption.[5]

Many companies strategically apply the goal-gradient principle to foster customer loyalty. For example, credit card companies often offer sign-up bonuses that incentivize new customers to increase their spending to reach a certain threshold within a set time frame. These bonuses not only help entice customers to join the program but also motivate them to use the new card more frequently by giving them an initial sense of progress. To maintain this momentum, many companies set milestones with motivational rewards, providing benchmarks that serve as reference points and accelerate usage. These milestones help overcome the "stuck-in-the-middle" effect, where customers have made some progress but are still far from reaching the ultimate goal.[6]

A practical application of this strategy can be seen in airline loyalty programs, where customers earn miles to reach different status tiers, each offering progressively better perks. Many airlines enhance this experience by displaying progress bars on their apps and websites, visually showing customers how close they are to the next tier. The nearer customers get to reaching a new status, the more likely they are to book additional flights or use affiliated services to accumulate the necessary miles. Similarly, retailers with loyalty programs use this principle by awarding points for purchases, which can be redeemed for discounts or special rewards once a certain threshold is met. The anticipation of the reward encourages customers to concentrate their shopping with the retailer to earn points faster.

Switching Costs as a Driver of Loyalty

Another strategy companies use to enhance customer loyalty is creating switching costs. These costs can take the form of financial penalties, such as fees for early termination of contracts or forfeiting accumulated benefits when switching to a competitor. For example, a mobile service provider might charge a cancellation fee for ending a contract prematurely, and an airline could invalidate frequent flyer miles if a customer fails to book a flight within a certain timeframe. Switching costs can also be nonmonetary, requiring significant time and effort from customers to change companies. For instance, if canceling a service involves complicated paperwork, customers may find the hassle too great and choose to stay with their current provider.

Switching costs can also be psychological, particularly when customers who are already familiar with a company's products and services face the prospect of expending mental effort to learn how to use a competitor's offerings. The greater the complexity of the offering, the higher the cognitive costs of learning its specifics, making customers more reluctant to switch. This reluctance intensifies as an offering becomes ingrained in their routine, making the prospect of learning and adapting to a new one seem even more daunting. As a result, customers may conclude that the time and effort required to achieve the same level of familiarity with a new offering are not justified, leading them to stay with the current offering.

For example, Apple has successfully created an ecosystem that tightly integrates its devices and services, enhancing user convenience and promoting continued loyalty to Apple products rather than switching to competitors. This ecosystem ensures that products work together seamlessly, enabling users to start a task on one device and effortlessly continue it on another. Additionally, the learning curve associated with switching to a different platform plays a crucial role in maintaining customer loyalty. The effort and time required to adapt to a new system can serve as significant barriers to switching, particularly for users who are comfortable and proficient with Apple's interface and software, thereby increasing the cognitive costs of changing platforms.

Creating switching costs can be seen as the flip side of launching a reward program. In fact, a reward program and switching costs together resemble a carrot-and-stick approach. The reward program serves as the carrot, enticing customers to buy the company's products, while switching costs function as the stick, penalizing them for disloyalty. Companies vary in how they balance these rewards and penalties to cultivate a loyal customer base. Some offer generous and flexible reward programs, while others focus on retaining customers by imposing significant restrictions that make leaving difficult.

Since many customers perceive switching costs as a company-imposed limitation on their freedom to choose the offering that best suits their needs, managers must exercise caution when implementing such measures. Imposing switching costs that seem unnecessary, unreasonable, or unfair can backfire, damaging customers' attitudes toward the company and creating the impression that the company is exploiting their loyalty and goodwill. This risk is especially pronounced when the switching costs involve a financial loss or require significant effort from the customer.

Emotional Loyalty

Customer satisfaction with the functional benefits of a company's offering is only one aspect of fostering loyalty. Equally important is how customers feel about the offering. The emotional component of the customer experience is crucial because many decisions are driven by emotions as much as by logic. As a result, customers' emotional responses can profoundly influence their overall experience with the offering.

Emotions as a Driver of Loyalty

Emotional loyalty stems from creating a deep emotional connection with customers by engaging their feelings and fostering a sense of enjoyment with the product or service. While enjoyment and satisfaction are closely related, they represent distinct aspects of the customer experience. Emotional loyalty is rooted in intuition rather than logic. Unlike functional loyalty, which is largely a System 2 process driven by satisfaction with the offering, emotional loyalty is primarily a System 1 process. Satisfaction is generally determined by the question, "Did this experience meet my expectations?" In contrast, enjoyment arises from questions like, "How did I feel about this experience? Did I enjoy it? Did it make me happy?"

Emotions can profoundly shape how customers perceive a company's offering. The emotional dimension of the experience can even overshadow the satisfaction or dissatisfaction with the offering itself. As a result, the memory of how customers felt during the experience often has a greater impact on their future decisions and loyalty than the actual performance of the offering. Because emotions can deeply influence the overall experience, people tend to gravitate toward offerings that evoke positive emotions and avoid those that generate negative ones.

The idea that people are driven to seek pleasure has been central to most theories of human motivation, from ancient Greek philosophers to 20th century psychologists. This concept, known as the pleasure principle, was most notably advanced by Sigmund Freud, who argued that all human activity is governed by the hedonic principle, where decisions are instinctively guided by the pursuit of pleasure and the avoidance of pain. A key outcome of this principle is the concept of emotional reinforcement, which suggests that behaviors leading to pleasurable outcomes are more likely to be repeated.

The importance of emotional reinforcement was vividly illustrated in the 1950s with the discovery that emotional stimulation can be a powerful driver of behavior. A classic experiment demonstrated this by presenting rats with a lever that when pressed delivered small electrical jolts to electrodes implanted in the pleasure centers of their brains. Unsurprisingly, the rats quickly learned to press the lever to receive this pleasurable brain stimulation. What was surprising, however, was the intensity of their response: The rats would press the lever thousands of times per hour to stimulate their brains. Even more astonishing, the rats preferred this stimulation over food and water, even when they were hungry and thirsty. Some rats would self-stimulate up to 50,000 times a day, neglecting all other activities, and had to be removed from the study to prevent death by self-starvation.[7]

This experiment, along with many others involving both animals and humans, highlights the profound influence of emotional stimulation. Research has shown that all forms of pleasure, from simple sensory enjoyment to more complex aesthetic experiences, increase dopamine levels in the same pleasure-related area of the brain, the nucleus accumbens. This neural connection suggests that basic sensory pleasures are linked to broader hedonic processes in the brain that shape emotional experiences.

We are drawn to experiences that deliver a sense of emotional gratification. This is why offerings that generate a positive emotional reaction often enjoy greater loyalty than offerings that merely deliver functional benefits. Because emotional loyalty entails a deeper level of commitment to the company and its offerings, reward programs that rely purely on monetary rewards often miss an opportunity to create deeper engagement through emotional loyalty. In a world inundated with information, emotions help shape customers' attitudes toward the company and its offerings. While customers may not remember the specifics of their interactions with a company, they are likely to remember how those interactions made them feel. These emotional memories are often the key drivers of their loyalty to the business.

Managing Emotional Loyalty

Even though we seek positive emotional experiences and avoid negative ones, we do not react the same way to their presence and absence. We actively pursue positive emotions and gain emotional gratification from them, yet the mere absence of positive emotions does not necessarily lead to a negative emotional state. Conversely, when it comes to negative emotions, we strive to avoid experiences that trigger them, yet their absence does not automatically generate positive feelings.

Consider the case of Febreze, a Procter & Gamble product designed to eliminate odors using its patented chemical, cyclodextrin. Initially, Febreze was marketed as a problem-solving product that emphasized its main functional benefit: odor removal. It targeted consumers who were believed to have the greatest need for an odor-eliminating product: pet owners and smokers. The marketing team produced commercials featuring scenarios like a woman complaining that her house smelled like her dog and another lamenting that her clothes reeked of cigarettes after sitting in a restaurant's smoking section. In both cases, Febreze was presented as the solution, effectively eliminating the unpleasant odors. The company's print ads reinforced this message with taglines like "Get your home back" and "Because odors love to hide in your home."

Despite its innovative technology addressing a common problem, Febreze struggled to gain market traction. This slow start stemmed from two main reasons. First, consumers who needed Febreze the most—pet owners and smokers—were unaware that they had a problem. Due to habituation, they had become so accustomed to the smells of their pets and cigarettes that they no longer noticed them. And since these consumers did not perceive a problem, they did not see the value in a solution to what they considered a non-issue. Second, the human brain is naturally more attuned to noticing things that appear rather than those that disappear. This tendency is rooted in evolutionary development, where detecting potential threats is crucial, while tracking the absence of something is less critical. As a result, the elimination of an odor was not a benefit consumers readily noticed or appreciated.

Recognizing these challenges, Procter & Gamble repositioned Febreze to emphasize the emotional experience it provided. They added a distinct scent to Febreze, transforming it from just an odor neutralizer into an air freshener as well. The new advertising slogans, "Breathe happy" and "Spray Febreze to make the room smell as nice as it looks," repositioned the product as the perfect finishing touch to a cleaning routine, offering sensory gratification. This revised approach resonated with consumers, propelling Febreze to become a billion-dollar brand. The key to its success was shifting from a functional positioning that addressed an unrecognized problem to one that highlighted the emotional satisfaction associated with using the product.

Another example of the role of emotions in building loyalty is the *Got Milk?* campaign, which aimed to reverse the declining milk consumption trend. Traditional advertising campaigns that promoted milk on its functional benefits as a healthy drink were not very effective—perhaps not very surprising given that most consumers already believed that milk was a healthy drink and further reinforcing this message was unlikely to make a big difference. The advertising agency tasked with addressing this challenge identified two main reasons for the decline in milk consumption. The first was the lack of consumer mindshare—milk is a rather mundane product, and it is hard to get excited about it. The second reason was the shared nature of consumption or "rationing" of milk, whereby consumers monitor how much milk they drink to make sure there is enough left for other family members.

To address these concerns, the agency devised a dual-strategy approach. First, to increase the mindshare of milk, it created a memorable ad campaign that appealed to consumers' emotions rather than simply touting milk's health benefits. The key insight was recognizing that although milk is seen as boring on its own, it complements many delicious food items such as cookies, cake, and cereal. The second aspect of the strategy focused on encouraging consumers to always keep an ample supply of milk at home, eliminating the need for rationing and naturally increasing milk consumption.

The result was the famous "milk deprivation" campaign, featuring scenarios where people were enjoying sweets like cookies or cake and then found themselves in the predicament of having no milk to wash it down. The *Got Milk?* tagline appeared at the end of each commercial, driving home the core message: Make sure you have enough milk on hand. By most accounts, the campaign was highly effective. It used an emotional appeal that combined humor with a touch of fear, successfully halting the downward trend in milk consumption. The success of the *Got Milk?* campaign illustrates that infusing emotion into something as mundane as milk can help create engagement and loyalty.

Beyond simply highlighting the inherent benefits of their offerings, companies can deepen the influence of emotions on customer loyalty by creating *shared emotional experiences* that foster social connections. Southwest Airlines is a prime example of this approach. As a low-cost carrier, Southwest forgoes traditional amenities like in-flight meals. One might assume that these omissions would result in lower service evaluations, as customers trade off service quality for lower prices. However, Southwest consistently ranks high in customer satisfaction. A significant factor in this success is the airline's ability to emotionally engage passengers and create a sense of community, thus driving customer satisfaction and loyalty.

For example, Southwest introduced concerts on some flights, turning a routine journey into a delightful and memorable experience. While hosting concerts on every flight might be logistically challenging, making every flight enjoyable is achievable. Take, for instance, the pre-flight announcements. On most airlines, these announcements are typically dull, annoying, and often ignored. Yet, Southwest saw these mandatory announcements as a chance to emotionally engage passengers. Many of these humorous and creative announcements went viral on YouTube, with some videos garnering tens of millions of views. Reimagining the flight experience to prioritize emotional engagement and crafting experiences that foster social connections were some of the key contributors to Southwest's success in creating a loyal customer base.

Identity Loyalty

Customers are loyal to offerings that they see as part of their identity. Identity loyalty goes beyond functional and emotional loyalty, addressing our deeper needs for self-realization, belonging, esteem, and respect. These identity-related needs hold the highest personal relevance in the hierarchy of needs and play a crucial role in motivating customer loyalty and repeat purchasing behavior.

The Need for Self-Expression as a Driver of Loyalty

Identity loyalty stems from the ability of a company's offering to fulfill the self-identity needs of its customers. These needs have two key components: the need for self-identification and the need for self-expression. The need for self-identification reflects customers' desire to define themselves as individuals through their choice of products, services, and brands. We purchase offerings not just for their functional benefits, but also for how they capture aspects of our identity. Patronizing certain offerings enables us to discover our own preferences—thus defining our self-identity and reaffirming our perception of the type of person we are or aspire to be.

The need for self-expression, on the other hand, reflects customers' desire to communicate their preferences and values to others. Fulfilling this need often involves conspicuous consumption, where individuals acquire products for two main reasons: to attain or maintain a certain social status and to express their unique personality. Status-focused conspicuous consumption involves offerings associated with high social standing, wealth, and power, while personality-based conspicuous consumption includes offerings that highlight the unique aspects of an individual's personality, such as their value system, beliefs, and tastes.

Customers' perception of the personal relevance of a company's offering can significantly influence their loyalty. The identity-related aspects of an offering can have a profound effect on customer loyalty, often surpassing the impact of its functional and emotional aspects. While functionality-based loyalty is important, it can easily shift to another offering with superior performance. Similarly, loyalty driven by emotional experiences, although often more powerful than functional loyalty, tends to be fleeting and may not result in lasting commitment. In contrast, identity loyalty, which fulfills needs deeply rooted in a customer's identity—such as status, aspirations, and personality—achieves the highest level of personal relevance. This form of loyalty is closely tied to an individual's self-image, making it the most enduring and resistant to change (Figure 4).

Figure 4. Identity Loyalty and Personal Relevance

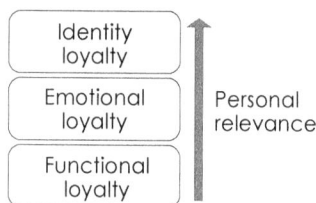

A notable example of the impact of self-identification and identity-based loyalty is the Texas Department of Transportation's promotional campaign in the 1980s. At the time, Texas was spending around $20 million annually to clean up highway litter. Previous campaigns with slogans like "Keep America Beautiful" and "Keep Texas Beautiful" had little effect on drivers' behavior, with no significant reduction in littering.

An analysis of the campaign's limited success revealed that it primarily appealed to those who were environmentally conscious and were not littering the highways anyway. Crucially, it failed to resonate with the group most likely to litter: 18- to 35-year-old males. The challenge, therefore, was to create a message that would truly engage those in this demographic, which self-identity research showed perceive themselves as independent and tough, with a strong pride in their Texas heritage.

Leveraging this insight, the Department of Transportation crafted a new campaign designed to align with the identity of these potential litterers: "Don't Mess with Texas." Rather than using prominent environmentalists, the campaign featured celebrities like Stevie Ray Vaughan, George Foreman, and Chuck Norris, who connected with the target audience. The campaign also included songs such as Willie Nelson's "Mamas, tell your babies 'Don't Mess with Texas'" and Lyle Lovett's "Keep your trash off the road." This strategic focus on identity proved highly effective, reducing highway litter by over 70% within five years. Over time, the slogan "Don't Mess with Texas" grew beyond its original purpose of keeping highways clean, becoming a symbol of the Lone Star State's independent spirit.

Another powerful example of how identity appeals can shape beliefs and actions is the "Keep Walking" campaign by Johnnie Walker, the world's leading Scotch whisky brand. This campaign transcended its role as a product tagline, inspiring people worldwide with its message of progress and optimism, motivating them to take their own steps toward achieving their dreams and aspirations. Similarly, Nike's "Just Do It" campaign struck a chord not only within the athletic community but also with those outside of sports, even becoming a life creed for some. These well-crafted messages demonstrate how companies can effectively tap into and influence the broader identities and values of their customers.

The profound impact of identity-based associations on customer loyalty prompts an important question: When should a company start cultivating identity loyalty? The conventional wisdom suggests that loyalty should be built after customers have had their initial experience with a product or service. Typically, loyalty is seen as an allegiance—both in beliefs and behavior—to something customers have already engaged with. However, this approach is somewhat narrow when it comes to identity loyalty.

The best time to build identity loyalty is when customers' identity is being formed. An old Porsche ad perfectly illustrates this concept. The ad features the 911 Carrera, Porsche's flagship sports car, with the tagline: "Honestly now, did you spend your youth dreaming about someday owning a Nissan or a Mitsubishi?" Indeed, many men who bought the 911 as adults developed an affinity with the car when they were teenagers, and owning a Porsche became part of their identity. By designing cars with a strong identity appeal, Porsche successfully cultivated loyal customers long before they were able to afford the car.

Identity loyalty can be nurtured even before one's identity is fully formed. Real Madrid, one of the world's most valuable and widely supported football clubs, exemplifies this approach. A key factor in its popularity is its loyalty program, which offers members exclusive benefits like season tickets, early access to seats for major games, and the opportunity to visit first-team training sessions. Members also receive a "Madridista" card, which strengthens their sense of belonging to the team.

Although this membership comes with an annual fee, Real Madrid encourages early sign-ups by waiving the fee for children until they turn 11. The fee is also waived after 50 consecutive years of membership—meaning that if your parents enrolled you when you were a toddler, you could enjoy free membership by the time you turn 50. Real Madrid also offers branded merchandise targeting all ages, starting with onesies for infants. This strategic approach not only fosters a deep sense of belonging among fans from an early age but also ensures a loyal and growing fan base that will support the club for generations.

Brands as a Source of Identity-Based Loyalty

Customers use brands as a form of self-expression to signal their social status and personality. For instance, riding a Harley-Davidson, wearing the latest Diesel jeans, or carrying a Birkin bag can make a strong statement about a person's identity, beliefs, and values. This signaling not only shares personally relevant information with others but also reinforces one's own self-image.

One specific way individuals use brands is to compensate for discrepancies between their current and desired self-image. When we perceive a gap between our actual self and our ideal self, we often surround ourselves with symbols that help close this gap and "complete" our self-image. Through this process of symbolic self-completion, brands can help us feel more secure in areas where our self-image feels lacking. For example, novice tennis players might buy gear prominently featuring well-known brand logos, and less experienced business school students may choose brands like Rolex and Montblanc, which symbolize professional success.[8]

Because self-expressive brands are associated with beliefs and values held by customers, they tend to command greater loyalty. A prime example of the impact of brand self-identification on customer loyalty occurred with the introduction of New Coke in 1985. Coca-Cola developed New Coke to outperform Pepsi in taste, and confident in their superior product—supported by blind taste tests showing that most consumers preferred New Coke—Coca-Cola decided to replace the original formula with the new one. What Coca-Cola management failed to consider was that consumers were buying Coke not just for its taste but also for what it meant to them.

The announcement that the "old" Coke would be discontinued sparked a widespread backlash, as customers felt betrayed by a brand they perceived as an integral part of their identity. The depth of customer dissatisfaction with Coca-Cola's decision is encapsulated in the sentiment expressed by one of its loyal customers: "I am forty-six years old, and I bought my first Coke with a nickel when I was five years old. I helped build this multinational corporation. My oldest daughter is twenty-two; her first word was Coke; her second word was mommy."[9]

Self-expressive brands enjoy greater loyalty because customers see them as extensions of themselves and integral to their personal identity. Brands like Harley-Davidson, Disney, and Nike sometimes even adorn the skin of their most devoted fans. As tattoos have increasingly become a way for individuals to express their uniqueness, those who feel a deep connection to a particular brand solidify their loyalty by permanently inking the brand's logo and aligning with the brand's values. While not every brand achieves tattoo status, striving to become genuinely relevant to customers' self-image and a part of their identity can foster enduring brand loyalty and make the brand resilient against competitors.

Building identity-based loyalty begins with defining a set of core values that resonate with customers and mirror the company's culture. Pinpointing these core values helps position the brand in a way that connects with the target audience and ensures the company can deliver on its brand promise. A notable example of this is Unilever's "The Evolution of Beauty" campaign for its Dove brand. The campaign's creators sought to "create a new definition of beauty, which will free women from self-doubt and encourage them to embrace their real beauty." By challenging traditional beauty standards, this approach deeply resonated with its audience.

Despite a relatively modest budget, the campaign successfully built a loyal customer base and established Dove as an enduring self-expressive brand.

Strong brands often create brand communities—customers as well as company employees—who have a sense of connection with the brand, identify with the brand, and share rituals and traditions that enhance and perpetuate the meaning of the brand. These communities can emerge organically among brand loyalists eager to share their connection, or they can be intentionally organized, sponsored, and facilitated by the company.

For example, LEGO has successfully nurtured a passionate and engaged community of fans and builders of all ages. This community goes beyond a simple love for LEGO bricks and models; it includes various forums, social media groups, and events where members share their creations, ideas, and building techniques. LEGO actively encourages this interaction by hosting events and supporting user-generated content platforms where fans can submit their own designs for new sets. This deep engagement has allowed LEGO to foster a strong sense of belonging and loyalty among its community members.

One challenge in building identity-based loyalty is that people differ in the values central to their self-image. This means that the values a brand represents resonate deeply with some customers while being irrelevant or even antagonizing to others. Consequently, successful identity branding may not universally increase loyalty: while it can enhance loyalty among certain customers, it might also alienate others.

Brands that take a stand on divisive social, political, economic, or environmental issues may strengthen loyalty among customers who share their views but risk losing those who disagree. For example, Nike's "Believe in Something" campaign, featuring Colin Kaepernick—the former NFL quarterback known for kneeling during the national anthem to protest racial injustice in the United States—provoked backlash from some of Nike's customers, with some even threatening to boycott the company.

Nike's campaign was based on a key insight: To build and sustain identity-based loyalty, a brand must stand for values that truly matter to its customers. Identity loyalty cannot be achieved by trying to appeal to everyone. Instead, as Nike's own slogan suggests, a brand must "believe in something, even if it means sacrificing everything."

Behavioral Loyalty

The three types of loyalty discussed so far—functional, emotional, and identity—represent different facets of psychological loyalty involving mental processes like thinking, feeling, and self-expression. Behavioral loyalty, on the other hand, does not necessarily involve mental deliberation or emotions. Rather, it is characterized by routine behavior, often driven by habit. In the sections that follow, we delve into the nature of habitual behavior and outline strategies for fostering behavioral loyalty.

Habitual Behavior as a Driver of Loyalty

Habits are repetitive behaviors marked by routine decision making, minimal information seeking, and little to no evaluation of alternatives. These habits develop through the consistent purchase of products or services that reliably satisfy the customer. Many everyday items, such as milk, bread, orange juice, and peanut butter, are often chosen out of habit. These decisions are characterized by low involvement and usually do not involve a detailed comparison of available options.

Habit formation can be likened to the concept of inertia in physics, which describes how an object in motion continues moving indefinitely until disrupted. This principle of inertia was famously demonstrated by Galileo. He used two planes—one inclined and the other horizontal—and rolled a ball down the incline. Gravity pulled the ball downward, but even after reaching the bottom, the ball continued to move along the horizontal plane, despite no longer being influenced by gravity. Galileo concluded that the ball maintained its motion due to inertia, and without friction, it would keep rolling at a constant speed (Figure 5).

Figure 5. Galileo's Demonstration of the Force of Inertia

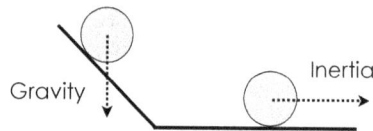

The process of consumer habit formation mirrors the force of inertia. An initial purchase, typically made after some deliberation, acts like the gravitational force that sets the ball in motion. Once the initial decision is made, subsequent purchases often become routine, low-involvement actions driven by the inertia of the consumer's established habit.

Habitual purchasing offers two significant advantages to customers. First, it reduces decision-making effort—an essential benefit given the countless decisions we face daily. By eliminating the need for a new information search, evaluation of alternatives, and deliberate decision making for each purchase, habitual buying allows us to conserve cognitive resources for more critical decisions. In addition, habitual buying reduces the risks associated with purchasing. When we choose a product that has consistently met our expectations, the likelihood of disappointment or unmet needs decreases, thereby minimizing the perceived risk with each purchase.

Not all repeated behaviors evolve into habits. The likelihood of a behavior becoming habitual is influenced by three main factors. First, the behavior must occur *frequently*, enhancing the possibility of it becoming automatic. Second, the action involved must be relatively *simple*, facilitating the shift from the rational and deliberate processing of System 2 to the unconscious and effortless functioning of System 1. Finally, behaviors that typically develop into habits are those that yield *consistent outcomes* and do not require corrective actions.

Consider, for example, routine grocery purchases. These purchases occur frequently, with many consumers making them every week. They also involve relatively simple actions. Consumers know where to find what they are looking for; they go to the store, take the product from its usual place on the shelf, and put it in their shopping cart. And as long as there have been no major changes in product availability, store layout, or package design, the purchase produces consistent outcomes, with consumers ending up with the product they intended to buy.

Automaticity is crucial for creating habits. Consider how companies design birth control pills to facilitate habit formation. The pills follow a four-week cycle—taken daily for three weeks, with a one-week pause. The intermittent nature of this regimen could potentially disrupt the formation of a daily habit. To ensure compliance, the pills are packaged in four-week containers that clearly indicate the sequence, including the inactive pills for the final week. This design simplifies the instruction to "Take one pill every day," making the behavior automatic and driven entirely by System 1, without requiring System 2 deliberation.

Companies have recognized the importance of habit formation, particularly for frequent purchases. For instance, Amazon introduced Dash buttons to simplify the reordering process and encourage habit formation. These small, stick-on buttons allowed customers to quickly reorder household essentials like Bounty paper towels, Tide laundry detergent, and Gillette razors with a single press. Each Dash button was branded with the product logo and could be set up to purchase specific items and quantities directly through the customer's Amazon account. A key advantage of these buttons was their placement in convenient locations where the products were frequently used, enabling consumers to reorder items as soon as they noticed supplies running low. Over time, Amazon's Subscribe & Save program took over most of the reordering functions previously handled by Dash buttons, further streamlining the repurchase process and reinforcing habitual buying behavior.

Managing Behavioral Loyalty

Once established, behavioral habits must be carefully maintained to prevent disruption. The automatic nature of habits can be easily unsettled if interrupted, forcing individuals to engage in more deliberate consideration of alternatives. This shift can break the "loyalty loop," which normally bypasses the need to search for options and leads customers to repeat past purchases without much thought. A disruption in habitual buying forces customers to re-enter the decision-making process, where they re-examine available options, evaluate them, and possibly select an offering different from their usual choice.

Managing behavioral loyalty requires understanding both the factors that foster habit formation and those that can disrupt it. Because habits are governed by System 1 information processing, they heavily rely on peripheral cues such as location, shape, color, imagery, and size. Altering these cues can disrupt routine purchasing behaviors. Yet, companies sometimes unintentionally undermine established customer habits by redesigning their offerings—such as changing the brand logo, visuals, and packaging—in ways that disrupt established customer habits and weaken behavioral loyalty.

Maintaining the consistency of the buying experience is crucial, especially since customers are often overwhelmed by the abundance of choices and are hesitant to invest extra effort in scrutinizing each option, particularly for items they purchase regularly. Because customers typically do not spend much time contemplating the products they habitually buy, they tend to evaluate them on a visceral level, relying on easily recognizable visual cues rather than conducting a thorough analysis.

Consider Coca-Cola's campaign supporting the World Wildlife Federation's efforts to preserve polar bear habitats. Coca-Cola had used polar bears in its branding since 1922 and saw this initiative as a great way to reinforce positive associations with its brand while benefiting the environment. To emphasize the conservation message, Coca-Cola made a bold move by changing its iconic red cans with white lettering to white cans with red lettering, featuring silhouettes of a mother bear and her two cubs crossing Arctic snowbanks. The company intended the color change to be "attention-grabbing" and "disruptive" in support of the campaign's themes.

Consumers, however, were not enthusiastic about the new color scheme. The new red-on-white Coke cans very closely resembled the familiar red-on-silver Diet Coke cans, leading to widespread confusion and a sharp increase in complaints from customers who accidentally bought the wrong product. Recognizing the issue, Coca-Cola quickly reverted to the original color scheme just a few weeks into the promotion—months ahead of the planned schedule.[10]

When a familiar brand undergoes a radical packaging redesign, shoppers can become confused, struggling to connect the new look and feel with the brand they usually buy. This confusion is especially likely when a company changes several packaging elements—such as shape, color, logo, messaging, and imagery—simultaneously. These changes can leave consumers uncertain whether the new packaging still represents the product they have trusted and regularly purchased, potentially disturbing their habitual buying behavior. As a result, instead of effortlessly and automatically repurchasing the familiar product without considering alternatives, consumers might start evaluating—and possibly choosing—products from competing brands.

Take the case of Tropicana. Ten years after it was acquired by PepsiCo, Tropicana decided to change the packaging of its flagship Pure Premium orange juice to "reinforce the brand and product attributes, rejuvenate the category and help consumers rediscover the health benefits they get from drinking America's iconic orange juice brand."

The marketing team was concerned that the original packaging, which prominently featured an image of an orange with a straw inserted directly into it, did not adequately represent the juice inside. As a response, a new design was introduced, replacing the familiar orange-and-straw image with a picture of a glass of orange juice that extended around the side of the package.

The redesign also altered the Tropicana logo by changing its orientation from horizontal, which is easy to read, to vertical, making it more difficult to discern. The logo's distinctive curved design was replaced with a straight one, and its unique three-dimensional font was switched to a more generic two-dimensional style. The color scheme of the packaging also underwent a significant overhaul, and key product descriptors such as "Pure Premium" and "No Pulp" were relocated to the top of the package, making them less visible. Overall, Tropicana invested $35 million in advertising to promote the new packaging. Yet, the redesign immediately drew criticism from consumers and the media. Sales dropped over 20%, forcing Tropicana to return to its original packaging less than two months after the launch of the new one.[11]

The Coca-Cola and Tropicana cases highlight the importance of maintaining consistency in a product's look and feel over time. To achieve this, managers must balance two considerations. On one hand, there is a desire to introduce substantial changes to showcase the product's new features, advance the brand's new positioning, and better differentiate the offering from the competition. On the other hand, there is a need for continuity, ensuring that any changes in the product's appearance are subtle enough not to disrupt sales to existing customers.

The challenge of ensuring continuity while managing behavioral loyalty raises an important question: How can a company reposition its offering without alienating its current customers? Successful repositioning starts with understanding the information shoppers seek and the visual cues—such as shape, color, logo, and imagery—they use to identify the company's product among competitors. The next step is to prioritize these elements based on their importance to the customer and make gradual changes rather than overhauling multiple key elements at once. Packaging redesigns should be implemented with careful consideration of how customers, particularly habitual buyers, will react to the new packaging.

Consider how Oil of Olay successfully reinvented itself by gradually changing its positioning, logo, and packaging. Originally developed during World War II as a glycerin-based treatment for burns for Britain's Air Force, the product was later transformed into a consumer offering by its inventor, a South African chemist. He marketed the product as "a mysterious beauty fluid that makes you look younger" without claiming specific skin benefits, leveraging a fictional narrative about a tropical plant named Ulan from which the "oil" was supposedly derived.

After initial success in South Africa, the brand expanded internationally under different names: Oil of Ulay in the UK, Oil of Ulan in Australia, Oil of Olaz in France, Italy, and Germany, and Oil of Olay in the United States. When Procter & Gamble acquired the company, it sought to unify the brand under a single global name. However, all existing names shared a common issue: The word "oil" led consumers to believe the product was greasy, despite the company's advertisements emphasizing "the non-greasy feeling of Oil of Olay." To address this challenge, Procter & Gamble shortened the brand name to "OLAY," and revamped its logo and visuals.

The repositioning of Oil of Olay differed from Tropicana's approach in two important ways. First, the changes were necessary to consolidate the brand image as well as to address the negative associations with "oil" in the name. Perhaps more important is that the changes were done gradually, spanning nearly a decade. As a result, even though Oil of Olay's change was more comprehensive than that of Tropicana—it involved changing the brand name in addition to changing the logo and the visuals—it had a less disruptive effect on the customer experience. This strategic pacing allowed customers to adapt to the changes without alienating them, preserving brand loyalty throughout the transition.

SUMMARY

Loyalty benefits both companies and their customers: Companies seek loyal customers, and customers often desire to be loyal. For customers, loyalty adds value by simplifying decision making, enhancing their consumption experience, and serving as a form of self-expression. There are four types of customer loyalty: functional, emotional, identity, and behavioral; they reflect how customers think, feel, perceive themselves, and habitually act.

Functional loyalty arises from customers' satisfaction with how well the performance of a product or service meets their needs and expectations. Both needs and expectations must be met for customers to be satisfied. Expectations are shaped by factors such as customers' past experiences with similar products, the brand's image and reputation, and the company's communication. The relationship between customers' expectations and their actual experiences has an asymmetrical impact on satisfaction: Failing to meet expectations results in a significantly stronger negative impact on satisfaction than the positive effect of exceeding them. An effective way to build loyalty is through reward programs that acknowledge and reward customers for their ongoing patronage. These programs utilize the reinforcement principle, which states that behaviors followed by rewards are more likely to be repeated.

Emotional loyalty is built by creating a strong emotional connection with customers through experiences that resonate with their feelings. This type of loyalty is grounded in the idea that customers are naturally drawn to experiences that provide emotional gratification. Consequently, offerings that evoke positive emotions often achieve higher levels of loyalty compared to those that solely offer functional benefits. Customers' reactions to emotional experiences are asymmetrical: They actively seek positive emotions and receive emotional gratification from their presence, although the mere absence of positive emotions does not lead to a negative emotional state. Similarly, while customers aim to avoid experiences that elicit negative emotions, the mere absence of negative emotions does not guarantee loyalty.

Emotional experiences that foster a sense of social connection are particularly effective in driving loyalty and increasing customer engagement.

Identity loyalty is rooted in an offering's ability to meet customers' needs for both self-identification and self-expression. The need for self-identification reflects customers' desire to establish their identity and reaffirm their perception of the type of person they are and aspire to be. The need for self-expression, on the other hand, reflects customers' desire to communicate this identity to others. Because it reflects factors central to an individual's self-image, such as status, aspirations, and personality, identity loyalty has the highest personal relevance. The best time to cultivate identity loyalty is when a person's identity is being formed.

Behavioral loyalty is characterized by repetitive actions, typically driven by habit. These habits form through the routine purchase of products or services that consistently meet or exceed the customer's expectations. For a behavior to become a habit, it must occur frequently, involve a relatively simple action, and yield consistent results that do not require corrective action. Maintaining the consistency of the buying experience is crucial for preserving habitual buying: Radical product redesign can confuse customers and disrupt their established buying habits.

KEY TAKEAWAYS

Define the key sources of loyalty. Create functional, emotional, identity, and behavioral loyalty by focusing on a customer's mind, heart, self-image, and habits.

Deliver on performance expectations. Satisfaction with the core benefits of the offering is a key component of customer loyalty.

Build an emotional connection. Customers gravitate to experiences that maximize positive emotions and avoid negative ones.

Become a part of customers' identity. Offerings associated with ideas and values held by customers enjoy greater loyalty.

Foster behavioral habits. Most routine purchases are automatic; they are difficult to create but easy to disrupt.

SPOTLIGHT: MANAGING DISSATISFIED CUSTOMERS TO BUILD LOYALTY

Despite a company's efforts to create fulfilling experiences for all customers at all times, achieving this goal is not always possible. Not every customer can be satisfied all the time, whether due to the economic and logistical challenges of designing perfectly customized offerings for each individual or because of inevitable manufacturing defects and service delivery inconsistencies. As a result, instances of customer dissatisfaction are inevitable. This raises the question of how to manage customers who, for various reasons, are unhappy with the company's offerings.[12]

Customer dissatisfaction arises when there is a significant discrepancy between customer expectations and the actual performance of a product or service. This gap often opens up a range of negative emotions, including disappointment, discontent, anxiety, regret, and even anger. In fact, the negative impact of not meeting customer expectations far outweighs the positive impact of exceeding them; customers tend to react more strongly to offerings that fall short than to those that meet or surpass their expectations.

The way a company addresses and attempts to resolve these issues can greatly impact its customers' emotional state, either improving their feelings or worsening negative sentiments. Customer reactions can vary widely, ranging from continued support and advocacy for the company and its products to abandoning the company altogether and discouraging others from engaging with it (Figure 6)

Figure 6. Customer Reaction to Negative Experiences

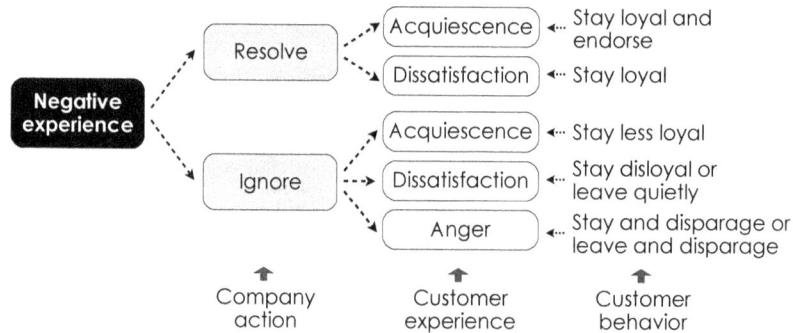

Customers who voice complaints and receive a satisfactory resolution from the company often maintain their loyalty. In fact, when a company exceeds customer expectations in responding to a negative experience, these customers may not only remain loyal but also become advocates for the brand, actively recommending its products or services to others. In such cases, the company's efforts to rectify the situation can transform the negative emotions associated with the initial issue into a positive perception of the company's dedication to customer satisfaction, thereby strengthening the customer's favorable attitude.

Customers who voice their concerns but do not receive a satisfactory resolution face a crossroads: They can either leave the company or decide to stay despite the negative experience. Those opting to leave may do so immediately following the unsatisfactory incident or wait until a viable alternative becomes available. Customers who choose to stay might be influenced by factors such as inertia, high switching costs, or a lack of feasible alternatives. However, continuing with the company does not imply that their attitudes and behaviors remain unaffected. Some may become less loyal, while others might become vocal adversaries, actively seeking opportunities to disparage the company. These customers are usually motivated by their resentment of the company's actions and its unwillingness or inability to address the experience failure.

Finally, dissatisfied customers who have not complained are also likely to change their attitude and behavior toward the company. They may quietly become less loyal, eventually leaving the company without any direct confrontation. Some may even engage in negative word of mouth, further harming the company's reputation, all while discontinuing the use of its products or services. Several factors can discourage dissatisfied customers from reporting their negative experiences, such as a lack of time, insufficient motivation to contact the company, or skepticism about whether their feedback would be valued or lead to meaningful change.

Just because customers have not lodged complaints directly with a company does not mean they will keep their grievances to themselves. Research shows that dissatisfied customers are far more likely to share their negative experiences than those who are satisfied. With the rise of social media, it has become much easier for customers to share their experiences, and the reach of these stories has expanded dramatically. As a result, negative feedback about a company's offerings tends to spread much faster than positive feedback. This potential snowball effect of customer complaints has led many companies to closely monitor customer experiences, proactively address potential issues before they escalate, and consistently deliver superior customer service.

Promptly and effectively resolving a customer's issue not only can restore but also increase customer loyalty. Customers often understand that mistakes can occur even when a company strives to do its best. A swift response to correct a problem demonstrates to customers that the company genuinely cares about their satisfaction. By effectively managing negative experiences, a company can turn dissatisfaction into loyalty. While each negative incident may require a customized response, there are general service recovery principles that are applicable across different industries, companies, and customer types. These principles are outlined below.

- *Identify the source of a customer's dissatisfaction.* Customers might be frustrated by functional aspects of the service, such as receiving an unsatisfactory hotel room, experiencing flight delays, or encountering poor-quality repair services. They might also be displeased with the monetary aspects, including the overall cost, unexpected fees and surcharges, or issues with payment processing. Additionally, customers might be upset by the psychological aspects, such as rude and inexperienced employees, unfair prioritization of some customers over others, or management's indifference to customer issues. Understanding the source of customer dissatisfaction is crucial to a company's ability to remedy the situation; it can be very difficult to solve a problem without knowing its cause.

- *Develop a relevant solution.* A company can take various actions to address a negative customer experience. These may include functional benefits, such as upgrading a hotel room, rebooking a more convenient flight, or replacing a defective product; monetary benefits, such as free service vouchers, discounts, or cash compensation; and psychological benefits, such as apologies from frontline employees and management. The key is to ensure that the proposed solution is seen by the customer as appropriate and satisfactory. For instance, some customers unhappy with their hotel room might prefer an upgrade, others might want monetary compensation, and still others might value an apology from management that acknowledges their dissatisfaction and reaffirms their importance to the company. Addressing the issue without a clear understanding of what the customer values most and which solution best meets their needs might not only fail to remedy the problem but also aggravate it.

- *Resolve the issue promptly.* The speed with which a company responds to service failures can significantly influence a customer's reaction. Quick responses tend to result in more favorable outcomes. The longer it takes for a company to respond, the greater the customer's anxiety about the service failure, and the higher their expectations about what the company should do to rectify the problem. Delays in addressing the issue can also make customers more inclined to escalate the situation by reaching out to various levels of management or sharing their negative experience with friends, acquaintances, and their social media networks.

- *Inform customers about the recovery process.* The uncertainty that accompanies a service failure is often as frustrating for customers as the failure itself. Transparency in the recovery process is a powerful tool to reduce customer dissatisfaction and mitigate the negative aftermath of a service failure. For instance, dissatisfaction from a flight delay can be significantly alleviated by providing passengers with information about the cause of the delay and updates on the flight status. Communicating the specifics of the service failure and the steps being taken toward recovery not only diminishes customer anxiety but also demonstrates respect and acknowledges customers' value to the business.

- *Accept responsibility.* While not all service failures stem from a company's direct actions—such as city-wide power outages, weather conditions affecting flights, or pre-existing manufacturing defects—many issues are rooted in internal factors. These can include mismanagement of supply and demand, inefficient service policies, or the inexperience of front-line staff. In such cases, accepting responsibility for the negative experience not only conveys respect and courtesy toward customers but also enhances the company's credibility in future interactions.

- *Adjudicate the experience failure fairly.* Customers place a high value on fairness in rectifying service failures. Their perception of outcome fairness is significantly influenced by whether the company's recovery actions are seen as equitable and whether the compensation aligns with the inconvenience caused by the negative experience. Even if the resolution is not ideal, customers may still feel satisfied with the company's recovery efforts if they perceive the process leading to that resolution as fair. A sense of procedural fairness can be crucial in alleviating customers' dissatisfaction with the company's offerings.

Anecdotal evidence suggests that negative experiences followed by outstanding recovery often increase customer satisfaction and loyalty. This seemingly paradoxical outcome occurs because most customers recognize that mistakes are inevitable and are willing to overlook them if the company takes swift and fair action to resolve the issue. By accepting responsibility and quickly rectifying the problem, the company reassures customers and reduces uncertainty about how it will handle future issues, demonstrating a commitment to high-quality service. Proactively engaging with customers, offering timely and meaningful resolutions, and continuously improving based on feedback can enhance customer satisfaction, strengthen their relationship with the company, and ultimately foster greater loyalty and advocacy for the brand.

THE CX CANVAS: MANAGING CUSTOMER LOYALTY

Every stage of the customer experience must be designed to foster long-term loyalty. Creating experiences that nurture loyalty involves two key components: (1) analyzing customers' interactions with the company's offerings to identify factors that either strengthen or weaken loyalty, and (2) developing a course of action to enhance customers' loyalty. These two components of managing customer loyalty are depicted in Figure 7 and outlined below.

Figure 7. Managing Loyalty: The Big Picture

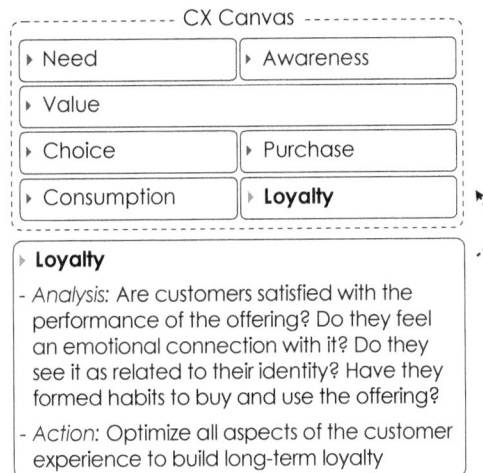

The first step in building customer loyalty is to evaluate customers' current commitment to the company's offerings and identify the factors that either contribute to or detract from their continued support of the company's products, services, and brands. The key questions to consider include:

- *Are customers satisfied with the performance of the offering?* This question determines the extent to which customers' experience with the company's offerings matches their needs and expectations. This is crucial, especially for offerings that deliver functional benefits, as satisfaction with performance is a key factor in creating and sustaining customer loyalty.

- *Do customers feel an emotional connection with the offering?* This question examines the extent to which the offering has successfully connected with customers on an emotional level, creating enjoyment and positive feelings. Emotional connections are important because customer decisions are often driven by affect, not just logic, and these feelings can significantly influence loyalty.

- *Do customers see the offering as related to their self-identity?* This question explores how well the offering aligns with customers' self-identity and self-expression needs. Since one's identity holds significant personal relevance, offerings that resonate with a customer's self-concept are powerful drivers of loyalty.

- *Have customers formed habits to purchase and use the offering?* This question determines whether customers have established routines that favor the company's offering. This is important because habitual behavior, characterized by low involvement and automatic actions, reflects the way many purchase and usage decisions are made.

The ultimate purpose of loyalty analysis is to evaluate customers' attachment to the company's offerings, which in turn helps identify opportunities to enhance the customer experience and strengthen loyalty. In this context, four main challenges can be identified, each requiring a distinct course of action:

- *Subpar performance.* Customers' dissatisfaction with the offering's performance can significantly diminish the company's chances of creating a loyal customer base. Therefore, it is crucial that the company ensures that the offering's performance meets customers' needs and preferences. This can be achieved by enhancing the offering's benefits, reducing costs associated with acquiring and using the offering, and managing customers' perceptions of the offering's performance.

- *Weak emotional connection.* Customers actively seek positive emotional experiences, and the lack of such experiences can impede a company's efforts to foster loyalty. To build a meaningful emotional connection, the company must ensure that customers derive emotional gratification from interacting with its offering. This can be done by maximizing positive affect, minimizing negative emotions associated with the offering, and designing shared emotional experiences that facilitate social interaction.

- *Weak identity relevance.* Connecting the company's offering to a customer's identity is a powerful way to foster loyalty. Identity needs are highly personal and often play a critical role in driving customer loyalty and repeat purchases. An effective strategy to ensure the company's offerings resonate with customers' identity is to build self-expressive brands that reflect ideas and values held by the company's customers.

- *Weak behavioral habits.* Many repeat purchase decisions are made automatically, without much deliberation. Therefore, the company's goal should be to facilitate the formation of behavioral routines that favor its offering and carefully nurture these routines to avoid disruption in customers' purchase patterns. This can be achieved by streamlining the buying process so that it becomes automatic and ensuring consistency in the offering's appearance, functionality, and the context in which it is sold.

The four challenges to loyalty and the corresponding company actions are summarized in Figure 8. The first three factors—functional, emotional, and identity loyalty—are different types of psychological loyalty, involving mental processes such as thinking, feeling, and self-expression. In contrast, behavioral loyalty is action-oriented and characterized by low involvement and routine activities. Both psychological and behavioral loyalty are crucial for building and sustaining a loyal customer base.

Figure 8. Managing Loyalty: The Action Plan

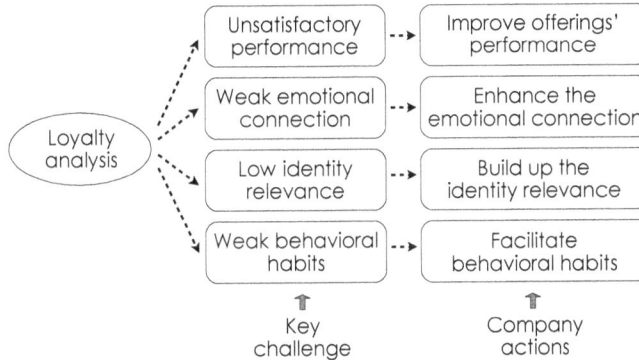

Imagine you have developed a new breakfast cereal and want to build a loyal customer base. To understand customers' experiences with the cereal, you might examine whether its taste meets their expectations and if they perceive it as good value for the money. Further analysis could explore the depth of customers' emotional connections with the brand and whether it holds personal meaning relevant to their identity. Additionally, you might consider whether the cereal's packaging is distinct, making it easy for consumers to recognize among other cereals in the store.

Actions to enhance customer loyalty should directly address the challenges identified. For example, if some customers find the cereal too expensive, you could introduce a rewards program offering discounts on future purchases. If customers struggle to locate the cereal in the store, consider redesigning the packaging to make it more distinct and memorable. If customers see the cereal as just another commodity with similar benefits to other cereals, you might differentiate it by making the packaging more cheerful, adding fun elements like games or trivia, or including collectible toys for children. To increase personal relevance, consider creating a brand character like Tony the Tiger or partnering with a celebrity that resonates with your target customers.

CHAPTER NINE

GATHERING CUSTOMER INSIGHTS

It is a capital mistake to theorize before one has data. Insensibly one
begins to twist facts to suit theories instead of theories to suit facts.
—Sir Arthur Conan Doyle, *Sherlock Holmes*

One of the key drivers of market success is the effective use of customer insights to guide managerial decision making. While it may seem obvious that managers should leverage customer research to inform their decisions, it is not uncommon for them to overlook research data, opting instead to rely on intuition. This may be due to a mistrust of the data or uncertainty about how to apply these data to specific challenges. The flaw in this approach is that regardless of managers' experience, gut feelings can never replace the value of current, relevant, and valid customer insights. The cornerstone of consistent market success is making decisions based on sound customer insights.

Market Research as a Source of Customer Insights

Market research provides managers with relevant information about how customers think, feel, and behave to inform decision making. It also enables managers to test the potential outcomes of their decisions before committing substantial resources. By breaking down business problems into specific questions and testable hypotheses, customer research allows managers to validate and refine their ideas.

Customer research and behavioral science complement and reinforce each other. Behavioral science offers a broad understanding of human behavior, accumulated over decades or even centuries, whereas customer research is a practical tool for gaining specific knowledge to address particular business challenges. Customer research benefits from the conceptual and methodological frameworks of behavioral science while providing specific data that can enrich as well as challenge its theoretical foundations.

Problem-Driven Customer Research

Customer insights generated through market research are crucial for understanding how customers think, feel, and behave. However, not all companies effectively leverage these insights to make business decisions. Often, data are collected and analyzed simply because they seem relevant to the project rather than for their ability to solve a specific business problem. Effective customer research depends on clearly defining the problem at hand. In the words of Albert Einstein, "If I had an hour to solve a problem, I'd spend 55 minutes thinking about the problem and 5 minutes thinking about solutions."

Conducting market research is a collaborative process aimed at generating insights to address business challenges. This process typically involves four distinct company entities. *Business managers* set the direction for the market research project, assess the implications of the research findings, and apply these insights to make informed business decisions. *Research project managers* oversee the entire research process and communicate the results to business managers. *Market-insights researchers* collect and analyze data using various techniques such as experiments, surveys, interviews, and focus groups. *Data-analytics researchers* work with large datasets to uncover relationships between events and predict market outcomes.

Coordinating the research activities across these entities is essential for gathering meaningful market insights. Business managers must have a basic knowledge of market research to formulate actionable research questions. Research project managers need the relevant context to accurately understand the research problem and address it effectively. Market-insights and data-analytics researchers must be proficient in data collection and analysis to carry out the project efficiently. By working together, these four entities provide essential market data that inform managerial decision making.

Customer research begins with identifying the business problem that needs to be resolved and ends with proposing a course of action (Figure 1). The initial step involves defining the business problem the company intends to address—a task typically overseen by business managers, often with minimal input from the market research team. The types of business problems addressed by customer research can vary widely, from identifying target customers and developing new products to meet their needs, to analyzing the reasons behind underperforming products.

Figure 1. Problem-Driven Customer Research

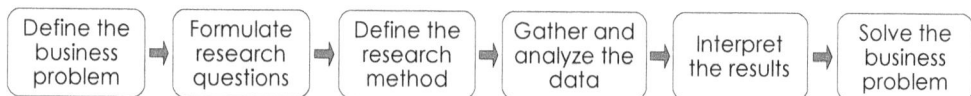

Define the business problem ⇒ Formulate research questions ⇒ Define the research method ⇒ Gather and analyze the data ⇒ Interpret the results ⇒ Solve the business problem

Following the definition of the business problem, the market research team collaborates with managers to formulate specific questions designed to generate insights. Managers work closely with the market research team to translate the business problem into well-defined research questions that align with existing research methodologies. Once these questions are set, the research team selects the appropriate methods for gathering and analyzing the data, typically with little to no involvement from the company's managers.

Once the data have been collected and analyzed, research project managers collaborate with the market insight and data analytics teams to interpret the results. They relate these findings to the initial research questions and rule out alternative explanations. Informed by the data, marketing managers then make decisions aimed at addressing the business problem. This collaborative approach ensures that solutions are grounded in reliable market data and are closely aligned with the company's strategic goals.

The key principle of conducting impactful customer research is that it must be actionable, meaning it should directly influence managers' decisions and actions. When planning customer research, managers should ask themselves the following questions: What specific decision do I need to make? What information do I need to make this decision? How will the research results influence my actions? What would I do differently based on the outcome of this research?

These questions help filter out the "nice-to-know" information and focus on the essential "need-to-know" customer insights. This focus is crucial because many companies conduct research without a clearly defined question that requires an empirical answer. As a result, customer research can become an endless pursuit of additional information under the mistaken belief that more data are always beneficial. More information is not always better, as it can lead to the misallocation of time, money, and effort on irrelevant data. Effective customer research should solve a specific problem by providing insights that directly impact managerial decisions and actions.

Customer Research in the Age of AI

A rapidly growing method for gathering customer insights involves the use of artificial intelligence (AI). Unlike traditional market research, AI incorporates automated judgment and decision making through self-guided algorithms. At the heart of AI is machine learning, which enables systems to learn and make inferences without being explicitly programmed for specific tasks. Instead of relying on rigid models created by engineers to produce certain outputs, AI systems can autonomously improve by adjusting their own algorithms.

A common application of AI can be seen in the following example: A software company launches a new video game that initially attracts a small group of early adopters. The challenge is to identify potential new users to accelerate adoption and scale the game. In the past, managers would have conducted traditional research, such as market surveys and focus group interviews with current users, to identify a target profile for effectively reaching potential users in a cost-efficient way. Today, this task can be achieved by AI, which analyzes the demographics, preferences, and online behavior of early adopters to identify other individuals with similar profiles.

An important aspect of this approach, often referred to as "look-alike matching," is that it is self-guided rather than dictated by software engineers. Managers provide the system with the basic principle of look-alike matching—finding customers with similar profiles who are likely to share an interest in the company's product—and then allow AI to carry out the matching process. Companies like Facebook, Netflix, and Amazon use similar self-guided algorithms not only to understand their target customers' behavior but also to develop personalized offerings for these customers in real time.

Using AI to gather customer insights offers numerous benefits. In an increasingly complex business environment, the ability to evaluate vast amounts of information in real time without relying on predefined algorithms is invaluable. AI not only can process existing data but also design and execute studies that generate new market insights. This ability to quickly conduct large-scale experiments is particularly important for managers operating in fast-paced, dynamic environments.

AI algorithms, however, are not without downsides. One limitation is that AI, especially in its early stages, learns from patterns in existing data. This reliance on available data means AI can have limited ability to predict new behaviors and trends that are not represented in the data. Another significant challenge is the issue of trust. The actions suggested by AI algorithms might not always align with managers' intuition or the findings from traditional marketing research. When faced with conflicting recommendations and a limited understanding of AI algorithms, managers may be hesitant to trust these algorithms and could disregard their advice. This is partly because AI often functions as a "black box," producing outputs through self-guided algorithms that are neither designed nor fully understood by managers.

Because of the drawbacks of AI algorithms, traditional research methods continue to play a crucial role in validating and enhancing AI-generated insights. AI should be viewed as a complement to, rather than a replacement for, traditional customer research methods. The research process should still begin with defining the business problem and formulating research questions and conclude with a recommendation that outlines a viable solution to the identified problem. These critical steps require direct input from the management team. However, other aspects of the research process—such as selecting the research method, gathering and analyzing data, and interpreting results—can be significantly enhanced by AI.

Defining the Business Problem and Formulating the Research Question

Market research promotes rigorous thinking about business problems. By asking concrete, testable, and relevant questions, managers can clearly define these problems. This added clarity helps identify the actionable causes and develop effective solutions.

Defining the Business Problem

For customer research to be truly effective, it must be directly linked to the specific challenges a company is facing and the decisions it needs to make. This decision-focused approach to gathering customer insights begins with clearly identifying the business problem and formulating the corresponding research questions. Without a well-defined and relevant problem to guide the research, it is unlikely to yield useful insights. Echoing the words of American inventor Charles Kettering, "A problem well stated is a problem half solved."

A practical approach to defining the business problem is to identify and analyze the challenges faced by the company in creating the "ideal" customer experience. By examining different aspects of customers' interactions with the company's offerings, this analysis provides a deeper understanding of the dynamics of the customer experience and identifies areas for improvement. Using the customer experience map discussed throughout this book, we can pinpoint several potential challenges, or experience gaps, in creating the optimal customer experience.

The hurdles in the customer experience can be visualized by examining the distribution of customers across different stages of the experience, as illustrated in Figure 2. Here, the light portion of each bar represents a value-creation gap, indicating the target customers for whom the company's offering fails to deliver superior value. The ratio of the light portion to the dark portion of each bar indicates the effectiveness of the company's actions at each stage in managing the customer experience.

Figure 2. The Gap Model for Optimizing the Customer Experience

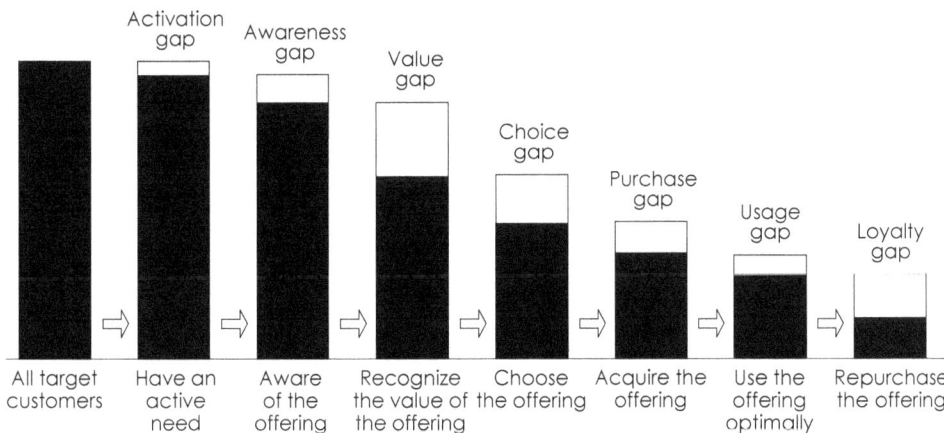

- *Need-activation gaps* occur when the need targeted by the company's offering is not prominent in a customer's mind. If the need is not active, target customers are likely to disregard the company's offering because it seems irrelevant to their current goals. For example, customers who are satisfied with their current car are likely to ignore promotions for a new car, even if it offers superior benefits. To address need-activation gaps, companies must trigger the targeted need — for example, by highlighting how the customer's current situation is suboptimal and can be improved.

- *Awareness gaps* arise when potential customers have an active need but are unaware of the company's offering. Because the offering is not part of their consideration set, it is not evaluated, resulting in a missed opportunity for the company. For instance, a car buyer might be unaware of certain features of a specific car model and, as a result, exclude it from consideration. To bridge awareness gaps, companies must engage customers with their offering so that it becomes an option they actively consider. This could involve increasing communication spending, refining marketing messages, creating more compelling content, or improving strategies to reach target customers effectively.

- *Value gaps* reflect a mismatch between customers' needs and the benefits they perceive an offering can deliver. These gaps can arise from two factors. First, the offering might not create customer value if its costs outweigh its benefits. Second, customers might not understand how the offering's attributes translate into meaningful benefits, causing them to overlook its value. For example, a customer considering a new car might not see the value of advanced features like self-driving mode, feeling that they do not justify the higher price. Alternatively, the benefits of these features might not be clear or compelling if they are not effectively communicated. Addressing value gaps involves enhancing the perceived benefits of the offering, reducing its costs, and improving how these benefits and costs are communicated to potential customers.

- *Choice gaps* occur when there is a disconnect between a customer's valuation of an offering and the likelihood of them choosing it. These gaps can be influenced by the decision-making context, including the number of options considered, the sequence in which they are evaluated, the time frame for making the decision, and the perceived importance of the decision. For example, a car that perfectly meets a customer's needs might be overlooked if the customer feels overwhelmed by the many available options and ends up choosing the first car that meets their basic criteria. To bridge a choice gap, a company can examine the decision-making context and guide customers through the process, increasing the likelihood that its offering will be selected.

- *Purchase gaps* occur when customers' decisions to buy do not lead to actual purchases. This can happen due to a delay in purchasing, a change of mind, or opting for a competitor's product instead. For instance, a customer might add an item to their online shopping cart but abandon it before completing the purchase. To close purchase gaps, a company can introduce time-sensitive incentives, such as short-term discounts, and streamline the purchasing process to minimize uncertainty and effort, making it easier for customers to complete their transactions.

- *Usage gaps* arise when customers are dissatisfied with their experience of using a product or service because it does not meet their needs or expectations. This can happen if a product malfunctions or if a service delivery is subpar. Usage gaps can also occur when customers fail to fully realize the value of the offering, such as when a customer uses the incorrect dosage of laundry detergent, leading to a suboptimal outcome. Addressing usage gaps involves improving the offering's performance and educating customers on how to get the most value from the offering.

- *Loyalty gaps* emerge when customers decide not to repurchase a company's product or service and instead choose an alternative option. These gaps can result from various factors, such as the poor performance of the company's offering, the availability of superior alternatives, or customers' desire for variety. For example, customers might switch to a competitor's offering due to dissatisfaction with the current product, or they might be drawn to the novelty of another option. To close loyalty gaps, a company should consider enhancing customers' overall experience with the offering, streamlining the process of repurchasing the offering and introducing loyalty programs that provide rewards for continued patronage.

A company's focus on different aspects of the customer experience often depends on its market position. For instance, market leaders like Microsoft in business productivity applications, Google in search engines, Apple in premium smartphones, and Nvidia in AI chips are more likely to emphasize managing loyalty to retain existing customers. In contrast, new market entrants typically concentrate on the early stages of the customer experience to attract new customers.

Identifying and assessing gaps in customer experience is essential because these gaps can reduce customer satisfaction and impair a company's ability to attract and retain customers. Conducting a gap analysis provides a clear understanding of where improvements are needed, allowing the company to prioritize and develop strategies that address these deficiencies effectively and cost efficiently. This, in turn, ensures that resources are allocated in a way that maximizes their impact.[1]

Formulating the Research Question

After defining the business problem, a manager must identify the information needed to address the issue and formulate the relevant research question. Business problems and research questions differ in their level of specificity. Business problems are often broad and encompass a wide range of challenges, from identifying target customers and developing new products to reducing customer churn and understanding why certain offerings underperform.

Market research, on the other hand, is problem specific. It typically addresses a specific question within a specific context, such as: How would a two percent price reduction influence the demand for the Ford F150 truck? How effective is the latest Geico advertisement in generating brand awareness? What are the key factors influencing customers' satisfaction with their mobile phone service? Market research questions are typically narrower in scope than the broader business problem they aim to solve. While they do not capture all the complexities of the underlying business issue, they focus on uncovering information critical to making a specific business decision.

The research questions a manager must ask are outlined in the CX Canvas, introduced in the first chapter and explored throughout this book. When analyzing the customer experience, the central question for managers is whether and how the company's offering creates value across all stages of the customer experience—need activation, search, evaluation, choice, purchase, consumption, and repurchase. The key research questions for these different stages of the customer experience are as follows:

- *Need activation.* What need does the company's offering address? Do customers see this need as a problem that must be solved? Are they actively trying to address this need?

- *Search.* Are customers aware of the company's offering? Are they aware of the specifics of the offering? Is this offering a part of customers' consideration set?

- *Evaluation.* Do customers understand the benefits and costs of the offering? Do they see the offering's benefits as relevant to their needs? Do customers think that the benefits of the offering outweigh its costs?

- *Choice.* Is it easy for target customers to make a choice? Does the decision context facilitate the choice of the company's offering?

- *Purchase.* Are there opportunities to enhance customers' motivation to act? Are there any functional, emotional, or implementational barriers to purchase?

- *Consumption.* Do all aspects of the consumption experience create customer value? Does the experience engage customer emotions? Is the experience memorable?

- *Repurchase.* Are customers satisfied with the offering? Are they emotionally connected with it? Do they see it as related to their identity? Have they formed habits to buy and use the offering?

Breaking down the business problem into a series of specific research questions and testable hypotheses allows managers to validate and refine their intuition. This process of formulating concrete and testable questions compels managers to clearly outline the key aspects of the business challenge they aim to address. Meaningful research questions possess four properties: They are relevant, actionable, concrete, and simple.

- *Relevant* questions provide information directly related to solving the focal business problem. Relevance is important, as there is a common tendency among managers to generate questions that are only tangentially related to the issue at hand. While it might seem that more information is always better, each additional question adds costs related to gathering, processing, and interpreting data. This added complexity can dilute the resources available for market research. More important, focusing on irrelevant or tangential questions can distract managers from addressing the core business problem.

- *Actionable* questions are directly related to the different courses of action a company can take to address an impending problem or seize a market opportunity.

A popular approach to generating actionable research is to first lay out the alternative actions the company might take after the research study is complete and then outline the specific information needed to make those decisions. To this end, managers can create scenarios of potential outcomes and connect them to the identified courses of action. By developing research questions with the company's decision-making needs in mind, the data gathered are more likely to be actionable, beneficial for decision making, and obtained in a cost-efficient manner.

- *Concrete* questions are clearly articulated and specific. They should be empirically testable, meaning it should be relatively easy to see how these questions can be addressed through market research. General questions such as "understand the customer" and "analyze the industry" can take many directions and are likely to produce broad answers that are not very informative with respect to the specific business problem at hand. The more specific the research question, the more precise the answer from the market research is likely to be.

- *Simple* questions address a single issue and are articulated in a straightforward fashion that leaves no room for ambiguity. Simplicity is important because overly complicated questions can lead to unfocused market research and results that do not effectively inform the business problem. A practical solution for dealing with complex issues is to break down compound questions into several simpler questions that can be more easily addressed.

Formulating research questions that are relevant, actionable, concrete, and simple greatly increases the chances that market research will produce informative results. Because formulating the research questions requires knowledge of both the business problem and the research tools available to address it, managers are best positioned to do this in collaboration with the customer research team. Such collaboration can go a long way to ensure that the research output can inform managerial decision making and enhance the company's ability to create customer value.

Following the formulation of the research question, a manager must select the best research methodology to address this question. The choice of experimental methodology, often underestimated, can significantly increase the ability of the gathered data to facilitate decision making. Based on the nature of data sought, there are three basic types of research methods: exploratory, experimental, and descriptive (Figure 3).

Figure 3. Key Research Methods

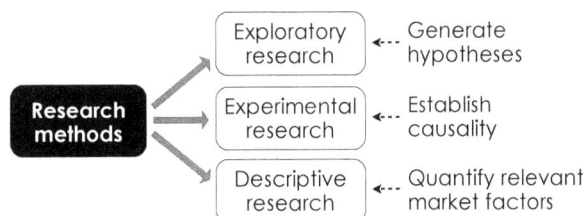

These three methods all aim to gather customer insights to help managers make informed decisions. Where these methods differ is in how they collect these insights and in the specific purposes for which the data are gathered. We discuss the key aspects of these methods and their advantages and limitations in the following sections.

Designing Exploratory Studies

Exploratory research helps managers in the early stages of a market research project attain a general understanding of the business problem, generate new ideas, and formulate hypotheses. This type of research is not concerned with quantifying insights or establishing causal relationships; rather, it serves as a starting point for setting the direction of a project and generating more specific research questions. Common exploratory methods include observation, surveys, activity-based tasks, and personal and focus group interviews.

Observation, Surveys, and Activity-Based Studies

Observation examines people's behavior in their natural environment to gain insights into their needs and the ways they address these needs. Many observational methods are derived from ethnography, a branch of anthropology that examines the sociocultural aspect of people's lives. This foundation in ethnography enriches observational research by incorporating a deep understanding of cultural context and social dynamics into the analysis of behavior.

Observation can involve monitoring people's physical behavior, including the way they go about evaluating, buying, and consuming products and services to fulfill their needs. For example, researchers might visit consumers in their homes or offices to observe their behavior in their natural environment and gain insight into their needs, daily rituals, and product usage. A less intrusive method of observation involves remotely monitoring the behavior of consumers who have consented to participate in the study by using video cameras embedded in their homes, offices, and even cars.

Observation can also include tracking people's online behavior, such as the websites they visit, the content they focus on, and the information they share online. This type of observation, also referred to as exploratory data mining, helps identify patterns and relationships before making any assumptions and formulating hypotheses. Unlike traditional forms of observational research, online tracking does not elicit new data but rather relies on existing data such as online search behavior and social media interactions. Exploratory data mining is often used to examine changes in consumer preferences, needs, or attitudes; to examine the growth of various product categories; and to analyze demographic trends that influence consumer behavior.

A key advantage of observation is that it captures individuals' behavior in their natural environment, offering authentic insights. Additionally, observation often does not require researchers to have preliminary hypotheses about specific relationships in the market. On the downside, however, observation typically yields qualitative data, which can be challenging to quantify for empirical testing (with the notable exception of methods using big data to observe online behavior, which can offer quantifiable insights). Another major limitation of observation is that it cannot establish causality and, instead, is used to formulate hypotheses that can be tested through experimentation.

Surveys are one of the most popular forms of gathering customer-specific information. They collect information by asking individuals to self-report their thoughts, feelings, and behaviors. Surveys vary in complexity, ranging from a few targeted questions to more rigorous studies that include a broad array of questions. Survey research can gather quantitative data by using questionnaires with numerical scales as well as qualitative information through open-ended questions.

Despite its popularity, survey research has several important limitations that can directly affect the validity of its insights. A key problem with surveys is that people are often unwilling to share their true beliefs, feelings, and intentions. And even if they are willing, they are often unable to adequately express their behavioral intentions or predict their future behavior. In the words of one of the most influential advertising thinkers, David Ogilvy, "The trouble with market research is that people don't think what they feel, they don't say what they think, and they don't do what they say."

Activity-based studies probe people's thoughts by asking them to perform specific tasks such as drawing a picture, role-playing a situation, or arranging a series of images to create a narrative. These methods are rooted in the idea that people's beliefs, feelings, and motivations are better captured by actions rather than words. For example, research participants might be asked to collect pictures representing their thoughts and feelings related to a particular aspect of their lives. These pictures are then used as the basis for in-depth interviews to gain better insight into their individual beliefs, needs, and preferences. Alternatively, participants might be asked to draw cartoons of typical users of a brand; write an obituary for a brand; or compare a brand to an animal, a car, or a magazine. Because they offer an alternative approach to understanding customer beliefs, motivations, and behavior, activity-based studies are often used to complement observational studies, personal interviews, and focus groups.

Personal and Focus Group Interviews

Personal interviews explore in depth people's views, experiences, beliefs, and motivations to uncover their needs, understand how they make decisions, and identify factors that influence their behavior. Interviews can be conducted in person or indirectly, using questionnaires administered by mail or online.

Interviews can be conducted in either a structured or unstructured format. Structured interviews are similar to questionnaires and can be administered in person, online, or by mail. They typically involve asking participants predefined questions, with little room for follow-up or conversation, although some structured interviews may allow for follow-up questions when responses need further elaboration. In contrast, unstructured interviews do not follow a predetermined script and are more conversational, with respondents' answers guiding the direction of the interview.

Personal interviews can also vary in their depth. Some interviews are straightforward, focusing on topics such as individual preferences, shopping behavior, and demographic information. In contrast, in-depth interviews delve into the deeper motives behind individuals' behavior. These interviews often employ projective techniques from psychology—such as word association, sentence completion, and picture interpretation—to gain a deeper understanding of the underlying motivations driving people's behavior.

Asking "why" is crucial for uncovering the higher level needs that drive an individual's behavior during an in-depth interview. This often involves a series of "why" inquiries about specific preferences or behaviors, a process known as *benefit laddering*. To illustrate, consider the following interaction between an interviewer and a respondent: "What do you like the most about your Harley?" "The sound." "Why do you like the sound?" "Because it's very distinct." "Why does this matter to you?" "Because it reminds me of riding with my friends." "Why is this important to you?" "Because it makes me feel free." In this interview, the initial answers provide relatively low levels of insight, focusing on a specific attribute—the distinct sound. The subsequent inquiries and responses delve deeper, uncovering the emotional benefit associated with that attribute. Finally, the last answer reveals the higher level self-identity benefit tied to the Harley-Davidson brand.

The main advantage of personal interviews is that they can provide a wealth of detailed information on specific topics of interest to researchers. Additionally, the interactive nature of interviews allows researchers greater flexibility to adapt their questions based on the respondents' answers. On the downside, interviews can be costly, especially when conducted in person. Another potential drawback is desirability bias, where respondents may tailor their answers to what they believe will please the interviewer. For instance, when asked whether they like a company's product, respondents might overstate their interest and the likelihood of purchasing it.

Focus groups are interviews conducted with groups rather than individuals, engaging participants in a free-flowing discussion to uncover their collective opinions on a specific topic. These participants are typically the company's target customers, whose views, insights, and ideas are explored within an interactive social context.

Focus groups are typically moderated by a professional facilitator whose role is to keep the discussion on point, explore potentially interesting ideas suggested by participants, and ensure that all participants have the opportunity to share their thoughts. The facilitator can also offer a meaningful interpretation of the discussion and relate it to the business problem the company aims to address. These interviews can be conducted in person or online, with online focus groups becoming increasingly popular.

A key advantage of focus groups over one-on-one interviews is their ability to generate a broader range of insights, ideas, and opinions because of the interactive nature of group discussions. They also provide insights into social dynamics, showing how individual ideas might be received by others. Focus groups are also faster and more cost-efficient than individual interviews. A potential drawback of focus groups is that the group interactions can sometimes skew the discussion, leading to an overemphasis on certain ideas while overlooking others.

Crafting Experiments to Establish Causality

Experimentation enables managers to understand cause-and-effect relationships. In their simplest form, experiments involve altering one factor to determine whether it has a causal impact on another—such as assessing how changes in product design, price, or advertising influence the desirability of a company's offering. The causal relationships identified through experimental research offer a deeper understanding of customers and their behaviors compared to other research methods. Because experiments are the most effective method for establishing causality, the terms "causal research" and "experimental research" are often used interchangeably.

Understanding Causality

Causality defines the relationship between two or more events where one is a direct consequence of the other(s). Simply put, causality explains the "why" behind the occurrence of any given event. Understanding causality is crucial because it links specific marketing actions to particular market outcomes, enabling managers to make informed decisions and increase the likelihood of achieving the desired impact.

Causality is often confused with correlation, leading managers to mistakenly interpret correlated events as cause-and-effect relationships. For instance, a manager at a soft drink company might launch a price promotion campaign during every major holiday and notice a subsequent increase in sales. The manager could then assume that the price promotion directly caused the sales increase and continue allocating resources to similar campaigns. However, despite the manager's belief that holiday price discounts drive sales volume, the data only show correlation—or more accurately, covariation—not causality. There is no direct evidence that the price promotion was the actual cause of the sales boost. It is possible that the sales increase was driven by the naturally higher demand for soft drinks during holidays, and the same sales volume might have been achieved even without the discount.

Correlation means that certain events tend to occur at the same time. In contrast, for causality to exist, it is not sufficient for events merely to occur at the same time. The relationship between the factors must meet three criteria: covariance (a consistent association between the events), precedence (one event must occur before the other), and the absence of rival explanations (other factors that could account for the relationship must be ruled out).

- *Covariance* refers to a relationship between two factors where changes in one are associated with changes in the other. For example, an increase in advertising expenditures might be associated with an increase in sales volume. Covariance indicates that the relationship between the two events is not random and does not happen by chance alone. Covariance is a necessary but not sufficient condition to establish causality. Indeed, two factors can exhibit similar patterns without being causally related. For example, examining the relationship between spurious factors such as the per capita consumption of cheese and the total revenue generated by golf courses shows that they are highly correlated even though there is no logical connection between them.

- *Precedence* means that there should be temporal sequencing such that the cause must occur before the effect. Indeed, logic dictates that for one factor to cause another, it must occur first. For example, if advertising is the cause of an increase in sales volume, one would expect to observe an increase in advertising activity prior to observing a change in sales volume. Establishing precedence is important because two factors might co-occur without having a causal relationship. For example, while better company performance is often associated with more charismatic CEOs, bringing a charismatic CEO into an organization does not cause the subsequent improvement in performance. On the contrary, research has shown that it is the improvement in a company's performance that leads the public to perceive the CEO as charismatic.[2]

- *Absence of rival explanations* requires that there should be no alternative cause that could explain the relationship between the two events. Even when two factors co-occur, a third factor might be responsible for both. For instance, a researcher might observe a correlation between increased ice cream sales and a rise in crime and mistakenly conclude that ice cream sales cause crime. However, this association might be due to a third factor, such as hot weather, which increases both crime and ice cream consumption. Similarly, an increase in sales following an advertising campaign might actually be due to a coinciding price drop, not the advertising itself.

To establish causal relationships, it is essential to demonstrate that a change in one factor necessarily leads to a corresponding change in another factor. For instance, an experiment can determine whether altering the price of a product actually drives sales, whether a specific advertisement influences individuals' preferences and purchase behavior, or whether a particular reward program boosts customer loyalty. Only experimentation can prove causality by controlling for other variables that might influence the relationship between the factors of interest. Other forms of research can reveal correlations that may suggest a causal relationship, but they cannot definitively prove it.

Creating Insightful Experiments

The simplest version of an experiment, often referred to as A/B testing, involves two conditions. The first is the focal condition, in which the researcher varies the factor of interest, such as price, to observe its impact on a particular outcome, such as sales. The second is the control condition, which serves as a basis for comparison. Having a control condition is necessary to be able to isolate the impact of the factor of interest from other irrelevant factors that happen to coincide with the factor of interest. For example, when examining how price influences sales, it is important to account for external variables, such as the company's advertising, competitor prices, and the overall economic environment, which could also affect sales.

For an experiment to effectively test causality, the control condition must be identical to the experimental condition in all aspects except for the factor of interest. This is why experiments typically involve respondents with similar profiles who are presented with versions of the offering that differ only in the factor being tested. Consequently, any difference in response between the experimental and control conditions can be attributed to the factor of interest, rather than to differences in the respondents' profiles or variations in the offerings that are unrelated to the factor of interest.

Because multiple factors can influence an offering's success, managers are often tempted to vary several attributes simultaneously to more expediently and cost effectively understand their impact. The problem with this approach is that testing multiple factors at once makes it difficult to determine the unique impact of each factor. For instance, if customer demand increases following a simultaneous improvement in the offering's functionality and a reduction in its price, it is difficult to pinpoint whether performance, price, or a combination of both drove the increase. Since an offering's success often depends on multiple attributes working together, the most effective way to understand the impact of different attributes is to test each attribute individually and in combination with others.

An important aspect of planning an experiment is deciding on the research sample and study design. Traditionally, experiments were conducted in labs with a relatively small number of participants—an approach that dominated research practices for many decades. However, with the rise of social media and e-commerce, there has been a shift toward leveraging technology in experimental research.

Increasingly, companies are conducting large-scale online experiments that present real choices to customers. For example, Amazon might display the same product to different customers at varying price points, with different descriptions and promotional incentives. Companies like Microsoft, Facebook, Google, and Netflix run hundreds of experiments daily to fine-tune pricing, communication, and promotional strategies for each customer segment. Because these experiments are conducted in real-world settings with a relatively large number of respondents, they can greatly enhance the efficiency of the company's research efforts and improve the validity of the experimental findings.

The discussion so far has focused on designing experiments where researchers intentionally vary one factor to examine its impact on another. This type of experiment, known as a *controlled experiment*, can be conducted in an artificial setting, such as a lab, or in a real market environment. For example, to study the impact of price on sales volume, a researcher might invite participants to a research facility and ask them to indicate their likelihood of purchasing the product of interest at different price points. Alternatively, a researcher could set up a field experiment where a retailer varies product prices for different customers to observe their purchasing behavior.

Another form of experimentation involves *natural experiments*. Instead of intentionally varying a factor, natural experiments leverage existing differences in the market to draw inferences about relationships of interest. For example, to understand the impact of price changes on purchase behavior, a researcher might analyze historical sales data (the observed effect) in relation to past price fluctuations (the potential cause). Because they rely on existing data, natural experiments are typically less costly and easier to conduct. However, since managers do not have direct control over the factors being studied, establishing causality is more challenging; the observed effect might not be caused by the factor of interest but by another factor that coincides with it. As a result, natural experiments are generally less effective at establishing causal relationships compared to controlled experiments.

Conducting Descriptive Research

Descriptive research, like exploratory and experimental research, helps a company gather valuable information about the market in which it intends to compete. However, unlike the other two methods, which often involve actively collecting data from individuals through surveys and experiments, descriptive research typically relies on analyzing existing information such as web traffic, personal browsing behavior, retail sales figures, and geolocation data.[3]

Descriptive research can help companies assess business opportunities by estimating the size and potential of a given market to determine how attractive that market might be. It can also assist in dividing customers into segments based on their reaction to the company's offering, thus helping managers decide which segments to target and how best to optimize this offering for the chosen segments.

Descriptive research typically involves systematic computational analysis of large amounts of data to facilitate managerial decision making. Based on the nature of the data, two types of data analysis can be distinguished: analysis of structured data and analysis of unstructured data.

Analyzing Structured Data

Structured data encompass information that is highly organized, often in the form of text or numbers arranged in rows and columns. Examples include responses to closed-ended survey questions, lists of names and addresses, and company financial records. Due to its high degree of organization, structured data are relatively easier to analyze.

Structured data can provide insights into various aspects of the market including its size, the demographic characteristics of target customers, the market position of competitors, and the potential sales volume a company can achieve. Simply put, structured data help answer questions such as *Who? What? Where?* and *When?*

Analyzing structured data typically involves exploring the relationships between different variables of interest. One of the most common modeling methods is regression analysis, which aims to uncover the relationship between factors that the company can control (independent variables) and the relevant outcomes (dependent variables). For example, regression analysis might examine the relationship between price, advertising, and sales promotions, on the one hand, and sales volume, on the other. Another popular approach is time-series analysis, which examines changes in a particular factor over time, often to forecast future performance. For example, a company might analyze the historical sales of a product to predict its future sales.

Companies are increasingly leveraging customer data to uncover relevant behavioral patterns, such as purchasing habits, service usage, and engagement with loyalty programs. To gain these insights, many companies rely on internal data that capture customers' interactions with the business. Additionally, an increasing number of companies are utilizing data aggregated from various sources—a process known as "data stitching"—to create a more comprehensive view of their current and potential customers. This aggregated data are then used to customize products and services, predict future purchasing behavior, and enhance customer retention, ultimately allowing companies to personalize their outreach and improve the effectiveness of their marketing efforts.

A well-known example of using descriptive research to understand customer behavior involves Target's ability to identify which of its female customers were pregnant. This gained significant media attention, with headlines like "How Target Figured Out a Teen Girl Was Pregnant Before Her Father Did." Target's predictive ability came from analyzing the buying patterns of women enrolled in their baby registry. Decision scientists at Target observed that women often begin purchasing larger quantities of unscented lotion around the beginning of the second trimester. In the first 20 weeks, they buy a lot of supplements like calcium. And as they get closer to the delivery date, they start buying large quantities of cotton balls.

Target's decision scientists applied these insights to their broader customer base using look-alike matching—an approach based on the premise that individuals with similar demographics and behavior patterns are likely to have similar underlying needs.

Accordingly, scientists identified two dozen products that when purchased together allowed them to assign each customer a "pregnancy" score and estimate a due date. Empowered with this information, Target developed a marketing program for customers with high pregnancy scores that included sending product coupons timed to the specific stages of pregnancy. To mitigate the potential backlash from customers who might feel singled out and "targeted" by the company, Target's marketers included promotions for products like lawnmowers that were likely to be of no interest to these customers, thus creating the perception that the pregnancy-related coupons were coincidental rather than deliberate.[4]

This example is a powerful illustration of the ability of data analytics to inform managerial decision making. Notably, this example dates to over a decade ago. Since then, data analytics has made significant progress not only in terms of computation power but also in terms of its adoption by managers, who increasingly rely on data-driven insights generated by descriptive research.

Analyzing Unstructured Data

Unstructured data consist of information that does not involve text or numerals organized in a matrix format of rows and columns. Most of the data people encounter daily fall into this category, including images, sounds, videos, books, and social media posts. Some data, known as semi-structured data, contain both structured and unstructured elements. Examples of semi-structured data include freeform text from consumer surveys, social media databases, and databases containing audio-visual content.

Analyzing unstructured data typically begins by imposing some structure on the dataset, which then allows for analysis using methods similar to those employed for structured data. For example, when analyzing social media posts, the process might start by creating a matrix that shows the frequency of certain words or phrases. Because of this extra step, analyzing unstructured data typically requires substantially more effort than analyzing structured data. Two commonly used techniques for analyzing unstructured and semi-structured data are natural language processing and metadata analysis.

Natural language processing (NLP) involves analyzing natural streams of recorded or written text. For instance, a company might use NLP to perform sentiment analysis on freeform text, a technique often employed to gauge public sentiment on social media regarding the company's products, services, and brands.

Metadata analysis involves examining the information linked to the gathered data. Unstructured data, especially when gathered online, usually come with a set of automatically collected metadata. For example, social media posts often include metadata such as the time of the post, the sender's name and location, and how the person arrived at the site. By analyzing this metadata alongside unstructured data using techniques like NLP, a company can gain deeper customer insights.

Unlike structured data that primarily include quantitative information, unstructured data can consist of both quantitative and qualitative information. Structured data typically address questions such as *Who? What? Where? When?* but do not delve into the *Why?* In contrast, unstructured data can dig deeper into the drivers of customers' behavior to gain a better understanding of the "why" behind customers' actions.

Google Flu Trends, developed by Google, is a notable example of the advantages and limitations of using predictive analytics with unstructured data. The service analyzed Google search queries to estimate flu activity in various regions worldwide. Specifically, its algorithm examined the frequency of search terms historically linked to flu, such as "flu symptoms" or "fever and cough." The underlying assumption was that an increase in these searches would signal a rise in flu cases. Google's algorithm then compared the search frequencies with historical data from traditional flu surveillance systems, like those run by the U.S. Centers for Disease Control (CDC), to create real-time models predicting flu trends.

Despite its innovative approach, Google Flu Trends encountered significant challenges that ultimately led to its discontinuation. One major issue was its tendency to overestimate flu prevalence during the flu season, at times predicting more than twice the number of cases estimated by the CDC. This overestimation occurred partly because the model was overly sensitive to spikes in search terms, which could be influenced by factors unrelated to actual flu activity. For example, a number of search terms, such as "high school basketball," which tend to coincide with influenza season in the United States, could skew the results.

Additionally, media coverage of flu outbreaks likely prompted increased searches from people who were not actually ill but were looking for information out of concern or curiosity. Over time, growing public awareness of the tool might have further altered search behaviors, distorting the data even more. These issues were exacerbated by Google's lack of transparency about the specific search terms and complete methodology used, which limited the scientific community's ability to evaluate or refine the model. Despite these issues, Google Flu Trends underscores the potential of algorithmic analysis of unstructured data to generate valuable insights and enhance managerial decision making.

Interpreting the Research Findings and Solving the Business Problem

After managers have gathered and analyzed the data, the next crucial step is to connect these insights to the specific business problem that needs solving. Interpreting research findings can be challenging due to various limitations and biases. The primary challenge is ensuring the validity of the research findings while also developing a strategy to manage potential decision errors.

Assessing the Validity of the Data

Validating research data is crucial because customer research often involves assumptions about how people think, feel, and behave, as well as assumptions about the methods used to gather and analyze data. Research validity reflects whether the reported results are grounded in the core principles of behavioral science and are methodologically sound. Two commonly recognized types of research validity are internal validity and external validity. Internal validity refers to how well a study is designed, while external validity pertains to how well the study's results can be generalized beyond the experimental setup to the broader market it aims to examine.

Internal validity focuses on whether the study accurately measures what it intends to measure — whether the findings are logically sound and not influenced by extraneous factors. A common threat to internal validity are experimental design errors, which occur when a study fails to accurately capture the variables of interest. For example, vaguely worded or leading questions can result in responses that do not genuinely address the study's objectives. Another issue arises when questions are framed in a way that allows respondents to guess the purpose of the experiment, leading them to provide answers they believe the company wants rather than expressing their true beliefs and feelings.

Another threat to internal validity are analysis errors that involve inaccuracies in the assessment of the data. These errors can include data entry mistakes, miscalculations during data processing, or inappropriate application of statistical methods. For example, a common type of error involves deciding how to analyze the data only after examining all the data. The problem here is that managers might selectively focus only on those aspects of the data that are most likely to produce significant (and desired) results, which, in turn, will lead to inaccurate conclusions. Planning out analyses before engaging with the data can help prevent these types of analysis errors.

In addition to challenges with internal validity, marketing research can also be compromised by *external validity* errors, which can limit the extent to which study results can be generalized. External validity addresses whether the findings of a study would hold true in different contexts — such as with different people, in different locations, or at different times. For experimental research, a lack of external validity might arise if the study is conducted in highly artificial environments or if participants are placed in overly simplified or abstract scenarios. In descriptive research, external validity errors might occur when the data are drawn from situations that differ significantly from the situation being studied, meaning the insights generated may not be applicable to the problem at hand.

Another factor that can undermine external validity is the use of participants who are not representative of the target market. A common example of this is *self-selection bias*, which occurs when study respondents are allowed to decide for themselves whether to participate rather than being randomly selected. The issue here is that those who choose to participate may not accurately represent the broader population. For instance, a customer satisfaction survey might disproportionately attract responses from individuals who are extremely dissatisfied with a company's offerings, leading to a biased assessment of overall customer satisfaction.

The case of the *Literary Digest* poll serves as a cautionary tale about the danger of selecting a biased research sample. To predict the outcome of the 1936 U.S. presidential election between incumbent Franklin D. Roosevelt and challenger Alfred Landon, *Literary Digest* sent out 10 million mock ballots to people across the country. The list of names was acquired by scouring sources like telephone books, magazine subscriptions, and club memberships. Almost 2.5 million people returned the mock ballots, and the magazine confidently predicted that Landon would win with 57% of the vote.

As it turned out, Roosevelt won the election with 62% of the vote, almost opposite of what the *Digest* had predicted. The faulty predictions were a result of poor sampling. By selecting respondents from telephone books as well as magazine subscription and club membership rosters, it had inadvertently sent out ballots to a disproportionately large percentage of middle- and upper-class voters. Indeed, in the 1930s telephones were a luxury; as a result, lower income voters—who largely supported Roosevelt—were underrepresented in telephone books and, hence, among the poll participants.

Despite the common belief that more data are always better, large volumes of marginally relevant information can actually confuse managers and obscure critical insights. Therefore, managers must carefully screen research findings, discarding data that does not directly address the problem at hand. This process involves evaluating each finding to determine how well it informs the solution to the business problem and prioritizing the most relevant insights. When screening out the irrelevant data, managers should focus on findings that are supported by multiple data sources, as convergence across different methods and sources suggests greater reliability. The more consistent the data, the more dependable the insights.

When designing experimental studies, it is important to keep in mind that a theory can never be conclusively proven because an infinite number of experiments could be conducted to test it. Rather, theories establish their validity by enduring numerous rigorous tests without being disproven. Conversely, it only takes a single well-executed experiment with results that contradict the theory to prove it wrong. Albert Einstein captured this concept succinctly: "No amount of experimentation can ever prove me right; a single experiment can prove me wrong."

Managing Decision Errors

The ultimate goal of gathering market insights is to help managers in selecting the best course of action. Marketing research aims to identify key decision options and outline the pros and cons of each alternative. It is then up to the manager to weigh these pros and cons and determine the optimal path forward. No matter how accurate and timely, marketing research can only suggest a specific course of action—it cannot make the decision for the company.

Drawing conclusions from market research often involves the risk of decision errors. Some errors may arise from incorrect calculations, poor sampling, or faulty assumptions during data gathering and analysis. Others result from using samples to infer the characteristics of a broader population—a process that involves probability estimates rather than certainties, and therefore always carries some degree of error. Even the most meticulously designed research and thoroughly conducted analysis has some likelihood of leading to conclusions that may ultimately prove not entirely correct.

There are two types of decision errors: false positives, also known as Type I errors, and false negatives, also known as Type II errors. A false positive occurs when a test indicates that a particular factor is present when it is not. Conversely, a false negative occurs when a test indicates the absence of a factor when it is actually present.

For example, imagine an online retailer conducting a study to determine whether a specific change to its website will increase sales. The retailer performs an A/B test with a subset of customers, where some see the original website and others see the new one. A positive outcome suggests that the new website is likely to increase sales, while a negative outcome suggests it will not. In this scenario, a false positive means the test shows that the new website will boost sales when it actually will not. A false negative means the test indicates the new website will not increase sales when it actually will.

These two types of errors are inversely related: Reducing the likelihood of false positives increases the likelihood of false negatives, and vice versa. When evaluating data, it is important to consider which type of error is more acceptable in the context of the decision being made. The probability of each type of error depends on the decision criteria set by the researcher. Stricter criteria to avoid false positives will increase the chance of false negatives, and looser criteria will have the opposite effect.

When determining the right balance between false-positive and false-negative errors, a manager must weigh the probability of making a mistake and the consequences of that mistake against the likely benefits. In the example of the website change, a manager might decide to implement the change if the test shows less than a ten percent chance of a false positive, especially if the website change is minor and the consequences of a mistake are negligible. On the other hand, if the consequences of being wrong are significant, the manager might choose to be more cautious and only proceed if the test shows less than a one percent chance of a false positive. Understanding the likelihood and potential impact of these errors is crucial for managing risk and making informed decisions based on market research.

Because most options available to managers are imperfect and involve various tradeoffs, solving business problems often requires selecting the alternative that best aligns with the company's goals. Making tradeoffs is inherently challenging because it involves sacrificing performance in one area to gain in another. In such situations, managers may be tempted to gather more data or conduct additional analyses, hoping that new information will clearly favor one option and eliminate the need for trade-offs. While collecting additional data can sometimes be beneficial, in other cases it can waste time and resources, potentially increasing ambiguity rather than reducing it.

Difficult decisions often lead to so-called "analysis paralysis," where managers, hesitant to make a choice, continuously seek additional information in the hope that it will clarify the best course of action and free them from having to weigh the pros and cons of the available options. This reluctance to decide is well captured by the German philosopher Johann Wolfgang von Goethe, who observed, "The first sign we don't know what we are doing is an obsession with numbers." One way to avoid such decision stalemates is by recognizing that gathering more data comes at the cost of missed opportunities due to indecision. Delaying a decision in pursuit of more information is, in effect, a decision to stay the course and maintain the status quo.

The opposite error to analysis paralysis is overconfidence, where managers are unrealistically certain that their chosen course of action is correct and dismiss the possibility of being wrong. Overconfidence often leads to an overestimation of the likelihood of success, causing managers to act without thoroughly considering the potential drawbacks of their decision or the advantages of alternative options. Overconfident managers also tend to fall victim to confirmation bias, selectively focusing on information that supports their preferred decision and ignoring data that contradicts it. A common form of overconfidence is wishful thinking, where managers overestimate the likelihood of desirable outcomes and underestimate or ignore the risks of adverse consequences.

A practical way to curb overconfidence and better assess potential drawbacks is to imagine that the decision has turned out disastrously a year later and then consider the factors that might have led to this failure. This approach is grounded in the so-called hindsight bias, also called the "I-knew-it-all-along" effect, which refers to people's tendency to see an event that has already occurred as easily predictable, even in the case of events that are unforeseeable and could not have been reliably predicted. By envisioning the decision as already implemented and then reflecting on why it might have failed, managers can gain a more realistic perspective on the risks and downsides of their choice.[5]

SUMMARY

Gathering customer insights is essential for facilitating managerial decision making by providing the necessary information to identify, evaluate, and address challenges facing the company. The market research process begins with defining the problem the company needs to solve, followed by formulating a research question that will yield the specific information required to address the identified problem. This research question is typically narrower than the business problem and focuses solely on uncovering information pertinent to making a well-informed business decision. To ensure the research question is meaningful, it must be relevant, actionable, concrete, and straightforward.

Once the business problem has been identified and the research question formulated, the next step is to define the research method that will be used to collect market data. There are three basic types of research methods: exploratory, experimental, and descriptive.

Exploratory research assists managers at the beginning of a market research project by facilitating a general understanding of the business issue, sparking new ideas, and helping to develop hypotheses. It acts as a stepping stone to guide more structured, quantitative research later in the planning process. This type of research is not aimed at pinpointing cause-and-effect relationships or quantifying different market factors but rather at establishing a foundation for guiding the project's direction and formulating specific research questions. Common exploratory methods include observation, surveys, activity-based tasks, and personal and focus group interviews.

Experimental research is the primary method to establish cause-and-effect relationships in the market. The simplest version of an experiment, commonly referred to as A/B testing, involves changing one factor, such as product design, price, or advertising, to establish whether it has a causal impact on another factor, such as the desirability of a company's offering. The control condition is necessary to isolate the impact of the factor of interest on the outcome being studied from irrelevant factors that might influence this impact. Experimental research can involve controlled experiments that are designed by researchers or natural experiments that take advantage of naturally occurring changes in the market.

Descriptive research aims to gather quantitative information about the target market. Unlike exploratory and experimental research, which actively solicit information from individuals through surveys and experiments, descriptive research primarily utilizes existing data sources like web traffic, retail sales, and geolocation data. This type of research typically involves systematic computational analysis of large amounts of structured and unstructured data. Structured data consist of highly organized information such as responses to closed-ended survey questions, lists of names and addresses, and financial records of companies. In contrast, unstructured data include more free-form content such as images, sounds, videos, books, and social media posts.

Following data analysis, managers must *interpret the data* by relating the empirical findings to the specific business problem. This involves assessing the validity of the data and managing decision errors. Data validity reflects whether the reported results are methodologically sound. Internal validity reflects how well a study is designed, while external validity reflects how well the results of a study can be generalized beyond the experimental setup to the target market. When drawing conclusions from market research, some error is inevitable. False positives (Type I errors) occur when a factor is erroneously believed to be present, while false negatives (Type II errors) happen when a factor is wrongly assumed to be absent.

Key Takeaways

Start with the business problem. The ultimate purpose of market research is to help the company improve its market performance.

Formulate the research question. Pinpoint the specific information needed to solve the identified business problem.

Select the right research method. Use exploratory studies to generate hypotheses, experiments to establish causality, and descriptive data to quantify the relevant market factors.

Assess the validity of the data. Determine whether the research data measure what they are supposed to measure and whether the results are applicable to the focal research question.

Beware of decision errors. Find the optimal balance between false-positive and false-negative errors.

Spotlight: Popular Customer Research Scales and Methods

Customer research employs a variety of techniques to help managers answer research questions. Five of the most popular methods for gathering customer insights—Likert scales, best–worst scaling, conjoint analysis, purchase-intent score, and net promoter score—are outlined below.

The *Likert scale*, named after its inventor, psychologist Rensis Likert, is a popular tool used in survey research to measure people's beliefs about a particular issue. The Likert scale typically includes a series of statements that are shown to respondents, who are asked to indicate the extent to which they agree or disagree with them. Examples of such statements include "The product is easy to use," "I am satisfied with the service," and "the price is fair." Following each statement, respondents are typically asked to indicate the extent to which they agree with it.

The most popular version of a Likert scale involves a five-point response scale: "strongly disagree," "disagree," "neither agree nor disagree," "agree, "strongly agree." Typically, the Likert scale is an odd-point scale; however, an even-point version of the scale, lacking the neutral option of "neither agree nor disagree," is sometimes used to force respondents to decide whether they lean more toward agreeing or disagreeing with each statement. While the original Likert scale aims to assess people's beliefs by measuring their agreement or disagreement with a particular idea, Likert-type scales can also be used to measure other factors, such as frequency, importance, and likelihood.

Likert scales are a staple in survey research due to their simplicity and effectiveness in gauging respondent preferences. Their popularity also stems from their ability to measure many different types of variables, such as attitudes, values, and levels of agreement. On the downside, Likert scales can lead to a central-tendency bias where some of the respondents might avoid extreme positions and prefer middle options, as well as an acquiescence bias that reflects respondents' tendency to agree with statements regardless of their content.

Best–Worst Scaling (BWS), often referred to as maximum difference (MaxDiff) scaling, is used to measure relative preferences, perceived importance, or personal relevance of the attributes describing the available options. This technique presents respondents with a set of items (or a subset of items from a larger list) and asks them to identify the item they consider the "best" and the one they consider the "worst" from the set. This process is repeated across different sets of items, with each set containing a different combination of items from the larger list. The data collected from these responses are used to calculate scores for each item, indicating its relative standing in the list based on the frequency of being chosen as "best" or "worst."

BWS differs from traditional rating scales in that instead of asking respondents to evaluate each item in isolation on a numerical scale, respondents are presented with a set of items and asked to choose the best and the worst (or most and least preferred, important, or relevant). Furthermore, rather than measuring the absolute level of preference or perception for each item, it focuses on extremes to help discern the relative strength of preferences or perceptions.

One of the main benefits of BWS over traditional rating scales is that it places a lower mental burden on respondents, who need to select only the best and worst items rather than quantitatively evaluating each item. Because it relies on relative judgments, BWS also helps minimize the central-tendency bias of traditional rating scales, with some avoiding extremes and others using the full range. Overall, BWS tends to be more useful for relative comparisons and prioritization among a group of items, whereas rating scales are beneficial for assessing the level of sentiment or agreement with each item on its own.

Conjoint analysis is a technique used to assess the value people place on different attributes of a company's offering. This method is commonly employed to determine the relative importance of product attributes and to identify the optimal levels of these attributes. It is particularly useful for choosing between various combinations of attributes when designing or modifying a product. A typical conjoint study involves presenting respondents with a series of options, each representing different combinations of attribute values, and asking them to choose their preferred option from each pair. By analyzing how preferences vary with changes in attribute values, conjoint analysis helps to identify the relative importance of different attributes and the "ideal" values for these attributes in the company's offering.

Conjoint analysis is based on the premise that directly asking individuals to state the relative importance of attributes describing a company's offering might not yield truly informative results. This is because individuals' "true" preferences are more effectively revealed when they make a choice and must sacrifice better performance on one attribute to gain performance on another. Therefore, by creating a series of choices where respondents must trade off the pros and cons of available options, conjoint analysis can uncover the utility generated by various levels of performance across the attributes describing the offering.

Consider a cereal company evaluating different product options involving two flavors, three types of nutritional content, and four price points. This configuration results in 24 unique offering concepts (2 x 3 x 4), which are presented to respondents in pairs. Respondents are asked to choose their preferred option from each pair. The analysis of their response patterns allows researchers to determine the ideal combination of flavor, nutritional content, and price, as well as to assess the value respondents place on each attribute of the company's offering. Additionally, conjoint analysis helps identify the rates of attribute tradeoffs—that is, the extent to which individuals are willing to compromise on one attribute to gain benefits on another. For example, it can determine the premium consumers are willing to pay for their preferred flavor and how much more appealing a particular flavor is when combined with a specific level of nutrition.

The *purchase-intent score* measures the likelihood of customers' buying a specific product or service, usually within a defined time frame such as a month, quarter, or year. This method typically utilizes a five-point scale with responses "definitely would buy," "probably would buy," "might or might not buy," "probably would not buy," and "definitely would not buy." The simplicity of this method makes it popular because it is easy to execute and interpret. However, despite its widespread use, it has several drawbacks. An important limitation is that respondents often overstate the likelihood of making a purchase when asked directly. This overestimation can skew results, leading researchers to typically adjust the stated purchase responses to reflect true buying intentions more accurately.

A common approach to correct for overestimation bias in purchase-intent scores involves using adjustment coefficients derived from comparing predicted and actual purchase rates within the specific industry. For instance, in the consumer packaged goods sector, original answers are often adjusted as follows: Responses indicating "definitely would buy" are reduced by 20%, implying that only 80% of those who say they will definitely buy the product actually do; "probably would buy" responses are reduced by 70%, meaning only 30% of these respondents end up purchasing the product. Responses in the three remaining categories are considered as indicating no intention to purchase. Because analysis of the responses is focused on the first two answers, this method is often referred to as the top-box approach.

To illustrate the adjustment process, consider a scenario where survey responses are distributed as follows: 10% of respondents indicate they would "definitely buy" the product, 33% say they would "probably buy" it, 31% are indifferent, 21% say they would "probably not buy," and 5% indicate they would "definitely not buy." Assuming the industry standard adjustment of 80/30 holds, the purchase-intent score is 10%*80% + 33%*30% = 18%, meaning that in reality only about 18% of potential customers are likely to purchase the offering.

The *Net Promoter Score* (NPS) is based on the premise that a customer's true preference for a product or service is best indicated by their willingness to recommend it to others. The NPS metric is used to gauge the likelihood that customers will promote a company, its products, or its brands through positive word of mouth.[6] To calculate NPS, customers are asked to rate the likelihood that they would recommend the company, its offerings, or its brands to a friend or colleague. Responses are scored on a scale from 0 to 10, where 0 means "extremely unlikely" and 10 means "extremely likely."

Based on their responses, customers are categorized into three groups: promoters, who rate the company as 9 or 10; passives, who give a score of 7 or 8; and detractors, who score 6 or lower. NPS is calculated by subtracting the percentage of detractors from the percentage of promoters. For example, if 40% of a company's customers are promoters and 25% are detractors, the company's NPS would be 15%. This score reflects the net proportion of customers likely to advocate positively for the company.

NPS has gained popularity among managers because of its intuitive underlying assumption that a person willing to recommend an offering must find it attractive. This method's simplicity, involving just one straightforward question, further adds to its appeal. Despite its widespread use, this method is not universally applicable. For instance, customers might hesitate to recommend a product if they believe its value is unique to their specific needs and preferences and might not be appreciated by others with different preferences. Therefore, while useful, NPS is best used alongside other market research methods to provide a more accurate assessment of customers' reaction to a company's offerings.

FURTHER READINGS

Dan Ariely, *Predictably Irrational: The Hidden Forces That Shape Our Decisions* (HarperCollins Publishers, 2008).

Roy Baumeister and John Tierney, *Willpower: Rediscovering the Greatest Human Strength* (Penguin Books, 2011).

Jonah Berger, *Contagious: Why Things Catch On* (Simon & Schuster, 2013).

Jonah Berger, *The catalyst: How to Change Anyone's Mind* (Simon & Schuster, 2022).
Jonah Berger, *Invisible Influence: The Hidden Forces That Shape Behavior* (Simon & Schuster, 2016).

Christopher Chabris and Daniel Simons, *The Invisible Gorilla: How Our Intuitions Deceive Us* (Crown, 2010).

Robert Cialdini, *Influence: The Psychology of Persuasion* (New York, NY: HarperCollins Publishers, 2007).

Robert Cialdini, *Pre-Suasion: A Revolutionary Way to Influence and Persuade* (Simon & Schuster, 2018).

Mihaly Csikszentmihalyi, *Flow: The Psychology of Optimal Experience* (HarperCollins Publishers, 2009).

Angela Duckworth, *Grit: The Power of Passion and Perseverance* (Scribner, 2016).

Charles Duhigg, *The Power of Habit: Why We Do What We Do in Life and Business* (Random House, 2012).

Carol Dweck, *Mindset: The New Psychology of Success* (Random House, 2006).

Nir Eyal, *Hooked: How to Build Habit-Forming Products* (Penguin, 2014).

Chip Heath and Dan Heath, *Made to Stick: Why Some Ideas Survive and Others Die* (Random House, 2007).

Chip Heath and Dan Heath, *Switch: How to Change Things When Change Is Hard* (Crown, 2010).

Chip Heath and Dan Heath, *Decisive: How to Make Better Choices in Life and Work* (Random House, 2013).

Chip Heath and Dan Heath, *The Power of Moments: Why Certain Experiences Have Extraordinary Impact* (Simon & Schuster, 2017).

Sheena Iyengar, *The Art of Choosing* (Twelve, 2010).

Eric Johnson, *The Elements of Choice: Why the Way We Decide Matters* (Riverhead Books, 2021).

Daniel Kahneman, *Thinking, Fast and Slow* (Farrar, Straus and Giroux, 2011).

Michael Lewis, *The Undoing Project: A Friendship That Changed Our Minds* (W. W. Norton, 2016).

Martin Lindstrom, *Buyology: Truth and Lies About Why We Buy* (Crown Currency, 2010).

Nina Mažar and Dilip Soman, *Behavioral Science in the Wild* (Rotman-UTP Publishing, 2022).

Katy Milkman, *How to Change: The Science of Getting from Where You Are to Where You Want to Be* (Portfolio, 2021).

Daniel Pink, *Drive: The Surprising Truth About What Motivates Us* (Penguin, 2011).

Daniel Pink, *When: The Scientific Secrets of Perfect Timing* (Penguin, 2018).

Colin Shaw and Ryan Hamilton, *The Intuitive Customer: 7 Imperatives for Moving Your Customer Experience to the Next Level* (Palgrave Macmillan, 2016).

Simon Sinek, *Start with Why: How Great Leaders Inspire Everyone to Take Action* (Portfolio, 2009).

Richard Thaler and Cass Sunstein, *Nudge: Improving Decisions About Health, Wealth, and Happiness* (Yale University Press, 2008).

Richard Thaler, *Misbehaving: The Making of Behavioral Economics* (W. W. Norton, 2015).

Paco Underhill, *Why We Buy: The Science of Shopping* (Simon and Schuster, 2009).

NOTES

Chapter 1

[1] Alden Hayashi, "When to Trust Your Gut," *Harvard Business Review* (February 2001).

[2] Herbert Simon, "A Behavioral Model of Rational Choice," *The Quarterly Journal of Economics* 69.1 (February 1955).

Chapter 2

[1] A slightly different version of this classification of customer needs is discussed in Chapter 4. It involves three main types: functional, monetary, and psychological. In this classification, functional and monetary values represent the two aspects of utilitarian value, while psychological value encompasses emotional and identity values.

[2] Jerome Bruner and Cecile Goodman, "Value and Need as Organizing Factors in Perception," *The Journal of Abnormal and Social Psychology* 42.1 (1947); C. Miguel Brendl, Arthur Markman, and Claude Messner, "The Devaluation Effect: Activating a Need Devalues Unrelated Objects," *Journal of Consumer Research* 29.4 (2003); Richard Nisbett and David Kanouse, "Obesity, Food Deprivation, and Supermarket Shopping Behavior," *Journal of Personality and Social Psychology* 12 (August 1969); Arthur Markman and C. Miguel Brendl, "The Influence of Goals on Value and Choice," *The Psychology of Learning and Motivation* 39 (2000).

[3] Clayton Christensen, Taddy Hall, Karen Dillon, and David Duncan, "Know Your Customers' 'Jobs to Be Done,'" *Harvard Business Review* (September 2016).

[4] https://statista.com/statistics/596114/per-capita-consumption-of-ice-cream-in-europe-by-country (2020 data).

[5] Thorstein Veblen, *The Theory of the Leisure Class: An Economic Study of Institutions* (Macmillan 1899); Laurie Simon Bagwell and Douglas Bernheim, "Veblen Effects in a Theory of Conspicuous Consumption," *The American Economic Review* 86.3 (1996).

[6] San Bolkan and Peter Andersen, "Image Induction and Social Influence: Explication and Initial Tests," *Basic and Applied Social Psychology* (November 2009).

[7] Mason Haire, "Projective Techniques in Marketing Research," *Journal of Marketing* 14 (April 1950).

[8] Abraham Maslow, "A Theory of Human Motivation," *Psychological Review* 50 (1943).

Chapter 3

[1] Daniel Kahneman, *Thinking, Fast and Slow* (Farrar, Straus and Giroux, 2011); Steven Sloman, "The Empirical Case for Two Systems of Reasoning," *Psychological Bulletin* 119.1 (1996).

[2] Shane Frederick, "Cognitive Reflection and Decision Making," *Journal of Economic Perspectives* 119.4 (2005).

[3] Roger Shepard, *Mind Sights: Original Visual Illusions, Ambiguities, and Other Anomalies* (W. H. Freeman and Co., 1990); Richard Thaler and Cass Sunstein. *Nudge: Improving Decisions About Health, Wealth, and Happiness* (Yale University Press, 2008).

[4] Colin Cherry, "The Cocktail Party Effect," *The Journal of the Acoustical Society of America* 25.5 (1953).

[5] Adrian North, David Hargreaves, and Jennifer McKendrick, "The Influence of In-Store Music on Wine Selections," *Journal of Applied Psychology* 84.2 (1999).

[6] Robert Cialdini, *Pre-Suasion: A Revolutionary Way to Influence and Persuade* (Simon & Schuster, 2018).

[7] Samuel McClure et al., "Neural Correlates of Behavioral Preference for Culturally Familiar Drinks," *Neuron* 44.2 (2004); Hilke Plassmann, John O'Doherty, Baba Shiv, and Antonio Rangel, "Marketing Actions Can Modulate Neural Representations of Experienced Pleasantness," Proceedings of the National Academy of Sciences 105.3 (2008); Calvin Trillin, "The Red and the White," *The New Yorker* (August 11, 2002).

[8] Hedwig Von Restorff, "Über die Wirkung von Bereichsbildungen im Spurenfeld" [On the Effect of

Area Formation in the Trace Field], *Psychologische Forschung* 18 (1933); Reed Hunt, "The subtlety of distinctiveness: What von Restorff really did," *Psychonomic Bulletin & Review* 2 (1995).

9 Daniel Berlyne, "A Theory of Human Curiosity," *British Journal of Psychology*, 45 (1954); George Loewenstein, "The Psychology of Curiosity: A Review and Reinterpretation," *Psychological Bulletin* 116.1 (1994).

10 Bluma Zeigarnik, "Das Behalten erledigter und unerledigter Handlungen" [On the Retention of Completed and Uncompleted Activities], *Psychologische Forschung* 9 (1927).

11 David Schkade and Daniel Kahneman, "Does Living in California Make People Happy? A Focusing Illusion in Judgments of Life Satisfaction," *Psychological Science* (1998).

12 Ravi Dhar and Itamar Simonson, "The Effect of the Focus of Comparison on Consumer Preferences," *Journal of Marketing Research* 29.4 (1992).

13 Robert Cialdini, *Pre-Suasion: A Revolutionary Way to Influence and Persuade* (Simon & Schuster, 2018).

14 Fritz Strack, Leonard Martin, and Norbert Schwarz, "Priming and Communication: Social Determinants of Information Use in Judgments of Life Satisfaction," *European Journal of Social Psychology* 18.5 (1988); Norbert Schwarz, Fritz Strack, and Hans-Peter Mai, "Assimilation and Contrast Effects in Part–Whole Question Sequences: A Conversational Logic Analysis," *Public Opinion Quarterly* 55.1 (1991).

15 Edward Thorndike, "A Constant Error in Psychological Ratings," *Journal of Applied Psychology* 4:1 (1920); Solomon Asch, "Forming Impressions of Personality," *Journal of Abnormal and Social Psychology* 41.3 (1946); Richard Nisbett and Timothy Wilson, "The Halo Effect: Evidence for Unconscious Alteration of Judgments," *Journal of Personality and Social Psychology* 35.4 (1977); William Cooper, "Ubiquitous Halo," *Psychological Bulletin* 90.2 (1981); Alan Feingold, "Good-Looking People Are Not What We Think," *Psychological Bulletin* 111.2 (1992).

16 Richard Nisbett and Timothy Wilson (1977), "The Halo Effect: Evidence for Unconscious Alteration of Judgments," *Journal of Personality and Social Psychology* 35 (April).

17 Solomon Asch, "Forming Impressions of Personality," *The Journal of Abnormal and Social Psychology* 41.3 (1946).

18 Nathan Novemsky, Ravi Dhar, Norbert Schwarz, and Itamar Simonson, "Preference Fluency in Choice," *Journal of Marketing Research* 44 (2007).

19 Michaela Wänke, Gerd Bohner, and Andreas Jurkowitsch, "There Are Many Reasons To Drive a BMW: Does Imagined Ease of Argument Generation Influence Attitudes?" *Journal of Consumer Research* 24.2 (1997).

20 Chris Janiszewski, "Preattentive Mere Exposure Effects," *Journal of Consumer Research* 20.3 (1993).

21 Rolf Reber and Norbert Schwarz, "Effects of Perceptual Fluency on Judgments of Truth," *Consciousness and Cognition* 8 (1999).

22 Matthew McGlone and Jessica Tofighbakhsh, "Birds of a Feather Flock Conjointly (?): Rhyme as Reason in Aphorisms," *Psychological Science* 11.5 (2000).

23 Robert Cialdini, *Pre-Suasion: A Revolutionary Way to Influence and Persuade* (Simon & Schuster, 2018).

24 Richard Petty and John Cacioppo, *The Elaboration Likelihood Model of Persuasion* (Springer, New York, 1986).

25 Naomi Mandel and Eric Johnson, "When Web Pages Influence Choice: Effects of Visual Primes on Experts and Novices," *Journal of Consumer Research* 29.2 (2002).

26 Martin Ashford, "Maurice Saatchi on Advertising," *Financial Times* (June 22, 2006).

27 Chip Heath and Dan Heath, *Made to Stick* (Random House, 2007).

28 Geoffrey Moore, *Crossing the Chasm: Marketing and Selling High-Tech Products to Mainstream Customers* (Harper Business, 1991).

Chapter 4

[1] Amos Tversky and Daniel Kahneman, "Prospect theory: An Analysis of Decision Under Risk," *Econometrica* 47.2 (1979).

[2] Victoria Medvec, Scott Madey, and Thomas Gilovich, "When Less Is More: Counterfactual Thinking and Satisfaction Among Olympic Medalists," *Journal of Personality and Social Psychology* 69.4 (1995).

[3] Amos Tversky and Daniel Kahneman, "The Framing of Decisions and the Rationality of Choice," *Science* 211 (1981); Richard Thaler, "Toward a Positive Theory of Consumer Choice," *Journal of Economic Behavior and Organization* 1.1 (1980).

[4] Amos Tversky and Daniel Kahneman, "Judgment under Uncertainty: Heuristics and Biases," *Science* 185.4157 (1974).

[5] Dan Ariely, *Predictably Irrational* (HarperCollins Publishers, 2008).

[6] Amos Tversky and Daniel Kahneman, "Judgment under Uncertainty: Heuristics and Biases," *Science* 185.4157 (1974).

[7] William Shakespeare, *Hamlet* (Act 2, Scene 2).

[8] Richard Thaler and Cass Sunstein, *Nudge: Improving Decisions About Health, Wealth, and Happiness* (Yale University Press, 2008).

[9] Amos Tversky and Daniel Kahneman, "The Framing of Decisions and the Psychology of Choice," *Science* 211.4481 (1981).

[10] Gerd Gigerenzer, *Risk Savvy: How to Make Good Decisions* (Penguin, 2015).

[11] Daniel Kahneman, Jack Knetsch, and Richard Thaler, "Experimental Tests of the Endowment Effect and the Coase Theorem," *Journal of Political Economy* 98.6 (1990); Daniel Kahneman, Jack L. Knetsch, and Richard Thaler, "Anomalies: The Endowment Effect, Loss Aversion, and Status Quo Bias," *Journal of Economic Perspectives* 5.1 (1991).

[12] Aristotle, *The Nicomachean Ethics*, Book IX.

[13] Jack Knetsch, "The Endowment Effect and Evidence of Nonreversible Indifference Curves," *The American Economic Review* 79.5 (1989).

[14] Daniel Bernoulli, "Exposition of a New Theory on the Measurement of Risk," *Econometrica* 22 (1954). (Translation of Bernoulli 1738 "Specimen Theoriae Novae de Mensura Sortis;" in *Papers of the Imperial Academy of Sciences in Petersburg*, Vol. V, 1738).

[15] Klaus Wertenbroch, "Consumption Self-Control by Rationing Purchase Quantities of Virtue and Vice," *Marketing Science* 17 (Fall 1998).

[16] Paul Rozin, Michele Ashmore, and Maureen Markwith, "Lay American Conceptions of Nutrition: Dose Insensitivity, Categorical Thinking, Contagion, and the Monotonic Mind," *Health Psychology* (1996).

[17] Chernev, Alexander, "The Dieter's Paradox," *Journal of Consumer Psychology* 21 (April 2011).

[18] Adam Alter and Hal Hershfield, "People Search For Meaning When They Approach a New Decade in Chronological Age," *Proceedings of the National Academy of Sciences* 111.48 (2014); Daniel Pink, *When: The Scientific Secrets of Perfect Timing* (Riverhead Books, 2018).

[19] Abha Bhattarai, "One Way Companies Are Concealing Higher Prices: Smaller Packages." *The Washington Post* (June 1, 2021).

[20] Abha Bhattarai, "One Way Companies Are Concealing Higher Prices: Smaller Packages." *The Washington Post* (June 1, 2021).

[21] Andrew Geier, Brian Wansink, and Paul Rozin, "Red Potato Chips: Segmentation Cues Can Substantially Decrease Food Intake," *Health Psychology* 31.3 (2012).

[22] Edward Thorndike, "A Constant Error in Psychological Ratings," *Journal of Applied Psychology* 4.1 (1920); Solomon Asch, "Forming Impressions of Personality," *Journal of Abnormal and Social Psychology* 41.3 (1946); Richard Nisbett and Timothy Wilson, "The Halo Effect: Evidence for

Unconscious Alteration of Judgments," *Journal of Personality and Social Psychology* 35.4 (1977); Alan Feingold, "Good-Looking People Are Not What We Think," *Psychological Bulletin* 111.2 (1992).

23 Hilke Plassmann, John O'Doherty, Baba Shiv, and Antonio Rangel, "Marketing Actions Can Modulate Neural Representations of Experienced Pleasantness," *Proceedings of the National Academy of Sciences* 105.3 (2008).

24 J. Craig Andrews, Richard Netemeyer, and Scot Burton, "Consumer Generalization of Nutrient Content Claims in Advertising," *Journal of Marketing* 62.4 (1996); Brian Wansink and Pierre Chandon, "Can 'Low-Fat' Nutrition Labels Lead to Obesity?" *Journal of Marketing Research* 43.4 (2006).

25 Hayley Dixon, "Cadbury Facing Revolt over New Dairy Milk," *The Telegraph* (September 16, 2013); Mary Kim Ngo and Charles Spence, "Assessing the Shapes and Speech Sounds that Consumers Associate with Different Kinds of Chocolate," *Journal of Sensory Studies* 26.6 (2011).

26 Gregory Carpenter, Rashi Glazer, and Kent Nakamoto, "Meaningful Brands from Meaningless Differentiation: The Dependence on Irrelevant Attributes," *Journal of Marketing Research* 31 (August 1994).

27 Alexander Chernev, *Strategic Brand Management* (Cerebellum Press, 2019).

28 Yann Cornil, Pierre Chandon, and Aradhna Krishna, "Does Red Bull Give Wings to Vodka? Placebo Effects of Marketing Labels on Perceived Intoxication and Risky Attitudes and Behaviors," *Journal of Consumer Psychology* 27.4 (2017).

29 Alexander Chernev and Sean Blair, "Doing Well by Doing Good: The Benevolent Halo of Corporate Social Responsibility," *Journal of Consumer Research* 41.6 (2015).

30 Alexander Chernev and Gregory Carpenter, "The Role of Market Efficiency Intuitions in Consumer Choice: A Case of Compensatory Inferences," *Journal of Marketing Research* 38.3 (2001).

31 Raghunathan Rajagopal, Rebecca Walker Naylor, and Wayne Hoyer. "The Unhealthy = Tasty Intuition and Its Effects on Taste Inferences, Enjoyment, and Choice of Food Products," *Journal of Marketing* 70.4 (2006).

32 Alexander Chernev, "Jack of All Trades or Master of One? Product Differentiation and Compensatory Reasoning in Consumer Choice," *Journal of Consumer Research* 33 (March 2007).

33 Paul Slovic, Dale Griffin, and Amos Tversky, "Compatibility effects in judgment and choice." In *Insights in Decision Making: A Tribute to Hillel Einhorn,* ed. Robin Hogarth (University of Chicago Press, 1990).

Chapter 5

1 Richard Thaler, *Misbehaving: The Making of Behavioral Economics* (W. W. Norton, 2015).

2 Herbert Simon, "A Behavioral Model of Rational Choice," *The Quarterly Journal of Economics* 69.1 (1955).

3 Richard Thaler, "Mental Accounting Matters," *Journal of Behavioral Decision Making* 12.3 (1999).

4 Richard Thaler, "Mental Accounting and Consumer Choice," *Marketing Science* 4.3 (1985).

5 Daniel Kahneman and Amos Tversky, "Choices, Values, and Frames," *Handbook of the Fundamentals of Financial Decision Making: Part I* (2013).

6 Itamar Simonson, "Choice Based on Reasons: The Case of Attraction and Compromise Effects," *Journal of Consumer Research* 16.2 (1989).

7 Ellen Langer, Arthur Blank, and Benzion Chanowitz, "The Mindlessness of Ostensibly Thoughtful Action: The Role of 'Placebic' Information in Interpersonal Interaction," *Journal of Personality and Social Psychology* 36 (1978). Note that the sample sizes used in the study were relatively small compared to the standards currently accepted in the field.

8 Itamar Simonson, Ziv Carmon, and Suzanne O'Curry, "Experimental Evidence on the Negative Effect of Product Features and Sales Promotions on Brand Choice," *Marketing Science* 13.1 (1994);

Eldar Shafir, Itamar Simonson, and Amos Tversky, "Reason-Based Choice," *Cognition* 49.1–2 (1993); Daniel Kahneman, *Thinking, Fast and Slow* (New York, NY: Farrar, Straus and Giroux, 2011).

[9] Uri Gneezy and Aldo Rustichini, "Pay Enough or Don't Pay At All," *The Quarterly Journal of Economics* 115.3 (2000).

[10] Dan Ariely, *Predictably Irrational* (HarperCollins Publishers, 2008).

[11] Richard Thaler and Cass Sunstein, *Nudge: Improving Decisions About Health, Wealth, and Happiness* (Yale University Press, 2008).

[12] Eric Johnson, *The Elements of Choice: Why the Way We Decide Matters* (Riverhead Books, 2021).

[13] Irwin Levin, "Associative Effects of Information Framing," *Bulletin of the Psychonomic Society* 25 (March 1987). See also, Levin, Irwin and Gary Gaeth, "How Consumers Are Affected by the Framing of Attribute Information Before and After Consuming the Product," *Journal of Consumer Research* 15 (December 1988).

[14] In addition to its 99 $^{44}/_{100}$% pure slogan, Ivory's other famous slogan is "It Floats!"

[15] Katie Kiefner, "The New $400,000 Bed That Already Has A Waiting List," Forbes, August 20 (2020).

[16] Itamar Simonson, "The Effect of Product Assortment on Buyer Preferences," *Journal of Retailing* 75.3 (1999).

[17] Jason Silva, "Brain Games," *National Geographic*, https://www.natgeotv.com/asia/brain-games/videos/the-decoy-effect

[18] Amos Tversky, "Elimination by Aspects: A Theory of Choice, *Psychological Review* 79.4 (1972).

[19] Itamar Simonson and Amos Tversky, "Choice in Context: Tradeoff Contrast and Extremeness Aversion," *Journal of Marketing Research* 29.3 (1992).

[20] Kathryn Sharpe, Richard Staelin, and Joel Huber, "Using Extremeness Aversion to Fight Obesity," *Journal of Consumer Research* 35.3 (2008).

[21] Solomon Asch, "Opinions and Social Pressure," *Scientific American* 193 (1955).

[22] Leslie Kaufman, "Utilities Turn Their Customers Green, With Envy," *The New York Times* (January 30, 2009).

[23] Noah Goldstein, Robert Cialdini, Vladas Griskevicius, "A Room with a Viewpoint: Using Social Norms to Motivate Environmental Conservation in Hotels," *Journal of Consumer Research* 35.3 (2008).

[24] Sheena Sethi Iyengar and Mark Lepper, "When Choice is Demotivating: Can One Desire Too Much of a Good Thing?" *Journal of Personality and Social Psychology* 79.6 (2000).

[25] Sheena Iyengar, Gur Huberman, and Wei Jiang, "How Much Choice Is Too Much? Contributions to 401(k) Retirement Plans," *Pension Design and Structure: New Lessons from Behavioral Finance* (July 2004).

[26] Alexander Chernev, "When More Is Less and Less Is More: The Role of Ideal Point Availability and Assortment in Consumer Choice," *Journal of Consumer Research* 30.2 (2003).

[27] Alexander Chernev, Ulf Böckenholt, and Joseph Goodman, "Choice Overload: A Conceptual Review and Meta-Analysis," *Journal of Consumer Psychology* 25.2 (2015).

[28] Alexander Chernev, "When More Is Less and Less Is More: The Role of Ideal Point Availability and Assortment in Consumer Choice," *Journal of Consumer Research* 30.2 (2003); Alexander Chernev, "Product Assortment and Individual Decision Processes," *Journal of Personality and Social Psychology* 85.1 (2003).

[29] Shai Danziger, Jonathan Levav, and Liora Avnaim-Pesso, "Extraneous Factors in Judicial Decisions," *Proceedings of the National Academy of Sciences* 108.17 (2011).

[30] Baba Shiv and Alexander Fedorikhin, "Heart and Mind in Conflict: The Interplay of Affect and Cognition in Consumer Decision Making," *Journal of Consumer Research* 26.3 (1999).

[31] Kathleen Vohs et al., "Making Choices Impairs Subsequent Self-Control," *Journal of Personality and Social Psychology* 94.5 (2008).

[32] Kathleen Vohs and Ronald Faber, "Spent Resources: Self-Regulatory Resource Availability Affects Impulse Buying," *Journal of Consumer Research* 33.4 (2007).

[33] Scott Golder and Michael Macy, "Diurnal and Seasonal Mood Vary with Work, Sleep, and Daylength Across Diverse Cultures," *Science* 333.6051 (2011); Arthur Stone et al., "A Population Approach to the Study of Emotion: Diurnal Rhythms of a Working Day Examined with the Day Reconstruction Method," *Emotion* 6.1 (2006); Daniel Pink, *When: The Scientific Secrets of Perfect Timing* (Penguin Publishing Group, 2018).

[34] Eric Johnson and Daniel Goldstein, "Do Defaults Save Lives?" *Science* 302.5649 (2003).

[35] Jeffrey Clark and Jean Young, "Automatic Enrollment: The Power of the Default," Vanguard Research (March 2018). See also Brigitte Madrian and Dennis Shea, "The Power of Suggestion: Inertia in 401(k) Participation and Savings Behavior," *The Quarterly Journal of Economics* 116.4 (2001).

[36] Jessica Wisdom, Julie Downs, and George Loewenstein, "Promoting Healthy Choices: Information versus Convenience," *American Economic Journal: Applied Economics* 2.2 (2010).

[37] Eric Johnson, *The Elements of Choice: Why the Way We Decide Matters* (Riverhead Books, 2021).

[38] Marcel Zeelenberg, "Anticipated Regret: A Prospective Emotion about the Future Past." In *The Psychology of Thinking about the Future,* ed. Gabriele Oettingen, A. Timur Sevincer, and Peter Gollwitzer (The Guilford Press, 2018).

[39] These roles were originally proposed by marketing professors Frederick Webster and Yoram Wind to describe the ways in which organizations make purchase decisions. The original list of five roles was later expanded by Thomas Bonoma to include the role of initiator. See Yoram Wind and Frederick Webster, *Organizational Buying Behavior* (Prentice Hall, 1972); Thomas Bonoma, "Major Sales: Who Really Does the Buying?," *Harvard Business Review* 60 (May–June 1982).

Chapter 6

[1] Jeffrey Inman, Anil Peter, and Priya Raghubir, "Framing the Deal: The Role of Restrictions in Accentuating Deal Value," *Journal of Consumer Research* 24.1 (1997); Brian Wansink, Robert Kent, and Stephen Hoch, "An Anchoring and Adjustment Model of Purchase Quantity Decisions," *Journal of Marketing Research* 35 (February 1998).

[2] With the exception of Germany, where the McRib is available year-round.

[3] Phillip Nelson, "Information and Consumer Behavior," *Journal of Political Economy* 78 (March–April 1970).

[4] Leon Festinger, *A Theory of Cognitive Dissonance* (Stanford University Press, 1957).

[5] Marcel Zeelenberg, "Anticipated Regret: A Prospective Emotion about the Future Past," In *The Psychology of Thinking about the Future*, ed. Gabriele Oettingen, A. Timur Sevincer, and Peter Gollwitzer (The Guilford Press, 2018).

[6] Neal Roese, "Counterfactual Thinking," *Psychological Bulletin* 121.1 (1997).

[7] Daniel Kahneman and Amos Tversky, "The Psychology of Preferences," *Scientific American* (January 1982).

[8] Daniel Kahneman and Dale Miller, "Norm Theory: Comparing Reality to its Alternatives," *Psychological Review* 93.2 (1986).

[9] Marcel Zeelenberg, Kees van den Bos, Eric van Dijk, and Rik Pieters, "The Inaction Effect in the Psychology of Regret," *Journal of Personality and Social Psychology* 82.3 (2002).

[10] Chip Heath and Dan Heath, *Switch* (Crown, 2010).

[11] Jonah Berger and Gráinne Fitzsimons, "Dogs on the Street, Pumas on Your Feet: How Cues in the Environment Influence Product Evaluation and Choice, " *Journal of Marketing Research* 45.1 (2008).

[12] Kurt Lewin, *Field Theory in Social Science: Selected Theoretical Papers*, ed. Dorwin Cartwright (New York: Harper and Brothers, 1951); Richard Thaler and Cass Sunstein, *Nudge: Improving Decisions*

About Health, Wealth, and Happiness (Yale University Press, 2008).

[13] David Nickerson and Todd Rogers, "Do You Have a Voting Plan? Implementation Intentions, Voter Turnout, and Organic Plan Making," *Psychological Science* 21.2 (2010).

[14] Steven Sherman, "On the Self-Erasing Nature of Errors of Prediction," *Journal of Personality and Social Psychology* 39.2 (1980); Anthony Greenwald, Catherine Carnot, Rebecca Beach, and Barbara Young, "Increasing Voting Behavior by Asking People if They Expect to Vote," *Journal of Applied Psychology* 72.2 (1987).

[15] The results reported here reflect voting behavior among single eligible-voter households, which best account for the link between an individual's behavioral intentions and actions. The turnout from households with multiple eligible voters was not significantly influenced by the different messages.

[16] Peter Gollwitzer, "Implementation Intentions: Strong Effects of Simple Plans," *American Psychologist* 54.7 (1999); Peter Gollwitzer and Paschal Sheeran, "Implementation Intentions and Goal Achievement: A Meta-Analysis of Effects and Processes," *Advances in Experimental Social Psychology* 38.6 (2006).

[17] Although the identity of the retailer has been kept confidential by the consulting team, the available data suggest that it is Best Buy.

[18] Jared Spool, "The $300M Button," UIE (2009), https://articles.uie.com/three_hund_million_button/

[19] Robert Cialdini, *Influence: The Psychology of Persuasion* (New York, NY: HarperCollins Publishers, 2007).

[20] David Strohmetz, Bruce Rind, Reed Fisher, and Michael Lynn, "Sweetening the Till: The Use of Candy to Increase Restaurant Tipping 1," *Journal of Applied Social Psychology* 32 (2002).

Chapter 7

[1] Shane Frederick, George Loewenstein, and Ted O'Donoghue. "Time Discounting and Time Preference: A Critical Review," *Journal of Economic Literature* 40.2 (2002); Gal Zauberman, B. Kyu Kim, Selin Malkoc, and James Bettman, "Discounting Time and Time Discounting: Subjective Time Perception and Intertemporal Preferences," *Journal of Marketing Research* 46.4 (2009).

[2] George Loewenstein, "Anticipation and the Valuation of Delayed Consumption," *The Economic Journal* (September 1987).

[3] Brian Wansink, *Mindless Eating* (Bantam, 2006).

[4] Leif Nelson, Tom Meyvis, and Jeff Galak, "Enhancing the Television-Viewing Experience through Commercial Interruptions," *Journal of Consumer Research* 36.2 (2009).

[5] Robert Cialdini, *Pre-Suasion: A Revolutionary Way to Influence and Persuade* (Simon & Schuster, 2018).

[6] Nicholas Hayes, *Frank Lloyd Wright's Forgotten House* (University of Wisconsin Press, 2021).

[7] Paul Ekman, "An Argument for Basic Emotions," *Cognition and Emotion* 6.3–4 (1992); Robert Plutchik, *The Emotions* (University Press of America, 1991).

[8] Hans Greimel, "Toyota President Declares 'No More Boring Cars,'" *Autoweek* (January 31, 2017).

[9] Paul Ekman, "An Argument for Basic Emotions," *Cognition and Emotion* 6.3–4 (1992); Robert Plutchik, *The Emotions* (University Press of America, 1991).

[10] Mihaly Csikszentmihalyi, *Flow: The Psychology of Happiness* (Random House, 2013).

[11] John Schouten and James McAlexander, "Subcultures of Consumption—An Ethnography of the New Bikers," *Journal of Consumer Research* 22.1 (1995).

[12] Daniel Kahneman, *Thinking, Fast and Slow* (Farrar, Straus and Giroux, 2011).

[13] Daniel Kahneman, *Thinking, Fast and Slow* (Farrar, Straus and Giroux, 2011).

[14] Barbara Fredrickson and Daniel Kahneman, "Duration Neglect in Retrospective Evaluations of Affective Episodes," *Journal of Personality and Social Psychology* 65.1 (1993).

[15] Dan Ariely and George Loewenstein, "When Does Duration Matter in Judgment and Decision Making?" *Journal of Experimental Psychology: General* 129.4 (2000).

[16] Daniel Kahneman, Peter Wakker, and Rakesh Sarin, "Back to Bentham? Explorations of Experienced Utility," *The Quarterly Journal of Economics* 112.2 (1997).

[17] Alexandre Dumas, *The Count of Monte Cristo* (1844).

[18] Donald Redelmeier and Daniel Kahneman, "Patients' Memories of Painful Medical Treatments: Real-Time and Retrospective Evaluations of Two Minimally Invasive Procedures," *Pain* 66.1 (1996).

[19] Daniel Kahneman, Barbara Fredrickson, Charles Schreiber, and Donald Redelmeier, "When More Pain Is Preferred to Less: Adding a Better End," *Psychological Science* 4.6 (1993).

[20] Derrick Wirtz, Justin Kruger, Christie Napa Scollon, and Ed Diener, "What to Do on Spring Break? The Role of Predicted, On-Line, and Remembered Experience in Future Choice," *Psychological Science* 14.5 (2003).

[21] A. Parasuraman, Valarie Zeithaml, and Leonard Berry, "A Conceptual Model of Service Quality and Its Implications for Future Research," *Journal of Marketing* 49.4 (1985).

[22] Adapted from A. Parasuraman, Valarie Zeithaml, and Leonard Berry, "A Conceptual Model of Service Quality and Its Implications for Future Research," *Journal of Marketing* 49.4 (1985).

Chapter 8

[1] Itamar Simonson and Russell Winer, "The Influence of Purchase Quantity and Display Format on Consumer Preference for Variety," *Journal of Consumer Research* 19.1 (1992).

[2] Richard Oliver, "Effect of Expectation and Disconfirmation on Postexposure Product Evaluations: An Alternative Interpretation," *Journal of Applied Psychology* 62.4 (1977).

[3] Drazen Prelec and George Loewenstein, "The Red and the Black: Mental Accounting of Savings and Debt," *Marketing Science* 17.1 (1998).

[4] Xavier Drèze and Joseph Nunes, "Feeling Superior: The Impact of Loyalty Program Structure on Consumers' Perceptions of Status," *Journal of Consumer Research* 35.6 (2009).

[5] Ran Kivetz, Oleg Urminsky, and Yuhuang Zheng, "The Goal-Gradient Hypothesis Resurrected: Purchase Acceleration, Illusionary Goal Progress, and Customer Retention," *Journal of Marketing Research* 43.1 (2006).

[6] Andrea Bonezzi, C. Miguel Brendl, and Matteo De Angelis, "Stuck in the Middle: The Psychophysics of Goal Pursuit," *Psychological Science* 22.5 (2011).

[7] James Olds and Peter Milner, "Positive Reinforcement Produced by Electrical Stimulation of Septal Area and Other Regions of Rat Brain," *Journal of Comparative and Physiological Psychology* 47.6 (1954); James Olds, "Pleasure Centers in the Brain," *Scientific American* 195.4 (1956).

[8] Robert Wicklund and Peter Gollwitzer, *Symbolic Self-Completion* (Routledge, 1982); Ottmar Braun and Robert Wicklund, "Psychological Antecedents of Conspicuous Consumption," *Journal of Economic Psychology* 10.2 (1989).

[9] Jeff Martin, *Coca-Cola: The History of an American Icon* (MPI Home Video, 2002).

[10] Mike Esterl, "A Frosty Reception for Coca-Cola's White Christmas Cans," *The Wall Strteet Journal* (December 1, 2011).

[11] Scott Young and Vincenzo Ciummo, "Managing Risk in a Package Redesign: What Can We Learn from Tropicana?" *Brand Packaging* (June 16, 2009).

[12] This insight is based on Alexander Chernev, *Strategic Marketing Management: Theory and Practice* (Chicago, IL: Cerebellum Press, 2019).

Chapter 9

[1] Note that the process of identifying target customers was not included in the gap analysis. This is because the choice of target customers is influenced by a variety of factors, including a company's

core competencies and strategic assets, and thus is beyond the scope of this book.

[2] Bradley Agle, Nandu Nagarajan, Jeffrey Sonnenfeld, and Dhinu Srinivasan, "Does CEO Charisma Matter? An Empirical Analysis of the Relationships Among Organizational Performance, Environmental Uncertainty, and Top Management Team Perceptions of CEO Charisma," *Academy of Management Journal* 49.1 (2006).

[3] Exploratory data mining is one of the notable exceptions here as it relies on already existing data.

[4] Kashmir Hill, "How Target Figured Out A Teen Girl Was Pregnant Before Her Father Did," *Forbes* (February 16, 2012).

[5] Daniel Kahneman, *Thinking, Fast and Slow* (Farrar, Straus and Giroux, 2011).

[6] Fred Reichheld, "The One Number You Need to Grow," *Harvard Business Review* (December 2003).

www.ingramcontent.com/pod-product-compliance
Lightning Source LLC
Chambersburg PA
CBHW051116200326
41518CB00016B/2519